Supervision   The Direction of People at Work

SECOND EDITION

Supervision

THE DIRECTION
OF PEOPLE AT WORK

W. Richard Plunkett

WRIGHT COLLEGE

CITY COLLEGES OF CHICAGO

wcb

Wm. C. Brown Company Publishers

DUBUQUE, IOWA

To my mother and father: Mary C. and Paul M. Plunkett

Contents

Foreword

■ Every first-line supervisor is concerned (or should be) with the human relations impact on his role in the management hierarchy. Supervisors who understand human relationships between superiors, peers, and subordinates and who practice sound personnel techniques in reacting to these relationships, have mastered the most difficult and demanding aspect of their position.

Richard Plunkett's book *Supervision: The Direction of People at Work,* brings into focus a unique view of organizational structure, the managerial function, and the role of the supervisor. Through its substance, clarity, and style, Professor Plunkett's book develops sound concepts and principles, which are certain to lead supervisors who apply them to achieve success and prestige for themselves, respect and work performance from their associates, and survival for their companies.

Arthur D. Dula
Assistant to Vice-President for Personnel
The Atchison, Topeka & Santa Fe Railway Company
Chicago, Illinois

Preface

**ABOUT THIS
SECOND EDITION**

■ This second edition has been thoroughly updated and revised to utilize the many fine comments and suggestions from users of the first edition, both students and professors, and several academic reviewers. It incorporates new materials and research and, as a result, has been considerably expanded to provide more extensive coverage on the most essential topics. Some chapters have been combined and an entirely new chapter has been added on security, safety, and health. Equal time has been given to both men and women in the text examples and case problems.

The organization of the text has been improved. Each chapter begins with a specific set of Learning Objectives. Instructional materials are followed by the Instant Replay section that provides a quick review of the chapter's main topics. Next come the Key Words—the main technical terms or concepts developed in the chapter. All the key words are printed in **bold face** when they are first encountered in the chapter, and are gathered together in alphabetical order in the Glossary and given a chapter reference. Thus, the glossary is not only a handy reference tool for the student but also serves as a review in preparing for examinations. Next come the Questions for Discussion. Finally, each chapter ends with a Case Problem (most of which are new in the Second Edition) that provides a means for the students to apply their own understandings of the text materials.

The text now has a new and more attractive typographical design. Just as occasional cartoons were used in the first edition, several have been included here for your enjoyment. All the tables and figures have been redesigned and redrawn.

The auxiliary materials have been completely revised to reflect the changes and expanded coverage in the new edition. The Student Study Guide now includes nineteen short cases—with answers—to help the students apply their knowledge in real-life situations. The Instructor's Resource Manual now includes comprehensive case problems to help summarize and review each of the text's five parts. Additional test questions have been added as well. All in all, the reviewers, editor, and author think that this second edition brings together the essential principles, attitudes, and body of knowledge supervisors need to direct their people at work. It has been designed to serve its users as an up-to-date, practical guide that will help the students to move through principles and theories to practical applications of them both.

SUGGESTIONS TO INSTRUCTORS

■ Some years ago I discovered what every top salesperson knows: in order to sell my students on sound management theory I must first sell them on me. Unless students see their instructor as a credible source and competent spokesperson they will not accept the theories and principles that are so essential to their practice of supervision.

The first class session each new term is of the utmost importance to teachers and students. If it is utilized correctly, it can be the key to establishing rapport and credibility. My technique is to give the new students an in-depth look at me—at my educational background and management experiences both in and out of teaching. I let them know from the beginning that I love teaching and my teaching field. I explain that much of my growth and joy in my work has been a direct result of working with students. Most of the case problems in this text came from my students and I was privileged to help them resolve many of them. My students have been my best critics in the past, and I let the new ones know that I expect them to continue that tradition.

Next, I offer testimonials. I proudly relate the success stories of former students who have found an immediate use for their new knowledge acquired from the course. I tell the new students how many of the former student's lives have changed as a direct result of their management course.

After giving the students the scope and ground rules for the course I let them introduce themselves to one another through brief autobiographies. Each student explains to the others why he or she has taken the course and what each does for a living. This procedure helps to break the ice and gives each class member the security of knowing others in the group.

After the students know about me, the course, and their fellow students, they can relax a bit and more easily understand the course material. Their resistance to participation is lessened and their interest and attention increased. They quickly realize that they have much to learn and many sources to help them learn.

SUGGESTIONS TO THE STUDENTS

■ I envy all of you for the fun and the challenge you are about to embark upon. I congratulate you on your ambition and foresight in choosing a very fascinating course of study—the management of people.

Don't hide your talents. Share your experiences with your class, and soon you'll realize how valuable your personal experiences have been to yourself, and thus how valuable they may be to your classmates.

You can expect to find a frequent and almost immediate use of almost everything you learn in the management course, and this is a pleasant contrast to many courses you may have taken in the past. If you are already a manager, you can apply the lessons at work. If you are not one yet, start to think and act as if you were. If your boss is highly qualified, you will soon be able to see why this is so. If he is not, you will learn what is wrong with his or her performance. More important, you will also know what mistakes you yourself should *not* make. Often the example of a poorly qualified boss can be an excellent learning experience.

Never seek to conceal your own ignorance about the task of being a supervisor. Admit to yourself that you have a lot to learn, as we all do. Only by recognizing a void in your knowledge can you hope to fill it. And the proper way to fill it is by studying and by expanding your work experience. If you ask questions in class as they occur to you, you'll avoid the old problem of missing out on important pieces of information. You must take the initiative. The chances are that some questions that are bothering you are also of concern to others in the class. The more you contribute to the course, the more will you receive from it.

From now on you should think of yourself as a supervisor. For throughout this book I'll be talking to you as one superviser to another. In the following pages you'll find many tools—the tools of supervision. Their uses are explained in detail. As we all know, a skilled worker knows his or her tools, and knows which one is right for each task. When you complete this course, you'll have the knowledge you need to be a successful supervisor. You should put this knowledge to use as soon as possible. During the course, you will probably have a chance to present one of the case problems to your classmates. It's a fine opportunity to test yourself on how to apply the principles of supervision to a concrete situation in the world of work. You may also find other applications of these principles, both at home and on the job. Don't overlook them.

Good Luck!

W. Richard Plunkett

Acknowledgments

■ I am deeply indebted to my students and others without whom I could not have completed this revised edition. Specifically, I wish to thank the reviewers whose comments and criticisms were so helpful: Charles Beavin, Miami-Dade Community College, North Campus (Miami, Florida); Arthur H. Boisselle, El Paso Community College (Colorado Springs, Colorado); C. S. Everett, Des Moines Area Community College (Ankeny, Iowa); Benjamin Findley, Jr., Southeastern Oklahoma State University (Durant, Oklahoma); Lawrence A. Olivia, Educational Institute of the American Hotel and Motel Association (East Lansing, Michigan); Paul Wolff, Dundalk Community College (Baltimore, Maryland).

For the preparation of the manuscript I deeply appreciate the contributions of Clelia Leopold, Lorraine Bruce, Pamela Miskoci, and Cornelia Van Esso. I am most grateful to Kenneth A. Anderson for his expertise with the English language and his many hours spent in proofing the manuscript.

To Robert Grigg and Robert J. Cunningham I owe appreciation and admiration for their editorial and production efforts; and to Catherine Koehler for her interpretation of the graphic material.

Part One
The Big Picture

1 The Management Concept

■ After reading and discussing this chapter, you should be able to:

1 Define management.

2 List the four essential elements of any formal organization.

3 Define formal, informal, and functional authority.

4 Define responsibility, delegation, and accountability, and explain their their relationships to one another.

5 Identify the three levels of the management hierarchy, and describe the inhabitants of each level.

6 List the officers of a corporation and describe their roles.

7 Describe the line manager's role.

8 Describe the staff manager's role.

9 List the five functions of management.

INTRODUCTION

■ Management is one of the world's oldest professions. Early in human history, people had to learn how to manage themselves and their own affairs. Then they had to learn how to manage their relationships with others. Parents must learn to manage their families and their finances. The professional manager must learn to manage his or her job and, together with other managers, to manage a business. It is with the management of a business that we shall concern ourselves in this chapter.

A DEFINITION OF MANAGEMENT

■ **Management** is defined here as an activity that uses the functions of planning, organizing, directing, controlling, and coordinating human and material resources for the purpose of achieving stated goals. A **man-**

ager is a member of a team of decision makers that gets things done with and through others by carrying out these five management functions or activities. Managers occupy positions of trust and power in a formal organization such as a business.

The term **formal organization** is used here to distinguish our concern from other types of organizations, for example, social or informal organizations. A formal organization is one put together by design and rational plan, such as a business or industrial union. A formal organization is basically the coming together of several people for the accomplishment of stated purposes. The necessary tasks to be performed are identified and divided among the participants. A framework for decisions and control is established.

The essential elements of any formal organization are:

1. A clear understanding about stated purposes and goals;
2. A division of labor among specialists;
3. A rational organization or design;
4. A hierarchy of authority and responsibility.

Each of these elements is related to the others. We shall look at each of them separately, however, because in this way we shall be able to understand all of them better.

Stated Purposes and Goals

Every business enterprise is established so that its owners and managers can make a profit. How they intend to make this profit is summed up in very clear statements as to what kind of business they wish to engage in (for example, manufacturing, or retailing), and exactly what aims or objectives they are trying to attain.

Managers of each department establish for themselves both the short- and long-range goals. The goals the managers set for themselves and for their staffs and departments are influenced directly by the organization's goals established by the top management. These goals are targets to be reached within certain periods of time and as a result of certain limited expenditures of company resources. Through the exercise of management functions, these goals of the organization are to be achieved.

A Division of Labor Among Specialists

We live in a world of specialists. In teaching, medicine, law, and business, men and women are asked to choose areas in which to specialize so that they can concentrate their energies and efforts on the gathering of knowledge, skills, and proficiencies in order to become masters of their fields.

Any formal organization is set up to make good use of the special talents and abilities of its people. Each person is assigned those tasks that he or she is best qualified to complete through the application of his or her specialized knowledge. Through the coordination of these specialists—each of whom contributes a part to the whole job—the entire work of the organization is planned and then carried out.

A Rational Organization or Design

Formal business organizations must have order and planning within their operations if they are to be successful. There must be established policies, programs, and procedures as well as an uninterrupted flow of both information and work from the start to the finish of each project.

Before a building can be constructed, many specialists must be called upon to assist in its planning. Architects, engineers, and draftsmen must create its size and shape in line with the functional demands placed upon the structure. Then more specialists will be needed to clear the land, lay the foundation, construct the walls and roof, and finish the interior. Only with precision, planning, and timing can the design become a building.

A Hierarchy of Authority and Responsibility

By the term **hierarchy** we mean a group of people who are picked to staff an organization and make all the necessary plans and decisions that allow it to function. Men and women with specialized abilities are installed at different levels of authority and responsibility throughout the organization. These people make up the group called management and fill all formal positions of power. From the chief executive to the supervisors, these managers must plan, organize, direct, control, and coordinate the many activities that have to take place if the organization's goals are to be reached.

AUTHORITY

■ **Authority** is the ~~power~~ *Right* to do something or to get something done. Power is the ability a person has to mobilize or bring into action the various resources of the business. It is the right to make a decision or to perform a specific action that will have a direct impact on the organization.

Authority can be broken down into two distinct types: formal and informal. **Formal authority** comes with the position you occupy in any formal organization. It resides in that position and is yours to use as long as you occupy it. **Informal authority** is the power you have over others because they willingly give it to you. Other people decide to subject their wills to yours because of the kind of person you are.

Power comes to an individual in any of the following three ways:

Traditional Authority. All people in formal positions of authority have power as a result of tradition. A politician elected to office inherits the power of that office. A manager has the power of his or her office by reason of appointment or promotion.

Rational Authority. All people who are respected and admired by others for their knowledge or skills have this kind of power. They are looked up to and listened to when they explain or practice their particular craft. They are easily able to influence others. This is one way of gaining informal power.

Charismatic Authority. Persons who are well liked by others simply because of their personal qualities have informal power. This kind of power over others comes from their liking you and being willing to subject their wills to yours. It is one of the main bases for friendship.

The key points in this connection are that: (1) any of these ways to power gives people influence over others; (2) if you wish to be influential in your job, you must strive to strengthen and increase your power over others by acquiring power in all three ways. To rely solely on traditional authority as a result of your formal position means that you are going into battle poorly armed.

RESPONSIBILITY

■ Those in authority must answer to someone else or to others for the use of their power. This is called responsibility. You must answer to your boss for the use of your formal authority. And in a similar way you have to answer to your friends and subordinates for the use of your informal authority.

DELEGATION

■ All formal authority in a business enterprise belongs originally to the owners. In many cases, however, the owners cannot or do not wish to manage the businesses directly. They hire others, that is, managers, to run the enterprise for them.

Initially the owner creates a key position—that of the chief executive who is in control of all the other managers and employees. To enable the chief executive to function, the owner must establish a "reservoir" of formal authority in sufficient quantity to allow the entire business to operate. Simultaneously there is established a "reservoir" of responsibility that is exactly equal to that formal authority. Then the chief executive is installed in office.

The chief executive has to determine the various specialized positions that he or she and the owner think are needed for a successful operation. Once these positions are established, the chief executive will create reservoirs of power and responsibility for each of them. As the chief executive does so, he or she funnels off some of his or her power and responsibility into the reservoirs of the managers. In other words, every manager in a position of formal authority within a formal organization is equipped to function through the exercise of a portion of the owner's power. All the managers have acquired their authority in the traditional way.

Giving away some or all of the formal power that belongs to a formal position constitutes **delegation.** Power is given by the one who holds the power to a subordinate. This delegation decreases the formal authority and corresponding responsibility of the delegator, and it increases the power and responsibility of the subordinate to the same degree.

ACCOUNTABILITY
■ You are responsible for the use of your formal authority to the degree that you retain it and do not delegate it. **Accountability** means having to answer for a subordinate's use of your formal authority. Delegating your formal authority to another does not relieve you as delegator of the necessity to render an accounting for its use. So when a manager delegates formal authority and responsibility to another, he or she retains accountability for the use of that authority.

To understand better the concepts of authority, responsibility, delegation, and accountability, let us use an example. Mr. Big wants to start a retail store. He has the money and knowledge to do so, but he does not have the time to manage the business. So he decides to hire a general manager to run it for him. After choosing a location for the store, Big hires Ms. Jones as his general manager. Together they build up the store's inventory and open for business. At first, Jones is alone in the management of the store while Big provides capital and advice, and shares in the profits. Jones therefore possesses all the authority and responsibility necessary to run the business on a day-to-day basis. The authority and responsibility she possesses were delegated to her by Big, so Jones has formal authority. Jones has to answer to Big for her use of that formal authority so she must have exactly the same amount of responsibility as she has authority.

To illustrate what has happened so far, imagine that both authority and responsibility are liquids—like water or milk—and that we can visualize them as being stored in individual reservoirs. Ms. Jones' reservoirs would look like this.

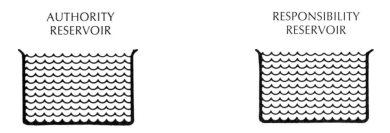

AUTHORITY
RESERVOIR

RESPONSIBILITY
RESERVOIR

Both reservoirs are full and exactly equal in volume.

It isn't long before business gets good and Jones finds that she can no longer manage the business alone. So, she creates a new position—that of an assistant manager—and delegates, or pours off, some of her formal authority and responsibility into the two new reservoirs created to go along with the new position. Then she hires Mr. Brown to fill the assistant manager's position. Brown now inherits the power and responsibility that belong to his new position. But that power and responsibility originally belonged to Jones and were given to the position and Brown through the process we call delegation. The reservoirs now look like this.

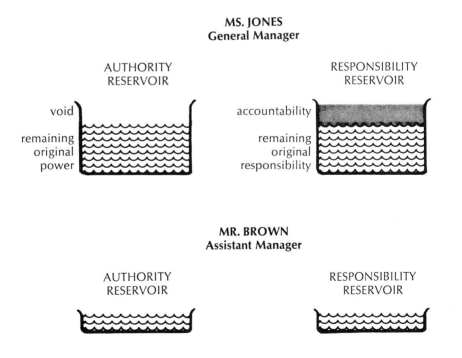

MS. JONES
General Manager

AUTHORITY
RESERVOIR

RESPONSIBILITY
RESERVOIR

void

remaining
original
power

accountability

remaining
original
responsibility

MR. BROWN
Assistant Manager

AUTHORITY
RESERVOIR

RESPONSIBILITY
RESERVOIR

Just enough of Ms. Jones' authority and responsibility were poured into the assistant manager's reservoirs to fill them. Brown's reservoirs are exactly equal to the amount of authority and responsibility that was lost through delegation by Jones. Jones still retains much of her formal authority and responsibility. In place of her delegated responsibility she has gained accountability, which has moved in to fill the vacuum. Remember that delegated authority and responsibility may be taken back by the delegator at any time—either totally or partially.

THE MANAGEMENT HIERARCHY

■ We have concluded that, among other things, managers make up a team of decision makers charged with operating the formal organization of a business. You will recall that one of the characteristics of a formal organization is that it has a hierarchy of authority and responsibility. It is this hierarchy that we shall now examine.

The simple pyramid shown in Figure 1–1 is our symbol for the management hierarchy. This pyramid is divided into three levels: the top management; the middle management; and the operating management. As depicted here, both the top and bottom levels are rather thin in comparison with the middle level. This pyramid is typical of a medium-sized (500–1,000 employees) or larger business. A smaller enterprise might well have an even distribution at each level, or only one manager performing all the activities at each level. The key point is that, whether the roles for each level are played by many people or by a few, these roles must be played.

Figure 1-1. The management hierarchy pyramid.

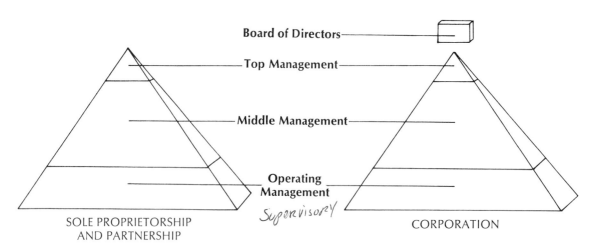

SOLE PROPRIETORSHIP AND PARTNERSHIP

Board of Directors

Top Management

Middle Management

Operating Management

Supervisory

CORPORATION

Top Management Level

Visually occupying only the small top of the pyramid, the **top management** level is the location of the chief executive (president) and of his or her immediate subordinates (vice-presidents or their equivalents). In a sole proprietorship the owner is usually the chief executive. In a partnership the role of the chief executive is usually shared between or among the partners, each of whom concentrates on his or her specialties.

In a corporation the top management is composed of the officers of the company: a president, one or more vice-presidents, a treasurer, and a secretary. Any two or more offices may be held by the same person, except the offices of secretary and president.

We shall discuss this section with the business corporation as our model. All that is said here also pertains to partnerships and sole proprietorships, except that the role of the secretary does not exist in partnerships and sole proprietorships.

THE CHIEF EXECUTIVE'S ROLE

The chief executive must play at least two roles: he or she must be a person capable of both careful analysis and effective action. He or she must develop and establish the major objectives for the business and make the major decisions necessary to attain them. The chief executive is the one manager who must be able to observe and comprehend the entire operation. Like the captain of a ship the chief executive is responsible for his or her own decisions and accountable for those of all the other managers. He or she must be able to plan, control, organize, direct, and coordinate the work of subordinates in order to attain the stated objectives of the company.

THE VICE-PRESIDENT'S ROLE

The vice-presidents are the immediate subordinates of the chief executive. They are charged with the overall operation of the company's functional areas:

Marketing—sales and all sales-connected activities
Production—manufacturing and procurement of raw materials
Accounting—record-keeping, forecasting, and costing
Finance—managing the company's funds
Personnel—recruitment of employees and managers, administration of employee benefits

All other business activities, such as engineering, research and development, purchasing, and the like, fall under one or another of these headings.

The vice-presidents must plan, organize, direct, control, and coordinate the operation of their departments in general so as to achieve their department's as well as their company's stated objectives. Their subordinates are the middle managers.

THE SECRETARY'S ROLE

The corporate secretary has the following duties: (1) to keep the minutes of the meetings of the stockholders and the board of directors; (2) to keep all stock ownership records; and (3) to act as the custodian of the corporate records and of the corporate seal, which is affixed to all corporate shares and documents as a proof that they are official acts of the company. He or she may also serve the company in other capacities, such as finance manager, personnel manager, or some other executive position. The job of corporate secretary is seldom a full-time position demanding a person's entire time.

THE TREASURER'S ROLE

The treasurer has the following duties: (1) to accept charge and custody of, and responsibility for, all funds and securities of the corporation, receiving and depositing all moneys due and payable to the corporation; (2) to control all disbursements of company funds; and (3) to prepare all financial statements, such as the balance sheet and the profit-and-loss statement. The treasurer is either the chief financial officer of a corporation or a member of his or her staff.

The Board of Directors

Outside of and above the corporate management pyramid is the board of directors, which is represented graphically in the second pyramid in Figure 1–1. The board members, who are elected by the stockholders or owners of the corporation, elect their own chairperson. The directors exercise jurisdiction over the actions of the chief executive of the corporation. They review the major decisions of the chief executive, who is held responsible for both the decisions he or she makes and those he or she fails to make. The board decides what the company's business is and should be. It formulates company *policy*—general guidelines for management action at every level when dealing with recurring situations—picks the chief executive, and diagnoses and recommends treatment for business ills in the absence of recommendations from the chief executive. In short, the board of directors is a watchdog for the owners' interests and a tough court of review before which the chief executive must try his or her case. The majority of a board's members are full-time executives working for other corporations. They are usually specialists.

Only in a crisis does the board depart from its role of judge and adopt an executive approach. It may give orders to remove or replace the chief executive in order to bring the firm through a period of difficulties. When the crisis ends, the board will quickly return to its judicial role. Only at such rare times can the board function as the top management of the corporation.

The Middle Management Level

Visually occupying the center of the pyramid, the **middle management** level is the location of all managers below the rank of vice-president and above the operating level.

Like all managers, the middle manager's functions are to plan, direct, control, organize, and coordinate.

Each functional area has many specific tasks to be performed. Figure 1–2 illustrates a typical hierarchy in the sales area of a retail store.

The store manager is not a specialist, but all the subordinate managers are. Each one must carry out the operation of a specific part of

Figure 1-2. Functional division in a retail store.
Only the merchandise manager's subordinates are shown.

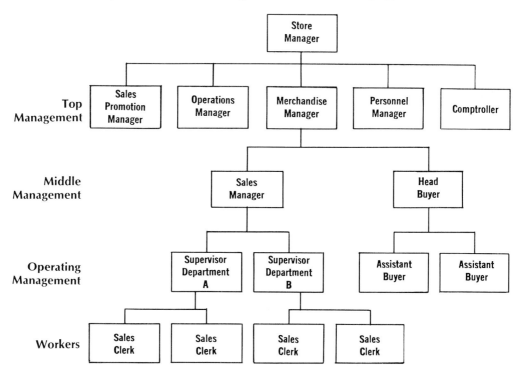

a large whole. The principle of division of labor could not be more evident. Although only the merchandise manager's subordinates are shown in the figure, a diagram of any of the other functional areas would show a similar pattern.

The Operating Management Level

Shown at the bottom or base of the management pyramid, the **operating management** level is the place where supervisors and foremen are found.

A **supervisor** is a manager whose subordinates all are nonmanagement employees **(workers).** If a manager directs the work of other managers, he or she does not belong on this level. The term *foreman* can be used interchangeably with the word *supervisor*. In common practice, *foreman* usually refers to a supervisor of workers in production activities.

It should be remembered that the first pyramid depicted only the management team. The majority of workers form the base upon which these managers depend for support, output, and success. To complete the pyramid concept we must add this foundation and the functional areas, as shown in Figure 1–3.

Figure 1-3. The corporation pyramid. All the functional areas of management rest on the base provided by the workers.

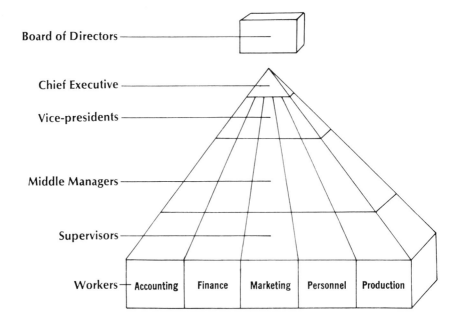

Line and Staff Authority

LINE MANAGERS

The formal authority that flows from the top of an organization to all its management positions is also termed *line authority*. From the top to the bottom of any formal organization, formal power flows from superiors to subordinates in a continuous line. The management positions connected by this line authority make up the organization's hierarchy.

Line authority allows its holder—a manager—to exercise direct supervision over his or her subordinates. Managers who have line authority can give direct orders to others as well as appraise and discipline those who receive their orders. They can take direct action and command those who contribute directly to achieving the business's major goals.

The managers in the organization hierarchy who manage those activities or departments that directly influence the success (profitability) of a business are called **line managers.** Their departments make direct contributions toward achieving the company's goals. Line departments traditionally include marketing and production, and sometimes include finance as well.

STAFF MANAGERS

Staff authority, like line authority, is a kind of formal authority. It is distributed throughout the organization to various managers at any level who advise and assist other managers. **Staff managers** are specialists who supervise activities or departments that do not directly contribute to achieving the company's major goals. The staff manager's primary mission is to help all other managers who need his or her specialized knowledge.

The concept of *staff* is only relevant as it is applied to the relationships between and among managers. If a manager's job is to advise, counsel, assist, or provide services to another manager, the first manager is a staff manager. You can tell if managers are staff or line managers by observing what their relationships are to the other managers.

Since staff managers are linked to the top of an organization, they receive line authority also. If they have subordinates, the staff managers direct, appraise, and discipline those subordinates, just as any line manager does with his or her subordinates. It is safe to say that when a staff manager directs the work of subordinates, he or she is acting like a line manager. But when the staff manager gives advice or assistance to another manager, he or she is acting the exclusive way in which staff managers act.

Figure 1–4 is an abbreviated organization chart of a management hierarchy that shows both line and staff positions as well as the rela-

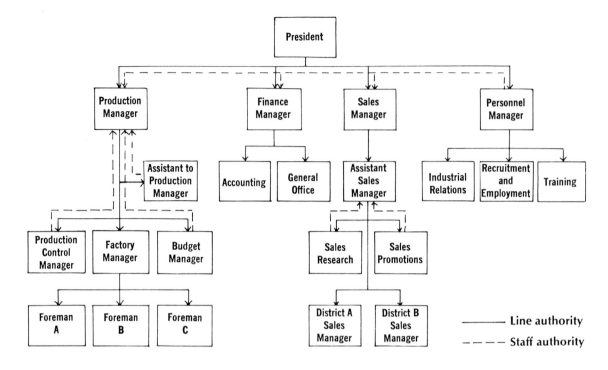

Figure 1-4. The flow of authority in line and staff organization.

George R. Terry, *Principles of Management,* 6th ed. (Homewood, Ill.: Richard D. Irwin, 1972), p. 353. © 1972 by Richard D. Irwin, Inc.

tionships of authority. Note that staff and line managers appear at both the top and the bottom of the hierarchy.

Functional Authority

Functional authority is power given to a manager of a department, usually a staff department, enabling him or her to make decisions that govern the operation of another department. Figure 1–5 illustrates the flow of functional authority from the staff managers to the other managers in an organization. The lines of functional authority indicate a measure of control by a staff manager over a line manager and his or her people and their activities.

The normal practice is for a line manager to have complete control over his or her area of responsibility and relative freedom to make his or her own decisions. Staff managers have been installed to help the line as well as other staff managers, but usually only when called upon to do so. It is as though the line manager is saying, "Don't call us, we'll call you." Under this arrangement a staff manager may never be consulted. In any case the line manager must take full responsibility for the results of acting on such staff consultations. After all, he or she might have ignored the advice of the staff manager.

For this and other reasons, many companies make use of the concept of functional authority. This concept holds that if a staff manager makes a decision about his or her area that has application to the area of another manager, the manager of that other area is bound by the staff manager's decision. For example, the payroll department issues a directive stating that henceforth all payroll data from each department must be submitted on a specific form, in a specified way, and by a certain date. If the managers throughout the business wish to get themselves and their people paid on time and in the correct amounts, they had better follow the directive.

Figure 1-5. The flow of functional staff authority and line authority in a manufacturing business.

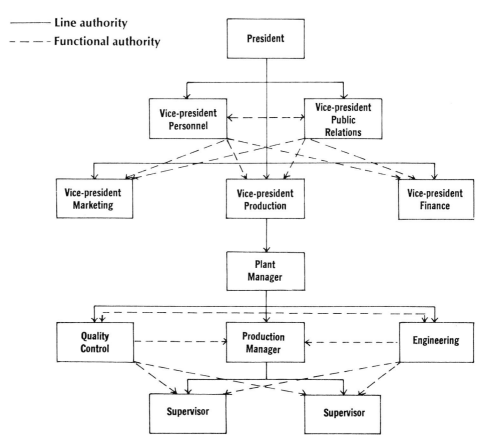

Functional authority seems to give a manager many bosses. But does it? Isn't a company merely removing many important, but not essential, areas from a manager's concern in order to promote uniformity and efficiency? When many decisions about routine and common-problem areas are made outside the department, each manager is freed of the time it takes to consider these matters. As a result, the manager has more time to devote to his or her specialized, essential tasks. What is lost in autonomy is more than compensated for by an increase in efficiency and economy in the overall operation of the business.

THE MANAGER'S FUNCTIONS

■ We shall now briefly explore the five major functions of management. By major functions we mean the most important and time-consuming activities common to all managers. These functions are *planning, organizing, directing, controlling,* and *coordinating.* Planning and organizing are the preparatory phases for management action. Directing is the actuating phase. Directing is supervising, which means literally *to oversee* the work or performance of another. Directing more than any of the other functions is our prime concern throughout this text. Controlling and coordinating are the follow-up phases, which attempt to guarantee the successful execution of the other functions.

Each of these functions will be treated in more detail in Chapters 3 and 4. Although we shall treat each function separately in our discussions, it should be noted that they are often integrated and interdependent and may take place in any sequence.

The five major functions apply to all managers. Whether the manager is a president or a supervisor, he or she plans, directs, controls, organizes, and coordinates the activities of his or her department. The difference at each level of management is one of time devoted to each function, as shown in Figure 1–6. Supervisors spend most of their time

Figure 1-6. Managers at different levels and the proportion of their time spent on the management functions.

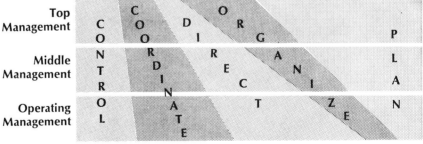

in directing, while presidents spend most of their time in planning. Planning and organizing are prerequisites to action. Directing is the execution function through which work is initiated and accomplished. Controlling is concerned with the outcomes of these three functions, and coordinating tries to prevent any interference between or among the other functions.

Beginning at this point, think as a manager would. Try to relate each concept to your past employment experiences, your present job, and your boss's job. When you discover parallels, jot them down. This will facilitate your ability to retain what you read and discuss in class. Our treatment of the subject matter will be from the point of view of *what should be*, not necessarily *what is*.

INSTANT REPLAY Management is a team of people who rationally coordinate the activities of a business enterprise and attempt to get its tasks and goals accomplished through and with others. Managers make the decisions that guide the formal organization. Their control rests in their company's organizational structure as well as their formal power and responsibility. This formal power and responsibility can be delegated. If it is, accountability takes the place of lost responsibility. Whether a manager exercises power or someone else does, he or she is answerable (accountable) to someone for the results.

We have discussed the various levels of management's hierarchy and defined the roles played at each level. Basically, top management is charged with the operation of the entire business, working within the framework of company policy and the top managers' own individual specialty areas. The chief executive is the person who must oversee the entire operation. In a corporation the board of directors reviews major decisions that affect the enterprise and makes policy. Only in an emergency does it move from a judicial role to an executive one.

The management of an enterprise today is a job for many specialists, because the tasks are so dynamic and diversified. Most businesses have seen fit to divide the labor into *line* (marketing and production) departments and *staff* (all other departments). In many organizations today we find the concept of functional authority very much in evidence. According to this concept, the manager of one department may enforce his or her decisions on many other departments. This is done so that the managers of the other departments will be freed from the problem areas they share with other departments and thus able to concentrate their energies on essentials.

KEY WORDS	accountability	hierarchy	responsibility
	authority	informal authority	staff manager
	delegation	line manager	supervisor
	formal authority	management	top management
	functional authority	middle management	worker
		operating management	

QUESTIONS FOR DISCUSSION

1. Who is a manager?
2. What are the differences between a formal organization and an informal or social one?
3. In what three ways can a person acquire power or authority over others? Give an example of each.
4. What happens when a manager delegates authority to a subordinate?
5. Can informal authority be delegated? Why or why not?
6. What is the difference between accountability and responsibility?
7. Give the four essential elements an organization must have to be called formal.
8. In the sole proprietorship or partnership business, who performs the role of the board of directors?
9. Give an example to illustrate how a personnel manager could use his or her functional authority in hiring.
10. Contrast the role of a staff manager with functional authority with that of a staff manager without it.

CASE PROBLEM

Who's Responsible?

Mr. Charles, President of Sera-Ramics, Inc., picked up his phone and dialed 74. Sam Deadwood, Vice-President of Product Development, answered.

"Deadwood here."

"Sam," said Charles, "I have to give a status report to the board of directors in ten days on our new line of housewares. Can you prepare a report filling me in on the details as to when we intend to testmarket it and where?"

"You bet, Mr. Charles. I'll put my best man on it right away. You should have the report by the eighteenth, the day before the meeting with the board."

Deadwood pressed his intercom switch.

"Ellsworth here," it crackled.

"Bill, Charles just called and wants a status report on our new line of housewares. He needs the details of the testmarket plans. Put together all the details in a report and give it to my secretary, Betty, to type. Charles needs it by the eighteenth."

"Can do, Mr. Deadwood." Bill Ellsworth walked over to Al Farley's desk. He explained the project to Farley and told him to get the report to Betty by the seventeenth for final typing.

Farley prepared all the data, laid it out in rough form, and took the report to Betty's desk on the morning of the seventeenth. Betty was not there so he left it in her in-basket.

On the morning of the nineteenth Charles called Deadwood. "Sam, where is that report you promised me on the housewares line? I'm due at the board meeting in an hour."

"I gave the assignment to Ellsworth, Mr. Charles. I'll check it out right away."

After some hasty phone conversations and checking, the report was discovered on Betty's desk, still untyped. Mr. Charles had to give his report to the board from the rough draft.

Betty had taken a three-day leave of absence on the sixteenth for a family emergency. She wasn't due back until tomorrow.

Questions

1. Who is responsible?
2. Who is accountable?
3. How could this situation have been avoided?

2 The Supervisor's Special Role

LEARNING OBJECTIVES

■ After reading and discussing this chapter, you should be able to:

1 Define the kind of manager known as a supervisor in at least two ways.

2 List the three groups to whom supervisors are responsible, and explain how they meet their responsibilities to each group.

3 List at least five specific activities on which supervisors spend their time each working day.

4 Explain the **linking-pin concept** as it applies to supervisors.

5 Explain how superiors, subordinates, peers, family, and friends help shape the supervisors' perception of their proper roles at work.

6 Define and give an example of role conflict for supervisors.

7 Define and give an example of role ambiguity for supervisors.

8 List the four most common reasons why supervisors fail.

9 Explain the **Peter Principle** and how a company can prevent it from applying to its personnel.

INTRODUCTION

■ Today as probably never in the past, the operating level of management is receiving greater attention and emphasis throughout industry. This is due primarily to a wealth of information published in recent years that points out the unique impact of supervisors on productivity and profitability. Because of the heavy emphasis today on reducing costs and increasing productivity, supervisors are recognized as playing a very direct and key role in achieving business success. Unlike other managers, they directly supervise the nonmanagement employees in the execution of their tasks.

We have defined supervisors as the managers who direct the workers. As such, they are a vital link between plans and their execution. After all is said and done, the goals will be reached or missed to a great extent as a result of how well the supervisors are achieving their own goals.

Federal labor legislation gives another definition of supervisors—one that emphasizes their particular activities. According to the Labor Management Relations Act (the Taft-Hartley Act) of 1947 as amended, a supervisor is a person who has formal authority to:

> hire, transfer, suspend, lay off, recall, promote, discharge, assign, reward, or discipline other employees, or responsibly to direct them, or to adjust their grievances, or effectively to recommend such action, if in connection with the foregoing the exercise of such authority is not a merely routine or clerical nature, but requires the use of independent judgment.

The Fair Labor Standards Act of 1938 as amended distinguishes supervisors from workers with respect to how they spend their time and how they are compensated. Employees are considered supervisors if they spend no more than 20 percent of their time performing the same kind of work that their subordinates do, and if they are paid a salary with no compensation for overtime.

No matter how supervisors are described, they perform many functions. In fact, the functions of planning, organizing, directing, controlling, and coordinating can be further broken down with the help of the word *supervisor.*

S upervise—to direct human and physical resources;
U tilize—resources of people, materials, machines, money, and methods;
P lan—work, objectives, and communications;
E nforce—rules, policies, and standards;
R elate—to their subordinates, individually and collectively;
V alidate—performances, promotions, and transfers of subordinates;
I nstruct—in methods, procedures, skills, and safety;
S how—true leadership and set an example for subordinates;
O rganize—a department and its operations;
R egulate—people, processes, and resources.

THE SUPERVISOR'S RESPONSIBILITIES

■ There are three primary groups to which supervisors have responsibilities: (1) their subordinates; (2) their peers in management; and (3) their superiors in management. They must work in harmony with all three groups if they are to be effective supervisors.

**Relations
with Subordinates**

The responsibilities managers have to their subordinates are many and varied. To begin with, supervisors *must* get to know their subordinates as individual human beings. Each subordinate, like his or her supervisor, has specific needs and wants. Each of us has certain expectations from work, certain goals we wish to achieve through work, and fundamental attitudes and aptitudes that influence our performances at work. When supervisors get to know each subordinate as an individual, they are able to approach each person in a specific, careful way.

One of the first principles of good communications (see Chapter 5) is for you to keep your audience in mind when you attempt to communicate. If you are to be effective in your dealing with another person, you should know as much about that person as you can *before* attempting to communicate any message.

Subordinates want to know that their supervisors care about them and are prepared to do something about their problems. A sure sign that supervisors care about their subordinates is demonstrated through common courtesy—using a person's name, a respectful tone of voice, personalized greetings, and sincere inquiries about your subordinate's health and well-being.

Getting to know subordinates well can be difficult. Some people are easy to know while others are not. Also you can never really know your subordinates thoroughly for long because most people develop and change with the passage of time and with new experiences in life and on the job. These obstacles, however, should not be used as excuses for you to avoid trying to know your subordinates. Rather, such difficulties should be viewed as barriers that can be overcome through a sincere effort and openness on the supervisor's part.

You will only get to know your subordinates well if you spend time with them and on their problems. Study each subordinate's personnel file. Talk to each of them whenever you get a chance. If contacts with your people are informal, use the time for some casual conversation about them and what is going on in their lives. A sincere interest on your part usually results in open responses from them. If contacts are formal, start out with a personal greeting, get through the formal communications of orders or instructions, and then end on a friendly note. For example, you might say, "Well, I've had my say, is there anything you want to talk about?" Only after you have a good understanding of each subordinate can you expect to be successful in your dealings with them.

Additional responsibilities supervisors have to their subordinates include the following:

1. Tailoring jobs to fit the job holder, or finding people who are well equipped to handle their duties;

2. Standing behind your people when they act under your orders or with your permission;

3. Providing them with constructive criticism and adequate instruction, training, and evaluation;

4. Handling their complaints and problems in a fair and just way;

5. Safeguarding their health and welfare while they are on the job;

6. Providing an example of what good behavior on the job should be like.

These are just a few of the many responsibilities supervisors have to their subordinates. If such obligations are carried out well, the supervisors will be looked upon by their subordinates as leaders. Such supervisors gain the respect of their subordinates, and this is the key to effective supervision and personal achievement. Your subordinates represent the most important group to whom and for whom you are responsible.

Relations with Peers

Supervisors' **peers** are your fellow supervisors throughout the company with whom you come into contact. They are the individuals and groups with whom you must cooperate and coordinate if your department and theirs are to operate in harmony. Your peers directly or indirectly affect the outcome of your own operations. The reverse is true as well. Be on the lookout for ways to cement good working relationships with them and to lend a hand to them when you can. In turn, you can expect assistance from them when you need it.

Your peers normally constitute the bulk of your friends and associates at work. If they do not, you should suspect that something is wrong with your relationships with them, and you should take steps to correct this situation. Your peers represent an enormous pool of talent and experience which will be yours to tap and contribute to if they view you in a favorable way. For this reason if no other, it is to your advantage to cultivate their friendship both on and off the job. Your peers can teach you a great deal about the company, and they are often a fine source of advice on how to meet difficult situations that may arise. They can do more to keep you out of trouble than any other group in the company. In so many ways you need each other, and both you and they stand to benefit from a partnership or alliance based on mutual respect and the need to resolve common problems.

Your responsibilities to your peers are:

1. To know and understand each of them as individuals;

2. To approach and cooperate with each of them as individuals;

3. To provide what help you can to enable them to achieve the measure of satisfaction they desire from their jobs;

4. To foster a spirit of cooperation and teamwork between yourself and all your peers.

Your success as a manager is linked to your peers and what they think of you as a person and a supervisor. Your personal and professional reputation with them is important. If they think highly of you, they will be drawn to you and be willing to associate with you. They will freely give of their time and energy on your behalf.

If you are off in your own little world or unwilling to share your knowledge and know-how, you deny yourself the growth and experience that your peers stand ready to offer. As a result, you may be labelled as uncooperative or antisocial and destined, at best, for a career as just a supervisor. People in higher positions in business as a rule have no need for withdrawn or isolated managers. You will discover, if you have not already done so, that the more you give of what you have, the more you will receive from others.

Relations with Superiors

Your responsibilities to your superiors, both line and staff, can be summarized as follows:

1. To transmit information about problems along with recommendations for solving them;
2. To operate within your budget and to respect company policy;
3. To promote the company's goals;
4. To strive for efficiency whenever and wherever possible;
5. To prepare records and reports on time and in the proper form;
6. To use the company's resources effectively;
7. To schedule work so as to meet deadlines;
8. To show respect and cooperation.

Your boss or supervisor is a middle manager who is accountable for your actions. He is similar to you in that he is both a follower and a staff or line manager. He executes all the functions of management and is evaluated on the basis of his or her subordinates' performances. Like yourself, your boss must develop and maintain sound working relationships with his or her subordinates, peers, and superiors. Also, your boss has probably served an apprenticeship as a supervisor so you can count on his or her understanding of your own situation.

Your superiors should be consulted, and their advice should be followed. To your boss you owe allegiance and respect. You must be a loyal follower if you intend to be a successful leader. To the company's team of staff specialists you are like a laboratory through which their ideas and recommendations are implemented. Chapter 19 has more to say about how you can get along and cooperate with your peers and superiors in management.

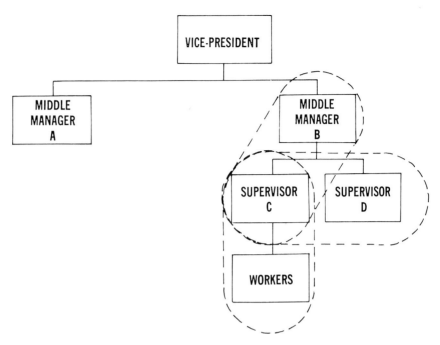

```
                    ┌──────────────────┐
                    │  VICE-PRESIDENT  │
                    └──────────────────┘
          ┌──────────────────┴──────────────────┐
 ┌──────────────┐                      ┌──────────────┐
 │    MIDDLE    │                      │    MIDDLE     │
 │   MANAGER    │                      │   MANAGER     │
 │      A       │                      │      B        │
 └──────────────┘                      └──────────────┘
                              ┌──────────────┴──────────────┐
                     ┌──────────────┐             ┌──────────────┐
                     │  SUPERVISOR  │             │  SUPERVISOR   │
                     │      C       │             │      D        │
                     └──────────────┘             └──────────────┘
                              │
                     ┌──────────────┐
                     │   WORKERS    │
                     └──────────────┘
```

Figure 2-1. Use of an organization chart to identify linking pins. The circles link group members. Where the circles overlap, you have a linking pin.

MANAGERS AS LINKING PINS

■ Since human beings are social animals, we need to consider some recent theories about how people interact in a social organization like a business enterprise, and how the role of individual managers is shaped and influenced by other managers. These theories will add greatly to your understanding of the behavior of people on the job.

Most business organizations contain many people who interact with one another on a regular basis both individually and in groups. The typical organizational chart shows a division of labor among individuals employed by the organization to accomplish its tasks. It also shows certain key individuals who head up and link together the independent groups within the organization. These key individuals are often called **linking pins**[1] because, as members of two or more groups, they link or lock these groups together. To illustrate this concept, consider the following situation. A supervisor is the organizational leader of a working section but is also the subordinate of a middle manager. Each supervisor therefore is a member of at least two groups—a working section

---

1. Rensis Likert, *New Patterns of Management* (New York: McGraw-Hill Book and Education Services Group, 1961), p. 61.

or department and a group of fellow supervisors (peers) who report to the same middle manager. In turn, the middle manager is in charge of a group of supervisors, and he is also a member of a group of middle management peers who report to a member of the top management of the company.

As Figure 2–1 shows you, Supervisor C is a member of three groups: of Middle Manager B's department; of the group of B's subordinate supervisors, who are Supervisor C's peers; and of Supervisor C's own working section. The circles that overlap Supervisor C in the figure reveal that he or she is a linking pin, that is, a manager who joins together three groups and who can serve as a communications link among them.

SUPERVISORY ROLES

■ Like actors who have to learn their parts well, all managers are expected to learn and play specific parts or roles in order to successfully execute their duties. The precise role of each manager depends upon his or her understanding of the job he or she holds as well as on the pressures, rewards, sanctions, and guidelines brought to bear on the manager from inside and outside the organization. What follows here is a brief but important discussion of the ways in which roles are assigned to, designed for, and perceived by each manager in a business enterprise. The author is indebted to Robert L. Kahn and his associates[2] and to Professor John B. Miner[3] for much of what follows on managerial roles.

Role Prescriptions

The subordinates, peers, friends, family, and superiors of supervisors help shape and define the kind of roles the supervisors play and the way in which they play their roles. Demands made on the managers by these groups and the business organization in which the supervisors work literally prescribe the roles or write out **role prescriptions** for managers to follow as they define and play out their roles at work. Through the expectations and demands placed on managers, people help shape each manager's perception of his or her job. Organizational influences, such as policies, procedures, job descriptions, and the union contract, also exert influence on the roles of each manager. Of course, the demands of different people and of the organization itself can and do create conflicts in the minds of managers as to just what their roles should be and how precisely they should play them.

---

2. R. L. Kahn et al., *Organizational Stress: Studies in Role Conflict and Ambiguity* (New York: John Wiley & Sons, 1964).
3. John B. Miner, *Management Theory* (New York: Macmillan, 1971) pp. 39–48.

Role Conflict

When conflicting and contradictory demands are made on managers, they find themselves in awkward or difficult positions. How they react to such pressures and what precisely they do to cope with such conflicts—all this depends upon their own values and perceptions and the circumstances of the **role conflicts.** To illustrate this concept, consider the following incident that happened in a suburb north of Chicago. Two paramedics discovered a conflict between the instructions in their medical manual and the provisions of Illinois law about the proper method of treatment for heart-attack victims. If the paramedics followed their manual, they believed they would be in violation of state law. If they followed the law, however, they believed that they would be giving incorrect or outmoded treatment to their patients. Perplexed, they asked their hospital administrator for clarification of the treatment procedures. To their surprise they received in reply a letter that called them incompetent and suspended them from their duties as paramedics! This example highlights a common job situation—one in which an employee's training in organizational procedures contradicts the demands of the immediate boss. Role conflicts can and do occur, and when they do, they create tensions and job dissatisfaction for the employees.

Role Ambiguity

Whenever a manager is not sure of the role he or she is expected to play in a given situation or how to play it, he or she is a victim of **role ambiguity.**

Role conflict results from clearly contradictory demands. Role ambiguity results from unclear or nonexistent job descriptions, orders, rules, policies, or procedures. Where role ambiguity exists, managers may do things they should not do, fail to do things they should, and find it hard to distinguish where one manager's job begins and another's ends.

Role Performance

Even if there is no role conflict or role ambiguity, managers may still fail to meet the demands of their role prescriptions for one or more of the following reasons:[4]

1. The managers may not perceive their jobs in the same way as the role prescriptions specify;

2. The managers may not want to behave in the way the role prescriptions specify;

---

4. Ibid., pp. 44–46.

3. The managers may not have the knowledge, mental ability, or physical skills needed to behave in the way the role prescriptions specify.

> Where role behavior deviates from role prescriptions because of faulty role perceptions or insufficient role capacity, the usual solution is either to provide more information or to alter the individual's role prescriptions so that he [or she] can meet them. Where motivation is lacking or inappropriate, it is typical to manipulate sanctions with a view to inducing a greater desire to act in accord with role requirements.[5]

Role Sanctions

To encourage managers to play their roles in accord with the role prescriptions established by their superiors, business corporations often make use of positive incentives or rewards. If the rewards for proper role playing prove to be ineffective, the superiors may use negative means to secure conformity. Such means, which may include threats or actual punishments, are known as **sanctions.** If a business organization does not provide adequate sanctions, the roles played by various managers and the ways in which they understand them may deviate widely from their superiors' role prescriptions. Unless people want to play their roles as prescribed or feel that they have no real alternatives to doing so, they will usually tailor the roles they play to suit themselves.

THE DIVISION OF THE SUPERVISOR'S TIME

■ Many studies have been done on how supervisors spend their time. Surprisingly the studies show many similarities, although in specific details there are wide differences among supervisors. Table 2–1 is a composite constructed from several studies, including some done by the author. It is intended merely as a guide and is useful when you examine the use of your own time.

Items 1, 2, and 4 together fill more than one half of a supervisor's day. All of them involve direct contact with subordinates.

If you know how you spend you time, compare your use of time to what is reported in Table 2–1. If your figures differ significantly, you might reexamine your routine for a possible reallocation of your time. You may be spending too much time with one person or activity at the expense of others. If you don't know how your time is spent, keep track

---

5. Ibid., pp. 45–46.

Supervisor's activity	Approximate portion of 8-hour day	Approximate number of minutes
1. Production supervision	25%	120
2. Personnel administration and grievances	20%	96
3. Concern with machines and equipment	15%	72
4. Appraising worker performance	8%	38
5. Concern with materials	8%	38
6. Planning and scheduling work	5%	25
7. Meetings and conferences	3%	15
8. Other	16%	76
	100%	480 minutes

Table 2-1. A typical distribution of a supervisor's time.

of it according to the above categories and compare the results. A two-week record should be enough. You may be in for some surprises.

SUPERVISORS AND EDUCATION

■ Education benefits individuals and their employers as well. By providing students with both general training and specific skills, education holds out the potentials of a greater earning power for individuals and of higher productivity for employers.

Figure 2–2 shows the rising educational level of the American labor force since 1940.[6] Included are persons from eighteen to sixty-four years of age. Over the last fifty years the educational level of Americans has risen steadily. More than 60 percent of Americans today have graduated from high school, and nearly 25 percent have gone on to some form of higher education.

Figure 2–3 shows the educational attainment of male and female employees in various occupations.[7] How does your own educational level compare with those in your occupation? How does the educational level of your subordinates compare to those doing similar work?

What does all this mean to supervisors? Demands on them to improve their education have never been greater. Increasingly they must

6. "Educational Attainment of the Work Force," *Road Maps of Industry* 1758 (The Conference Board, March 1975).
7. Ibid.

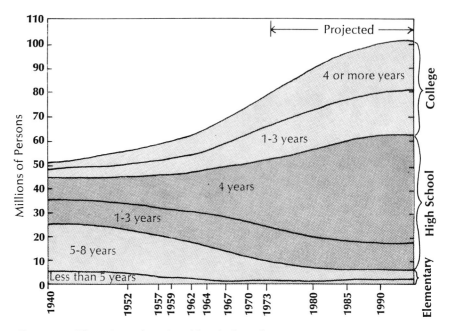

*Figure 2-2. The rising educational level of workers
(civilian labor force) 18-64 years of age.*
Adapted from The Conference Board, *Road Maps of Industry* 1758, March 1975.

supervise people whose educational levels are rising and may one day surpass their supervisors' level. As people advance intellectually, their wishes and attitudes change. They want more meaningful work and better opportunities. Many seek a stronger voice in the decisions that affect them and their work. The need such workers feel for adequate explanations and their demand for greater consideration are factors that affect directly the success a supervisor has in working with and through them. The days of simply issuing orders and expecting blind obedience are over.

If supervisors are to make progress in their jobs, they can only do so through the cooperation of their subordinates. For the way supervisors build their reputations depends on their workers' performance. Workers can earn a good reputation for themselves only on the basis of what they themselves do. But the supervisors build their own reputations mainly as a result of good performances on the part of their group of workers. Supervisors need to be like catalysts that cause good results to take place. If supervisors fail to have good results, this may be because they have not acquired through education the skills and knowledge needed to guide others effectively and to communicate convincingly the organization's goals to their subordinates.

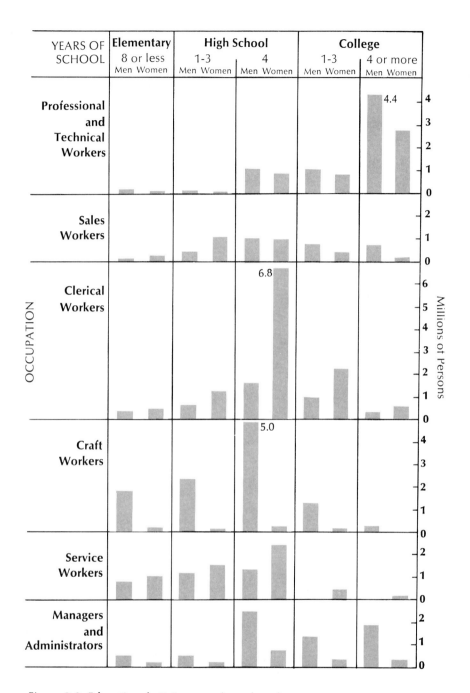

Figure 2-3. Educational attainment of employed persons
in nonagricultural occupations, 1973.
Adapted from The Conference Board, *Road Maps of Industry* 1758, March 1975.

REASONS FOR THE FAILURES OF SUPERVISORS

■ Many companies have studied the reasons for supervisor failures. They have done so in order to prevent similar failures in the future through a better program for training and selecting new supervisors. These managerial studies have revealed certain general, recurring causes of supervisory failures. Among these causes are: (1) problems in human relations; (2) character or personality defects; (3) improper attitudes; and (4) a lack of skill in carrying out managerial functions.

Problems in human relations head most lists of supervisory failures. Such supervisors have difficulty in getting along with their subordinates, fellow managers, or the boss. This failure in human relationships is usually due to a lack of understanding of human behavior and needs as well as an inability to relate successfully with others. It can be prevented through education and through a greater attentiveness to others and a greater concern for their welfare. The remaining chapters of this book deal directly or indirectly with this problem area as well as with the other causes of supervisory failures. The emphasis is on how to prevent such failures from happening to you.

Character and personality defects are the next most common reasons for failures of supervisors. Many supervisors lack the personal qualities that are a must for success in the management ranks. Qualities such as integrity, initiative, a sense of justice, a spirit of service, and emotional stability must be in a supervisor's personal inventory if he or she is to achieve success as a manager. It is possible to overcome deficiencies of this type through an honest evaluation and awareness of yourself, your strengths and weaknesses, and a concerted effort to improve. Your boss's appraisals can be most beneficial in pointing out problem areas on which you need to concentrate your attention.

Improper attitudes show up in our everyday actions and conversations. Attitudes are your readiness to react in a predetermined way to some stimulus. They directly affect your behavior and work performance. Attitudes may color your approach to people and problems. Often workers who have been promoted to supervisor have difficulty seeing things from a management point of view. They may fail to identify with management. They may retain their identity with the workers or lack a feeling of identity with either the workers or management. They may fail to see the need for discipline and as a result, undermine their own formal authority and control over their workers.

Besides failures in directing subordinates, the lack of ability to adequately plan, organize, control, and coordinate your operations can cause failure for a task or an entire program of action. Just as this is so, so too can these tasks be mastered. Time and experience, your own as well as others', can be your chief aids in overcoming such problems. Participation in company training programs, self-help sessions with good texts on the subject, and formal education are the preventive measures you can use at any time. There is really no excuse for being poor at any of the management functions when there are so many ways open to you to become more proficient.

These four causes of failures on the part of supervisors can all be prevented through a personal commitment to do so. The remaining chapters of this book will do much to help you prevent your own failure. Study them, and relate the ideas and recommendations in each chapter to your personal situation.

SOURCES OF SUPERVISORY PERSONNEL

■ Many companies prefer to choose some or all of their supervisors from the worker ranks. The best worker in a group is often chosen to lead that group because of his or her excellent performance record. There is an inherent danger in this approach which can be quickly understood through an examination of the **Peter Principle.**[8] Dr. Laurence J. Peter, a scientist who has devoted many years to studying the reasons for incompetence, explains his principle in the following way:

> In a hierarchy every employee tends to rise to his level of incompetence.

Dr. Peter sees people progressing from the level at which they are competent to another higher level as a result of their past performance. Given enough time and enough levels in a hierarchy, each employee eventually rises to and remains at a level where he or she will be incompetent.

Dr. Peter's corollaries to his main principle run as follows:

> In time, every post tends to be occupied by an employee who is incompetent to carry out its duties.

> Work is accomplished (in an organization) by those employees who have not yet reached their level of incompetence.

Peter's supporting evidence seems to be well documented. He sees people being promoted to a superior position on the basis of their performance in an inferior one. The very skills that make a man a good worker (technical ability and the ability to follow orders) may cause him to fail as a supervisor. Dr. Peter cites the example of promoting a teacher to an administrative position because he or she is the best teacher in the school or department. Thus the reward for excellent

---

8. Reprinted by permission of William Morrow & Co., Inc., from *The Peter Principle* by Dr. Laurence J. Peter and Raymond Hull. Copyright © 1969 by William Morrow & Co., Inc.

teaching is to be removed from the students and the classroom which accounted for the teacher's success.

Depending upon the selection criteria and process used to promote an individual worker, the Peter Principle may or may not apply. In most cases promotion from within the organization improves morale and personal initiative. Whether or not the individual worker can make a successful transition from worker to manager, which almost always requires making new associations and a change in attitudes, remains for a program of training and apprenticeship to verify.

Many companies prefer to choose some or all of their supervisors from the ranks of junior or senior college graduates. After some preliminary training and understudy these candidates are installed as functioning supervisors. The practice of hiring all or some of a firm's new supervisors from outside the company takes its toll on the morale of the employees. Personal incentive and the competition for supervisory positions are enhanced, however, since there are fewer positions available to which the workers can hope to advance. As a result, some workers may begin to pursue a college education, while others may be encouraged to complete the advanced training they began years ago. The practice of hiring supervisors from outside the company may also prevent excessive inbreeding and infuse new ideas and approaches into the organization.

A major disadvantage to the practice of going outside the organization for new supervisors is that the new college graduates who may be hired may lack firsthand experiences of the company's workers. They may also fail to understand the attitudes of the workers and their interactions among themselves. The new supervisors may be young, and as a result they may experience a built-in resistance to their supervision from older, more experienced members of the department.

We should keep in mind also the fact that many workers do not wish to be promoted to the ranks of management. Some are reluctant to give up the security that goes with knowing their job and doing it well. Others may be convinced that the extra prestige is not worth the extra time, problems, and responsibilities that go along with a management position. In some cases a worker may be asked to take a pay cut if he or she accepts a promotion to supervisor. This is due to the loss of hourly pay status, annual pay increases, and overtime pay. Although the cut may be only temporary, it is still a lot to ask of a worker who makes such a shift.

In addition, the attitude of the company toward supervisors may make many workers try to avoid a supervisory role. In far too many companies, supervisors are given lip service as managers, but in fact they are not treated with the respect managers are entitled to receive.

We have seen how supervisors are the most important level of management for achieving organizational goals and for carrying out management's programs. Inevitably all the programs that management has planned can only be executed through the workers under the skillful direction of their supervisors. We have examined the responsibilities of supervisors to their subordinates, peers, and superiors, and the ways in which they are expected to discharge such responsibilities.

A look at how typical supervisors spend their time reveals that over half the time is spent with subordinates on matters that directly affect the subordinates. The more supervisors are with their subordinates, the more are they aware of their subordinates' individual needs and contributions. The supervisors must lead the workers to superior performances. This they must do both for their own advancement as supervisors and for the advancement of the workers as well. A supervisor's reputation is a direct result of the collective efforts of himself or herself and of the workers.

We have seen how the educational level of American workers has risen since 1940, and how it continues to rise. This places an ever increasing demand for all supervisors and managers to advance their own educational levels if they wish just to stand even with where they are today, let alone to move forward.

Finally, we have examined the reasons for the failures of many supervisors. All such failures can be prevented. Often they are caused by the lack of an effort at self-improvement. If the desire for self-improvement exists, there is really no reason why any supervisor should fail. All that supervisors need do is to channel their efforts to situations and problems where there is the greatest need of attention. At the same time they need to apply their own energies to these problems as well as the energies of others who stand ready to help them.

linking pin	Peter Principle	role prescription
peers	role ambiguity	sanctions
	role conflict	

1. How does the Labor Management Relations Act (the Taft-Hartley Act) of 1947 describe a supervisor's job?
2. To what three groups is a supervisor responsible?
3. In what way is a supervisor responsible to staff managers?
4. Give an example of the Peter Principle from your own experience. Must the principle always apply? If not, why not?
5. State two specific advantages that accrue to a company when it promotes workers to supervisors.
6. What is a major disadvantage to bringing in college graduates who have no experience as workers and installing them as supervisors?
7. If you were planning a training program for workers to become supervisors, what specific elements would you include?
8. In what ways would the training program described in question 7 change if recent college graduates were to be enrolled?
9. What are the four chief reasons for supervisory failure? How can each be prevented?

CASE PROBLEM

The Mix-up About
the Miami Convention

Ken Anderson was perplexed. He wondered how his subordinate Jane Adams could have left for the Miami convention as his department's representative after he had clearly refused to authorize her attendance. After a trip out of town on company business, he returned to his office where he found Jane's leave request on his desk with his boss' signature on it.

"That little schemer! She pulled a fast one behind my back. I'll bet she went in to see Mary as soon as I left the office."

Ken picked up his phone and called his boss' secretary.

"Hi Silvia, it's Ken. Is Mary free sometime tomorrow? I've got something urgent to kick around with her. . . . 1 p.m.? O.K. I'll need about half an hour. . . . Thanks. See you tomorrow."

All that next morning Ken kept thinking about Jane in Miami while her work was piling up in the office. He was doing a slow burn when he reached Mary's office at five minutes to one.

"Come in, Ken, I've been meaning to talk with you."

"I've been anxious to see you too," said Ken.

After some routine exchanges about company affairs and work in process, Ken finally managed to get Mary onto the real purpose of his visit.

"Jane Adams dropped this on my desk yesterday", said Ken, handing Mary the leave request. Mary looked it over briefly.

"What's the problem? She had every right to go on the basis of what she told me. You weren't here, so naturally I had to make the decision."

"Did Jane tell you that I had turned down her request to attend that conference?"

"No, she did not. I'm amazed to hear that. She gave me no clue that she had even mentioned it to you."

Ken moved uneasily in his chair, and then explained: "I want you to know that I refused her request for two reasons. First, she has not been doing her work up to standard for the past few weeks, and I wanted her to concentrate more on her job. Secondly, no funds were earmarked in my department budget for travel to that convention. We have money approved for two conferences that are more important to the department than the Miami meeting."

Mary got up and began to pace the office. Then she remarked, "You were gone, and as in the past I had to make a decision in your absence. Jane has been here a long time—longer than you. She has received fine appraisals from you for the past two rating periods. I felt it in the company's best interest to send a representative from your department to the Miami meeting. Jane is the most senior member of your department and deserved a chance to participate. As for the money, just pay her travel out of your budgeted funds and cancel one of the other conferences."

"Mary, it's not that simple. As far as the money goes, the Miami trip will eat up nearly all the funds, which makes it impossible for anyone to attend either one of the other conferences. Also, what's at stake here is our working relationship. We need to get a few things straight between us now so that similar difficulties can be prevented in the future."

Questions

1. What are the "few things" Ken wants to get straight between himself and his boss?
2. Was Mary right in approving Jane's travel request? Why?
3. How is the concept of role ambiguity illustrated in this case? What can be done to clarify Mary's role toward Ken?
4. Give role prescriptions for Mary and Ken that would prevent such problems in the future.

3 Management Functions:
PLANNING and ORGANIZING

LEARNING OBJECTIVES

■ After reading and discussing this chapter, you should be able to:

1 Define planning as a function of management.

2 List and briefly explain the elements of planning, and describe how they relate to one another.

3 Describe PERT and explain how it can serve supervisors as a planning tool.

4 Describe the use of a Gantt chart for production planning.

5 Define organizing as a function of management.

6 List and briefly explain the five principles that govern the organizing process.

7 Describe the information found on a job description, and explain how it can help a supervisor in the organizing process.

8 Describe the information found in a job specification, and tell why it should be considered when a supervisor is engaged in the organizing process.

INTRODUCTION

■ As stated in Chapter 1, the five major functions of a manager are planning, organizing, directing, controlling, and coordinating. These are the most important and time-consuming activities common to all managers. In this chapter we shall examine briefly two of these functions: planning and organizing, which are preparatory phases for management action. Both are efforts to predict and prepare for the future and, therefore, will help to prevent problems and provide a way in which such problems can be resolved.

PLANNING

■ The first and most basic management function is **planning.** Through it a manager attempts to prepare for and predict future events. Planning involves the construction of a program for action in order to achieve stated goals through the use of people, procedures, and practices. Figure 3-1 illustrates the **flow of planning** in a formal organization.

We need to keep in mind the fact that problems can arise in a business for any of the following reasons: (1) lack of an overall policy; (2) poor or confusing statements of policy; (3) programs that are ill planned; (4) faulty thinking on the part of a manager; and (5) wasteful or poorly thought-out procedures. Often a combination of these problems may occur. Let us now consider the various steps in the flow of planning.

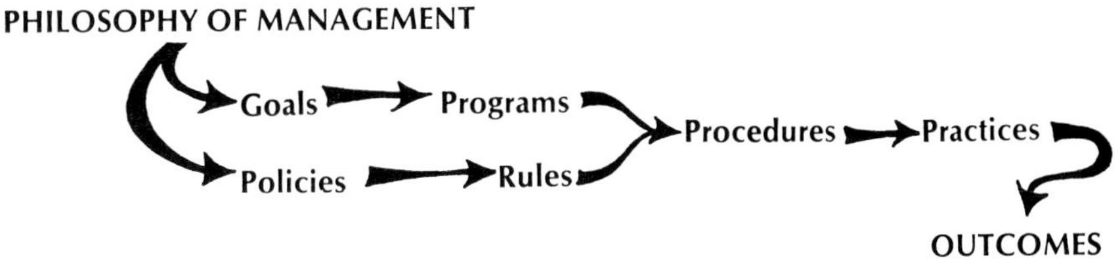

PHILOSOPHY OF MANAGEMENT

Goals ▶ Programs ▶ Procedures ▶ Practices

Policies ▶ Rules

OUTCOMES

Figure 3-1. The flow of planning in a formal organization.

Flow of Planning

PHILOSOPHY OF MANAGEMENT

The way in which the top management of a company looks at all the people and events that have an impact on the business is known as the **philosophy of management.** Their philosophy is the result of their principles, attitudes, and thought processes. It results in general and usually predictable approaches to setting goals and solving problems.

GOALS

The objectives that the top management decides are worth aiming at or working to achieve are known as the company's **goals.** Once the goals are decided upon, they must be described formally. At the same time, some of the company's resources of people and materials must be committed to enable the company to reach the goals. As a rule, goals should be precise and specific. Typical goals for a company might include promoting the best qualified middle managers or workers, or increasing sales for specific lines or the whole company by 10 percent over the next two years.

POLICIES

The broad guidelines for management action that have been formulated by members of the top management are known as **policies.** They are an attempt to coordinate and promote uniformity in the conduct of the business and in the behavior of employees. In a corporation the board of directors usually formulates the policies, which are basically plans for insuring smooth and harmonious operations of the company.

RULES

Inflexible guides for the behavior of employees while at work are known as the company **rules.** They are specific directions that govern the way people should act. Many are prohibitions, such as "no smoking" while on the job or in certain locations; others are simply instructions, such as "turn lights off when they are not in use." Rules promote safety and security; they attempt to conserve resources as well as prevent problems from arising during the course of the company's operations.

PROGRAMS

Plans for each division, department, or section that are developed by the managers at every level are organized into **programs.** They list the goals to be accomplished and answer general questions about the use of the company's resources, including *who, what, where, when, why,* and *how much* in specific details.

PROCEDURES

General **procedures** are the ways or methods for carrying out individual programs and handling the day-to-day routine of the business. They are plans that answer questions about how each employee should carry out his or her duties.

PRACTICES

Further refinements in procedures that deal with the "nitty-gritty" or small details that must be decided upon for the completion of work are known as **practices.** They fill in the gaps left by general procedures and are usually established by individual managers for their own departments.

OUTCOMES

The main reason for establishing goals, policies, rules, programs, procedures, and practices is to come up with satisfactory results, which are known as **outcomes.** Examples of satisfactory outcomes are producing

A Comprehensive Example

a new product on time or effecting a sharp increase in the profitability of a specific line or product.

To tie these terms together and to illustrate how the flow of planning works in a formal organization, examine the following excerpts from a management memo recently issued to all supervisors of a Chicago bank. The memo begins with a statement of the bank's philosophy on the subject of the memo: employee promotions.

> It has been this bank's experience that the majority of our employees have both the desire and ability to advance in position, pay, and responsibilities. Our promotion system therefore should and does allow for the consideration of employees who: (1) aspire to a higher rated job; and (2) currently possess the specific job qualifications necessary for a higher position; or (3) currently do not possess specific job qualifications for a higher position but who are qualifiable with additional training and experience.

> In line with federal and state rules and guidelines, our promotion system should insure that all bank employees are considered equally for job openings. The bank's objective is equity—all employees are to be treated fairly, regardless of race, sex, age, religion, color, or nation of origin. This is the reason why our department executives identify areas where underutilization of women and minorities may exist and why our promotion system is examined regularly to ensure its effectiveness in meeting the organization's primary goal: promoting the best qualified and most deserving employees.

As you can see, the bank has clearly stated what it believes to be true about the majority of its employees and how federal and state rules and guidelines have helped shape the company's primary goal. The statement of this goal is followed in the memo by these words:

> It is this bank's policy therefore to promote from within to obtain from the bank's work force qualified applicants for each new position and job whenever it is possible to do so.

The bank has stated its policy, but has left itself an "out." Notice that the memo does not say that people will be promoted from within to fill every position vacancy. It says that qualified applicants will be sought from among existing employees "whenever it is possible to do so." Federal and state rulings may force the bank to look outside for qualified or qualifiable women and minorities to meet the bank's or the Government's hiring goals or quotas for these groups.

The memo continues by outlining its program and procedures for promoting from within:

Our promotion program consists of the following procedures:

Testing
Tests have long been used as initial selection devices for measuring clerical skills. Mental ability, personality, preference, psychological and motivational tests, and indexes have gained prominence in the business world and have been used at times in the promotional process. Unfortunately, tests do not take into account performance, attitude, potential and career aspirations.

Consideration for Seniority and Experience
On-the-job experience is important to personal growth. However, the amount of experience does not always correlate with performance excellence. A major weakness in seniority systems is the concept that the individual with the most experience is the most competent and therefore deserves first consideration for promotional opportunities. Such a system also ignores performance, attitude, potential and career aspirations.

Posting Job Vacancies and New Positions
Our job-posting procedure calls for us to display a list of selected job openings accompanied by abbreviated job descriptions. Employees then bid for job openings for which they feel qualified. This system has been praised because employees can initiate their consideration for advancement.

Individual Requests or Recommendations by Others
Our promotion system is multifaceted. Employees can initiate their own personal promotional considerations by expressing their career desires to their supervisors and a member of the Personnel Division. A large number of promotions are made through the use of this procedure, but additional methods are used more frequently. Supervisors initiate promotions within their own areas or recommend exceptional employees for consideration elsewhere. Also, promotional considerations are initiated by Personnel; when employees approach the top of their salary ranges, the Personnel Division automatically adds them to an eligibility list for consideration for promotion to a higher rated job.

The Personnel Division utilizes every internal promotional channel available to find suitable candidates for promotion when job openings occur. Only when there are no suitable candidates among our existing employee ranks is the search extended to the marketplace.

These procedures are all efforts at fleshing out the promotion program developed as a result of management's philosophy and policy on promotion from within. The remainder of the memo evaluates how well the bank has been doing in meeting its goal and following its policy:

> In order to evaluate how well we follow our promotion policy, a study of internal employee assignments was conducted during 1977. The results revealed that about 75% of our job openings were filled by individuals already in the bank's employ—50% were by promotions where the employees moved to positions with higher job ratings, 15% were by placements of trainees and 10% were lateral transfers. A similar study is underway covering the year 1978.
>
> The success of any promotion method is measured by results, and the bank's method compares favorably to other procedures, including those utilizing testing, seniority, and an old but currently publicized method—job posting.

TYPES OF PLANS

■ Human and material resources place a limit on planning. The five M's of management—men and women, money, machines, materials, and methods—are not only the subject matter of plans but determine their scope as well. One major resource is time. How much of it is available and how it is used are of the utmost importance in planning. Indeed, many plans are based entirely on time.

Time Plans

Time is the unit of measure for most of a manager's personal and departmental activities. The timing for one plan may directly affect the timing for others, as is the case in sequential activities. The scheduling of work is almost always based on time. Time plans answer the questions "when?" and "how long?"

Money Plans

The most common types of money plans are budgets. They authorize the availability and expenditure of funds for various activities such as operating expenses, maintenance, overtime, and payroll. Managers may be involved in the preparation of budget requests or they may simply be told how much money will be available to them. Whether or not they assist in the preparation of their budget, they are bound to adhere to it. Therefore, budgets are both plans and controls. These types of plans answer the question "How much?" You will learn more about budgets as forms of control in Chapter 4.

Personnel Plans

The effective and efficient allocation of all human resources also must be planned. How will each member of the organization be employed for the company's profits as well as his or her own benefit? The answer to this question demands a detailed knowledge of people and their interests and abilities as well as a clear understanding of the goals and work to be accomplished. These plans answer the question "Who?"

Procedures Plans

A program for action must include both general procedures and their details, which are called practices or methods. Procedures plans then are plans within plans. They set forth the way in which programs can be implemented. They constitute the tools you need to make your plans work. Programs may be implemented entirely through existing procedures or may require modifications or additions of such procedures. Procedures plans answer the question "How?"

Material Resources Plans

These plans determine the expected use of machines, equipment, supplies, raw materials, and space. They state the roles each of these factors will play in a program. Such plans answer the questions "What?" and "Where?"

The question "Why?" should be answered before each step of planning is accomplished, and the answer communicated to all concerned.

"Things must be going badly—he keeps referring to it as my plan."

REG HIDER

PLANNING TOOLS

■ The path a product takes from the beginning to the end of its assembly or manufacture is called its route. The route should allow for the even flow of goods in production. Scheduling concerns itself with the sequence of events and the time that each production step takes. An effort is then made to calculate the total production time.

There are several methods currently in use to schedule production. All of them involve: (1) a detailed listing of all production operations; (2) a careful assessment of the time each operation will take; (3) the determination of which production steps precede each of the other steps, and which can take place simultaneously; and (4) the calculation of the total time required to produce the product—the **critical path.**

PERT

One of the most precise and popular methods used in critical-path scheduling of production is called the Program Evaluation and Review Technique, which is known more simply as **PERT.** This method was originally developed in the 1950s by the United States Navy to assist in the development of its Polaris submarine missile. It has been used to schedule office work, construction projects, and many other simple and complex tasks.

PERT lends itself to any task that has an easily defined sequence of jobs or **activities.** These activities must be performed in a precise sequence and must have definite starting and ending points called **events.**

Production activities are listed, and completion times are determined for each activity. Then each activity is studied to determine which other activity or activities must immediately precede it. The results are then listed as shown in Table 3–1.

Table 3-1. A PERT listing of production activities with completion times.

Activity code	Activity	Time in days	Immediate predecessor
A	Decision to make new product	30	None
B	Product design and development	45	A
C	Raw materials ordered and received	25	B
D	Machinery acquired or modified	30	B
E	Work force assembled and trained	15	C D
F	Production of new product	10	D E
G	Finished goods shipped	1	F

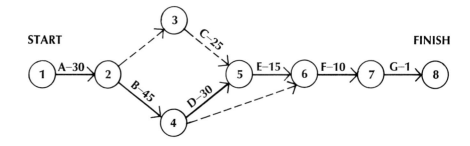

Figure 3-2. A PERT flowchart for production activities in Table 3-1. (Solid line shows the critical path.)

After all the activities have been listed along with estimates of the times needed to complete each of them, a diagram is constructed to show the interrelationships among the different activities. **Events** are added to mark the starting and ending times for each activity. Event 1 marks the beginning of activity A. Event 2 marks ending of activity A and the beginning of activities B and D. The results are shown in Figure 3-2.

Note that before activity C can be performed, activity B has to be completed. Activity B is an important activity because without it, activities C and D cannot begin. If B were delayed for any reason, so too would activities C, D, E, F, and G.

From the flowchart in Figure 3-2 the critical path can be determined by listing the activities from event 1 through event 8 that have the longest completion times. The longest path through the PERT flowchart is the critical path because the events along it determine the earliest possible completion time for the production that is being scheduled. The critical path in the flowchart in Figure 3-2 is calculated as follows:

Activity		Time in days
A		30
B		45
D		30
E		15
F		10
G		1
Critical Path	=	131 Days

If a production planner can shorten the time required for any one or several of the activities along the critical path, he or she can usually achieve an earlier completion time. Conversely, if after each activity begins, any one of them takes more time than originally scheduled, the entire completion time is increased. For these reasons the critical events —those along the critical path—must be monitored carefully once they have begun. Seldom does production flow as scheduled without some changes occuring as each new activity is executed. As events change along the critical path, the entire flowchart should be reexamined to determine if a new critical path has replaced the old one.

The Gantt Chart

For scheduling work on a smaller scale, say, by department or on machines, a **Gantt chart** (named for its inventor, Henry Gantt) may be used. It is the most familiar tool for planning work on the basis of time. Examine Figure 3–3 to become familiar with its symbols. The solid lines drawn between the planned start and finish of each job on each machine indicate what stage of completion each job is in at any given moment in time. The example assumes that we are at the start of operations on Thursday, at 8:00 a.m. Each day is divided into four two-hour blocks, or eight hours in all. All this time is available for production.

Looking at the work schedule for the lathe, you can determine that job A–4 was scheduled for and completed in eight hours on Monday and Tuesday. The seven hours immediately following its completion have been set aside for some reason, indicating that the lathe was not available for production during that period. Job A–5 was initially

Figure 3-3. Gantt-type chart for scheduling work on reserved time basis.

Machine	Machine number	Monday	Tuesday	Wednesday	Thursday	Friday
Lathe	114	A-4	⊠	A-5	A-6	
Drill Press	315	C-3	C-4			
Grinder	42	B-7	B-8	B-9		

⩒	=	Today's date
⌐	=	Signifies day and hour for work to begin
¬	=	Signifies day and hour for work to end
⊠	=	Reserve time (for maintenance or to catch up)
A-1	=	Job number

"Miss Blanchfield! . . . Why don't I have anything to do?!!"

planned to take a total of nine hours, but as of Thursday morning it is two hours behind schedule. As of Thursday morning, job C–4 and job B–9 are each three hours ahead of schedule.

Planning Guidelines

To summarize the planning process, consider the eight guidelines for planning that appear below:

1. Study your situation in detail, examining the past as well as the present;

2. Make reasonable assumptions as to future events and outcomes;

3. Develop an initial detailed plan;

4. Determine your time and resource requirements;

5. Check available resources against plan requirements;

6. When adjustments are required, make them where they will least affect the overall plan so as to balance resources against requirements;

7. Develop alternate plans for reasons of flexibility;

8. Plan within the framework of existing policy, and prescribe detailed procedures and practices.

ORGANIZING

■ **Organizing** involves the following steps: (1) determining the tasks to be performed; (2) establishing a framework of authority and responsibility among the people who will accomplish them; and (3) allocating appropriate resources to accomplish the tasks and reach the objectives. Organizing is directly related to and interdependent with planning. These two preparatory functions cannot be accomplished separately.

At the top management level, concern should be for the entire operation. What is the best way to organize the overall operation so as to perform our tasks with a minimum amount of conflict? The answer may result in a division of labor along functional lines (marketing, production, etc.); along product lines; or according to a geographical division. Whatever method is chosen must effectively involve the necessary people and resources in a cooperative effort to complete the assigned tasks.

The organizing process involves a knowledge of many factors and demands a step-by-step approach:

1. To determine the tasks to be accomplished in order to reach the planned objectives;

2. To subdivide the major tasks into individual and group-related tasks;

3. To identify and design into the organization the interpersonal relationships necessary to perform the tasks;

4. To select and assign personnel and material resources to each task;

5. To delegate the necessary authority and responsibility;

6. To provide the necessary training;

7. To follow the five principles that govern the organizing process, as described below.

Organizing Principles

There are five widely recognized **organizing principles** that you should keep in mind as you plan an organization, evaluate one, or attempt to redesign one. These principles are unity of command, span of control, delegation of authority, homogeneous assignment, and flexibility. Each will prevent the designer of any business organization from falling victim to the most common pitfalls in organizing.

UNITY OF COMMAND

This principle requires that there be only one individual responsible for each part of an organization. In each organization, each element of the organization should be under one chief. No person should have more than one person to whom he or she is responsible. Each individual throughout an organization should have only one boss.

SPAN OF CONTROL

This principle is based on recognition of the fact that there is a limit to the number of individuals a supervisor can manage effectively. Many variables can influence the span of control. Two of these variables are the kind and complexity of the tasks to be performed by your subordinates, and the degree of experience and expertise your subordinates possess. In general, the higher up one goes in the management hierarchy, the smaller is the number of subordinates each manager has to supervise.

DELEGATION OF AUTHORITY

Delegation of authority means that individuals are given authority in keeping with their responsibilities. In addition, each manager should delegate routine or repetitive tasks to subordinates in order to concentrate his or her own efforts on the most important duties and to gain time to handle new duties received from his or her boss. Through delegation you train your subordinates to handle aspects of your job while you learn aspects of your boss' job. You groom others for promotion while you groom yourself for promotion.

HOMOGENEOUS ASSIGNMENT

Homogeneous assignment is the predominating principle by which functions are grouped. Similar or related functions give rise to similar problems and require individuals with similar levels of intelligence, experience, and training to deal with them.

FLEXIBILITY

Flexibility means that an organization must have the capability of reacting to changing conditions even as it carries out its current, assigned tasks. Once any organization is set up, changes begin to take place. Managers must periodically review the organization's relevancy and adaptability to new situations. The manager must balance "what is" with "what should have been." Attention should be given to the subtle changes worked out by an organization's individual members. Often they will incorporate changes that lend greater efficiency and effectiveness to the operation as a whole.

TOOLS FOR ORGANIZING

■ Any established organization can be represented visually by an organization chart. This can be used to give a clear understanding of the part each person and department plays as well as to illustrate the thinking behind the organization. Organization charts are a graphic representation of the principles of unity of command, span of control, and homogeneous assignment.

An organization chart should clearly show the following:

1. Who reports to whom;
2. The flow of authority and responsibility;
3. The work to be accomplished and how it is divided;
4. Lines of promotion;
5. Lines of communications;
6. Linking pins.

In addition to the organization chart, two additional aids should be used by a supervisor engaged in organizing and staffing. They are the job description and the job specification.

Job Description

A **job description** is a listing of the duties and responsibilities of a job or formal position in an organization. All jobs you supervise should have such a listing. Reference to this document proves helpful in assigning work, settling disagreements, appraising subordinates, and filling vacancies. Figure 3-4 is a job description for a secretarial position. You will note that nothing on it deals with the personal characteristics desirable in the job holder. These are detailed in the job specification.

Figure 3-4. Job description for a secretarial position.

```
       TITLE:  SECRETARY    JOB NO. C-10    GRADE 4    EFFECTIVE DATE 1-79


   GENERAL:    Performs clerical and secretarial duties involving
              typing, dictation, correspondence and report
              preparation, filing, maintaining records, scheduling
              appointments, distributing mail.  Handles confidential
              information regularly.

   SPECIFIC   Take dictation in shorthand and transcribe.
   DUTIES:    Compose and type routine memos and business correspondence.
              Compile and type routine reports.
              Sort and distribute mail daily.
              Maintain and set up files of memos, letters, and reports.
              Obtain data and information by telephone or personal
                 contact on behalf of supervisor.
              Receive visitors.
              Schedule supervisor's appointments.
              Answer phone and take messages.
              Handle confidential files.

   EQUIPMENT: Electric typewriter, dictation machine, mimeograph
                 and ditto machines.



   Analysis by:  _____    Approved by:  _____
```

Job Specification

Figure 3–5 shows the **job specification** or personal characteristics required of a person to fill the secretarial position in Figure 3–4. Such factors as typing speed, clerical and secretarial experiences, formal education, and the like are listed. Knowledge of this data is extremely important in selecting someone to fill a job, assigning work, and determining promotions.

Figure 3-5. Job specification for a secretarial position.

```
        TITLE:    SECRETARY    JOB NO. C-10    GRADE 4    EFFECTIVE DATE 1-79


        FACTOR                    EXPLANATION

        Education                 High school graduate.


        Experience                Secretarial, including stenographic duties.


        Training Period           1 month.


        Dexterity                 Precise movement of hand and fingers required
                                  to operate typewriter at no less than 60 words
                                  per minute and take dictation at 90 words per
                                  minute.


        Adaptability              Must be able to adjust to frequent changes in
                                  duties such as typing, filing, composing letters,
                                  handling telephone.


        Judgment                  Must be able to follow existing procedures
                                  and establish new practices where necessary.
                                  Must be able to compose business letters,
                                  establish filing systems, and receive visitors.


        Responsibility for        Maximum loss possible: $200, due to clerical
          Losses to Company       errors.


        Contact with Others       Frequent contacts with visitors, vendors,
                                  and company managers.


        Physical Demands          Lifting requirements: under 10 pounds.



        Analysis by: _____        Approved by: _____
```

As time passes jobs change. So too must their descriptions and specifications. It is standard practice to review and update these documents at least once every two years. If you have them and they are up to date, use them. If this is not the case, you should set about the task of constructing them.

The checklist below will prove helpful in reviewing your organization's operation and effectiveness. A yes response to each question assures you that your approach is correct.

1. Do my people know their authority and responsibilities? Are both equal?

2. Do they know how their parts of an operation relate to the whole?

3. Do they know with whom they must coordinate and why?

4. Does each person have just one person to whom he or she must answer and from whom he or she must take instructions?

5. Have I tried to match my people's abilities and interests to the tasks to be performed?

6. Are the procedures and methods explained, understood, and working out well?

7. Can the necessary decisions be made quickly at the level most directly involved?

INSTANT REPLAY   This chapter has explored the two primary management activities upon which all others depend: planning and organizing. Planning is an activity that helps a person or business to prepare for the future. Goals are established; resources acquired and made available; and the necessary time tables, procedures, and standards are established to aid the people involved in reaching the goals.

Planning attempts to predict and deal with the future. It can be accurate and successful if the proper lessons have been learned from past planning efforts, and if sufficient guidelines and crosschecks have been created to monitor the progress of the plans. If improper philosophy, policies, programs, procedures, or practices have been created, or if these elements are unclear or lacking, then the planning process will not lead managers to achieve the goals they are seeking.

Organizing is the function through which tasks are created and grouped to accomplish the plans and to reach the goals set forth in the planning process. A framework of authority and responsibility is established, and the tasks are assigned to the people best equipped to execute them. The five principles that govern the organizing process must be adhered to if the organization is to reach its goals on time.

KEY WORDS	activities	job description	planning
	critical path	job specification	policies
	events	organizing	practices
	flow of planning	organizing principles	procedures
	Gantt chart	PERT	programs
	goal	philosophy of management	rules

QUESTIONS FOR DISCUSSION

1. Give an example that illustrates how the planning function influences the organizing function.
2. Relate the terms *programs, procedures, practices,* and *plans* to each other.
3. Why is planning referred to as a prerequisite for the other management functions?
4. Give an example that illustrates how the tasks to be performed influence the way we organize in order to accomplish them.
5. Do you think that organizing demands that the organizer should have an in-depth knowledge of his or her subordinates' abilities and interests? Why?
6. Which approach do you favor—assigning work to people or people to tasks? Why?
7. Do you think that PERT could be used to program office work? Explain.
8. Is the following a policy, a procedure, or a practice:

   This company shall make every effort to hire qualified applicants for the jobs available, regardless of their age, race, religion, sex, or country of origin.

CASE PROBLEM

One Man, One Boss?

Philip Turnbull, age twenty-five, was recently appointed to the temporary position of assistant to the director of personnel in order to train for a new position to which he will be assigned at some future date: director of recruitment for corporate personnel. Philip had a bachelor's degree in business administration and two years' experience as a personnel interviewer with his present employer. He liked the work, was considered a bright "up and comer," and had been good at his old, nonsupervisory job. What he had been doing was performing the final or selection interview with applicants for supervisory positions. He interviewed both current employees who were being considered for promotion as well as outsiders who were applying for available positions. As director of recruitment he would be involved with interviewing graduates of junior and senior colleges, and supervising two college recruiters whom he would have to hire.

As assistant to the personnel director, Philip had to perform many routine duties that his boss normally would have handled. In addition, he was to learn the company's personnel policies, programs, and procedures thoroughly so that when he moved to the director's job, he would follow them in his recruitments. As an understudy to the various section supervisors (see Exhibit A) Philip was to study how each of them operated and evaluate their operations in a formal

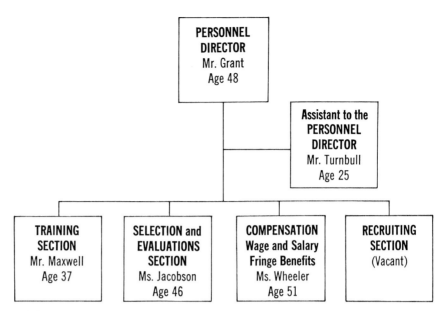

```
                    ┌─────────────────┐
                    │   PERSONNEL     │
                    │   DIRECTOR      │
                    │   Mr. Grant     │
                    │   Age 48        │
                    └─────────────────┘
                              │      ┌──────────────────┐
                              │      │  Assistant to the│
                              │      │   PERSONNEL      │
                              ├──────│   DIRECTOR       │
                              │      │  Mr. Turnbull    │
                              │      │   Age 25         │
                              │      └──────────────────┘
```

TRAINING SECTION	SELECTION and EVALUATIONS SECTION	COMPENSATION Wage and Salary Fringe Benefits	RECRUITING SECTION
Mr. Maxwell Age 37	Ms. Jacobson Age 46	Ms. Wheeler Age 51	(Vacant)

Exhibit A

report, which was due on Mr. Grant's desk in two weeks. His report was to consist of three parts: (1) present operations—programs and procedures; (2) effectiveness of existing personnel programs and procedures; (3) recommended changes in existing programs and procedures.

Philip soon found out that, although he had responsibilities, he had no real authority to carry them out. He met with strong resistance and what he considered to be delaying tactics on the part of the supervisors of nearly every section. When he requested an interview with one of the supervisors, he would either find the interview had to be rescheduled or cut short because the supervisor was involved with "more important" business. As Mr. Maxwell put it:

Look here, Turnbull, I haven't time for you now. I have four subordinates out there who need my time and direction. We have work to do that directly affects this company's work force. The information you need will take time to dig up. Just give me a list of what the old man wants to know about my operations, and I'll see that he gets it.

Philip also found that two of the section supervisors were under the impression that he was to assist them with their routine work. Ms. Jacobson wanted him to do a statistical analysis of the reliability and effectiveness of several tests she used to help predict success on the job. Ms. Wheeler wanted him to conduct an informal wage survey in the community to see if the company's wages were in line with those of other local employers. When Philip tried to explain that he was supposed to serve only Mr. Grant, both supervisors pointed out that he was their understudy and was charged with evaluating their operations. What they wanted him to do for their sections was clearly in line with his duties, as the two supervisors understood them.

Frustrated and fearful that his report would be inadequate and late, Philip decided to have a conference with Mr. Grant. After patiently listening to Philip's description of his problem in carrying out his assigned tasks, Mr. Grant gave the following monologue:

Philip, I cannot understand why you have been unable to progress any further than you have. You are a disappointment to me at this point and raise serious doubts in my mind as to your ability to handle the new director's job.

Ms. Wheeler and Ms. Jacobson are both highly qualified professionals. You are their understudy while you are working under my supervision, and the work they have requested you to do will help you evaluate their operations and make recommendations to me about how to change things for the better.

Mr. Maxwell is also correct in his assertion that his people need his time more than you do. He has two new people who have to be broken in and twenty new workers to help train throughout the company.

Now what I propose is this. Take care of the Wheeler and Jacobson studies first. Then give Maxwell a list, and he will have the answers for you. He's a good man. I'll give you one more week to get your report finished, but it has to be in my hands in three weeks to the day. Agreed?

Philip moved uneasily in his chair. "Agreed," he said with a sigh.

"Fine. Now how are those routine matters we discussed on Monday coming along?"

Questions

1. What are the major planning problems in this case? What would you do to solve each of them?

2. What organizing principles have been violated? How has each of them been violated?

3. Evaluate Mr. Grant's monologue in the light of your answers to questions 1 and 2.

4. If you were Philip, what would you do? Why?

5. Do you see any problems in the way the personnel department is organized? If so, how would you reorganize it?

4 Management Functions:
DIRECTING, CONTROLLING, and COORDINATING

LEARNING OBJECTIVES

■ After reading and discussing this chapter, you should be able to:

1 Define directing as a management function.
2 List and briefly explain the specific activities performed by managers when directing their subordinates.
3 Define controlling as a management function.
4 List and briefly describe the types of controls used by managers.
5 Describe management by exception.
6 Describe management by objectives.
7 Define coordinating as a management function.

INTRODUCTION

■ Chapter 3 introduced the preliminary management functions: the activities of planning and organizing. These two "first" functions usually precede the other three that we shall examine now: directing, controlling, and coordinating. It is often impossible to tell where functions begin or end. For your understanding and study of them, we shall explore the three functions separately.

DIRECTING

■ **Directing** may be defined briefly as supervising. This word literally means *to oversee*. The directing function includes recruiting, selecting, and placing new employees; these three activities are often lumped together under the heading *staffing*. In addition to staffing, directing includes training; offering incentives to subordinates to encourage acceptable performances (loosely called *motivating*); evaluating; disciplining; and promoting.

The directing function involves the ability on the part of a supervisor to motivate, educate, guide, and communicate with subordinates, individually and in groups, throughout the execution of their assigned roles. *Motivating* implies a personal knowledge of your subordinates, of their needs, desires, and ambitions. *Educating* means fostering the intellectual development of subordinates. *Guiding* relates to your leadership, that is, your ability to get them to respond positively to instructions. *Communicating* implies an ability to convey clear understanding and the reasons behind company instructions and events.

To direct your subordinates properly, you as a supervisor must gain their respect, confidence, and willing cooperation. Each supervisor must strive to build an effective organizational unit—one in which the company can achieve its goals—and an efficient organizational unit—one in which the members can find the means to achieve their personal goals.

The direction of subordinates is by far the most demanding and time-consuming of all the functions of a supervisor. If it is done well, your success is practically guaranteed. If it is done poorly, both personal and organizational failure are usually assured. Your reputation as a supervisor depends upon the efforts of your subordinates. Their response to your efforts to direct them will either promote your own advancement or retard it. These are the primary reasons why directing subordinates has been chosen as the focal point of this book. This chapter only gives you a broad overview of the directing function. A detailed analysis of the many facets of successful supervision is contained in Chapters 6–19. They set forth the principles and concepts you must master in order to direct your subordinates successfully.

Staffing

Recruiting, selecting, and placing new employees in their jobs are part of the process called **staffing.** Through staffing, managers at all levels attempt to fill the jobs they have available and to assign the tasks to people and people to tasks. In short, staffing tries to build an effective and efficient organization.

Recruiting is the search for talented people who are or might be interested in doing the jobs that the organization has available. It often occurs inside as well as outside the organization. Announcements about job opportunities may be posted on bulletin boards and/or placed in newspapers or trade journals. Everyone who responds is considered a potential employee until the decision to hire is made.

Selecting screens the potential employees and job applicants to determine who among them is most qualified. Tests, interviews, physical examinations, and records checks are used to eliminate the least qualified. The applicants are narrowed down to the one or more who are most qualified, and eventually a decision to hire one or more persons is made. Selection is often considered a negative process because every applicant has flaws, faults, or deficiencies. The people hired have the least serious or fewest deficiencies for the job opening.

Placement follows as soon as the person is hired. It involves introducing the new employee to the company—its people, the jobs, and the working environment. The new employee is given the proper instructions and equipment needed to execute the job for which he or she has been hired. Once work rules are explained and coworkers introduced, the break-in period begins.

Managers are often assisted in their staffing efforts by members of the personnel department. The decision to hire should be the supervisor's, however.

Training

Training teaches skills, knowledge, and attitudes to both new and existing employees. It can do this through classroom instruction, laboratory experiences, and on-the-job instruction. While the supervisor of each trainee has the primary responsibility for training, the actual instruction may be done by any persons who are qualified to train. Often the personnel department assists the supervisors in training by providing training materials or by teaching them how to train their subordinates. In some cases the supervisors may delegate the responsibility to train to an experienced subordinate and retain accountability for the training.

Offering Incentives

Incentives are things or states of being that the company hopes will have a strong appeal to their employees. Those who desire one or more of the incentives offered by their employer will be encouraged to give a better than average performance in their jobs in order to earn the incentives.

Incentives offered to employees vary from one business to another and from one department within a business to another. They all are offered with the intention of helping managers build an effective and efficient organization. Most companies attempt to offer a wide variety of incentives in the hope that they will have something for everyone. The idea is that what may not appeal to one employee as desirable and worth having will appeal to another.

The kinds of incentives most businesses offer include many of the following: raises, bonuses, promotions, better working conditions, greater challenges and responsibilities, and symbols of status in the or-

BLONDIE

ganization. Status symbols can be as small as a phone on the desk, as large as an executive suite, or anything in between. Which one, if any of them, will appeal to any given employee at any given time depends upon the individual—his or her current level of job satisfaction and/or financial condition.

Evaluating

Evaluating requires each supervisor to make periodic appraisals of each subordinate's on-the-job performance. To do this adequately, each supervisor needs precise guidelines and standards to follow. People are rated on the basis of what they are expected to do and how well they have done it.

Evaluating employees is done informally each day through routine, regular observations of their work by their supervisors. Formal appraisals are usually done once or twice each year. Supervisors who are not with their people regularly usually find it difficult to rate them properly. Supervisors who don't know themselves well—their own biases and prejudices—often make employee appraisals that are something less than objective or honest. Supervisors who don't know their subordinates and their work well find that it is impossible for them to make honest and fair appraisals.

The aim behind employee evaluations is to help people improve their performances on the job and, therefore, their usefulness to their employer and their pride in themselves.

Disciplining

Disciplining requires supervisors to act on the knowledge they have about their subordinates' mistakes and shortcomings on the job. *Positive discipline* demands that employees be informed about and understand the rules and expectations their bosses and employers have for them. The emphasis should be on preventing trouble rather than on dealing with it. When infractions of the rules occur, supervisors must act to enforce the rules and standards of performance by dispensing the appropriate disciplinary measures. This is known as *negative discipline*.

Appropriate disciplinary actions can be as simple as an informal discussion or as serious as a formal discharge. Discipline is allied with appraisals and is absolutely essential for a successful operation. Rules and procedures without some methods for their enforcement are just a waste of paper and ink. If infractions go unpunished, many employees will lack the incentives they need to behave themselves properly on the job.

Promoting

While supervisors seldom have the exclusive power in **promoting** subordinates, they have a great deal of influence over promotions. Their recommendations, ratings, and formal evaluations of their subordinates' performances are the case upon which promotion decisions are made. Promotions usually require the approval of two or more levels of management and the endorsement of the personnel department, if the company has one.

Recommending a subordinate for promotion can be a difficult dilemma for many supervisors. A subordinate who is qualified for promotion usually has a fine work record. If that person leaves the department, this may leave a gap in the supervisor's organization and an act that is hard to follow. Thus, many supervisors find themselves hoping that a subordinate will not get promoted, and they may even work against a promotion. Such feelings and actions have their roots in a supervisor's own insecurity or in his or her failure to develop and train a successor before a promotion takes a talented individual out of his or her department. Ambitious, hard-working people must have the potential for promotion as well as supervisors who help them achieve their promotions through adequate training, appraisals, and counseling. Keeping superior subordinates down will only cause them frustration. Ultimately they will leave the organization for another company that will recognize and reward their efforts.

The function of directing is the most difficult and demanding of the manager's functions because it deals with the most complex of the business' resources—people. As stated above, it involves the manager's ability to motivate, educate, guide, and communicate to subordinates, individually and in groups, as they carry out their assigned roles. It also demands that each of its parts described above be skillfully executed.

CONTROLLING

■ **Controlling** involves the ability to prevent, identify, and correct deficiencies in all phases of business operations. It is an integral part of all the other functions of a supervisor and must be designed into them as each of them is carried out.

If a manager is going to prevent, identify, or correct deficiencies, he or she must be able to relate to some established standards or norms. It is only through comparisons that "good" or "bad," "hot" or "cold," "fast" or "slow" take on meaning. The quality of work or products is relative to the standards or norms that have been established. The controlling process establishes standards, communicates them, measures performance against them, and identifies deviations from them.

Types of Controls

Prevention controls are familiar to all of us. Safety devices on a machine or firearm to avoid unintentional operation and accidents; a lock on a door to prevent unauthorized entry; safety locks on medicines to keep them out of the hands of children; the various checklists we'll discuss in this chapter—all are examples of prevention controls.

It is usually best to prevent trouble rather than to have to deal with it. If all our problems could be foreseen, we would need no other types of controls.

Diagnostic controls attempt to identify trouble when it occurs. Ideally, they should do so immediately. Just as a physician cannot prescribe a treatment for an illness until its cause is identified, a manager needs to know why something has gone wrong in his or her department.

Some familiar examples of diagnostic controls are warning lights, meters, and gauges. Personal observation and the detection of abnormal sounds and sights are daily routines that managers use to detect trouble. Once you detect them, you must identify their causes and deal with them efficiently.

Therapeutic controls are usually automatic in their operation. They are designed to deal with and correct deficiencies once the causes are known. Thermostats that regulate the operation of heating and cooling systems are a good example. A pressure-release valve that opens when the pressure reaches a certain level and releases excess pressure is another example.

All of these controls are necessary to most operations and should form an integrated approach to controlling. No one type is completely adequate. It is only through their combined use that a manager can effectively control resources and activities.

A budget and the budgeting process will help to illustrate effectively the three types of controls. A budget is both a plan and a control. It plans for the expenditure of money that is expected to be available over a fixed period of time. The people who will be spending the money usually participate in its preparation. They are also bound to follow the budget or money plan once it is approved.

A budget is a prevention control because it prevents (or helps prevent) unauthorized expenditures of funds. It is a diagnostic control because it helps monitor the funds being spent as they are spent and matches actual expenditures against planned expenditures. Where the actual expenditures significantly differ from what was planned, an investigation should be made to determine why. If the budgeting process is at fault, changes can be introduced to make it more realistic. Budgets have a built-in therapeutic control. When more money is requested than has been authorized, it cannot be spent without higher approval.

Control Characteristics

Regardless of the types of controls that are used, they should have the following characteristics. They should be:

1. timely—that is, provide immediate feedback;
2. appropriate—just right for the task they must control;
3. adequate—that is, they should go far enough for the purpose;
4. understandable—that is, clear to those who must use them;
5. economical—to install and operate.

To illustrate these characteristics, we shall look at a toolroom situation. Foreman Fred wants to control the use of his department's tools. He starts by locking them up in a toolroom. Next he assigns one person the task of issuing and accounting for each tool. Then he issues an I.D. card to each subordinate and sets up a procedure whereby tools are exchanged for these cards. Finally, he establishes records of the condition the tools are in and fixes responsibility for changes in conditions. This may or may not be a good control system, depending upon the circumstances. It may be too expensive, depending upon the value of the tools he is safeguarding. It may be inadequate and impractical if, in the absence of the toolroom supervisor, no one can get a tool. It may be inappropriate if only one or two workers have need for the tools. In short, all of the above characteristics are necessary; and if any one of them is missing, the controls will accomplish something less than is desired.

Controls used in offices should also have the five control characteristics listed above. Controls used to prevent problems include company policy, procedures manuals, periodic status reports of work in process, follow-up visits and memos, periodic staff meetings, and routine observations by office supervisory personnel.

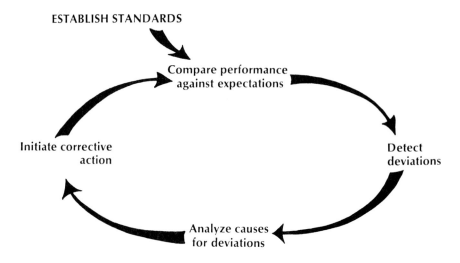

ESTABLISH STANDARDS

Compare performance
against expectations

Detect
deviations

Analyze causes
for deviations

Initiate corrective
action

Figure 4-1. The control process in a formal organization.

The Control Process

Figure 4–1 summarizes the control process in any formal organization. Any collection or system of controls for whatever purpose should set up standards and norms, detect deviations from established standards and norms, and initiate corrective action. All of these three basic operations should be constructed and carried out with the five control characteristics in mind.

Management by Exception

The principle of managing by exception applies most directly to controlling. A manager should spend his or her time only on those areas that demand personal attention. The routine should be delegated to others and procedures established to deal with it. When exceptions occur, they are usually situations for which there are no precedents. Then the manager's attention is warranted. Where controls reveal exceptions for which there is no prescribed cure, the manager must take action.

Management by exception can be illustrated through the examples in Figure 4–2. They show a few of the everyday demands on a supervisor's time and how the supervisor should handle each of them. Whenever possible, supervisors should delegate routine tasks to their subordinates to free themselves for additional tasks they may receive through delegation from their superiors and to enable them to spend more time on their most essential and important tasks—those that demand their personal attention and expertise.

TASK	KEEP	DELEGATE	OTHER ACTION
Appraisals of subordinates	✓		
Interviewing applicant for job vacancies	✓		
Handling regular reports to higher-ups		✓	Read before sending
Answering correspondence	Those only supervisors can answer	Those others can do well or better	Read before sending
Attending meetings and conferences	When your expertise is needed	When your input is not required	Have substitute brief you

Figure 4-2. Applying the principle of management by exception in the execution of supervisory tasks.

Management by Objectives

Objectives are goals or targets to be achieved or reached within some specific time. Management by objectives (MBO) requires each manager (and sometimes each worker) to sit down periodically with his or her boss and work out goals that can be mutually agreed upon. These goals will, when achieved, result in a more efficient and economical operation for a section or department. Such goals can only be set after a clear understanding is reached about what a department's weaknesses are and what its capabilities seem to be. Goals set by any manager must be in line with, not contradictory to, those of his or her superiors and those of departments with whom the manager must coordinate.

If MBO is to work efficiently, those participating in it must set clear, specific, and realistic goals for both the short and the long run. Once goals are set, progress (or lack of it) in reaching each goal is monitored by both the person who set the goal and his or her superior. The goal-setter's reputation and performance appraisals will be based in large measure upon his or her efforts and success in reaching the established goals.

MBO reduces the need for close supervision by involving subordinates in setting their own sights on specific targets and then having them work out the methods by which each goal can be reached. In such a system, results are what really matter. In setting goals, each subordinate and his or her superior get to know more about themselves, their individual capabilities, their current operations, and their personal commitments to achieve.

COORDINATING

■ **Coordinating** is the managerial function of making sure that all the various parts of your organization operate in harmony with each other. It involves the integration of all the details necessary for reaching your goals. Each activity must be executed without interference with or from other activities in order to have a unified effort in both the planning and execution phases of every operation.

The coordinating function should happen simultaneously with all the others. Through it, you attempt to foresee potential conflicts or deal with existing ones. The organization may have to be redesigned for better efficiency, or plans may have to be modified to include a better mix or balance between people and events. Controls may be so rigid that they restrict completion of the work. The direction of subordinates may be so poor that they rebel and resist instructions or work against organizational objectives. Lack of coordination means chaos.

Basically, there are two kinds of coordinating: *coordination of thought* and *coordination of action*. You coordinate thought by making certain through effective communications that all parties involved in planning an operation have the same concepts, objectives, and overall understanding. You coordinate action by including in your plans for a project the steps to be taken in its execution, the sequence of these steps, the roles that each person must play, and how all the persons involved are to cooperate. In other words coordinating is both an aid to planning and an objective to be realized through planning.

Coordination of thought and action are best provided for by fixing responsibilities. Each person should have an up-to-date, clear definition of his or her duties in general as well as the particular role for each project in which he or she becomes involved. In this way the efforts of everyone are directed toward common purposes with as little wasted effort and overlap as possible. Coordination is the thread that binds an entire operation together. It must be practiced by all managers at every level, both horizontally and vertically.

These are some of the more common management tools for coordinating:

1. meetings and conferences;
2. standard operating procedures (SOPs);
3. routing of informational bulletins, newsletters, and copies of pertinent documents to all parties concerned with a project;
4. company policies;
5. strict adherence to the organization structure and use of established channels of communications.

The checklist that follows will aid you in your performance of all your other functions. Keep it handy and make frequent reference to it.

1. Are intelligent cooperation and mutual understanding exhibited throughout my organization?
2. Are my people cross trained to keep them aware of the overall operation and the need to cooperate?
3. Are operating procedures available in writing when and where needed?
4. Are vertical as well as horizontal communications channels existent, open, and used?
5. Are external activities monitored, interpreted, and integrated, where appropriate, to our operations?
6. Is someone available at all times to execute my role in the event of my absence?

INSTANT REPLAY

The five major functions of a manager have been discussed. Whether you are the president or middle-level supervisor of a company, you must plan, direct, control, organize, and coordinate the activities of your operation. The differences at each level of management have to do with the amount of time devoted to each function. A supervisor spends most of his or her time in directing, while a president spends most of his or her time in planning.

Planning and organizing are prerequisites to action. Directing is the execution function through which work is initiated and accomplished.

Controlling is concerned with the outcomes of these three functions, and coordinating tries to prevent any interference among the different functions.

KEY WORDS

controlling	**disciplining**	**promoting**
coordinating	**evaluating**	**staffing**
directing	**incentives**	**training**

1. Is the assignment of tasks to a subordinate part of the organizing or directing function? Explain.

2. Using an automobile as your model, give an example of the three types of controls—prevention, diagnostic, and therapeutic.

3. The five management functions are common to all managers. Discuss why each function differs in terms of the amount of time spent on it by a supervisor as contrasted to a chief executive.

4. Briefly outline a system you would use to control the use (or abuse) of a photocopying machine in an office.

5. What activities go on in a business under the heading of staffing?

6. How can the personnel department help a supervisor with his or her staffing activities?

7. What is "management by exception"? Give an example from your own experience to illustrate how you or your boss has practiced management by exception.

8. In what ways is a budget both a plan and a control?

9. What is management by objectives (MBO?) Give an example of how it can be useful to students in their college work.

CASE PROBLEM

Day Shift Versus Night Shift

John Jackson is one of two shop supervisors at Ace Plastics. Lately he has noticed that production has been falling behind schedule. The work being fed to his shift by the other shop supervisor was beginning to pile up. As the result of an investigation to uncover the causes, he has discovered that the employees are away from their work areas an average of fifty-five minutes each morning and forty-five minutes each afternoon. His observations yielded the following averages over a one-week period.

Cause or reason	Average daily time away from work (in minutes)	
	AM	PM
Coffee breaks	35	20
Washroom visits	10	15
Tardiness	5	10
Miscellaneous	5	
Total	55	45

Suspecting lost time to be a major cause of the production problem, John last week posted the following memo in the employee lounge:

TO: All Workers
FROM: J. Jackson, Supervisor
Effective immediately the following rules shall be enforced:
1. Coffee breaks are limited to the fifteen minutes the company allows. Breaks start at 10:00 a.m., and the lounge is to be cleared of all personnel by 10:15 a.m.
2. Washroom visits should be held to ten minutes.
3. Any worker not at his or her work station by the start of the day-shift operations (8:30 a.m.) will be docked 15 minutes pay for each minute he or she is tardy.
I trust a word to the wise is sufficient.

J. Jackson
Supervisor

Since the posting of this memo, the situation has gotten steadily worse. Although the workers this week kept their coffee breaks to the fifteen-minute limit, John has noticed them bringing their coffee from the lounge to their work areas. Also John has discovered that every washroom visit by each employee has been almost exactly 10 minutes. Although most employees are at their work stations by 8:30 a.m., start-ups seem to be taking longer than they used to. He has only docked two workers' pay.

John wondered if his method of scheduling production might be at fault. He didn't think so because it worked quite well over the past seven months and no significant changes have taken place in personnel, machinery, or equipment.

John stayed late last night and talked about his problem with the other shop supervisor, Dick Mankowski. Dick has been using the same scheduling techniques as John, but has had no significant problems. Dick mentioned that his subordinates were tardy on occasion, and that they were a little lax in holding breaks to the fifteen minutes allowed. But since production was on schedule, he has decided to overlook these things. Both supervisors had complete autonomy in scheduling their output.

"Oh, by the way," said Dick, "next time you post a memo for your workers, make sure that's what it says. My people got pretty upset about your last memo until I assured them it was meant for your people only."

Questions

1. What do you think about Dick's statements to John?
2. Given the lost-time data John has found, what actions would you take if you had his job?
3. Why has production gotten worse on the day shift since John's note was posted?
4. Why do you think Dick's shift has not fallen behind even though its losses of time are similar to those of the day shift's?
5. What should John do now?

5 Communications

■ After reading and discussing this chapter, you should be able to:

1 Define communications.

2 List the four components of all communications.

3 List the four objectives of all communications.

4 List and briefly explain four barriers to successful communications.

5 Briefly outline the steps in planning communications.

6 Define listening, and relate your definition to the concepts of concentration and perception.

7 Differentiate between "open" and "closed" questions.

8 List the three basic ingredients of any oral communications.

9 State the three steps you should take to improve your written communications.

INTRODUCTION

■ The importance of communications to you as a manager cannot be overstated. Routinely you must give orders and instructions, and relay information and ideas to and from your subordinates, superiors, and peers. If your plans are ever to come to fruition, they will do so only through effective communications.

Communication is the transmission of information and understanding from one person to another through the use of common symbols. By communicating you are sharing or exchanging information or ideas. The common symbols used are both verbal and nonverbal. You use language, either written or spoken, color, pictures, objects, facial expressions, gestures, and actions to carry your message.

GOALS OF COMMUNICATION

■ All your communications have as their objective or goal the production of one or more of the following responses:

1. To be understood—to get something across to someone so that he or she knows exactly what you mean;

2. To understand others—to get to know their exact meanings and intentions;

3. To gain acceptance for yourself and/or for your ideas;

4. To produce action—to get the other person or group to understand what is expected when it is needed, why it is necessary, and sometimes how to do it.

All of the above goals point out the two-way nature of communications: communications take place between one person or group and another person or group. There must be a *common* understanding—each person must know the other's meaning and intent.

Communications can flow in four directions: up, down, left, and right. If you recall the discussion of the organization chart in Chapter 3, you will note that the lines connecting the various blocks of the hierarchy of management are also lines of communications. All managers have a frequent need to communicate with others. When they do, they generally follow these formal lines or channels of communication. Figure 5-1 illustrates the basic components in any effort to communicate our thoughts or ideas to others: the **message,** the **transmitter,** the **medium,** and the **receiver.**

Figure 5-1. Basic components in any effort to communicate.

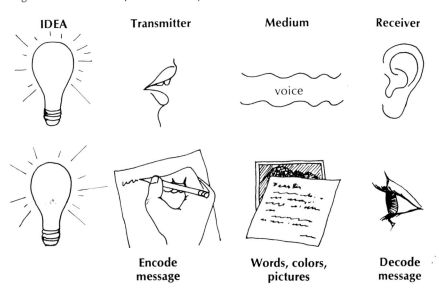

> **Ideas and feelings**
> What do I wish to communicate? Why?
>
> **Audience—their backgrounds and experiences**
> To whom do I wish to communicate? Why?
> Who should not receive the communication? Why?
>
> **Timing and the environment**
> When should I attempt to communicate? Why?
>
> **Location and the environment**
> Where should I attempt to communicate? Why?
>
> **The medium**
> How should my message be communicated? Why?
>
> **The content**
> How should I phrase my message? Why?
> How much should I say? Why

Figure 5-2. Getting ready to communicate.

THE COMMUNICATIONS PROCESS

■ People with ideas to communicate must formulate answers to several basic questions before they can successfully get their thoughts across to others. Figure 5-2 provides a quick checklist for you to follow as you prepare to communicate. Once its questions are answered in the mind of the sender of the message, he or she will be ready to communicate. Whether a message is to be sent by voice or by some visual medium, it must be encoded by the sender and decoded by the receiver. Therein lie additional problems for the communicator.

COMMUNICATIONS BARRIERS

■ The essential ingredients in the communications recipe are the message, the message sender (transmitter), the message carrier (medium), and the receiver. If any one of these ingredients is defective in any way, clarity of meaning and understanding will be lacking. **Communications barriers** can arise that will spoil these ingredients and the communications process. There are six major barriers to successful communications.

Uncommon Symbols

Words take on meaning only in the context of the message they compose. Facial expressions can be misinterpreted. Gestures viewed out of context can take on entirely different meanings than were intended. Every parent knows the blank expression that his or her child's slang expressions can create. Every employee knows the worry that accompanies the boss' departure from his normal and predictable patterns of behavior.

Example. Sally, the supervisor of a data-processing section, has an established pattern of communications. Each morning upon entering her section she makes it her duty to greet each of her seven subordinates warmly and to inquire about their well-being and work. Today she entered the office and went straight to her desk, ignoring her subordinates. As a result, what do you think might happen in the minds of her subordinates? What might the impact of her change in behavior be on today's work output?

Improper Timing

Unless the receiver is in the right frame of mind and tuned in on the proper channel, he or she won't hear your message. The sender can be upset, agitated, or improperly prepared to communicate. Sometimes the need for the message is too far removed from its transmission, or the message gets delayed in transmission and arrives too late to be effective. We all know the regrets that go with speaking in haste while we are in the heat of emotion or without thinking. When we are distracted, we may hear words but not their intended meanings.

Example. Charlie is upset because of a personal problem with his wife. He has been thinking about it on and off since his arrival at work two hours ago. His supervisor approaches him and begins a detailed explanation of a task he wants Charlie to perform before leaving today. Although Charlie is clearly distracted, he nods assent throughout his boss' instructions. What might happen? What should the boss have done that he did not do?

Atmospheric Disturbances

The atmosphere or environment of your communications should be as free as possible from noise, interruptions, and physical discomfort for both you and your receiver. You have certainly felt the frustration of trying to be heard above the din of machines or the confusion of others talking simultaneously. Remember the "What?" that you received so frequently? Wouldn't it have been better to have changed your environment before you tried to communicate?

Example. A supervisor had no sooner begun to interview a job applicant in her office when the phone rang. After handling the call, she resumed the interview. Five minutes later a change in shift occurred, creating noise and confusion outside her office. How successful do you think this interview was for both people?

Improper Attitudes

Unfavorable predispositions toward the subject, the sender, or the receiver will interfere with understanding. In fact, they may provoke emotional and harmful responses in place of the desired ones. A poor attitude in the sender or the receiver will confuse rather than clarify.

Example. One of your subordinates, Shirley, comes to you again today to see if she has gotten the pay raise you recommended her for two weeks ago. She has been asking you about it for the past five days, and you have told her that as soon as you know you will tell her. Since you haven't heard anything yet, you answer her tersely, "No! Now don't bother me!" Haven't you created problems for yourself by such a response? How do you think Shirley will react?

Background Differences

A lack of similar backgrounds in the sender and the receiver with respect to their education, previous experiences, or present environment may hinder receptiveness to a message and prevent a proper reaction to it. The newcomer attempts to give advice to the old-timer without success. The grade-school graduate attempts to gain acceptance from the college graduate and fails. These and many similar situations arise every day at work to prevent a mutual understanding. Someone has made improper assumptions about the other—a barrier has been erected.

Example. Allen, age twenty-five, is being "broken in" by Arthur, who is about to retire. Arthur is teaching Allen his job. While certain established procedures are being discussed, Allen recommends a change he feels will speed things up. Instead of evaluating Allen's proposal, Arthur shuts him off by stating, "Who's the expert here, you or me? This is the way I have always done it, and it works." What do you think will be Allen's reaction?

Sender/Receiver Relationships

Functional relationships, such as line manager versus staff manager or engineer versus accountant, can hinder communications. Suspicion on the part of one about the other's intentions or about his or her ability to communicate about the other's specialty will block the transmission of information. Positional or status relationships, such as supervisor versus subordinate or skilled worker versus apprentice, can cause one to tune out the other.

Example. A production manager is told by a personnel manager (who has the functional authority over hiring) that the production section will receive a qualified minority worker—the first for the production manager's section. Since the production manager resents being told whom to hire, he or she begins to plot the newcomer's failure for the sole purpose of embarrassing the personnel manager. What are the possible consequences of such an action? How could they have been prevented?

Regardless of the type of barrier encountered, they all have the same effect on communications: something less than a proper understanding will occur. Knowing that these barriers exist is half the battle. The other half is working to tear them down or minimize their effects.

PLANNING COMMUNICATIONS

■ No matter to whom or why you feel the need to communicate your ideas, planning must precede the act of communication. The following checklist will serve you well as a sequential list of steps to follow as you prepare to communicate:

1. Is this communication really necessary? (Will whatever I want to communicate be an improvement on the present situation? If you have no clear answer to this, proceed no further until you do.)

2. What are the objectives I wish to achieve by communicating? (Do I want action? Understanding? Acceptance?)

3. What are the essential facts? (Do I know them and, more importantly, am I able to properly express them?)

4. Are my thoughts outlined? (Whether your outline is mental or in writing, keep it brief and to the point.)

5. Have I considered my receivers? (What are their needs and how can I sell my message to them? Do I know their backgrounds and frames of reference for this message? What about our relationship? Have I included the "why" in the message?)

6. Have I chosen the right symbols? (Whether words, pictures, or some other symbols, are they correct for this communication? Remember that words take on meaning both from the context in which they appear and in the minds of the persons involved in the communication process.)

7. How should I communicate this message? (Face to face? In writing? If in writing, should I use a memo? A letter? Have I time for formal channels, or should I go directly to my intended receivers?)

8. When should I communicate? (Am I aware of the time element and the receptiveness of my receivers? When will the environment be most free from anticipated disturbances?)

9. Have I provided for feedback? (Will I be able to judge my receivers' reactions and will they be able to seek further information from me if they want to? How will I be sure my message has been received and properly interpreted?)

Listening

Just as important as planning your communications is the need to be tuned in to your potential receivers. **Listening** involves paying close attention to the speaker for the purpose of hearing his or her words. It requires on the part of the listener both **concentration** and **perception.** If you wish others to listen to you, you must learn to listen to them as well.

Nearly one third of your working day as a supervisor and about 90 percent of your class time as a student are spent in listening. Most of what you know and believe you have learned by listening to others. Your business and academic success depends as much upon listening as upon writing, speaking, or reading. Listening attentively will allow you to respond intelligently to what you hear, but this requires a conscious effort on your part.

Concentration—mental receptiveness coupled with physical alertness—is the key to effective listening. You must be intent on hearing what is said and try to detect what is not said—the underlying or hidden meaning that sometimes accompanies a speaker's words. You should try to **perceive**—to separate the speaker's facts from his or her feelings so as to comprehend the meaning. Try to prevent your emotional reactions to the speaker or the subject from conflicting with your perception of the meaning. Often a tone of voice, mannerisms, or physical appearance will get in the way of your reception if you don't consciously act to prevent it.

Another problem that can prevent effective listening is the fact that the mind is capable of comprehending the spoken word at a much faster rate than it is normally delivered. This extra time gives your mind time to wander from the subject or to begin extending or anticipating what the speaker will say next.

To counter these problems that can plague the listener you should look at the speaker, put facts above feelings, and suppress your preconceived ideas about the subject or the speaker. Ask questions when possible to seek clarification or further development of the speaker's points. By getting active in the listening process, you can demonstrate your interest.

One of the best ways to be active as a listener is to take notes. By doing so, you again express interest, improve your retention and understanding of what is said, and perhaps cause the speaker to be a bit more careful in the choice of his or her words or the structuring of them. Take a few minutes to review Appendix A of this book, which is entitled "How To Take Class Notes." The principles listed there will help you become a better listener as well as a better note taker. Taking notes causes a physical involvement as well as a mental one in the communications process.

The following two rules will help you improve your listening ability:

1. Don't assume anything. Let the speaker tell you what he or she means. A subordinate may be asking you (on the surface of his or her communication) to let him or her leave early today, but the real purpose of the request might be to see whether he or she will receive the same privilege you recently granted to another member of your section.

2. Don't interrupt the sender. Communications, like ideas, are fragile things and may shatter when interruptions (to a train of thought) occur.

Listening Responses

Listening responses are brief reactions that convey to the speaker the fact that you hear and understand what he or she is saying. They should be kept quite brief since, if they become too long or pronounced, they may interfere with the speaker's train of thought, or they may become disruptive. Normally they are used when the speaker pauses.

Here are four common forms of listening responses: (1) the *nod*, that is nodding your head slightly to show assent; (2) the *pause*, which means that you look at the speaker expectantly, but say nothing; (3) the *casual remark,* such as "OK," "Uh huh," or "Is that so?"; and the *echo*, which means that you repeat without any change the last few words of the speaker. Another form of the echo is to restate the speaker's view in your own words. Such an echo response might begin with a phrase like "You mean that . . ." or "Let me see if I understand you to say that. . . ."

Open and Closed Questions

At times a listener's questions should be asked in order to seek clarification and a better understanding of what the speaker has in mind. Questions can be "closed" or "open" depending upon the type of response the questioner seeks. A closed question can be answered with yes or no; an open question cannot be. The opening word in a question classifies it as either open or closed. Try these openers, noting the different kind of responses you get:

Open questions normally begin with:	*Closed questions usually begin with:*
What	Can
When	Is
Where	Do (Does)
Which	Have (Has)
Who	Shall (Will)
How	

Listening is no substitute for communication. It is an integral part of the communication process. But if a speaker begins to repeat herself or himself or to wander from the subject, it is time for the listener to take action. If the speaker is wrong about the facts, the listener should tactfully set him or her straight. If his or her meaning is not clear, seek a clarification. Remember that communicating is a two-way situation. It places a burden to be understood on the speaker and a burden to seek understanding on the listener.

Here are some simple exercises from *Changing Times* that you can try to test and improve your listening skills and sharpen your ability to remember:[1]

Describe the last lecture or sermon you heard. What was the theme of the talk? What arguments were made to support the message?

Name the subjects covered in the last newscast you listened to.

Say a word and ask the next person to repeat it and add another word that makes sense. Keep going around the room with each person adding a word. How long can the sentence be repeated before someone forgets a word or includes one that doesn't make sense?

List all the sounds you hear in the next fifteen minutes.

Using articles from newspapers, magazines and books, read descriptions of well-known people and ask others to guess the names of the subjects.

SPOKEN COMMUNICATIONS
■ There are two basic qualities that all successful managers have in common: the ability to think logically and the ability to communicate effectively. The most frequently used form of communication for a supervisor is oral. The ability to express yourself effectively through the use of spoken words is the most important tool at your disposal.

Effective speaking is much more than knowing correct grammar. You must have a clear purpose in mind, know your audience, and be certain of the type of response you wish to receive. Your way of talking to Bill is probably different from your discussions with Sue, even though your subject is the same. Bill may require a slower rate of speech, while Sue may respond best to a soft delivery.

As you speak, watch your listeners' facial expressions. Give your listeners time to ask questions. If they don't, ask some of your own in

---

1. "Listen! (It's an art you can learn)," *Changing Times, The Kiplinger Magazine* (January 1978), p. 20.

order to check their understanding and keep their attention. Saying things twice in different ways lends emphasis and clarification, so don't be afraid of repetition.

Tailor your message to your audience. Choose your words carefully. Use the minimum number of words possible to get your point across. Be honest and open, and your message will be welcomed. Stick to the facts and leave out the personal opinions. If your listeners desire more information than you have, don't bluff. Tell them you will get it and give it to them as soon as you can.

Basic Ingredients   An effective oral presentation to individuals or to groups usually contains three stages or parts: the **introduction,** the **explanation,** and the **summary.** All three parts have a definite purpose and specific ingredients. Our primary focus here is on communications between individuals. Chapter 10 will have a good deal to say about how to communicate to and within groups.

THE INTRODUCTION

The introduction or beginning of your oral presentation should attempt to do three things: (1) get the listener's attention; (2) arouse interest; and (3) introduce the subject matter and purpose of the communication.

The introduction can gain you the listener's attention through a number of devices: a statement designed to startle or amaze; a quotation from a famous source; an anecdote or story with a moral or lesson; a rhetorical question that will be answered later in the oral communication. (See Figure 5-3.) To convey the subject matter and the purpose of the communication, you as speaker can simply state what you intend to talk about, why the communication is necessary, and what goals and responses you have in mind. To obtain and keep the listener's inter-

Figure 5-3.
The three purposes
of the introduction
in an oral presentation.

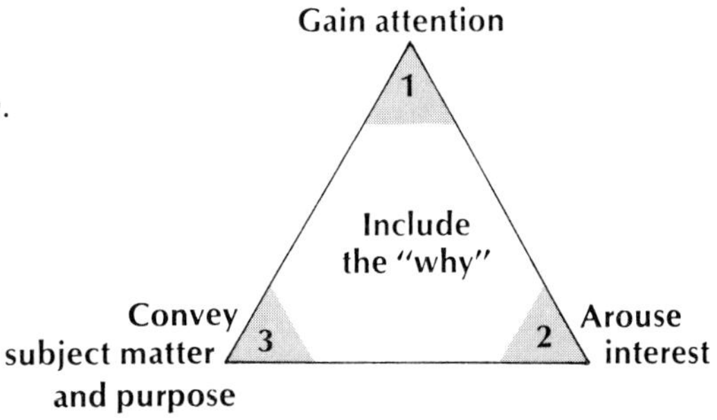

Gain attention
1
Include
the "why"
Convey subject matter and purpose 3
2 Arouse interest

est, you need to say why the communication is necessary and how the message will affect your listener. An effort should be made to relate the oral presentation to your listener's past experience, job, or special interests.

THE EXPLANATION

The explanation follows the introduction and should also be well organized. It will be well organized if it flows logically from one key point to another. To make sure that it does, you must identify the key points or ideas; you must group them in a sequence that makes sense; and then you must present them in that sequence to your listener. Transitions from one point to another should be thought out, and they should carry your listener logically from one point to the next point or idea.

Emphasis should be used to help your listener define in his or her own mind what the key points are and why they are worth knowing and remembering. Some devices for adding emphasis include repetition, voice tone and inflection, specific wording such as "This is really important," visual aids or specific questions. As the speaker you can use such devices to fix important points or ideas in your listeners' memories.

THE SUMMARY

A summary may occur at any point in an oral presentation where it might be helpful to restate important points you as the speaker have been making. Frequent summaries aid the memory and add emphasis. Any oral communication should be concluded with a comprehensive summary of all the key ideas as well as the responses expected from your listener. This final summary is your opportunity to reemphasize major points, to clarify the message through questions, and to leave a lasting impression with your listener. It may list rewards to be received by the listener who reacts favorably to your message as well as a statement of any penalties that may result from unfavorable or negative responses. It should restate the goals expected as a result of the communication in line with the way they were first stated in your introduction.

WRITTEN COMMUNICATIONS

■ Probably the most difficult form of communication is the written form. Yet nothing will mark you more clearly as a poor manager than your inability to write your thoughts effectively and correctly. Your written communications may be around a long time and will put you on record for future reference. A badly written, poorly constructed piece of writing can discredit you as nothing else can.

Just what is "good" writing? It is writing that transmits an idea or information clearly to the intended reader in accordance with the rules of grammar and proper sentence construction. Before you put your thoughts in writing you should: (1) have something specific that must be communicated; (2) have something that is best stated in writing; (3) have the command of language fundamentals, such as proper punctuation and spelling; and (4) have a specific reader in mind.

Writing effectively is not easy. But you can make it a lot less difficult for yourself if you lay a proper foundation before you try to write. First, you should have a specific objective in mind. Next, you should gather your facts (this may involve searching your files or consulting with others). Then, you should make an outline, that is, a simple breakdown of your major points. Expand your major point by writing underneath it the minor ones that you wish to use to support it. You can use a sequence of numbers, letters, or both to identify major and minor points. Use whatever system is comfortable for you. Then arrange your points in the order best suited for a logical presentation.

Although much of your writing will be done with little or no research, it may sometimes be necessary for you to research a problem before you write about it. When you have to do research, remember the sources of information available to you: your own files, library indexes, individuals in your own section or unit, and higher authorities. You may want to use 3" x 5" note cards to record information. When you decide that your research is complete, test the results by drawing conclusions from what you have learned and recorded. From these conclusions you should be able to prepare an outline while the details of what you have learned are still fresh in your mind.

Practice using simple, familiar, and concrete words. In reviewing your writing, be sure that *you* clearly understand the words you have used. Then ask yourself the following questions: "Will my readers understand my words?" "Will they get the same meaning that I do from them?" With some words there is little danger of any misunderstanding. For example, the word *book* means much the same thing to all of us. Other words, however, may have wide differences of meaning for various people. Consider, for example, the term *implement*. A farmer would probably think you meant a plow, but in business memos the word means *to carry out a policy* or a *plan*. If you have any doubt about a word, find another word that you are sure will be understood as carrying the meaning you intend. If your readers must continually stop to ponder the meaning of your words, they will lose track of what you are telling them.

If you want your written communications to have impact, use short sentences. Make use of the active voice as much as possible. Professional writers know that writing is easier to read and remember if most of the sentences and paragraphs are brief. You should not use short sentences all the time, however. Such writing tends to become choppy and monotonous. Try to alternate a long sentence with one or two short ones, and try to keep sentences to fifteen or twenty words.

In preparing your paragraphs, try to limit each of them to a single topic. As a rule, start each paragraph with a topic sentence that tells what the paragraph is about. Use transitional devices to tie both your sentences and your paragraphs together. The final sentence in a paragraph can often emphasize the points you wish to get across.

The introductory paragraphs tell what the writing is about. The paragraphs that make up the body of a communication state the writer's case (facts, figures, etc.). The closing paragraph or paragraphs recommend an action and/or summarize the important points of the paper. Once you are convinced that you have said what you wanted to say in the way you want to say it, stop writing.

Figure 5–4 shows an actual memo (memo A) sent by Jane, a middle manager, to her subordinate managers. Read it first and then read memo B, which is a suggested improvement. Do you believe that memo B carries the basic message intended by the author of memo A? Which memo would you prefer to receive if you were one of Jane's subordinates?

If you need help in the area of communications, get it. A course at your local college can improve your spoken and written communications. The results will be well worth your investment of time and money. You will harvest the benefits for the rest of your life.

There is an old saying: "Nothing is ever written, only rewritten." From the time you pen the first few words of your message, you will probably want to revise or rewrite your thoughts. From rough draft to the finished communication you will be polishing, tightening up, and filling in. Keep a dictionary handy. Don't be afraid to refer to a basic grammar text either. Remember that your words carry your reputation.

THE GRAPEVINE

■ Transmission mediums or channels of communication can be formal or informal. Formal channels are those specifically set up for the transmission of normal business information, instructions, orders, and reports. The organization chart of a business illustrates them. Informal channels—the **grapevine**—are not specifically designated for use in the dissemination of information, but they are used for this purpose by nearly every employee.

Informal channels exist because of the natural desire on an employee's part to be in the know and to satisfy his or her curiosity. Be-

Memo A

TO: ALL SECTION SUPERVISORS

The newly designed personal data sheet -- Form 14-A -- has
a necessary, essential, and vital purpose in our organization.
It provides the necessary and statistically significant personal data required by the personnel department to be kept on
file for future references regarding promotions, transfers,
layoffs, and more.

During our recent relocation efforts from the rented facilities
at Broad Street to our present location here at Cauley Boulevard,
files were lost, damaged, or misplaced, necessitating the current request for replacement of vital personal data on each
and every manager in this department. It is also the company's
policy to periodically update personal data on file through
periodic, personal perusal of one's own records -- updating and
adding new information as required and deleting obsolete or
outdated personal data on file.

Therefore, please complete the attached personal data sheet
at your earliest possible convenience but no later than Thursday,
May 14th, and return it to me by the close of the business day
on the 14th.

Jane Barton

Memo B

TO: ALL SECTION SUPERVISORS

Attached is our company's revised edition of the Personal
Data Sheet. Please fill it out completely and return to me
no later than the close of business on Thursday, May 14.

Thank you.

Jane Barton

Figure 5-4. Two memos compared: Memo A, the original memo, and Memo B, an improved revision.

cause employees mix and socialize frequently during and outside their normal working relationships, they speculate and invent "information." The less they know about something, the more they invent. At coffee breaks, during lunch, or at social events people often "pass the poop," even though they may not have all the facts. This informal dissemination of "information" is called the grapevine.

The grapevine will often give managers a clue as to what is bothering their people and where the need for immediate or future action lies. Although it is generally a means by which gossip and rumors about the company are spread, managers should be tuned in to it. But don't use the grapevine for the dissemination of orders or instructions to your people. It cannot be a substitute for formal channels.

To prevent the grapevine from yielding a crop of sour grapes, satisfy your people's need to know what is happening in their department by applying the following rules to your daily situation:

1. Tune in on their informal communications;
2. Combat rumors and gossip with the facts;
3. Discredit people who willfully spread improper information;
4. Be available to and be honest with your people;
5. Know when to remain silent.

By applying these rules you create in your subordinates a feeling of confidence about what is true and not true. You strengthen your personal reputation as a source of sound information. You build better morale and cooperation. As a result, resistance to change can be lessened, and the impact of it can be softened.

INSTANT REPLAY

For a concise summary of our discussion on communications, review the following Ten Commandments of Good Communication from the American Management Association.[2]

    I. *Seek To Clarify Your Ideas Before Communicating.*

    II. *Examine the True Purpose of Each Communication.*

    III. *Consider the Total Physical and Human Setting Whenever You Communicate.*

    IV. *Consult with Others, Where Appropriate, in Planning Communications.*

    V. *Be Mindful of the Overtones as Well as the Basic Content of Your Message.*

    VI. *Take the Opportunity, When It Arises, To Convey Something of Help or Value to the Receiver.*

    VII. *Follow Up Your Communication.*

    VIII. *Communicate for Tomorrow as Well as Today.*

    IX. *Be Sure Your Actions Support Your Communications.*

    X. *Seek Not Only To Be Understood but To Understand—Be a Good Listener.*

KEY WORDS

communications	**grapevine**	**perception**
communications barriers	**introduction**	**receiver**
concentration	**listening**	**summary**
explanation	**medium**	**transmitter**
	message	

---

2. Reprinted by permission of the publisher from "The Ten Commandments of Good Communication" © 1955 by the American Management Association, Inc.

1. Define communication.
2. What does it mean to say that "communications are two-way?"
3. What barriers to effective communications can arise when a supervisor talks to a subordinate about his or her work performance?
4. How can taking notes during a business conversation improve your communications skills?
5. What form of communications—written or oral—do supervisors use most often? Why?
6. What makes communicating in writing so difficult for many people?
7. Explain the importance of planning communications before attempting to communicate.
8. How can the grapevine help a supervisor? How can it be harmful?
9. What does it mean to say that, as you communicate, your feelings and attitudes are communicated along with your facts?
10. Why is it important for a supervisor to have empathy for subordinates when communicating to them?

CASE PROBLEM

Lester Atkins

Lester Atkins was visibly upset as he read the memo he had just received from his production supervisor:

I am quite distressed over your failure to follow up on our discussion about cost reduction. As I have not yet received your plan for reducing costs in your department, I must now order you to submit it in writing by noon tomorrow.

Jack Curtis

Mr. and Mrs. Curtis had been to the Atkins' home as guests for supper two weeks earlier. After the meal, Curtis and Atkins got to talking about the current slump in sales and the corresponding belt-tightening that was on throughout the plant. Curtis mentioned that several of the other foremen had come up with some "pretty darn good ideas" for reducing the costs of their various operations.

Atkins wasn't quite sure what Curtis was getting at, but he replied that he was always looking for ways to save the company money and mentioned a couple of his ideas and how they had worked out in the past.

Curtis then went into a glowing account about one of Atkins' fellow foremen, Harvey Sheldon, and the ideas that he had come up with. Sheldon had put his proposals in writing and submitted them to Curtis for his approval. As a result of implementing them, Sheldon would be at least 15 percent below his budget for the current year. Curtis then said, "My job would be a heck of a lot easier if more of my foremen had Sheldon's interest and initiative." This was the only time Atkins remembered talking with Curtis about cost reduction.

Questions

1. Was Lester Atkins wrong in not submitting a plan for cost reduction? Why or why not?
2. What do you think about formal communications taking place outside formal channels?
3. Comment on Jack Curtis' memo.
4. How is the barrier of Improper Timing illustrated in this case?
5. Which of the Ten Commandments of Good Communication have been violated by Lester Atkins? By Curtis?

Communications / **85**

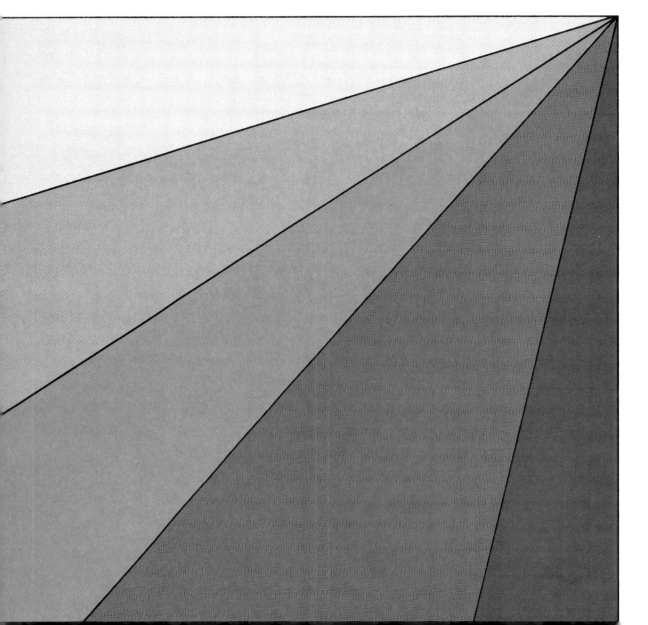

Part Two
You and Your People

6 Attitudes— Yours and Theirs

■ After reading and discussing this chapter, you should be able to:

1 Define the word *attitude*.

2 Briefly explain how attitudes are formed in people.

3 Explain why attitudes held by others should not be labeled as either "good" or "bad."

4 List and briefly explain the four basic steps required to change people's attitudes.

5 Briefly explain the concept of Force Field Analysis, and explain how it can be used to change attitudes.

6 List five persuasion techniques that supervisors may use to help change their subordinates' attitudes.

7 List and briefly explain two participation techniques that may be used in changing attitudes.

INTRODUCTION

■ Part One introduced you to the big picture of a business corporation. We discussed the management concept and the management hierarchy. Then we took up the role of supervisors, their major responsibilities, and the importance for them of establishing good communications.

Part Two will explain how you as a supervisor should relate to your subordinates and peers, and it will also discuss group relationships in a corporation. We shall begin this chapter with a study of **attitudes,** by which we mean our readiness or predisposition to react in a predetermined way to certain stimuli, such as individuals, groups of individuals, or events. We shall examine both your own attitudes and those of your subordinates: how attitudes are formed; how your attitudes affect those of your subordinates; and how their attitudes affect yours. Finally, we'll consider ways in which you as a manager can change the attitudes of your subordinates that you regard as unacceptable for your company.

At this point it is necessary to make a distinction between two terms that are frequently used as substitutes for one another, even though they do not mean exactly the same thing. An attitude is a state of mind that indicates you have certain opinions or beliefs about a certain person or event. An *opinion* then is a judgment about this person or event that you can put into words and that probably reflects your general attitude or outlook on life. An opinion is a verbal expression of your attitudes and shows what you think about the quality or value of some other person or event. From a person's opinions you can assess his or her attitudes. For example, Mary may speak to and about Bill in a very warm and friendly manner. Her opinion of Bill and her actions toward him express a friendly attitude. An examination of Mary's opinions of other people may show you that she has either the same attitude toward everyone she meets or toward only a few people. It may turn out that she has such feelings only for Bill.

THE FORMATION OF ATTITUDES

■ As indicated above, our attitudes are the feelings and habitual ways we have of thinking about and acting toward other people, events, and concepts. They project our *personality* because the forces that shape our attitudes are the same cultural forces that help form our personality.

Our experiences have predisposed us in certain ways toward nearly everything that is a part of our daily lives. We have definite opinions about our company, boss, job, family members, and friends. When someone mentions one of your subordinates, for example, a composite picture of that individual comes to mind. You visualize him or her in a general way and are able to make specific judgments about that person from your past observations and experiences with the person. Beneath your judgments about the person are your attitudes.

When you are confronted with people or concepts not already part of your experience, you are usually not predisposed in any specific way toward them. You lack definite attitudes or opinions about them. It is at this point that you are most open and impressionable about the new contacts. Initially, you try to make your own observations, gain some insights, and draw your own conclusions. This is the normal process by which we form new attitudes. Friends or associates can play a part to some degree, depending upon how valuable we feel their opinions are. Your attitude toward a source of information determines whether you

BLONDIE

accept a source's conclusions in whole or in part or reject them. In forming these new attitudes, we make reference to our existing attitudes.

Think back to the time when you were seeking employment with your present employer. Why did you decide to apply to that company rather than to other companies? If you had no prior experience with your present company, you probably relied on its reputation as relayed to you by others whose opinions you respected. A friend may have suggested that you apply because he or she worked there and liked the company. You were willing to put your future in the hands of an employer on the basis of another's attitude and your attitudes toward that person. During the selection process as a new applicant, you made your own observations and got answers to specific questions. Your attitudes toward your new employer were taking shape, and when you accepted the job, you had formed a positive set of attitudes toward both your employer and your new job. Your attitudes, therefore, had a definite influence on your behavior and that of your employer. They will continue to do so.

GOOD ATTITUDES VERSUS BAD ATTITUDES

■ We must agree at the start of our analysis of attitudes that there is no such thing as a "bad" attitude—only one different from our own on that topic. Ask yourself, "Would I willingly hold onto an attitude that I believe to be bad?" The answer quite obviously is no. Of course you wouldn't. Because if you realize that an attitude you hold is a source of trouble for you, you would soon understand that your trouble would vanish as soon as you rejected that particular attitude. Therefore, if you continue to have an attitude, you must consider it to be a good one, and you must believe yourself justified in clinging to it. Until you see, or are made to see, that your attitude is improper from your own view-point—that is, one no longer tenable in the light of new knowledge and experience—you will continue to cling to it and act accordingly.

When someone labels another's attitude "bad," what he or she is really saying is something like this: "That person's attitude is in opposition to mine—mine is right, his or hers must be wrong." It is only through comparisons with familiar standards or norms that something "good" or "bad" takes on meaning. A "good" attitude is one that agrees with or at least is not in opposition to our own. A "bad" attitude is one that differs significantly from our own.

Let us take an example of what we mean. Suppose as a supervisor in a machine shop you observe a subordinate named Joe not wearing his safety goggles while operating a grinding wheel. Safety regulations tell him to wear safety goggles while grinding. You remind him to wear them, and he agrees to do so. Ten minutes later you pass the same workman again. He is again not wearing his safety goggles. At this point you may ask yourself, "Why?" The question should have been asked earlier. If it had been, the second infraction of the rules might have been prevented. The answer to the question lies in the worker's attitude toward the wearing of safety goggles. He believes that his attitude is a sound one, or he wouldn't behave in this manner. You as his supervisor do not hold the same attitude because you believe his behavior is improper. Your tendency is to label his attitude "bad." At this point the dialogue might go as follows:

Supervisor: "Joe, you know we have a shop rule about wearing safety goggles, don't you?"
Joe: "Yeah, I know the rule."
Supervisor: "Do you want to lose an eye?"
Joe: "Nope."
Supervisor: "Didn't I tell you a few minutes ago to wear your goggles?"
Joe: "Yep."
Supervisor: "Well, why don't you wear them then?"
Joe: "The strap's too tight. It gives me a headache."

The lesson should be obvious. Whatever attitudes people reflect by their behavior are viewed by them to be adequate. Until they see a need for change or can be shown an alternative which gives them better results, they have no incentive to change. Joe was willing to take on a risk to his eye in order to avoid a headache. Why he didn't complain without being asked is another problem. If he has to buy the goggles out of his own money, he may be reluctant to buy another pair. If the company furnishes them, the storeroom may be out of Joe's size. There could be a dozen reasons. The point here is: what is the person's attitude and why does the person have it? When you know the answers to these questions, you can begin to effect a change in attitude.

YOUR OWN ATTITUDES

■ A worker's attitudes probably are prolabor. Nonmanagement personnel generally identify with each other and hold many common or similar views toward the things and people that affect them on the job. This may be partly due to the environmental forces at work such as the union or to general working conditions. Most likely, it is true because of peer group pressures on the individual to conform.

Figure 6-1 illustrates the attitude situation for both workers and management. Depending upon your attitudes, you fit into one of three locations in the diagram. Before and during the initial stages of training workers to become supervisors, their attitudes place them to the left of center in the prolabor area. The major job of supervisory training programs is to effect changes in the trainees' attitudes toward and their conceptions of management. If the program is successful, it will lead to a shift in the trainees' attitudes toward the center line—the fence between prolabor and promanagement attitudes.

The center line or fence is the awkward yet mandatory position for most operating managers because of their unique roles as spokespersons for both labor and management. They are concerned most directly about the welfare of their subordinates and must protect and fortify the position of the management. Needless to say, this "fence straddling" can be uncomfortable and demanding at times, but it is necessary nevertheless. Truly, supervisors are the "persons in the middle," who are caught between the needs of their subordinates and their superiors.

As supervisors take part in later management development programs, their attitudes usually again undergo a shift to the right, removing them from the center line and planting them firmly on the promanagement side by the time they become middle managers.

As a manager your attitudes should be in harmony with your company's policies and your understanding of sound management principles and practice. You should be willing to question your own attitudes whenever you observe contrary ones in either a peer or a superior. Try to be objective and to determine which are the better attitudes to hold. Maintaining an open mind and being receptive to the new and different will stimulate your growth and improve your knowledge and understanding of yourself and your position.

Beware of accepting the attitudes or opinions of others as your own. We all have a tendency to fill a void in our knowledge by the quickest

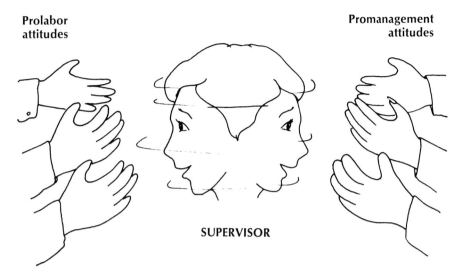

Prolabor attitudes

Promanagement attitudes

SUPERVISOR

Figure 6-1. The positions of workers and managers in relation to their attitudes.

means available, but this can be a dangerous practice. When you first became a supervisor, you may have heard from your boss or predecessor, "Watch out for Al, he's a sneak." Or, "You sure are lucky to have Agnes, she's a peach." Dismiss these "insights" and wait to form your own attitudes and opinions through your personal observations. What subordinates or superiors were like with your predecessor and what they will be like with you are almost always two different things.

If you look around you at work, you will probably find many examples of men and women, both in and out of management, who are putting forth a mediocre effort. This is often the result of their managers' expecting nothing more from them. Subordinates learn to give what is expected. Nearly every mediocre subordinate is but a reflection of a mediocre manager.

If you believe in yourself and set your standards above the average, your results will, in time, match those standards. So should it be with your subordinates. Believe in your people, assume the best about each one of them, and do all in your power to help them realize the inherent potential you know they possess.

Your attitudes will soon shape those of your subordinates. They will look to you for respect, guidance and example. What you expect from them and what you exemplify each day to them will determine their attitudes and reactions toward you and their own work.

Allow me to share with you an experience I had with a student one evening following class. The student—let's call him Greg—asked me how to make a résumé. He explained that he wanted to seek a new job. Greg related how he had been in contention for his boss's job in middle management, but had been frustrated when the president of the company brought in his brother from outside to fill the vacancy. Greg, who had had over fourteen years with the company, went on to state that the new man had no experience, didn't know the business, and didn't know the jobs of his subordinate supervisors. Greg was really depressed and understandably so.

I asked Greg two questions: (1) how long did he think the president's brother would occupy a low-level middle management position? and (2) wasn't it true that the president's brother was totally dependent upon Greg and his fellow supervisors both for learning his job and gaining a successful reputation?

Greg thought for a moment and began to smile. He reasoned that the answer to question 1 was "not very long" and the answer to question 2 was "yes." When our conversation was over, he was dedicated to helping that new man become the best middle manager possible. After all, it doesn't hurt to have a future executive in high places who respects your abilities and is indebted to you in part for his success.

PROBLEM SUPERVISORS

■ Without realizing it, some supervisors may be the prime causes of an employee's difficulties. Through the supervisors' actions or lack of action, supervisors can and often do influence their subordinates' behavior. Supervisors have the ability to aggravate their subordinates' difficulties and put them off balance. A supervisor can confront subordinates who are on the edge of trouble and either help them steer clear of it or push them into it. Like a parent or older brother or sister, the boss should be someone we can look up to for a good example and good advice. Your people are very conscious of your behavior and read into it guidelines for their own behavior.

Consider the following checklist. If some of these questions sting you a bit, you should set about charting a new course of behavior right now.

1. Do I control my people with threats?
2. Do I like to keep them off balance and feeling a little insecure?
3. Am I predictable to my people in my behavior and attitudes?
4. Am I mature?
5. Do I keep my promises?
6. Do I keep their confidences?
7. Do I issue conflicting orders and instructions?
8. Do I give them praise when they deserve it?
9. Do I discipline them in private?

10. Do I hold a grudge?
11. Do I play favorites?
12. Do I set realistic standards?
13. Do I enforce standards uniformly?
14. Do I take my subordinates for granted?
15. Do I trust my people?
16. Are my subordinates aware of my expectations for them?
17. Do I prepare my subordinates for changes?

Before you condemn or rule your subordinates' attitudes or behavior as improper, be certain first of all that you yourself are not unwittingly the root cause of the very things you are condemning.

YOUR SUBORDINATES' ATTITUDES

■ Your people have attitudes about their work, the company, and you as their boss. When you first take office in your new job as a supervisor, your people will adopt a "wait and see" attitude about you and your abilities. They are, for the most part, open and objective, waiting for evidence upon which to base their opinions. The attitudes they will eventually adopt in regard to you are almost entirely within your power to mold. The attitudes they already possess toward other things are hidden from view and will take some time to uncover. These were formed in an environment and through experiences of which you were not a part. Nevertheless, their attitudes will surely influence their performances, output, and the reputation of the department. Your success and theirs are linked directly to attitudes—both yours and theirs.

One of the most important tasks for managers, particularly for supervisors, is to identify improper or unacceptable attitudes—that is, attitudes held by subordinates that interfere with their rendering better-than-average or average performances. Once these attitudes are uncovered, managers must begin the demanding task of changing them in order to bring their people to a greater realization of their potential and their departments to a higher state of effectiveness.

UNCOOPERATIVE ATTITUDES

■ Cooperation means working together to reach common objectives or goals. If you are the kind of supervisor this book is trying to develop, you will have minimized your problems and found little resistance to overcome. The primary barrier to cooperation, therefore, is yourself—your weaknesses, inadequacies, and failure to offer a good example. Look first at yourself and your practices of management before you accuse others of wrongdoing. If you can honestly say that the barrier to cooperation lies outside yourself, then the remainder of this chapter should prove helpful to you.

At the core of a person's noncooperation is his or her lack of motivation to cooperate. This means that the person has no desire at present to do so. It falls to you, therefore, to attempt to provide the climate and incentives that will foster a spirit of cooperation in each of your people.

As a rule, people are unwilling to cooperate for two kinds of reasons: personal or social.

Personal Reasons

Individuals may be unwilling to cooperate with you or their fellow workers because they see no personal advantage in doing so. They may not understand the changes you propose in your operations and fear the implications of such changes to them in their jobs, status, pay, or future. How well people accept changes may be contingent upon how well changes have been introduced in the past. They can remember what happened at that time, and they will assume the likelihood of similar results happening again. If a change was handled well in the past, the gate remains open for new changes. If not, you can anticipate resistance or opposition to the change.

On the other hand, people may resist changes because of the personal advantages they can keep if the changes are thwarted. For example, if people know their jobs well and are successful at them, they have job security. They are using tried and proved methods, and feel no need to make an effort to learn something new. Thus they have no need to alter their present routines.

Most of us have a built-in fear of change. This fear seems to grow as we advance in years and experience. Nearly all such fear is based on ignorance—not knowing what the changes might mean to us and our position. We have seen people displaced through advances in technology. We have seen old and traditional skills and crafts eliminated. A change in methods may be viewed as a criticism of our present performance—especially when the change is enforced from outside our department.

The supervisor is an initiator, translator, and implementer of change. As such, it is his or her job to plan for change, to communicate its need effectively, and to show to subordinates the advantages that will accrue to them as a result of the adoption of the change. In short, the supervisor must point out the need for and advantages of cooperation, and must remove any attitudes that stand in its way.

Social Reasons

As you are well aware, most people in a business do not work by themselves. They are probably members of both informal and formal groups.

Changes proposed or suspected may give rise to a fear that the worker's social relationships may be upset, either by the loss of his or her present associates or by the need to find new ones.

An individual may be in favor of a change because he or she can see personal advantages in the new development. The group to which he or she belongs, however, may be against the change. What then can the individual member of a group do? He or she can adopt the group's viewpoint about the change and risk difficulties with the supervisor, or may favor the change and risk expulsion from the group.

CHANGING THE ATTITUDES OF SUBORDINATES

■ A supervisor can bring about a change in a subordinate's improper attitude or behavior through a four-step process. After you have observed an improper behavior on the part of a subordinate, or after you have heard an improper attitude expressed by a subordinate, you should:

1. Identify the improper attitude or behavior;
2. Determine what supports it;
3. Weaken whatever supports it;
4. Offer a substitute for the improper attitude or behavior.

In order to illustrate these four steps, consider the following example contributed by one of my students.

Mike was a supervisor of thirty assemblers in an electronics plant in Chicago. It was his practice to turn each new employee over to an experienced worker for training until the new person adjusted to the job and became capable of meeting both quality and quantity standards on his or her own. One day Mike hired a young, recent immigrant from India named Ehri. Ehri was placed under the direction of Dave, an experienced and willing worker-trainer. Once on his own, however, Ehri's production was marked by an unacceptable level of rejects.

Step 1: Identifying the Improper Attitude

When you determine that a subordinate's behavior is improper, you must look for the attitude behind it and state it in precise terms.

Mike went to Ehri and observed him at work. Ehri was working at an almost frantic pace. Mike assumed that this was the reason for the large number of rejects and asked Ehri to slow his pace and concentrate on quality, not quantity.

Often, just by investigating the action, showing concern, and giving corrective instructions, you will be able to solve the problem. The worker may realize at that point that his or her behavior is unacceptable and change it to meet the demands of the supervisor. This did not happen with Ehri.

Mike had failed to identify the attitude that supported the fast pace of work. He identified an action, which he attempted to stop with orders and instructions. He had dealt with the symptom of an attitude, not the attitude that was causing the problem.

Step 2: Determining the Root Causes

On the basis of your investigation and analysis, see if you can spot the roots of the attitude—the primary causes that both support and feed the attitude in the employee's mind. The best way to do this is to get the employee talking—get him or her to tell you his or her true feelings.

Some frequent root causes that support and nurture incorrect attitudes are:

1. Group pressures;
2. Faulty logic;
3. Misunderstood standards;
4. Previous supportive experiences.

Mike thought the problem was ended. After all, when a supervisor lays down the law, especially to a new worker, the subordinate should respond. Ehri's production, however, continued to yield an unacceptable number of rejects. Next, Mike and his boss both talked with Ehri. They again emphasized quality and included an implied threat that unless the situation reversed itself, Ehri's job was in jeopardy. But still the problem persisted.

Mike had not uncovered the root cause. Even though he was armed with the additional authority of his boss, Mike was still treating a symptom of the attitude. He had not yet uncovered the attitude and the root supports for it.

Finally it occurred to Mike that the problem may have originated in Ehri's training. He approached Dave and related the problem of too much quantity and too little quality. After stating that Ehri's job was at stake, he asked if Dave knew how this situation might have evolved. Dave became somewhat embarrassed and, upon further questioning, Mike discovered that Dave had told Ehri that quantity was all management really cared about, regardless of what they said to the contrary. Mike had finally struck pay dirt. He now knew what Ehri's attitude was and the root cause for it—misunderstood standards.

Step 3: Weakening the Root Causes

Once the root causes are known, they can be analyzed and their vulnerabilities noted. A program of action can then be constructed to systematically remove these causes through the use of reason. One way is to point out flaws in the employee's assumptions, or changes that have taken place to weaken those assumptions since they were formed.

Mike instructed Dave to go to Ehri and explain that he had been mis-informed. Dave apologized to Ehri and made it clear that he had only been "kidding" about quantity over quality.

Dave had the reputation of a practical joker, and he really had meant no harm by what he did. He was only taking advantage of a novice who was naive to the ways of a skilled worker like Dave. Ehri had a language difficulty with English and tended to take things rather literally. Thus he had been an easy prey for a joker. Dave felt certain that once Mike talked to Ehri and "straightened him out," Ehri would realize that he had been "had." When Dave understood that Ehri had not responded to Mike's talks, he was most eager to help correct the problem.

Step 4:
Offering
a Substitute

Dave had no trouble persuading Ehri to change his thinking since Ehri had received quite a bit of pressure by that time. Once Ehri realized that his attitude was based on misinformation as a result of the state-ments of both Dave and Mike, he became a superior workman.

You may be able to change behavior by constant harping and criti-cism, but, like the action of water in wearing away a rock, it may take too long a time and leave some noticeable scars. In general, people will change only if the attitudes they hold are seen by them to be no longer worth keeping. Threats and orders usually only suppress a nat-ural and observable behavior and drive it underground. The person becomes sneaky and does what you say only when you are there to police your order. When you are absent, his or her old behavior pat-tern will surface. The fact that you don't agree with or accept this be-havior is usually not enough. You must identify the attitude, find its roots, and get the individual to question his or her own position. Only then will you be able to effect a permanent change.

TECHNIQUES
FOR CHANGING
ATTITUDES

■ Fortunately, there are many tried and proven methods for changing attitudes, reducing resistance to change, and instilling a desire to coop-erate. These methods depend upon your understanding of the previous chapters and your ability to apply the knowledge they contain. There are six basic techniques at your disposal for introducing changes and resolving conflicts. They are:
  1. Force Field Analysis;
  2. Communications;
  3. Persuasion
  4. Participation
  5. Job enrichment
  6. Organization development.

Force Field Analysis   Kurt Lewin, a social psychologist of the Gestalt school, has given us the research in human relations upon which **Force Field Analysis** is built. It is a useful device for visualizing the situation you face when you attempt to overcome resistance to change in your subordinates.

There are two types of forces within individuals with regard to any issue affecting them at any given time: driving forces and restraining forces. Driving forces encourage us to change, while restraining forces encourage us to resist change. Whether we are predisposed towards a change in a negative or a positive way depends on the nature and quantity of these forces. If there is a balance between them, we are in a state of inertia. If a change is to take place, driving forces must outweigh the restraining ones; the restraining ones must be reduced; or a combination of these must take place. Figure 6–2 illustrates this concept.

In order to understand more clearly this type of analysis, let us consider an example. Assume that you want one of your workers, Barbara Adams, to work over a coming holiday. Since overtime is a voluntary situation in your shop, Barbara has a choice. Let us assume that you have asked her, and she has refused. The situation might appear as follows.

Driving Forces	*Restraining Forces*
1. Additional pay at overtime scale.	1. A desire to be with the family.
2. If she works, she will please you.	2. No immediate need for extra pay.
3. Working over the holiday is better than being idle.	3. Preference for time off over extra pay.

At this point there appears to be a standoff. You cannot order her to work, so you must try to weaken her restraining forces and/or add to the driving forces. Before attempting to do either, be sure that you see the situation as she does. Assuming the forces listed above represent a true picture of her conception of the situation, and that she understands the driving forces that are present, let us see what you can do to change her mind.

In view of the restraining forces, the easiest step is to increase the driving forces. You might be able to get her best friend at work to come in over the holiday. Once Barbara knows that someone she respects and admires has agreed to help out, she may too. In addition, you could let her know that the reason you have asked her is that you really need her and her abilities. If she is the best person for the work to be done, let her know you feel that way. Also, you can appeal to her group loyalties—explaining that the team needs her for a successful perform-

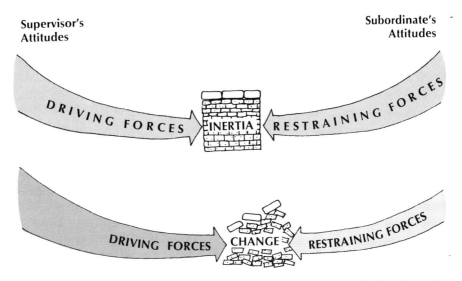

Supervisor's Attitudes   Subordinate's Attitudes

DRIVING FORCES → INERTIA ← RESTRAINING FORCES

DRIVING FORCES → CHANGE ← RESTRAINING FORCES

Figure 6-2. A representation of a force field. Above: the situation before desired changes. Below: the situation after resistance to change is overcome.

ance rating and that without her they stand a good chance of falling below expectations. In other words, the reputation of her group, either formal or informal, will be tarnished without her unique contributions.

If you are a leader in Barbara's eyes, you may get her to work overtime by putting your request on a personal basis such as, "Barbara, can you work overtime this Monday? I really need you." But not all managers are leaders, nor are all of them leaders to all their subordinates. You should not try these steps unless you are sincere. We are not talking here about playing "games" with people or their feelings.

You can change a person's mind and his or her prior attitude toward an idea or a suggestion if you manage to change his or her perception of a situation. This means that you must attempt to perceive the situation as the other person does and then go to work on the forces. You won't always succeed, but the effort is worth making if the change you are trying to effect is important to your department.

Communications

Chapter 5 dealt with the fundamentals of successful communications in general. All that is contained in that chapter is essential to every manager. Unless you have open channels with your people, peers, and outside specialists, you will have no real chance at winning their cooperation. To overcome fears, attitudes, and the lack of motivation to change, you must employ effective communication techniques. Regardless of the form you use, you must lay the groundwork for change and get its advantages across to your people before you can expect them to go along with you. Remember that your goal is to get your particular understanding of a situation into their minds. To do this, you must listen to and observe them. Take a few moments to review Chapter 5, in particular, the Ten Commandments of Good Communication (p. 84).

Persuasion

Each of the following suggestions works well in certain situations. Which one you choose depends upon your understanding of the people and events involved in the particular situation you face. Become familiar with all of them so that you will always carry with you one or more techniques that can be applied to any set·of circumstances.

1. Give your subordinates the "why" behind the proposal. Let your people know why the change is necessary. Put it in their terms, and tailor your message to each individual.

2. Give them the "how." Explain how the change will affect them and how it will help them. Appeal to their individual needs.

3. Give them the truth. If the change will be painful, let them know it. If Joe is to be displaced, assure him that the company will either relocate him or retrain him for a new position if this be the case. Don't lie to them or kid them. They will respect your integrity and remember it in the future.

4. Try a compromise. It is not always possible to give a little or meet them halfway, but when you can, do so. You may not have foreseen all the possibilities, and maybe they have some good points on their side. Often the method isn't as important as the results you expect of them.

5. Give your subordinates an example of a past success. Tell them about similar situations and the positive results that were obtained. Explain how each person benefited as a result of the change.

6. Plant a seed. Give them an idea and let it germinate. In advance of the change, converse with them about "How nice it would be if . . ." or "Have you guys thought about. . . ." Then nurture that idea with the proper care and feeding. Your subordinates may come to you with the very suggestion you anticipated. Even better, they may think it is their own idea.

7. Ask them some questions. Ask the kind of questions which, if they are honest with themselves, will yield support for a change or remove the cause of a possible conflict. Properly presented, these leading questions will lead them to the proper predisposition.

8. Offer them a choice. The choice you present is not whether to do something or reject it but rather when or how or by whom it will get done.

9. Offer them a challenge. Put the idea as a goal to be reached or a standard to be surpassed. Present the change as a test of their team's abilities and skills. Turn the event into a game or contest, a way of probing their potentials.

10. Make them a promise. If it is possible, give them your promise that if the idea is not successful or does not yield the desired results (given an honest effort), you will retreat from your position and withdraw the directive.

11. Try making a request. Instead of ordering compliance and being autocratic, ask them to cooperate. You will be amazed at what a difference requests make in a person's attitudes. You will appeal to the individual who feels insulted by demands but who bends over backward to meet an appeal for help.

12. Give them a demonstration. Show them by your own performance what the new system calls for, how it will work, and how it will benefit the group or individual. Introduce the change with a planned and carefully executed tryout, and the doubts will fade in the light of reason. "Seeing is believing."

13. Involve your subordinates in the decision. Using a problem-solving session, get them into the problem with both feet. State the dimensions of the problem, and then lead them in reaching a consensus.

Before you decide on any one of these suggestions, put yourself in the shoes of your people. Identify with their attitudes and set your course to meet their restraints and increase their drives. By finding the supports for their resistance and weakening these supports through logic and facts, you will pave the way for their acceptance of a substitute.

None of these persuasion devices, however, is a substitute for proper management or leadership. In fact, their success or usefulness depends upon your being the best person and the best manager you can be. Only then. can the potential of your people be released and fully utilized.

Participation

As we have seen throughout this chapter, people have a need to be in the know about the things that affect them. Managers must utilize various ways to involve their people in decision making and allow them to participate more fully in the work of the department.

The first device for employee participation open to managers is their formal authority. By delegating it to the more responsible members of their groups, they go a long way toward exposing their subordinates to the complexities of their jobs and toward developing them and their potential. How much a manager gives away depends upon many things. Is he or she allowed to delegate by the boss? Does the manager have subordinates who are responsible enough and good enough at their jobs to handle new responsibilities? Has the manager paved the way for delegation through proper training, appraisals, and human relations? All of these points are essential questions that must be answered before managers can give away any of their duties.

Another device is the problem-solving session. It is a most demanding kind of effort at participation on the part of subordinates in management decisions. It requires a good deal of patience and preparation, and is much more difficult than making the decisions yourself. The value of such meetings is immeasurable, however, as they are perhaps the most effective way to explain the facts behind the decisions and to promote understanding and cooperation. We all react more favorably to and promote much harder those ideas we gain on our own and as a result of our own efforts. When we see we are in the minority on an issue, we are strongly inclined to go along with the majority. (Chapter 10 will take up in some detail how to run meetings and group discussions.)

The third method of enlisting participation depends on the style of supervision you adopt toward your subordinates. The democratic and spectator styles promote a feeling of shared responsibility and a voice in what affects people. Each of these styles places a solid trust in the workers and makes the supervisor more dependent on them. The workers know this and usually act accordingly. No one wants to betray the trust of another unless he or she is emotionally ill. People want to live up to the expectations others have of them for the most part, provided they have the abilities and skills to do so. (Chapter 11 will explore in some detail different styles of leadership, their advantages, and their disadvantages.)

All these methods are effective if the necessary prerequisites exist. They give people a voice in decisions that many educated employees desire. If these tools are utilized properly, a manager can't help but succeed in winning support from the majority of his or her subordinates.

Job Enrichment

The days of the highly specialized, routine, assembly-line jobs are evidently numbered, if we can judge by the numerous attempts in nearly all major businesses to enlarge the scope of the workers' duties and put back the challenges that have been so systematically removed over the years. Today the emphasis is strongly toward enriching people's jobs and working environment to provide them with variety, a deeper personal interest and involvement, greater autonomy, and an increased amount of responsibility.

This concept is not new for many companies. The automobile manufacturers long ago saw the need to train workers capable of performing more than a narrow range of highly specialized duties. After they had constructed assembly lines and engineered the assembly process so that it could handle dozens of refined and repetitive tasks, the auto makers discovered that the entire operation might suffer as a result of a worker's absence unless a trained replacement was available. Rather than training back-up workers who knew only one of the many tasks, a few people were selected to learn every job on the line so that they could move quickly and smoothly into one or another of them as the need arose.

At this point a distinction should be made between **job enrichment** and **job enlargement.** Job enrichment adds challenge, variety, a deeper sense of personal involvement, more responsibility, and a greater autonomy to a worker's job. Job enlargement merely increases the number of tasks that a worker has to perform; the extra tasks may or may not offer a degree of variety or challenge. Usually these tasks consist of some additional duties similar to the ones the worker is already performing. Job enlargement takes place when a worker is laid off and his or her duties are reassigned to the remaining workers in the same shift or unit. As a result, some of these workers simply have more of the same duties to perform while others may be given additional duties related to the ones they are already handling. Job enlargement never means greater autonomy or a more personal sense of involvement for the worker. Job enrichment always does.

An opportunity for job enlargement and job enrichment presents itself in the case of almost every highly refined, routine job. The question then becomes: "Do the people who have these jobs want enrichment?" For many workers, the answer is a surprising no. A large number of production line workers prefer their repetitive, specialized tasks. Their reasons are many. Some do not want a challenge and the additional effort it might require. Others are working to their capacities with their job as it now is, and they could not adjust to additional duties. Still others do not want new responsibilities or the ways in which their jobs are to be enriched. A number of companies that tried job enrichment as an answer to the "blue-collar blues" found out that more difficulties were created by the new system than eliminated. Consequently, some of them have dropped wholesale attempts to introduce enrichment, and they have become more selective in their approach.

There are several ways to enrich a job. A company can simply expand the duties an individual has to perform. Another method involves giving the worker more decisions to make about the methods, procedures, working conditions, and layout of the work. Job rotation has been used for years in management-development programs, and this approach has filtered down to the ranks of the workers in companies like Polaroid. Finally, there is the method by which a worker is made a leader or "straw boss." By becoming a kind of assistant to his or her supervisor, this worker is actually beginning an apprenticeship for a future position in the management.

The IBM Experience Perhaps one of the best-known and most often cited examples of a major company's approach to job enrichment is the IBM story. In the 1940s IBM began to build computers. Most of the production personnel were semiskilled machine operators. The product, however, was amazingly complex and sophisticated, requiring close tolerance and precision machining. Like many companies, IBM had engineered each job into the simplest tasks and had assigned each individual worker just a few basic tasks to perform.

As the president of IBM, Thomas J. Watson, was walking through the plant one day, he noticed an operator sitting idle. When he asked her why, she told him that she had to wait for a set-up operator to get her machine ready for her next job. Watson asked her if she could do the preparatory work herself, and she answered that she could, but was not supposed to! Additional investigation revealed that, although workers spent idle hours each week waiting for set-up operators, only a few days would be needed to train each operator to set up his or her own machine. Set-up was added to each worker's job description. Eventually, each operator was made responsible for inspecting his or her own output as well. It wasn't long before the favorable experiences in computer manufacture spread to other IBM operations. Typewriter-production jobs were similarly enlarged, with a corresponding increase in morale and efficiency.

Other companies soon discovered that what worked for IBM could work for them, too. Many jobs, even though they were specialized and precise, could be designed to contain some degree of flexibility for a worker—the need to use his or her judgment, and the ability to influence the flow of the work.

Maytag, the home appliance manufacturer, has worked wonders on employee efficiency with numerous experiments in job enrichment. Some workers assemble entire components that were previously designed to be a team effort. Volvo, the Swedish car manufacturer, has small teams of workers who assemble entire automobiles. Texas Instruments, a precision instruments company, has involved its workers not only in additional duties such as testing and inspecting their output but also in planning their work by setting their own quality and quantity goals.

Job enrichment is not the ultimate solution to people problems, but it offers one of the best hopes for increasing productivity, reducing employee absenteeism, and boosting employee morale and loyalty. David Sirota, a professor of management and a management consultant, has listed a few problems that cannot be solved through job enrichment.[1]

1. Dissatisfaction with pay and fringe benefits;
2. Employee insecurity;
3. Technical incompetence;
4. Obstacles to getting the work done, such as poor administrative support or inferior tools and materials.

Organization Development

Organization development (OD) has been defined by the Conference Board, a nonprofit research group, as "a planned, managed, systematic process (used) to change the culture, systems and behavior of an organization in order to improve the organization's effectiveness in solving problems and achieving its objectives." This process involves efforts in education and training that eventually affect everyone in an organization.

Efforts at OD among the largest business firms of the United States include several different approaches. They include attitude assessments, management by objectives, job enrichment, problem-solving training and problem-solving sessions, and sensitivity training. Outside consultants and company personnel are utilized to initiate programs and to train company employees to carry them out. OD requires an organization to identify its weaknesses and strengths; define its problems; establish OD goals; set up programs for achieving the goals; and evaluate the progress of each program. The best aspects of a company are retained and improved. The problems are identified, and programs are constructed to deal with each of them.

OD uses a technique to change people's attitudes and break down their resistance to change that is known as **sensitivity training.** When conducted under the close supervision of a trained discussion leader, sensitivity training can and often does give participants a greater awareness of and insight into their own feelings and attitudes. Attendance at the training sessions should be strictly voluntary.

---

1. "How Industry Is Dealing with People Problems on the Line," *American Machinist,* November 12, 1973, p. 86.

Sensitivity training utilizes small groups that engage in several usually unstructured discussions. Through the interaction of the group members under the direction of the leader, the participants are forced to voice their feelings and opinions about themselves, others in the group, their company and its objectives, and many other topics. Demands are made on each person to become more open and honest, and to become more aware of his or her feelings and of the feelings of others in the group.

Many people who have experienced sensitivity training regard it as useful. Others claim to have been badly hurt by the process. As a general rule, most emotionally healthy people can get through such an experience with improvement to themselves and no psychic injuries. Most companies carefully screen potential participants, however, before inviting them to engage in the training.

As a final comment on what you've learned so far in this chapter, read the following statement by Dorothy L. Nolte.[2] As you read it, simply substitute the word *subordinate* for the word *child*.

If a child lives with criticism,
    he learns to condemn.
If a child lives with hostility,
    he learns to fight.
If a child lives with ridicule,
    he learns to be shy.
If a child lives with shame,
    he learns to feel guilty.
If a child lives with tolerance,
    he learns to be patient.
If a child lives with encouragement,
    he learns confidence.
If a child lives with praise,
    he learns to appreciate.
If a child lives with fairness,
    he learns justice.
If a child lives with security,
    he learns to have faith.
If a child lives with approval,
    he learns to like himself.
If a child lives with acceptance,
    he learns to find love in the world.

---

2. Dorothy L. Nolte (John Philip & Co., 1963).

Attitudes are formed within us through cultural forces—the same forces that shape our personality. Our personality is observable in part as a result of our words and actions. Beneath our words and actions lie our attitudes, and beneath our attitudes lie their supportive causes.

Supervisors must make daily judgments about the adequacy of their own attitudes and those of their subordinates. If the supervisors are well grounded in management principles and practices, they are equipped with the standards they need to make sound judgments.

Once supervisors observe improper conduct or attitudes in a subordinate—that is, conduct or attitudes that prevent that subordinate from achieving an average or better-than-average performance—they must probe for the attitude or attitudes that promote such action. Once this conduct or these attitudes are out in the open, the supervisors must seek to identify the experiences the worker has undergone to cause them. Only then are the supervisors capable of understanding the other person's point of view. By determining the vulnerabilities or weaknesses in the employee's reasoning and the supportive causes for them, the supervisors are able to attack the undesirable conduct and attitudes by appeals to the worker's intelligence.

By uncovering the personal and/or social reasons for a worker's resistance to change or lack of cooperation, the supervisors can try to find out what supports those reasons and then begin a concerted effort to weaken or remove those supports.

Unless people see that the attitudes they hold are no longer justified, they will not develop the drive or incentive to change them. Changing attitudes is a demanding task, and sometimes you will not succeed in persuading your subordinates to do so. But that is no reason for you not to try.

Basically you have six proven techniques for introducing changes and changing attitudes: Force Field Analysis; proper communications techniques; persuasion techniques; participation techniques; organization development; and job enrichment. If the circumstances are favorable, probably no approach to your subordinates can be so useful as job enrichment. For you will be working toward a more effective way of utilizing their talents and stimulating a greater mental commitment toward their jobs.

attitude	**job enlargement**	**organization development**
cooperation	**job enrichment**	**sensitivity training**
Force Field Analysis	**opinion**	

1. Why is the concept of "good" and "bad" attitudes inappropriate for managers?

2. What is meant by the phrase *improper attitude?*

3. Can we determine people's attitudes by observing their behavior? Why or why not?

4. Refer to Figure 6–1 and explain why the supervisor must "straddle the fence."

5. How can your attitudes affect those of your subordinates?

6. How can your subordinates' attitudes affect your own?

7. One of your workers, a lathe operator, is negligent about cleaning his or her work area and equipment regularly, as required by shop rules and the union agreement. How do you deal with this problem?

8. How do you tackle the problem of introducing a new method to old-timers who could be faster at their jobs if they used the new technique?

9. If all your efforts to win cooperation fail, how do you get your subordinates to adopt a change in routine imposed by your boss which you are obliged to put into effect?

10. Using the Force Field Analysis technique, list all the driving and restraining forces you can think of for a heavy smoker who doesn't want to quit smoking.

CASE PROBLEM

Section C

Jim Daly had been expecting a promotion for almost a month. He figured there was no way he would not get it. He had two year's experience on the job, and was regarded as the best worker in section C. Of course, he realized that a coworker, Marge Madison, had been in the section longer than himself, but their boss, Hazel Sam, had given him every indication that he was first in line to replace Hazel when she moved up to a middle management position.

No wonder then that Jim was so shocked and upset when Hazel called the section together last week to announce that Marge would be her replacement. Jim had great difficulty keeping his emotions under control at that meeting. In fact, he could not bring himself to congratulate Marge on her new responsibilities.

Since that time, the best worker in section C had become its least enthusiastic and least productive member.

Jim was rapidly becoming a negative influence among his four coworkers—so much so that two of them were beginning to shun Jim.

Marge was aware of the whole situation and knew that she would have to act quickly. She had been upset when Jim did not congratulate her on winning the promotion. She realized, too, that his resentment of her was bound to enter any conversation she might have with him. On the other hand, doing nothing was bound to make things worse. Although she knew that some action was called for, she could not decide what steps to take. That's when she decided to have a talk with Hazel. Their conversation yielded the following information:

1. Hazel admitted that she had wanted to give the promotion to Jim, but had been overruled by the personnel department because more women were needed as supervisors to meet the company's affirmative action quota for promoting females;

2. Hazel also admitted that she had assured Jim that he would be the next supervisor of section C;

3. Hazel stated that she had not spoken to Jim since the meeting of a week ago when Marge was given the promotion.

4. Hazel was unsympathetic to Marge's request for help. Her only advice was as follows:

Well, Marge, how did you expect the man to react? He was the better choice—he knew it, personnel knew it, and I knew it. You're the problem, not Jim.

Questions

1. Do you agree that Marge is the "problem," not Jim? Why?

2. Why have two members of section C begun to shun Jim?

3. What do you think of Hazel's attitudes toward the promotion and toward her subordinate manager, Marge?

4. What should Marge do now?

7 Human Needs and Motivation

LEARNING OBJECTIVES

■ After reading and discussing this chapter, you should be able to:

1 List and give an example of each of the five basic human needs.

2 Define frustration, and give an example of how frustration on the job can affect people's performances.

3 Define personality and tell how it evolves.

4 Summarize Theory X about human motivation, and state briefly how managers who follow it might approach their subordinates.

5 Summarize Theory Y about human motivation, and tell how managers who follow it would differ in their approach to their subordinates from Theory X managers.

6 Define motivation, and reproduce the diagram about the motivation process (Figure 7–2).

7 List five maintenance factors and give an example of each.

8 List five motivation factors and give an example of each.

9 Explain how the presence of motivation factors or their lack can influence people at work.

INTRODUCTION

■ This chapter explores five common human needs we all share and shows how they act as motives for our behavior. You will learn about the connection between our needs and our motivation and you will see how supervisors can use this knowledge to better understand themselves and their subordinates.

Success as a manager and a leader of human resources is directly linked to an in-depth understanding of the basics about human behavior. In this chapter we shall explore further the topics you studied in Chapter 6. The concepts of human needs, leadership, and motivation are complex, but they can be understood and utilized by anyone willing to put forth a sincere effort to learn about them. If you aspire to be a manager at any level, you will be responsible for directing subordinates. Your reputation will be in their hands. This fact alone should be a strong incentive to you to master thoroughly the important topics of this chapter.

HUMAN NEEDS

■ We all share a number of **human needs** that provide the stimuli or motives for change from within ourselves. Psychologist Abraham H. Maslow identified five common needs that are the bases of our internal drives to achieve satisfaction in life.[1] Figure 7–1 shows these needs as steps in an upward progression from the most basic to the highest psychological needs. All of us bring these needs with us each day to our jobs.

Physical Needs

At the lowest level of the scale are our physiological or body needs. They include the need for adequate food, clothing, and shelter, and the instinct to survive. These needs drive us to seek a degree of satisfaction that, if adequate from our individual point of view, causes them to be suppressed as motivators for a time. But eventually they will once again arise to motivate our conscious behavior. For example, if we are hungry, we seek food of a type and quantity necessary to satisfy our hunger. Once we have eaten our fill, however, our hunger is appeased and no longer motivates our actions. New needs surface and take over as motives for our actions. But as we all know, hunger will return.

Safety Needs

The second level of human needs—safety or physical security—is our next concern. Having satisfied our physiological needs for the moment, we are concerned about providing for their satisfaction in the future. Once we have achieved an economic position that provides the means necessary to secure our physical maintenance, we desire to protect this condition. People who have jobs are anxious to keep them. They are concerned with preventing the loss of their jobs and the corresponding loss of the ability to provide for their physical needs. As a result, they may join a union to gain this kind of security. They may take out in-

---

1. A. H. Maslow, *Motivation and Personality* (New York: Harper & Row, Publishers, 1954).

SELF-REALIZATION NEEDS	Job-related satisfiers
Reaching your potential	Involvement in planning your work
Independence	Freedom to make decisions affecting work
Creativity	Creative work to perform
Self-expression	Opportunities for growth and development

ESTEEM NEEDS	Job-related satisfiers
Responsibility	Status symbols
Self-respect	Merit awards
Recognition	Challenging work
Sense of accomplishment	Sharing in decisions
	Opportunity for advancement

SOCIAL NEEDS	Job-related satisfiers
Companionship	Opportunities for interaction with others
Acceptance	Team spirit
Love and affection	Friendly coworkers
Group membership	

SAFETY NEEDS	Job-related satisfiers
Security for self and possessions	Safe working conditions
Avoidance of risks	Seniority
Avoidance of harm	Fringe benefits
Avoidance of pain	Proper supervision
	Sound company policies, programs, and practices

PHYSICAL NEEDS	Job-related statisfiers
Food	Pleasant working conditions
Clothing	Adequate wage or salary
Shelter	Rest periods
Comfort	Labor-saving devices
Self-preservation	Efficient work methods

Figure 7-1. Human needs and their job-related satisfiers.

surance as a protection against economic losses from illness or accident. As with our physical needs, once a degree of satisfaction is reached that is adequate for individuals, their need for security weakens as a motive for their actions. But if their jobs are threatened, the need for security may once again become an active motivating force in their lives.

Social Needs

With the satisfaction of our safety needs comes the desire to satisfy our social needs. They include our desire for human companionship, that is, for affiliation with people and groups that will enrich us as individuals and give us a sense of identity with something or someone larger than ourselves. We need to have the assurance that we are acceptable to others. We need friends, family, and love. Once we have achieved the measure of affiliation that we feel desirable and adequate, our social needs begin to wane, and the fourth level of needs comes to the surface.

Esteem Needs

The need for esteem is two-sided. First, we have a desire to be appreciated for what we are and for what we have to contribute—to be respected by others. Second, we need to have a feeling of *self*-esteem—to know we are worth something to ourselves as well as to others. We need a positive self-image. From this need comes the desire for praise and symbols that reflect our worth to ourselves as well as others' appreciation of our efforts. We seek prestige and status positions among our peers and behave in ways that are pleasing and acceptable to others whose opinions we value.

Self-Realization Needs

Finally, our need for self-realization takes over after we have achieved some measure of satisfaction at the four previous levels. We begin to experience a need to fulfill our potential and to be creative. To some, this means striving for higher levels in company management and obtaining the added power and prestige that such an office represents. To others, it may mean being the best machinist or supervisor or teacher or biologist he or she has the potential to become. The need for self-realization causes a person to pursue interests and knowledge for their own sake and for the joy of the pursuit. The necessary prerequisite for this need is some satisfactory level of achievement in the other need categories. Clearly, a hungry person struggling for survival will not be motivated by self-realization needs until some time after subsistence has been achieved.

All these needs are common in all of us to some degree. At any given moment, one or more of them are active while the others lie dormant. When we search for satisfaction in one or more areas and find it to a degree we feel adequate, that need will cease for a time to be an active motive for our behavior. What is enough satisfaction for some, however, may be too little or too much for others. No need is ever completely satisfied, and none can ever cease completely to be a motivator. It is the unfulfilled need that is the strongest motive for human behavior.

THE SUPERVISOR AND HUMAN NEEDS

■ What does all this mean to you as a supervisor? You have learned that people's jobs can be a source of satisfaction or of dissatisfaction to them in their search for self-improvement and self-development. You know that our common needs provide the motive force for human behavior, and that each person is a unique individual with personal goals that may be quite different from those of his or her peers. As a supervisor, you are in a unique position to assist your subordinates and provide them with some of the satisfactions they are seeking. You can be most helpful with regard to their safety, social, and esteem needs, as we shall now see.

With regard to your subordinates' needs for safety and security, you are probably the one who initially provided them with their training. When your subordinates joined your department, chances are that you received and welcomed them. You set about assessing their strengths and weaknesses, and getting to know as much about them and their abilities as possible. Then you determined their specific needs for training so that they might improve their performances and skills. What you were doing was providing them with the knowledge, skills, and attitudes they would need to keep their jobs. You were increasing their sense of security and helping them remove some of their initial fears. Your actions helped them achieve a measure of satisfaction for both their physical and safety needs.

You have been helping your subordinates with their need for affiliation by inducting them into their new jobs and work groups when they first arrived. Your effort to know them has made you aware of their individual needs for affiliation and of those workers who are satisfied and of those who are frustrated with regard to their social needs. If you were doing your job, you went to work on the problem of those who needed more social contacts and weren't experiencing them. You should have done all you could to help the isolated individuals gain acceptance, to foster a team spirit among your subordinates, and to make them all feel part of a larger whole. If you haven't been doing these things, begin to do so right now. You have been missing some great opportunities to be of service to your people and to promote greater efficiency. It is your job as their supervisor to do so.

In regard to their esteem needs, you have several key roles to play. In your appraisals you are providing your people with the raw material they need to help them know themselves and to improve. You are also giving them an accurate assessment of how they rate with you and the company. You can pass out the praise if they deserve it and note the specific areas they must work on to gain your continued praise and acceptance. You also have authority which, if delegated, can be used to enrich their feelings of importance and give them a way to learn bits and pieces of your job. They know that this is an important sign of your faith and confidence in their abilities. You know that if you are to advance you must know your boss's job. If they are to advance, they must know your job. Each day you may receive suggestions from your people. If they are good, use them and give the credit to the source of each suggestion. If they are not suited to the operation, give the subordinate the reason why. These are but a few ways to help your people and your operation to improve.

A major difficulty may arise if you attempt to discover which of the five need levels is a conscious concern to each individual subordinate at any given time. This is difficult knowledge to gain because, when you observe your people, you do so in a fragmented way. You see them at work under the influence of many forces from within and outside of the company. Even if you know each of your people well, you can be fooled by your observations. In observing the actions of others we seldom see the motives for them. You, like your subordinates, tend to play roles at work that mask or hide your true feelings and motives. Yet every supervisor concerned about his or her job and subordinates must try to know his or her people well enough to answer the following questions about each of them:

1. What are his or her immediate goals?
2. What are his or her immediate needs?
3. What are his or her unique attitudes about me, his or her job, and our company?
4. Why does he or she hold these attitudes?

The answers to these four questions will help you determine what your subordinates' current needs are and what will motivate them at a given time. This knowledge will allow you to provide some **incentives** that might trigger a greater effort and contribution from each subordinate, and that will assist that person and your department to achieve a greater output.

FRUSTRATION

■ What happens when people seek satisfaction for their needs, set goals that they feel will provide this satisfaction, and find barriers in the way of achieving the satisfaction? For example, you have worked very hard to obtain an object that you believe will provide you with some measure of satisfaction for a need. Once you get it, however, you discover that it is a piece of junk or a "lemon" or that it simply does not give you the satisfaction you were looking for. Or let us suppose that you were counting on a promotion at work. You believed you were the best qualified candidate and have been working very hard to achieve it. Then you are told that someone else was given the promotion. What will you do? How will you react?

When we seek satisfaction in one or more areas and find difficulty in achieving it, we experience **frustration.** Now two courses of action are open to us. First, we can set a new goal or strengthen our efforts to achieve our original goal, looking for ways around, under, or over the obstacles in our path. Or we can repress our desire to achieve the goal, convincing ourselves that it is impossible or not worth the effort to achieve it. If we choose to repress or bury our desire for satisfaction, we don't just forget about it and move on. We will tend to overemphasize one or another of our needs to compensate for the lack of satisfaction we have just experienced. Our self-image may be damaged, and we will work hard to make up for this.

A worker who seeks social satisfaction at work and is denied it, either through the design of the environment (he or she may work alone) or through being excluded by others he or she wishes to join, may react by seeking a transfer to another job or looking for employment with another company. Employees who are mistreated by the company, or believe this to be the case, may decide to work against their employer, withholding their contributions and becoming less productive. They may decide to join with others who feel the same frustration, becoming members of negative groups bent on frustrating the company efforts to achieve its goals.

HUMAN PERSONALITY

■ Managers must get to know themselves and their subordinates in more than a superficial way. This effort begins with the knowledge of human **personality** and its formation. Your personality may be defined as your habitual way of acting, feeling, and thinking toward people and events. It is expressed to others through your attitudes and behavior toward them. Your personality is unique and dynamic. It is unique because there has never been anyone exactly like you before and never will be again. It is dynamic because each day, each month, and each year you change, as do others around you. Sometimes this change is subtle, and sometimes it is dramatic. Because you are unique, you must guard against judging others by using yourself as a standard.

Your personality is a composite that makes you what you are at any given time. It begins with your inherited traits, both physical and mental, and it develops unceasingly through your exposure to the culture around you. Your culture contains the environmental factors that influence your thinking, feeling, and acting as well as the opportunities for new experiences that come about through your interaction with others.

Heredity gives you your physical appearance and athletic potential as well as your learning and energy potential. Heredity can and does influence the way you think, feel, and act toward others because it affects how others think, feel, and act toward you. A physical trait that causes a person to stand out among his or her peers as somewhat unusual will color others' judgments and reactions. For instance, physical traits may promote or hinder acceptability to others. A boy or girl much taller than his or her peers at an early age may be ridiculed or teased in childish pranks and jokes. On the other hand, as team sports become important, this same person may become the most valuable player on the school basketball team. Depending upon circumstances, your physical traits may be either a positive or negative influence on your personality and its formation.

Cultural determinants generally have a much greater influence on personality formation than do hereditary factors. How our friends, our family, our associates, and our teachers react to us, their level of acceptance of us and what we are, can cause us to gain self-confidence and self-respect or can persuade us to change in an attempt to gain their acceptance.

Our environment has many different facets. Throughout life we are exposed to and become part of many of these. Each one has contributed in some measure to our development as persons. The kind of neighborhood we grew up in, the schools we attended, and the economic conditions we knew are but a few examples of environmental forces that have shaped our personalities.

The personal experiences people have had with their teachers, bosses, family members, friends, and associates have also influenced their patterns of thinking, feeling, and acting. How these people have reacted toward you and how you have related to them have colored your judgment about many things. Often their prejudices became yours; their job became your job; their experiences shaped your experiences.

There is a cause-and-effect relationship between your environment and your experiences. Your groups of friends and associates have placed limits on your experiences. These groups have limited your exposure to new people and new ideas. Your neighborhood perhaps dictated the schools you attended and thereby restricted the exposure you received to only a certain group of teachers, classmates, and neighborhood friends. Your family environment restricted your growth and development in the formative years to family values, hopes, ambitions, and goals. To a large measure then you are a product of your environment and the experiences you found within it. Whether these experiences were favorable or not, whether they caused a favorable growth and development or not, is something we all must examine. If we are unhappy with the answer we get, then we are motivated to begin to change.

The key point in this knowledge of personality development and its relationship to motivation is this: if we are satisfied with ourselves, we will make little effort to change; but if we are dissatisfied with our self-image and/or with the ways in which others react to us, we are motivated to strive to achieve a change in both ourselves and our relationships with others. This effort at change is self-directed and comes entirely from within. We have to see the need for a change and want to achieve it, or we won't accomplish it. It is not enough for others to want it in us.

THEORIES X AND Y   ■ A professor of management at Massachusetts Institute of Technology, Douglas McGregor, constructed two theories that attempt to summarize the two prevalent yet opposing sets of attitudes adopted by managers today in regard to human nature and motivation.[2] Theory X portrays a somewhat traditional view that unfortunately all too often underlies managers' behavior. It states that the average person:

1. Has a natural dislike for work and will try to avoid it;

2. Has to be threatened, controlled, coerced, and punished to give a fair day's work;

3. Avoids responsibility, lacks ambition, and needs constant direction.

The real tragedy of Theory X is that it is a self-fulfilling prophecy about people. If a manager really believes what this theory holds about subordinates, he or she will treat them in an authoritarian and suspicious manner, threatening them and looking down on them. The new employee who has a different makeup from the boss' will soon learn that his or her ideas, initiative, and drive are not respected or rewarded.

---

2. Douglas McGregor, *Leadership and Motivation* (Cambridge: The M.I.T. Press, 1966).

He or she will learn to behave in the way the boss expects him or her to behave. Soon the employee will adopt the "what's the use" attitude that this boss assumed existed from the beginning. Then the boss can smile and say, "See, I told you so."

What Theory X does not say but assumes is that there is a small minority of people who are exceptions to the theory, and that they, as if by Divine Providence, are destined to rule others.

Theory Y, on the other hand, is an attempt to apply what is now known about the majority of people in light of recent research on human behavior and motivation. Theory Y states that the average person:

1. Desires work as naturally as he or she does play or rest;
2. Is capable of controlling and directing himself or herself if committed to achieving a goal;
3. Is committed to a goal on the basis of the rewards associated with it and its achievement;
4. Desires responsibility and accepts it willingly;
5. Possesses imagination, ingenuity, and initiative;
6. Is intellectually underutilized in the average industrial setting.

It can easily be seen that a manager who adopts this set of beliefs about others in his or her subordinates will take an entirely different approach in relationships with them. This manager will assume the best and expect no less from each individual, while also demanding the best from himself or herself. Look around you at work. You will probably find many examples of men and women, both in and out of management, who are putting forth a mediocre effort. This often is the result of their managers' expecting nothing more from them. Subordinates learn to give what is expected. Every mediocre subordinate is usually only the reflection of a mediocre manager.

MOTIVATION

■ **Motivation** is the drive within a person to achieve a personal goal. The term **drive** in our definition denotes a force that is fueled by human needs common to us all. These needs provide the motives for our actions. Our actions are efforts, both mental and physical, that we feel are necessary to achieve our goal. Our goal may be to acquire some tangible thing like an automobile or a color TV set; it may be to achieve some position of status, such as a promotion or membership in a group or club; or it may be to accomplish something, such as designing a better machine. The specific form the goal takes is a result of our personal desires and wants. These desires and wants, once they are fulfilled, will provide us with some measure of satisfaction or happiness we don't now possess. Figure 7–2 shows the motivation process in graphic form.

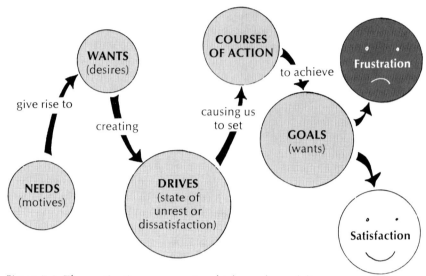

Figure 7-2. The motivation process, in which needs are felt and efforts made to satisfy them.

Our definition tells us that motivation is an internal process. It is something we effect within ourselves, not something we do to others. A person who is motivated is in a state of unrest because he or she feels or believes that he or she lacks something or some state of being that seems desirable or necessary (the goal). Motivated people are continually setting goals for themselves because their wants are insatiable. It is in the nature of people to want more—to continually strive to progress, to improve themselves or their conditions, and to acquire something new or some better position.

Behind every action you take there is a cause. You may not consciously know the underlying cause, but it is there, driving you on. The cause or **motive** for your action may be an urgent or pressing physical or psychological need, or it may be an emotional desire that is not necessary for subsistence but one that you consider worth a concerted effort to satisfy.

The Supervisor and Motivation

Your understanding of motivation begins with a recognition of the fact that a business can buy with money only some of a person's physical and mental energies. A business cannot buy, however, the individual's mental and emotional commitment to do the best job he or she can. It is partly up to each manager to inspire the employees in his or her charge to give of these things.

Have you ever wondered why some supervisors manage to get better results than others? Why their people perform so well for them? At the heart of their special ability is a clear understanding of themselves and an in-depth knowledge of their subordinates' needs, desires, and characteristics. These managers know that a better-than-average individual performance by both themselves and their subordinates depends on this personal knowledge, together with the development of strong personal and working relationships with their people. The development and maintenance of these personal and working relationships is what enables these supervisors to plan, organize, direct, control, and coordinate their subordinates' work and output.

If you get to know yourself well as a preliminary step to knowing others, you will be able to identify your strengths and weaknesses accurately and to begin the task of correcting your deficiencies. You will become aware of your personal biases and peculiarities which, if not noted and suppressed until you can correct them, might lead you to misjudge or act improperly towards those in your charge.

There are many sources available to help you know yourself better. All your mistakes, once investigated, will shed light on what went wrong and why. Each appraisal you have received from your boss or bosses, informal or formal, is a wealth of information about yourself. If it is received with the proper spirit, it can help you concentrate your efforts on areas of your performance and your personality that need improvement. This process of self-analysis and improvement is an ongoing one, so commit yourself to undertaking it *now*.

Maintenance and Motivation

As a further help in understanding motivation, let us examine the contributions of Dr. Frederick Herzberg and his associates, whose work on motivation in business has demonstrated some applications of Maslow's hierarchy of human needs.[3] They have found that two sets of factors must be provided in the working environment to promote motivation.

First, there is a set of factors they label *maintenance* or *hygiene* factors. These items will not cause employee motivation, but a lack of them will cause dissatisfaction. Provided in the right mix, they can prevent such dissatisfaction. The best a business can hope for by providing these factors is that the average employee will put forth an average commitment in time and effort at his or her job.

---

3. Frederick Herzberg, Bernard Mausner, and Barbara B. Snyderman, *The Motivation to Work* (New York: John Wiley & Sons, 1959).

The second set of factors is called *motivation* factors. They furnish the working environment with the conditions necessary to spark a better-than-average commitment from employees and provide the means by which individuals can achieve greater satisfaction of needs through their jobs.

MAINTENANCE OR HYGIENE FACTORS

The maintenance factors are:

1. *Economic:* wages, salaries, fringe benefits, and the like;

2. *Security:* grievance procedures, seniority privileges, fair work rules, and company policy and discipline;

3. *Social:* opportunities to mix with one's peers under company sponsorship, including parties, outings, breaks, and the like;

4. *Working conditions:* adequate heat, light, ventilation, hours of work;

5. *Status:* privileges, job titles, and other symbols of rank and position.

If the maintenance factors are absent or inadequate, this situation will cause employees to become dissatisfied. If they are provided in adequate quantity and quality (from the individual's point of view), they can merely prevent dissatisfaction. The best a business can hope for is a fair day's work for a fair day's pay. In the absence of these factors or their proper mix, employees will withhold some of their average contributions to the company's goals.

MOTIVATION FACTORS

On the other hand, let us now consider Herzberg's second set of factors: the motivation factors. If provided in the proper quantity and quality, they do have the potential to satisfy the employees' needs and cause an increased commitment of time and energy by the employees. The motivation factors are:

1. *Challenging work:* The average person wants to view his or her job as offering an avenue for self-expression and growth; each person needs something to tax his or her abilities;

2. *Feelings of personal accomplishment:* The average employee gets a sense of achievement and a feeling of contributing something of value when presented with a challenge he or she can meet;

3. *Recognition for achievement:* The average employee wants to feel his or her contributions have been worth the effort and that the effort has been noted and appreciated;

4. *Achievement of increasing responsibility:* The typical employee desires to acquire new duties and responsibilities, either through the expansion of his or her job or by delegation from the supervisor;

5. *A sense of individual importance to the organization:* Employees want to feel that their personal presence is needed and that their individual contributions are necessary;

6. *Access to information:* Employees want to know about the things that affect them and their jobs; they want to be kept in the know;

7. *Involvement in decision making:* Today's employees desire a voice in the matters that affect them and a chance to decide some things for themselves. They need freedom to exercise initiative and creativity.

These factors, unlike the common human needs they help satisfy, need to be designed into the structure and operations of a business. Some employees do not desire all or even a few of these factors and the opportunities they represent. This may be true because, for the moment at least, they lack ambition and don't feel the need to change. Still others, because of mental or emotional limitations, may lack the potential to take advantage of these factors and to master higher job responsibilities. For those who, in the manager's opinion, can take advantage of these factors but who for the present don't do so, some standards and goals must be set to prod them to keep growing. The manager should make it clear to these employees that more is expected of them, and that more rewards can be received in return for an increased effort. In short, the boss must try to get such employees off "dead center" and oriented to making progress both for themselves and for the company.

For those subordinates who have the potential and the drive to achieve something greater, supervisors have a duty to provide an environment that contains the motivation factors. If they are available like different kinds of fine foods on a buffet, the motivated ones in a group may pick and choose among them to satisfy their appetite for growth.

Motivational Studies During 1967 and 1968, a multinational electrical equipment manufacturer surveyed its 13,000 employees in 25 countries.[4] Professors Sirota and Greenwood averaged the employee rankings that respondents in the 25 countries, including the United States, gave to each factor, with 40 or more employees responding in each of the three occupational areas. Study Table 7–1 for the similarities and differences that appear. What does this survey tell you about people in the different occupations and countries?

---

4. D. Sirota and J.M. Greenwood, "Understand Your Overseas Workforce," *Harvard Business Review* (Jan.–Feb. 1971), pp. 53–60.

Factor	Salespersons Average	Salespersons U.S.	Technical personnel Average	Technical personnel U.S.	Service personnel Average	Service personnel U.S.
Training	2	8	1	3	1	5
Challenging work	1	1	2	1	2.5	1
Autonomy	3	4	3	5	7	10
Earnings potential	4	3	4.5	6	4	4
Advancement	5	2	6	2	5	2
Recognition	6	5	4.5	7	9	8
Job security	10	12	11	9	2.5	3
Friendly department	9	9	8	8	8	12
Personal time	11	7	7	4	6	6.5
Sense of importance	7.5	6	9.5	10	10	6.5
Efficient department	7.5	10	9.5	11	11	11
Fringe benefits	13	13	13	12	12	9
Physical conditions	14	14	12	14	13	13
Successful company	12	11	14	13	14	14

Table 7-1. How three different kinds of employees ranked the importance of job factors.

A more recent study yielded similar results. The Bemis Company of Minneapolis, Minnesota, surveyed its employees and a student group during the summer of 1974. Their findings are summarized in Table 7–2.

Modern business practices reflect the application of important research discoveries about human nature and motivation—what they consist of and how they operate. Managers everywhere draw heavily on

Table 7-2. A survey of job factor ratings by employees and students.
Adapted from NAM Reports data.

Factor	Average ranking Employees	Average ranking Students
Adequate compensation	1	2
Liking the work itself	2	1
Recognition for a job well done	3	6
Chances for growth and advancement	4	3
Chance for achievement	5	8
Quality of work supervision	6	9
Responsibility I am given	7	4
Friendly coworkers	8	5
Good working conditions	9	7
Company policies and administration	10	10

the contributions of social scientists, psychologists, anthropologists, and industrial researchers as they attempt to manage their human resources.

We have seen that motivation is an internal process. It exists in some people and not in others at any given moment. It comes about because of inner motives that give rise to drives creating unrest and a desire for change. The fuel for these drives is the five basic needs we all have in common.

Personality is what makes you you. It is the sum of your personal characteristics and reflects the influences of your heredity and cultural environment. Your personality is unique and dynamic. It is continually evolving with each new experience and the passage of time. It provides the frame of reference by which you determine who you are, what you want, and how you wish to get it. Personality gives particular substance to your motives, and forms the basis for your opinions.

People have five common levels of needs: physical, safety, social, esteem, and self-realization. These needs provide them with motives that influence their behavior. They seek individualized degrees of satisfaction for these needs. One or more of these needs may provide a person with a motive and drive for change at any given moment. None of these needs can ever be satisfied completely. They may lapse for a time as motivators but will return once again to become active within a person.

A business must provide both maintenance factors on the job and motivation factors to the best of its ability. The former prevent dissatisfaction, while the latter provide the means for achievement and growth. By designing work and the working environment in such a way as to include these factors, a business is setting the stage to get more from its people. They, in turn, receive the incentives they may need to spark their own motivation.

KEY WORDS

drive	**motivation**	**Theory X**
frustration	**motives**	**Theory Y**
human needs	**personality**	

1. Explain what is meant by the statement "Motivation is an internal process."

2. What is wrong, if anything, with using yourself as a standard when judging others?

3. How does knowledge of personality and its formation help you to understand motivation?

4. What courses of action are open to a worker who finds no motivational factors on the job?

5. What maintenance factors do you presently enjoy (a) on your job and (b) at your school?

6. What do motivation factors provide an employee on the job?

7. Why must we know ourselves well before we attempt to know others?

8. What needs do you feel are motives for taking college courses?

9. Refer to Table 7–2, and rank yourself on each factor. Why do you think you desire your number one choice so highly?

CASE PROBLEM

The Sleepy Hollow Motel

For five years Lillian Porter has been the receptionist at the Sleepy Hollow Motel. Her main duties include operating the switchboard, booking reservations, registering guests, and sorting the mail. In addition to her duties at the motel, Lill is a domestic engineer, that is, the mother of three youngsters who live at home with her. In addition, she has two grandchildren.

Lill is not a perfectionist but close to it. She demands the best she can give of herself and performs her duties consistently well. She is intolerant of errors that anyone makes, and was recently heard reprimanding a guest who had filled out the reservation card improperly. On that occasion she showed extreme annoyance with the same guest who was slightly intoxicated; as a result, the guest decided to seek other accommodations. Lill rarely smiles, and she has a rather stern matronly appearance as a result of her facial expression and way of dressing. She is rather fond, it seems, of two "basic black" dresses, both of which are out of style and unflattering to her figure. Lill hates to arrive late or to be asked to stay late. To date she has flatly refused to work even a minute overtime.

Lill's work area is well equipped, since the motel is only five years old. She receives above average pay for her job. She works pretty much alone and on her own, and likes it that way.

Her boss, Ben Sanderson, has often stated that he would be lost without Lillian. In Ben's words, "She seems to be able to handle six things at once."

"Everything about her is just great," said Ben in a conversation with his night manager, Angelo Fortini. "The only problem I have is with the four housekeepers. They always seem to be behind schedule. Nearly every day Lill sees one of them goofing off, and she is quick to point this out to them. When they fail to respond to her corrections, she is forced to come to me."

"Are you letting Lill supervise the housekeepers, too?" asked Angelo.

"No, it's just that Lill is the one who seems to catch them all the time. I have never seen any of them goof off."

"Ben, you know that Lill's husband was killed in a car accident a year ago."

"Yes, I know that."

"Do you remember how it happened?"

"Yes, it was a head-on collision at Route 41 and Ventura about 9 p.m. Why do you ask?"

"Well, did you know that it was a carload of migrant workers that ran the stoplight and killed Mr. Porter? The driver was drunk, and he escaped the crash with only a few scratches."

"So, what are you driving at?"

"Just this. What ethnic background are our housekeepers? Spanish, right?"

"Mexican, but they are all legal residents. I don't follow you. . . . Oh, now I see what you are getting at."

Questions

1. Which of the human needs seem most important to Lill?
2. Which maintenance and motivation factors is Lill receiving at work?
3. How can you explain Lill's lack of a pleasing disposition or personality?
4. Assuming that the motel's housekeepers are goofing off, how do you explain Ben's behavior?
5. What seem to be Lill's attitudes toward her work, coworkers, and liquor?

8 Human Relations— One on One

■ After reading and discussing this chapter, you should be able to:

1 Define the phrase *human relations.*

2 List and briefly explain the five purposes of human relations.

3 Explain the human-relations role of a supervisor acting as an educator.

4 Explain the human-relations role of a supervisor acting as a counselor.

5 Explain the human-relations role of a supervisor acting as a judge.

6 Explain the human-relations role of a supervisor acting as a spokesperson.

7 Explain the dangers of forming friendships with your subordinates.

INTRODUCTION

■ In recent years a great deal of attention has been focused on **human relations,** which can be defined for our purposes as sound, on-the-job relationships that managers should develop and maintain with their subordinates, peers, and superiors on an individual and group basis.

In this chapter we shall examine the nature of the relationships between yourself as a supervisor and your subordinates. Chapter 9 will take up your relationships with different kinds of groups at your place of business. Finally, Chapter 19 will explore another kind of human relations: your relationships with your peers and superiors. You may have achieved great technical proficiency in your work, but if you cannot develop good human relations with others, you will not succeed as a manager.

THE GOALS OF HUMAN RELATIONS

■ Managers should have the following goals in mind in their approach to human relations:

1. To know and understand each individual as an individual;

2. To approach and supervise each subordinate as an individual;

3. To provide what help you can to enable each individual to achieve the measure of satisfaction he or she wishes to achieve on the job;

4. To increase each individual's (a) contribution of intellectual effort; (b) commitment to the company and his or her job; (c) quantity and quality of output;

5. To foster a spirit of cooperation between yourself and your subordinates and peers, and between you and your boss.

These are worthy but difficult goals for any manager, but they are especially difficult for supervisors. The chief reasons for this difficulty are the wide diversity of ages, the differing backgrounds, and the lack of similar experiences so often found among workers. The heterogeneous mixture of people among the workers contrasts sharply to the homogeneous mixture so often found in the management ranks. Workers have always made the execution of the directing function much more difficult for supervisors than for any other level of management. What we are about to explore is not easy but absolutely necessary if you are to prevent the most common cause of failure in supervisory personnel: failure caused by faulty human relations.

DEVELOPING A SOUND WORKING RELATIONSHIP

■ As stated in earlier chapters, your success as a manager is directly related to and dependent upon the performance of your subordinates. Your reputation is in their hands since it is a product of their efforts. Your future therefore depends in large measure on how well you are able to relate to them and to promote in them a desire to excel. With this recognition should come a personal commitment on your part to aid all your people toward a more complete realization of their own potentials.

In Chapter 6 we discussed the need to know yourself well and to get to know your subordinates as individuals. Let us now consider the logical next step: the building of sound working relationships with each of your people.

The ideal relationship on the job between yourself and your subordinates will be the end result of your understanding, mastering, and executing the four fundamental roles listed below. (See Figure 8–1.) These roles are related and dependent upon one another. It is the supervisor's duty to initiate and maintain these relationships. Specifically there are four relationships that are defined in the following ways.

1. *Educator*—a builder of skills and developer of potentials;
2. *Counselor*—an adviser and director;
3. *Judge*—an appraiser and dispenser of justice;
4. *Spokesperson*—a disseminator of timely and accurate information.

Your Role as Educator

Your role as an educator is usually the first one you play in relation to a new subordinate. When new people first arrive, they are usually introduced to their coworkers, shown the facilities and places of work, and their duties and responsibilities are explained by their supervisors. If the supervisor played a part in the hiring, he or she has already begun to assess the individual's strengths and weaknesses. If not, the supervisor must begin to do so promptly. With this assessment comes a determination as to the type of training, if any, needed to bring the new employee up to par. This initial training is vitally important as it sets stand-

Figure 8-1. The four human relations roles for the supervisor.

ards and communicates skills, knowledge, and attitudes which have a lasting effect upon the individual and his or her department. Training, when properly planned and executed, does much to remove the initial fears we all have as we begin something new. It convinces the new people of our interest in and concern for their "getting off on the right foot." They should emerge from it with a clear understanding of what is expected of them and how they are expected to achieve it. The supervisor has demonstrated his or her commitment to helping the new person toward self-realization and a successful performance.

There is a second phase to your role as an educator. You will recall from Chapter 4 that we included in our definition of directing the element of educating. We stated there that to educate meant "the fostering of subordinates' intellectual development." By this we meant making new skills and knowledge available to subordinates and establishing proper attitudes. We also meant promoting an individual's own efforts to achieve these things. Your example in seeking further personal growth through formal education exemplifies your commitment to your company's emphasis on education. This just might be the incentive a subordinate needs to continue formal education on his or her own or to take advantage of company-sponsored programs that aid in self-development.

By understanding your role as an educator, mastering the knowledge and skills you wish to teach others, and executing this role in accordance with established principles of training (Chapter 17), you are well on your way toward promoting your own success by fostering success in others.

Your Role as Counselor

Think back to encounters with school counselors that you have had throughout your formal education. What was it they were trying to do for you? Why did the school feel they were necessary? Their advice was usually related to school and general growth-and-development problems common to most students. If the counselors were doing their jobs, they wanted what was best *for you*. They tried to get to know you and your individual needs, aspirations, and desires. They listened to you and, in turn, hoped you would listen to them—to their advice as to what was realistic thinking on your part and what was not. Sometimes they suggested solutions to your problems. If they were wise, they did not suggest solutions to personal or emotional problems but may have instead suggested that you talk with a specialist—an authority better equipped than they were to help you in that particular area.

In case you haven't guessed, this is also a description of the execution of your role as a counselor to your subordinates.

Mr. A. A. Imberman, a management consultant, states that there are two tests that employees use to judge their supervisors:

1. Is the supervisor aware of me? Can I turn to him or her for friendly help? Will he or she listen to me?

2. Will he or she do something about my problem?[1]

If the answers to these two questions are yes, the workers view their boss as a good one. By the first question the employees really want to know if the supervisor knows them in a personal way. Does the supervisor know about their ambitions, family and individual needs? By the second question they ask if the supervisor is willing to do something about a problem. Notice that the workers aren't asking for the boss to come up with a solution every time they present him or her with a problem. They only want him or her to try. Doing something can be as simple as being available to listen to them. We all know the release that accompanies our talking out a problem with a sympathetic listener. We often reach our own solution after or during such an experience. Sometimes we are not really looking for a solution because we know that only we ourselves or time can provide it, as in the case of a family argument or illness. Of course, job-related problems are something else. If it is within your power to solve the problems or recommend solutions, do so. If the problems must be resolved at a higher level, see that they are referred there, and that the disposition or decision is relayed to your subordinate. Even if the results do not satisfy the individual, you have tried to help. You have done the best you could, and a subordinate will know it. You will have passed a major test.

In order to get to know your people in depth, you should meet with each of them informally, face to face, at least once a month for twenty to thirty minutes. The purposes of these counseling or coaching sessions are to:

1. Get to know each person as an individual;

2. Periodically update your knowledge about each of your subordinates;

3. Pinpoint personal and business-related problems that you may be able to help resolve;

4. Find out how each subordinate is doing on the job;

5. Show your concern for each subordinate's growth and improvement.

Many supervisors ignore counseling until a problem arises. Then they call a hasty conference and belittle, berate, or "chew out" the subordi-

---

1. A. A. Imberman, "Why Are Most Foreman Training Courses A Failure?" *Bedding*, 96, no. 6 (July 1969): 40–41.

nate who is in trouble. Very soon subordinates get the message that the only time they see or hear from the boss is when he or she is unhappy or upset about their performance. Some supervisors claim that they do not have the time, or that the time spent on counseling could be better spent on other things. The plain fact is that if supervisors don't counsel their people, they will have plenty of fires to put out and very little time for counseling. But if they invest the time necessary to touch base with each person periodically, they will be able to spot trouble coming and thus prevent many problems that later on might require corrective measures or hastily called sessions to deal with the difficulty.

As you prepare for each counseling interview, keep in mind that you want to cement and improve good working relationships and to help each person as much as you can. Then refer to the four principles of coaching or counseling that follow.[2] These principles are:

> The *first principle* of successful coaching is to get your subordinate involved. The more active a part the subordinate can take in appraising the problem for himself, and in outlining possible courses of action, *the more committed he will be* to the solution. And, the more enthusiastically he will work for its success.
>
> The *second principle* is that you encourage him to participate actively in the interview. Your role in the coaching interview is not to *tell* your subordinate what to do or how to do it, but rather to *help him develop for himself* a plan of action for dealing with the problem at hand. You can raise key questions which will help him find a solution, but don't lead him by the hand unless it is absolutely necessary.
>
> The *third principle* is to make sure you both understand the meaning of what is being discussed and said. The only sure way of doing this is to get your subordinate to express his views in his own words. You should restate those views, in different words, to see if you can reach agreement. Otherwise, the two of you could come away from the coaching conference with entirely different ideas of the issues discussed and decisions made.
>
> Finally, the *fourth principle* is to force yourself to *do more listening than talking*. Even if you say relatively little during your meeting, the interview can prove of considerable value—provided you listen. If he is upset, you give your subordinate a chance to "let off steam." You also give him an opening to try out his ideas on you for a change.

---

2. *Training and Coaching Techniques* (East Lansing, Mich.: The Educational Institute of the American Hotel & Motel Association, 1976), p. 75.

An analogy can be made with respect to the supervisor's role in the motivation of subordinates and the director's role in bringing out the best in actors. A director knows that, like a supervisor, he or she cannot motivate an actor to put on a superior performance. The director realizes that motivation comes from within, and that certain limitations exist in and around every actor that can interfere with a superior effort. But the director knows that there is much he or she can do to provide the climate and incentives for the actor which can spark an inner drive to excel. He or she may remove distractions that might interfere with an actor's concentration. He or she can make certain that the actor has done the necessary homework and learned the lines. The director can counsel with the actor to find out how the actor perceives the role. The director is able to set the stage with the props and lighting that will allow the actor to perform to the best of his or her ability. Lastly, throughout the rehearsal and the performances the director offers advice and criticism. This coaching and sincere concern are often the spark the actor needs to give a superior performance. By sensing the actor's needs, strengths and weaknesses the director can tailor advice and direction to bring about a commitment to excel within the actor.

Supervisors must get to know themselves well, and get to know their subordinates in depth. Having committed themselves to these tasks, they will find that they are able to build sound human and working relationships with their subordinates. Supervisors should be able to tailor their approaches with the needs and responses of each subordinate in mind.

Your Role as Judge

Playing this role successfully involves being proficient at four important tasks:

1. Enforcing company policies and regulations as well as your department's procedures and rules;
2. Evaluating subordinates' performances;
3. Settling disputes among your people or between your people and yourself;
4. Dispensing justice.

ENFORCEMENT

In order to enforce company policy and regulations, you must first become aware of them. You have to know what they say as well as their proper interpretation. Then you must see to it that they are followed by both your subordinates and yourself. Finally, you must be certain that they are not violated by your section's procedures, practices, and rules.

You must follow a similar procedure in regard to your department's procedures and practices. Do the people know about them? Do they understand them? Are they following them? All these questions are usually answered through various controls you design into your operation. Proper induction and training should go a long way to insure that the department's procedures and practices are properly interpreted and utilized.

EVALUATION

Evaluating subordinates is one of your most important and time-consuming tasks as a supervisor. Chapter 4 showed us that the average operating manager spends 15 percent of his day on this activity. Appraising your people involves making judgments about their performances and their attitudes. Using established standards for each job, you must make an objective and honest evaluation of each person's output and individual contribution to the department. Is he or she meeting production standards? Is he or she correcting or trying to correct deficiencies noted in previous appraisals? Are his or her attitudes proper, or are they interfering with his or her efforts and those of other workers in the department?

Appraisals take place daily. In routine visits with your people, you have an excellent opportunity to note their successes and question their deficiencies. This will allow you to catch an error when it first appears and take corrective action to prevent its re-occurrence. Also, you are letting your people know on a regular basis how they stand with you. Your being with them regularly gives them the opportunity to ask questions and clear up misunderstandings. When the time finally rolls around for the formal semiannual or annual review, there should be no surprises. You have kept your people informed on a daily basis.

With regard to attitudes, your appraisals each day blend nicely with your role as a counselor. Much of appraising has to do with counseling. When your observations tell you that a worker's attitude is a cause for a deficiency in his or her output or conduct, try to find out why he or she harbors it. Chapter 6 contains much helpful information on attitudes and how to change them. You will recall that only when people see their attitude as "bad" will they reject it. Chapter 12 will probe more deeply into the specifics of the appraisal process.

SETTLING DISPUTES

You would be correct in interpreting part of your role as a judge as that of a peacemaker. People problems are the most persistent and numerous kind you have to deal with each day. Inevitably, two or more of your people or groups of subordinates will do battle with each other.

It would be best if these battles could be prevented, but that is not always possible. Sometimes the causes are hidden from your view and only surface under stress with an open display of hostility.

When you witness such disturbances, begin an investigation to uncover the causes on both sides. Analyze your evidence and make a decision. Try to avoid treating the symptoms, but concentrate your energies on the disease. When you have reached a conclusion as to the merits on both sides, confront the participants with your findings. Work toward a reconciliation that won't leave any scars as lasting reminders of the battle. Avoid any emphasis on who was at fault (chances are both sides share the blame), but point out why the problem got started and how it can be avoided in the future.

Once a student of mine who was a production foreman in the construction industry told me about one of his peers who, whenever they were together on breaks, would emphasize his own achievements on the job while criticizing and playing down those of my student. This had been going on for nearly a year. My student finally decided to avoid the other foreman for a while to relieve his feelings of frustration and remove their cause. Within a month the two men were reconciled. His peer began to miss my student's companionship on the job and realized why he had been avoided. When the other foreman dropped his critical attitude (he saw that to keep it would deprive him of his need for companionship), they were able to build a new and better relationship.

DISPENSING JUSTICE

Justice in this connection means seeing to it that each of your subordinates gets what he or she deserves. When they are doing a good job, they deserve your praise. When they break a rule or violate a procedure, they must be shown the errors of their ways. Rest assured that people desire to know the limits that exist on them and their activity. Once these limits are explained, they expect them to be enforced and usually anticipate some admonishment for each of their infractions. This admonishment may simply be a verbal warning or, in the case of repeated offenses, it may take some other sort of disciplinary action.

Improper or unacceptable conduct on the job cannot be tolerated. To prevent it, your company installs you as its chief enforcement officer in your department and gives you power to discipline violators. It provides you with policy and regulations while you provide your department with procedures and rules. When these prevention devices fail, corrective measures must take over.

To many, discipline means simply punishment. This is the negative side of a much broader concept. The positive side is the one that emphasizes informing organization members ahead of time as to the limits that surround acceptable conduct. It places the emphasis on self-control and mutual trust. When new employees are hired, you should inform them of the rules on the very first day, and you should make it clear to them what constitutes acceptable behavior and performance and what does not. When you take over a section as its supervisor, inform the members promptly of the standards you will enforce and the expectations you will have for each member. When infractions occur, take action. To do otherwise would ultimately undermine your formal authority and your integrity. You will find that it is much better to start out tough than to try to become so later. It is an unpleasant and difficult duty to discipline people for infractions of a rule that you failed to make clear to them.

When punishment is necessary, you must be certain that it fits the offense. Quite often, when dealing with unionized workers, the manager's disciplinary powers are limited by the union contract. Be certain that you have the power to take a specific action before you do so. Chapter 13 will deal with the tasks to be encountered in disciplining in more detail.

Your Role as Spokesperson

■ Your superiors expect you to represent adequately management's point of view to your subordinates. You are the only manager that can translate the management's plans into action. Your boss in particular is counting on you to defend and to reinforce management's position.

You must realize that you are (or should be) a fountainhead of timely and accurate information to your people. They look to you for an interpretation of the events they witness. They expect you to help them separate fact from fiction and truth from rumor. Their need to be kept "in the know" demands that you prepare them in advance for changes. They look to you also as *their* spokesperson—backing them up either when they are right or when they are wrong because they were executing your orders. If they believe that a policy or regulation is unfair, relay their feelings to those in a position to change it. You can do much to protect your people from harrassment and getting a "short stick." Just as you hope for their loyalty, they need yours.

What has been said above once again emphasizes that the supervisor is the person in the middle, caught between two different groups with individual demands that at times are opposed to one another. He or she is, as stated in Chapter 6, the manager straddling the fence between the demands of management and labor. Both sides expect the supervisor to be their representative to the other. But take heart. This is a necessary and totally logical evolutionary step in your movement through the ranks of management. Such experiences will serve you well for the rest of your career.

Just because your people request an answer to a question, and you know that answer, is no reason why you should give it. You must respect the confidences of both your superiors and subordinates. Information given to you in private with a request for your silence must be respected. If you betray a confidence, you'll soon find yourself on the outside of the group looking in.

There are times when your employees seem to know more about future events than you do. This is natural, and this situation may be explained in part by the grapevine. If they ask for clarification or verification and you cannot give it—don't bluff. Admit your lack of accurate information, and assure them that you will try to get it. Then be sure to deliver.

If you properly execute your role as spokesperson, your superiors and subordinates will learn to trust you and to rely upon you more in the future. This will strengthen your relationships with them and will promote harmony and cooperation in your department. You will be providing a key motivation factor for your people and earning their respect.

FRIENDSHIP

■ A word of caution. There is a distinct difference between the relationship between supervisor and subordinate that this chapter advocates and the relationship between two people called friendship. At the base of sound human relations are common interests (effective and efficient operation of the department, for example), mutual respect, and a concern for the other person's welfare. This is or should be true about your relationships with your friends as well. But you should try to prevent a true friendship from emerging out of sound human relations with your subordinates.

If you allow friendships to form between yourself and a subordinate, you do so at your own expense. How easy is it to give orders to a friend? Do you appraise your friend's performance and freely offer criticism to him or her? How about the times when you have to pass out an occasional "dirty" job? Would you consider your friend objectively as a candidate for it? You can't form a friendship with all your subordinates, so aren't you opening yourself to criticism about playing favorites? Isn't the subordinate you befriend open to criticism too, and aren't his or her relationships with his or her peers put in jeopardy?

Your honest answers to these questions should alert you to the inherent dangers of friendship with subordinates. Your friends at work should be your peers.

MAINTAINING YOUR RELATIONSHIPS

■ So far we have discussed how to build a sound relationship with your individual subordinates. How can you preserve it once you have established it? The answer lies in persistence. When we talked about personality formation, we agreed that it was a continuous process. So too with the on-the-job relationships. Like any living thing, human relations need constant attention. Each day brings about changes in the parties involved so that what worked well yesterday may not today. It is the recognition of this dynamic aspect of people and their relationships that dictates the need for maintenance.

Maintenance of your relationships with subordinates can be compared to the situation of gardeners who wish to keep their gardens in a healthful and beautiful condition. They have plans for the care and development of the gardens. There are schedules for feeding, pruning, and preventive measures such as spraying and weeding. Their daily observations tell them about the gardens' state of repair and keep them in touch with each plant and its present state of health. What precedes all this is a genuine love for gardening and a commitment to a program for maintaining the gardens. So it must be with your human relations efforts. Establishing a sound relationship with each person is only just a beginning. If it is to grow and be mutually beneficial, maintenance must be scheduled and performed.

Getting Along with Your Peers

■ Although Chapter 19 will have a great amount to say about your relations with your peers and related topics, a few words are in order here. You should have as your friends at work one or more fellow supervisors. Since you all experience common problems and share common interests, it is only fitting that you do your best to promote a cooperative spirit among your peers. You can do this by lending a hand when another supervisor needs help. By sharing your knowledge and experience, your time and talents, you are insuring the likelihood of similar responses when you yourself need assistance. With cooperation and mutual understanding, you can prevent conflicts and promote harmony between your operations and theirs. Without it, you are alone and cut off from the best sources of counsel outside your boss. Keep the channels open and give of yourself when you can. After all, they are your friends and what are friends for?

Getting Along with Staff Specialists

■ Probably dozens of times each week you come across the effects of staff specialists on your department. A good percentage of the forms and reports you generate are destined for their desks. The advice and service you receive at the press of a button or the twist of a dial can save you hours of agony and independent research. These people, like your peers, form an invaluable group of counselors on professional matters. Do everything you can to take advantage of their labors and foster a cooperative and receptive atmosphere. At times they may appear to you as prying eyes or fifth wheels. But over the long run your success as a supervisor as well as that of all other managers depends upon seeking and utilizing their advice. And if you recall the concept of functional authority, you may have no choice.

INSTANT REPLAY	We have defined human relations and examined the nature of the on-the-job relationship you must develop and maintain with each subordinate. The purposes of human relations may be summed up in a few words: to promote mutual understanding and growth.

Building an effective working relationship between yourself and a subordinate involves playing four distinct but related roles: those of educator, counselor, judge, and spokesperson. As an educator, you both teach and provide incentives for each individual to pursue, on his or her own, a program for self-development. As a counselor, you need to be available to your people as well as provide them with professional advice and service. As a judge, you evaluate their performances, enforce company and departmental standards of conduct and output, settle disputes, and dispense justice. The spokesperson's role requires you to accurately reflect and represent both the management's point of view and that of your subordinates.

Once these different roles are understood and mastered, their effective execution will result in the formation of sound human relationships. Once you have established them, you have to maintain them. With the initial commitment to build lasting relationships comes a great deal of work. But the rewards of your labor will more than justify the energy and time you expend. Both you and your people will better your performances and increase your value to the company and yourselves.

KEY WORD	**human relations**

1. What do you consider to be the major purposes of sound human relations?

2. How will the development of a sound working relationship between you and a subordinate help in the motivation process?

3. Once sound working relationships are established with your subordinates, they must be maintained. Why is this necessary?

4. As a counselor to your subordinates, with what limits will you have to live?

5. In executing your role as a spokesperson for both management and labor, can you foresee any conflicts that may arise? If so, what are they, and how can you resolve them?

6. Give an example from your own experience that illustrates your boss' efforts at human relations.

7. Relate the effort at human relations to a manager's function of coordinating.

8. What is wrong, if anything, with a friendship relationship between a boss and his or her subordinate?

9. How can the betrayal of a confidence harm a supervisor's efforts at human relations?

10. Is there ever a justification for transmitting to another person information received in confidence? If so, state it.

CASE PROBLEM

Just Friends

The Small Cleaners on Oak Street is one of three family-owned outlets in Mayfield, a town of thirty thousand people. Sylvia Halpern, age thirty-eight, has recently been promoted to supervise the operations of the third and newest branch outlet. Although she has received no formal academic or on-the-job training as a supervisor, she has been working in a Small Cleaners branch for nearly four years and has had a good boss, Mary Ritchards, to model herself after.

Since her promotion four weeks ago, Sylvia has had little difficulty with paperwork or customer relations. She has gone out of her way to be friendly to the customers and to her three subordinates. Al, the pressman, Cindy, and Beverly are all good people who know their jobs. In fact, the owner, Mr Small, assembled the workforce for the third branch outlet by taking the best people he had in the other two branches.

Sylvia has invited her subordinates to a small cocktail party, in her home, has taken them to lunch on two occasions, and is trying to stimulate interest among them to compete in bowling matches with the other two outlets. So far, however, her subordinates have shown little interest in such a team. Sylvia wants desperately to be more than a boss to her subordinates—she wants to be their friend as well.

Two weeks ago Al declined to join Sylvia, Cindy, and Beverly for lunch. Since then, Sylvia has noticed that Al, who was formerly a gregarious, cheerful guy, has become withdrawn. He rarely smiles and now speaks only when he is spoken to. He no longer joins in the friendly banter that has been a part of the Oak Street store from the first day it opened. Al is married, twenty-five years old, and the father of two children. Beverly is a good-natured soul with lots of interests outside the business. She and Sylvia were best friends when they worked together in the Fairfax Street store, and they have kept their friendship alive. Since neither Sylvia nor Beverly is married, they have time to share. Both like many of the same things, and their favorite activity is to go out to dinner and a show. Sylvia would like to model her relationship with Cindy after her relationship with Beverly.

Cindy, age twenty-two, is currently enrolled in a community college, where she is taking business courses. She is not quite certain what major she wants to pursue as yet, but she seems to favor accounting. Cindy gets along with Beverly and Sylvia but cannot stand Al. It seems that every time they are together, they exchange some unpleasant words.

Cindy also has trouble relating to the customers. On the few occasions where she has filled in for Beverly, she has been awkward with people and less than cordial. She has trouble operating the new electronic cash register and, although Sylvia has tried to explain its operation, Cindy has managed to misring sales more often than not. She hates making out a separate receipt for customers. As she has stated more than once, "Why can't they be satisfied with a cash register receipt? It carries the same information."

Sylvia's old boss, Mary Ritchards, has been a good friend and a source of counsel to her. She had a basic maxim that she has followed in all her relations with her subordinates: "Treat them like good friends, and everything else will take care of itself!" It certainly seemed to be good advice; Sylvia, who idolized Mary, was certain that her friendship with Mary didn't hurt her when Mr. Small was looking around for a supervisor for the Oak Street store. Sylvia has tried very hard to gain the friendship of her subordinates, but so far has been unable to do so with Cindy and Al. Perhaps, she thinks, they just need more time to adjust to the new situation. After all, they have been working together as a team for a month.

Questions

1. What human-relations roles does Sylvia need to carry out with Al? With Cindy? With Beverly? How should each be executed?

2. Do you think friendship with subordinates is an ideal to be sought by a supervisor? Why?

3. Is what Sylvia trying to do in line with what her old boss would recommend? Why?

4. Is it possible to be a friend with every subordinate you supervise? Why or why not?

5. What barriers exist that seem to prohibit friendship from forming between Sylvia and Al? Between Sylvia and Cindy?

9 Group Dynamics

■ After reading and discussing this chapter, you should be able to:

1 Define a group.

2 Define group dynamics.

3 List and briefly explain the forces that help shape a group's personality.

4 Contrast formal groups with informal groups.

5 Define a clique.

6 List three types of cliques and give an example of each of them.

7 Describe the Hawthorne Studies and their relationship to group dynamics.

8 Describe how group behavior can be affected by internal group competition—what happens to the winning side as well as to the losing side.

INTRODUCTION

■ Each individual has a personality which, as we have already observed, is undergoing constant change through exposure to his or her environment and to new experiences. When two or more dynamic people interact with one another, the process of change in each of them is accelerated. The coming together of two or more people for the purpose of obtaining some mutual goal or benefit is the basis for the formation of what we shall call a group.

More specifically, a **group** is (1) two or more people, (2) who are consciously aware of one another, (3) who consider themselves to be a functioning unit, and (4) who share in a quest to achieve one or more goals or some common benefit. When we say that the members are aware of each other, we mean that they know something about each other, are clear about why they are together, and recognize the need to cooperate.

Group dynamics is defined as the forces for change that are brought to bear on individuals when two or more of them come together in order to gain some mutual benefit or to achieve some common goal. These forces are:

1. The individuals themselves;
2. Their interactions with one another;
3. The passage of time;
4. The pressures, expectations, and demands of outsiders.

THE PERSONALITY OF GROUPS

■ A group, like the people that compose it, has a personality that is just as unique and subject to change as any individual's. The group's personality is partially a composite of the personalities of its members. We say partially because a group is always something more than the sum of its parts. That "something more" comes about because of the interaction of group members, which creates energy and qualities that may not be possessed by any of the group members nor by a majority of them. An example would be a basic training group in the military. Individually, its members may not have the desire or the will to excel and may not know their capabilities. But in group situations the pressure to conform and the feeling that, "If they can do it, so can I" will dominate. If twenty men were dispatched on a twenty-mile hike, one at a time at intervals of ten minutes, very few if any would complete the march. When all twenty men embark on the hike together, all the men will finish, even if their buddies have to carry some of them. Men in combat units often exhibit tremendous courage which none of them would exhibit without the support of and the commitment to their comrades.

There is a term for this two-plus-two-equals-five or more quality that many groups seem to possess. It is **synergy** (pronounced sin-er-ji). Common table salt is a chemical combination of two poisons—sodium and chlorine. Alone they are dangerous; together they are beneficial and take on beneficial properties that neither has alone. It has been common knowledge for about a century that two horses can pull more than the combined loads each is capable of pulling alone. A team of twelve horses can pull more than twice the load that a team of eight could pull.

Synergy can be either positive or negative. Satisfied groups or group members can exhibit greater positive action or forces for change than the individuals within the group could do on their own.

Group Dynamics.

all that happens (things & behavior) when people get together.

Some groups are quite strong and forceful, achieving what they set out to get. Other groups may be weak, lacking the leadership or the will to achieve. The personality the group exhibits is most directly influenced by the personalities of the stronger members. The strongest member will usually emerge as the leader of the group or at least its spokesperson. The strength we mention here is primarily intellectual, and the force primarily that of each person's will and drive.

It is just as difficult to comprehend a group's personality as it is to understand an individual's. Since we all work in groups of one kind or another, we need to study the behavior of people in groups and the effects of group membership on both ourselves and those we supervise. Attempting to observe and analyze these effects is quite properly a manager's job. You must begin to see your people as individuals who are also group members and therefore subjected to forces that accelerate change in them. This makes your task of knowing each one a little more difficult.

TYPES OF GROUPS

■ As you might imagine, there are countless groups of many different sizes and descriptions. For our purpose, however, we shall classify groups as either formal or informal:

Formal Groups

The **formal group** may be defined as two or more people who come together by management decision to achieve specific goals. All formal groups are a result of the organizing function through which people are assigned to different tasks and task units. In most cases we are placed in formal groups by some higher authority outside of or at the head of the group. Your company, your department, your shift, and the various management committees are but a few of the many formal groups you encounter each day.

Any individual, especially a manager, may belong to more than one formal group simultaneously. For instance, you are an employee of a company, working in a particular functional division and within a specific department. You are a member, therefore, of three formal groups at least. If you serve on a committee, you would belong to a fourth formal group.

Formal groups may be temporary in nature or permanent. An ad hoc committee—one set up to solve a particular problem and dissolved when the solution is determined—is an example of a temporary formal group. Most formal groups in your company are permanent, although even whole divisions can be dissolved or merged into others on occasion as the needs of the business may dictate.

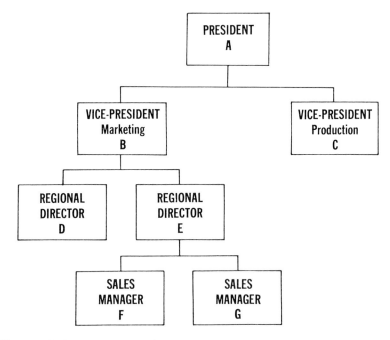

Figure 9-1. An organization chart.

Every formal group has a leader. The heads of most formal groups are managers who have been installed for just that purpose. The leader of a committee may be elected or appointed. Either way, the formal leader has the formal power of the position at his or her disposal.

Informal Groups

Two or more people who come together by choice to satisfy mutual needs or share common interests are considered an **informal group.** The distinguishing feature between the formal and the informal group is the matter of choice. Informal groups are formed because of the mutual social needs of people and because the environment at work favors or at least does not prohibit their formation.

There are three primary types of informal groups: **horizontal, vertical,** and **random** (sometimes called mixed).[1] These types of informal groups are often referred to as **cliques.** Figure 9–1 is an organization chart we shall refer to in order to illustrate the three different types of cliques.

1. Melville Dalton, *Men Who Manage: Fusions of Feeling and Theory in Administration* (New York: John Wiley & Sons, Inc., 1959).

HORIZONTAL CLIQUES

This type of group consists of two or more people from the same functional area and on the same level of the hierarchy. F and G constitute a horizontal clique providing they have chosen one another's company voluntarily on social occasions. D and E would also form a horizontal clique in the same conditions. B and C would *not* form a horizontal clique as they represent two different functional areas of marketing and production.

VERTICAL CLIQUES

This type of clique consists of two or more people from the same functional area but on *different levels of the hierarchy*. F and E would be an example as would D, E, and B. If all the members of the marketing department were together as an informal group, they would also constitute a vertical clique.

RANDOM CLIQUES

This kind of clique is composed of two or more people from two or more functional areas. B and C would be a good example. E, B, and C would also form a random or mixed clique. Whether the members of a random or mixed clique are from the same level of the hierarchy or not makes no difference. If A, the president, is a part of any clique, that clique automatically would be a random one. The reason is that the president is the only manager who oversees all the functional areas of the business. Therefore, he does not belong to any one of them but stands alone at his level of the hierarchy.

As a supervisor your subordinates will usually comprise one or more horizontal or, on occasion, random cliques. Seldom will you find them belonging to a vertical clique. Your analysis of your subordinates' group memberships can help you in your attempts to understand them as individuals and in the development of your relationships with their groups.

Let us assume that you have recently become the operating supervisor of the Health Insurance Systems Group illustrated in Figure 9–2. You have observed your people and their interactions and have drawn the connecting rings as shown. Since your subordinates work in close proximity to workers in the Life Insurance Systems Group, it would seem natural for members of the two groups to mix informally on social occasions such as coffee breaks and lunch periods.

The rings you have drawn encircle the members of the informal groups as you see them. The numbers in parentheses represent their ages. All of the groups represented are horizontal cliques. Even though

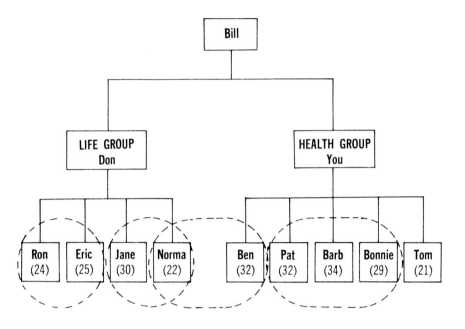

Figure 9-2. Life/Health systems group.

Ben and Norma are from two different work groups, they are in the same functional area called systems.

Now let us see what you have discovered. Pat, Barb, and Bonnie are a clique and prefer each other's company over that of others when they have a choice. This may be due in part to the fact that they are the only women in the health systems area. It may also be due to the close proximity of their ages. More knowledge is needed for a really thorough analysis. You should know their marital status, what their individual interests are, their backgrounds, and more before you can make any hard and fast conclusions as to the nature of their clique.

Ben has chosen Norma's company and vice versa. This is interesting because he has gone outside of his section for companionship. Norma is part of two informal cliques. Norma may be an informal leader to either Ben or Jane or both. But again more information would be needed before you can decide for sure. For example, Ben may be romantically inclined toward Norma.

Tom is another situation. He is the youngest member and as such may have little in common with the others. He might be an **isolate,** that is, a person who wants to belong to one or another of the cliques but is rejected or denied membership for some reason. His age, his personality, his education, or some other reason may be keeping him on the outside. If he is a new employee, he has not had enough time to become accepted or choose a group to which he might want to belong. He might be a **deviate,** a person who does not aspire to join or belong to a group. Quite often an isolate will evolve into a deviate if he or she is kept out long enough.

What we have just done in a small way is to observe the social interaction of subordinates and attempt to analyze our findings. If these observations were pursued in greater depth and detail, a better understanding might emerge of why these groups have formed, what keeps them together, and what they mean to you as a supervisor. Such a process will aid you by giving you more direct information about the forces at work on your people and the group influences on their attitudes and performances at work.

Every informal group has a leader. Unlike his counterpart in the formal group, the informal leader derives his power through the informal means discussed in Chapter 1. These, you will recall, were rational and charismatic authority. The clique members subject their wills to one of their number because he or she is a great person to be with and/or because of the knowledge, skills, and abilities possessed by that individual. It is seldom the case that the formal leader of the formal group is an informal leader with a clique of his or her subordinates. This is as it should be. As was pointed out in Chapter 8, a manager's friends should be his or her peers.

| JOINING A CLIQUE | ■ Once a new employee is hired, he or she is placed in a specific job which makes him or her automatically a member of several formal groups that constitute the business enterprise. If the design of work and the working relationships permit, informal groups or cliques will have been formed. The newcomer, like those who have preceded him or her, will naturally desire the companionship of one or more coworkers on a more or less regular basis, both during working hours and while on his or her own time.

The problem confronting the new arrival is that he or she is initially on the outside of the existing informal groups and, although he or she desires membership in one of them, is not certain about which one to choose. He or she needs time to assess the values, attitudes, and reputation of each group. The groups in turn are going to be evaluating the person for prospective membership. In this sense, the new employee is similar to a person seeking admission to a fraternity or sorority. He or she has to look at what it stands for and get to know its members while its members look the applicant over as well.

You as a supervisor can do a great deal for the new employee. If you know your people well and understand their groups, you can do all in your power to help him or her gain admittance to a group of subordinates that are a positive force and will exert a constructive influence on the newcomer. You hope that all of the informal cliques in your section are working with management and not against it. But, if one or another is not, do your best to steer the new arrival away from such a clique and into more beneficial surroundings. Chapter 16 will have more to say on this topic.

Stages of Induction   Before the individual on the outside of a clique can truly become a participating member of the clique, he must go through three separate but related stages of induction: (1) observation, (2) transformation, and (3) confirmation.

STAGE 1. OBSERVATION

This is the initial stage we all find ourselves in as newcomers. By necessity, we must remain neutral toward all the informal groups we encounter until we have time to know them. As time goes on, this neutrality becomes increasingly more difficult to maintain as we feel pressure from within and without to make a decision or choice. We may begin a kind of trial membership period wherein we are invited to participate with a group by one or more of its members. While in meetings with each clique we are somewhat passive and open to group members' opinions and attitudes, preferring to listen rather than speak our mind.

STAGE 2. TRANSFORMATION

The next step is for us to decide which group we like best. If the group honors our choice, we shall begin to confine our socializing almost exclusively to the new group. We will mask any personal opinions that are in direct contradiction to those the group holds as essential and begin to mouth agreement to these essential attitudes. Like a parrot, we begin to remember and repeat the sacred beliefs even though we may not be in agreement with them. Without this stage we can never really become an accepted member in a strong, informal group.

STAGE 3. CONFIRMATION

The confirmation stage is complete when the new member actually abandons attitudes he once held that were in direct opposition to those of the group and adopts the group's values as his own. He gives up his individuality with the group but may retain it on his own. The group has changed the person and his or her attitudes in much the same way as was discussed in Chapter 6. The difference may be that several people were at work on the individual instead of only one.

From this point on, the group will have more influence over a member's behavior than any other force at work. The person now weighs the relative merits of proposals against the group's willingness to accept them. If the group vetoes the action, each member will feel bound to support that veto.

Not long ago a student involved me in the following story. At the start of the business day one Friday, two of George's more able workers presented him with a petition signed by all twenty-six of his subordinates. It requested that the workday begin and end one half hour earlier. George was quite concerned as such a request was not in his power to grant, and he felt that the plant manager would not buy the suggestion. Wisely, he refrained from giving an immediate answer but assured the workers that he would consider the matter carefully.

The following week George and I discussed the problem. I asked if he was sure that all the workers really wanted the change. He reiterated that they had all signed the petition. But as we all know, people will sign almost anything for a variety of reasons. So George decided to interview each worker separately over the next two weeks to determine just how committed each of them was to the proposed change. The results were amazing. Two men were solidly in favor of the change—the same two who had confronted George with the petition and had initiated it. Eight workers were neutral but willing to go along with the others. The remainder were clearly against it. After George announced his findings, the demand was dropped, and only two people were really unhappy with the decision.

What made the twenty-four other workers sign? The two men were strong personalities, and one was an informal leader of a large clique. Beginning with his clique members and starting with the weakest, the informal leader got one signature after another until nearly two thirds of the workers had signed. The others fell into line when confronted with the sheer weight of numbers. Not wishing to obstruct the will of the majority, the few remaining holdouts also signed up.

The Hawthorne Studies

A research study that has had tremendous impact on our knowledge of group dynamics and the working environment is the famous Hawthorne study. In 1927, engineers at the Hawthorne Plant of Western Electric Company in Chicago conducted an experiment with several groups of workers to determine the effect of illumination on production. When illumination was increased in stages, the engineers found that production did increase. To verify their findings, they reduced illumination to its previous level—and again production increased! Perplexed, they called in Elton Mayo and a team of industrial experts from Harvard University to investigate.[2] The researchers selected several experienced women assemblers for an experiment. The records of the assemblers' past production were made available to the researchers, and the women's cooperation was obtained. Next, the management removed the women from their formal group of assemblers and isolated them in a room. The women were compensated on the basis of the output of their group. There followed a series of environmental changes, each discussed with the women in advance of its implementation. For example, breaks were introduced, with light refreshments being served. The women received no direct supervision as they had before, only indirect supervision from several researchers in charge of the experiment. Their normal six-day week was reduced to five, and the workday reduced for a time by one hour. Each of these major changes was accompanied by an increase in the group's output.

To verify assumptions made by the researchers, the women were returned to their original working conditions—breaks were eliminated, the six-day week was restored, and all other conditions that had prevailed before the women were isolated were reinstated. The results were that production again increased!

Findings. In the extensive interviewing that followed, Mayo and his group concluded that a team spirit had been created, quite by accident, when management singled out these women to be a study group and consulted with them before making each change. The women felt that they were something special, both individually and collectively. Their isolation as a group and their close proximity at work provided an environment for the development of close personal relationships. The formal group had been transformed into an informal one.

The Second Study. To test the researchers' findings, a second group of workers was selected and isolated. This time the researchers chose a group of men. Several of them were involved in wiring equipment while others soldered the wired connections. Two inspectors were part of the group and approved the finished jobs. An observer was on hand throughout the working day to observe the men and record their reactions.

2. F. J. Roethlisberger and W. J. Dickson, *Management and the Worker* (Cambridge, Mass.: Harvard University Press, 1939).

Observations. Several important occurrences were noted in this formal group. The men eventually split into two separate, informal groups. The basis for the split was that one group felt its work was more difficult than the other's. Its members adopted a superior attitude. This left the remainder of the workers to form a second clique. Both cliques included wirers, solderers, and an inspector. Also each group was engaged in setting its standards of output and conduct. Production quotas were mutually agreed upon by the members of the group that considered itself superior. Neither too little nor too much production was permitted, and pressure was exerted to keep group members in line. As intergroup rivalry developed, the output of the second group began to decline. The superior group became superior in output also, which caused additional condescending behavior and a still greater decrease in morale and output in the second group. Those who produced the most in each group were excluded from their group if they would not conform to the group's norm. Even though each man was to share in a bonus based upon the total output of the formal group, informal-group conflicts resulted in a decline of total production.

What these two experiments tell managers is that workers, through their informal cliques, can be positive or negative factors with respect to company standards, policy, and regulations. If they view management in a favorable way, they are capable of standards of output even higher than management may expect. If they feel negative toward management, the informal group will generate much less production. How workers, individually or in groups, relate to management is largely a result of their supervisor's approach. If he or she practices sound human relations and relates positively to his or her group of subordinates, the supervisor can and does influence the behavior and productivity of the subordinates.

GROUP COMPETITION

■ We have just seen that intergroup competition at Hawthorne caused ill will and declining productivity within the formal group. Edgar H. Schein of the Massachusetts Institute of Technology has added much to our understanding of what happens within and between competing groups.[3] Whether we are dealing with formal or informal groups, the following situation would apply.

What happens *within* competing groups? Each group:
1. Exhibits greater togetherness and cohesion;
2. Becomes more organized and highly structured;

---

3. Edgar H. Schein, *Organizational Psychology,* 2nd ed., © 1970, Prentice-Hall, Inc., Englewood Cliffs, N. J. By permission of the publisher.

3. Expects greater loyalty and conformity from its members;

4. Willingly accepts autocratic supervision;

5. Becomes more task-oriented and less concerned with the needs of individual members.

All of these are positive results and, at first glance, may appear to be desirable. But as we consider what happens *between* competing groups, the picture becomes less attractive. In Schein's words:

1. Each group begins to see the other group as the enemy, rather than merely a neutral object.

2. Each group begins to experience distortions of perception—it tends to perceive only the best parts of itself, denying its weaknesses, and tends to perceive only the worst parts of the other group, denying its strengths; each group is likely to develop a negative stereotype of the other ("They don't play fair like we do").

3. Hostility toward the other group increases while interaction and communication with the other group decreases; thus it becomes easier to maintain negative stereotypes and more difficult to correct perceptual distortions.

4. If the groups are forced into interaction—for example, if they are forced to listen to representatives plead their own and the others' cause in reference to some task—each group is likely to listen more closely to their own representative and not to listen to the representative of the other group, except to find fault with his presentation; in other words, group members tend to listen only for that which supports their own position and stereotype.[4]

If this intergroup competition—whether between informal or formal groups—results in one group emerging as the victor and the other as vanquished, then the problems are compounded dramatically. To paraphrase Professor Schein, the winning group:

1. Keeps its cohesiveness;

2. Tends to become self-satisfied;

3. Loses its task orientation and reemphasizes individual needs;

4. Becomes reassured that its self-image must be a correct one and loses the incentive to question its perceptions.

On the other hand, the losing group:

1. Becomes initially unrealistic as to its perception of why it lost, tending to transfer blame to some external cause;

2. Tends to lose its cohesiveness;

3. Becomes more dedicated to tasks and winning;

---

4. Ibid., p. 97.

4. Experiences less intragroup cooperation and less concern for individual needs;

5. Eventually reexamines its beliefs and self-image and becomes more realistic in its perceptions.

It should be clear to you that intergroup competition has more disadvantages than advantages. The loser may improve while the winner declines. This is not to say that competition is wrong—only that competition between groups within a company is dangerous. Competition can be a powerful tool to muster greater output and cohesiveness among your department's members if the "enemy" is not a group of coworkers but rather some outside force or group. If the thing to be beaten is a standard or a past record of output, then the group can muster its forces in a cooperative spirit to excel and exceed its previous record. Like a long-distance runner out to beat the best recorded time for his or her event or to surpass his or her previous best time, groups at work can try and succeed or they can fail with no lasting detrimental effects. To the contrary, they will most likely redouble their efforts and reexamine their operations, and they may seek outside help in the process. That is much to be desired.

OUTSIDERS AND INSIDERS

■ You are affected each day at your place of business by many factors, some of which are outside your company and some of which are inside it. The same is true for your subordinates.

Outside Factors

When was the last time you went to work with a personal family problem so much on your mind that your performance suffered? Your family is but one of many outside groups that can and do influence your efficiency. Your academic classes in management may be another example. We all hope that you will obtain from your instructor and classmates the means to achieve a more successful performance. But sometimes what you learn will bring you into conflict with your traditional beliefs or with those of your boss, and put you at odds with him when you attempt to act upon your new knowledge. You may find that you know more about a particular task and the best methods to deal with it than your superior does. The problem will then be one of your selling your belief to your boss and getting permission to implement it.

Customers can place demands upon the business, which in turn will directly affect your operations. Their requests may be translated into new methods or procedures for your department. New schedules of production may be the result, with added pressures and tensions for you and those under you.

Inside Factors

The groups within the company that directly or indirectly affect your performance are your superiors, your peers, and your subordinates. Superiors construct the programs, policies, and regulations that you must enforce and translate to action. Your peers place demands on you for conformity, cooperation, and uniform approaches to problems. They form the nucleus of your friendships and place demands on your time and talents. Your subordinates, as members of your formal groups and as members of their own informal cliques, ask a great deal from you, as we have already discussed in preceding chapters. How you cope with these groups and their demands directly relates to how well you can adjust to tension and frustration. Numerous times you will be faced with conflicts between what you think you should do and what others are asking you to do. Often you must yield completely to the demands of others. On occasion you must work out compromises. In all cases, however, you are being tested. How strong is your company loyalty? How strong is your friendship? How sincere are you in your commitment to your people? How much do your children really mean to you? Whoever said that life or holding a job were easy?

COPING WITH SUBORDINATES' CLIQUES

■ There are five main principles you should follow in order to minimize group conflicts and tensions and to maximize group cooperation and contribution.

1. Accept your subordinates' cliques as a fact of life. Just as you belong to one or more, so it is with them. Consider their informal groups as allies and additional forces to be won over and brought to bear on mutual problems. The trick is to learn to work with them—not to fight them or try to eliminate them.

2. Identify and enlist the cooperation of the informal leaders. They represent a force to be reckoned with. Many of them have the potential to be tomorrow's managers. The informal power they have over others can work for you both. Practice sound human relations with them as you would with anyone in your charge. Share whenever you can some of your formal authority with the best of them through delegation. They are usually perfect candidates for leadership roles. Also they are ambitious people who recognize the advantages that management has to offer.

3. Prevent intergroup competition and the occurrence of a win-lose situation. As stated earlier, groups in conflict have a tendency to tear each other and to reduce the overall effectiveness. The loser will profit while the winner suffers. Hold out standards to be achieved and surpassed. Use past performance records as targets to hit and scores to beat. These abstract enemies are harder to visualize but easier to beat.

4. Don't force your people to choose between you and their group. If you put it to them on an "either/or" basis, they will usually pick their group. Their loyalty to and membership in a clique does not have to be at your expense. They can serve both company and group demands. They can be loyal and unopposed to you if you are predictable and loyal to them.

5. Adopt a coach's attitude toward your group(s). Foster a team spirit and nurture the comradeship that cliques promote. Play fair and demand that your subordinates do the same. Team players know the value of rules and team play. Enlist their participation as a group and protect their self-image.

INSTANT REPLAY

This chapter has defined group dynamics, formal and informal groups, and the concept of a group's personality. Each group has a leader; the formal group is led by a manager, while the informal group leader emerges as the strongest and most popular member of his or her group.

We have discussed how an individual is inducted into an informal clique, passing through the three stages of observation, transformation, and confirmation. Once inducted, the individual gives up his or her individuality while part of the group and adopts the group's attitudes and values as his or her own. If the group is favorably predisposed toward management, it will cooperate and become a more potent force for the completion of tasks. If not, it can become quite obstructive and destructive. All managers must enlist the cooperation of the groups and minimize group conflicts.

Finally, we have taken a look at the pros and cons of group competition. We have seen that the winning side in intergroup competition becomes self-satisfied, less realistic in its perceptions, and complacent. The losing side experiences nearly the reverse reaction, looking for reasons why it has failed and increasing its efforts to win. The most upsetting feature of this type of competition is what happens between competing groups: hostility and open warfare break out, with one group hoping for the downfall of the other. This can become a vicious spiral that may bring both groups down in the process.

KEY WORDS

clique	group dynamics	random clique
deviate	horizontal clique	synergy
formal group	informal group	vertical clique
group	isolate	

1. What are the forces brought to bear on individuals as a result of their membership in a group?

2. Why is it that group membership accelerates change in individuals?

3. What does it mean to say that a group's personality is something greater than the sum of its members?

4. What does it mean to label a person an isolate? A deviate?

5. What type of clique do you belong to at work? How were you inducted? Did you go through the three stages discussed in this chapter?

6. State two possible dangers involved in a supervisor's membership in a clique of subordinates.

7. What do the two Hawthorne studies tell us about people in group situations?

8. How do you feel about groups competing against one another? About groups competing against some abstract enemy?

9. Referring to the five principles to follow in minimizing group conflicts, show how your own boss has attempted to practice one or more of them on a clique to which you yourself belong.

The Contest

The floor supervisors of the Sunset Plaza Hotel were waiting for their regular Monday morning problem-solving session to start. In attendance were the four floor supervisors and the housekeeper's secretary, Betty Morton. The housekeeper, Arnold Yankow, had not yet arrived to open the meeting.

On the agenda for this morning's meeting were three topics of great interest to the supervisory personnel. Item one was the training of new room attendants. Item two dealt with the problem of how to reduce the heavy turnover in employees. Item three dealt with the results of a month-long contest that had come to a close only last week. The third item was being kicked around by the floor supervisors.

"I don't know who the winner is, but I know who one of the losers is," said Rita Jackson, the third-floor supervisor. "It's me. It seems we couldn't get one room ready on time last week. What with my losing Marisa last month, I'm surprised we had all the rooms made up by five o'clock each day. A few of them even had to be done over. I don't ever want to go through another week like the last one."

"Don't feel like the lone ranger, Rita," said Beverly, the second-floor supervisor. "I had two people out sick for several days—people who have never been sick a day in years. And during the contest month too. They sure guaranteed we'd lose, and I told them so, too. I guess they cracked under the strain."

"Hey, girls, don't get uptight yet," said Madge, who is in charge of the fourth floor. "We won't know who won until Arnold shows up with the results. One thing's for sure, though. My people on the fourth floor really put out extra effort. They did a better job all around than at any time in the past. If they don't win, they will be very disappointed. I kept telling them that they were doing great. I'd hate to have to tell them now that they didn't win. Those rooms and floors literally sparkled! They're all walking around today with their heads held high. They're sure they must have won."

"Well, as far as I'm concerned, it was an unfair contest from the start," said Mario, the first-floor supervisor. "I started the month shorthanded and with one person in training. We were out of the running from the start, and my people knew it. They didn't even try to do things any better or faster. And, by the way, Rita, keep your people off my floor. They were down there several times, using our washrooms and slopping up the vending-machines area. My people don't want to have to clean up after yours."

"Sour grapes, Mario?," Rita came back at him. "I want you to start looking for the real reasons your floor is so bad and stop blaming my people. If you lose, you deserve to lose. If you can't handle your job, why don't you just admit it?"

At this point in the conversation, Arnold entered the room and called the meeting to order. Before he could get into item one on the agenda, he was interrupted by Madge, the fourth-floor supervisor.

"Let's start with item three."

"Well, I was saving the best for last, but since you all want to know who gets the bonus and holiday for the best-kept floor, I'll tell you. The criteria were:

1. Best-kept public areas;
2. Consistency in on-time room completions;
3. Fewest complaints from the hotel guests.

Based on my tallys, the second-floor team is officially declared the winner!"

Questions

1. What behavior patterns can you expect the winners to exhibit in the future?

2. Who are the losers? In what ways can you expect the three losing groups to behave in the future?

3. What negative traits or actions were exhibited by the four groups during the contest?

4. What problems do you think the fourth-floor supervisor will encounter? Why?

5. Are the three items on Arnold's agenda related? If so, in what ways?

10 Meetings and Group Discussions

■ After reading and discussing this chapter, you should be able to:

1 List and briefly describe the two basic kinds of meetings held by supervisors.

2 List three specific duties for the chairperson to perform before holding a problem-solving session.

3 Describe in general the duties required of group members before attending a problem-solving session.

4 List two specific duties for the chairperson to perform during a problem-solving session.

5 Describe in general the duties of group members during a problem-solving session.

6 Briefly describe group-serving and self-serving roles.

7 List the specific duties of a chairperson after a problem-solving session.

8 Describe in general the duties of group members after a problem-solving session.

9 Distinguish between a nondirective and a directive interview, and state the purposes of each of them.

INTRODUCTION

■ So far in Part Two we have considered your attitudes and those of your subordinates; human needs; human relations; and group dynamics. We shall now take up the types of meetings and interviews you will be expected to take part in or organize in your role of supervisor.

**TYPES
OF MEETINGS**

■ As the leader of a formal group, you will be expected to conduct group meetings at which you will act as the chairperson or discussion leader. There are two general types of meetings, classified as to their format, that you will conduct most often: the **informational meeting** and the **problem-solving meeting.**

**The Informational
Meeting**

As the title suggests, this type of meeting is used to disseminate various kinds of information to all your people or to certain groups of them. Usually you will use the lecture format, with yourself on the speaker's platform communicating information about such topics as status reports on work, new projects or programs in progress, or the interpretation of changes taking place elsewhere in the company which will affect your department and its members.

Many supervisors hold such meetings on a fairly regular basis, as they feel it offers them an excellent opportunity to relate to their people and communicate with them more efficiently with less time and effort. It is easier to say things once to all those affected than to try to reach each individually. Also, items of interest that accumulate daily can be assembled and dispensed with before they get out of date or become too numerous to handle efficiently in a single informational session.

Informational meetings promote cooperation among group members by providing for individual growth, by keeping people informed, and by giving people the reasons behind changes that will be necessary in the future. Informational meetings work best when they permit the supervisor and group members to:

1. Keep informed about what is going on in all areas of the company, their division, department, or section;

2. Obtain observations and information from people outside their group, for example, from higher management authorities, guest lecturers, or consultants;

3. Report on decisions and changes that are coming or will be handed down from a higher level of the hierarchy.

Employees benefit greatly from such meetings. Their time is efficiently utilized; they get a chance to relate to one another; and they understand more fully how each part is contributing to the whole. They are reminded that they are members of a team and are kept informed and up to date on individual and group progress or on the lack of such progress.

Although the format is usually a lecture, time should be set aside for questions so that misunderstandings can be cleared up at the earliest possible time, or be entirely avoided.

The Problem-Solving Meeting

This type of meeting is usually set up and conducted in order to reach a group consensus or solution to a problem affecting the group. It works best when it utilizes the discussion format, which allows the members to participate actively under the skillful direction of the chairperson. All the group members affected by the problem should be included. Their firsthand knowledge and experience can be of value in both the discussion of the problem—its causes and effects—as well as the listing and analysis of possible solutions.

If it is to be successful, the problem-solving session requires a great deal of thought and preparation on the part of the supervisor. By using this type of meeting you are involving your people in the formal decision-making process of your office. This is not without its hazards.

If you have never included your subordinates in your decision-making process in the past, they may be suspicious of your attempt to do so. Also, each subordinate brings to the meeting his or her particular interests and attitudes and is influenced, you will recall, by his or her informal group. The informal group leader will be part of the meeting too, so his or her ideas and attitudes may well affect the quality and quantity of ideas of his or her followers. He or she can inhibit open participation or promote it. The meeting, in other words, might be dominated by the informal leader. In the case of two or more informal leaders, the meeting might degenerate into a contest of strength. You as the formal group leader may have your ideas and attitudes challenged for the first time openly. You may be subjected to group criticism for the first time, and you may find yourself pitted against the informal leader or leaders.

All of these problems and more can be prevented or minimized by proper planning. The first question you must answer is whether your boss will allow you to share your decision-making authority with your subordinates. If he or she agrees, you must answer another question: what kinds of problems are my people best equipped to solve? The answer lies in part in the following list:

1. Problems involving the reduction of waste or scrap;
2. Problems related to health and safety;
3. Problems related to housekeeping;
4. Problems about methods improvement.

These problems relate to entire departments, sections, or shifts. By soliciting concrete suggestions and taking advantage of your subordinates' involvement in these problem areas, you will be sharing your authority and enlarging your perspective.

Once you know that you have permission to involve your people and have determined the kind of problems they are best able to solve, you are ready to embark upon a truly difficult but rewarding effort at winning and utilizing group participation. Through it you stand a good chance of changing group behavior by changing the individual and group attitudes of your subordinates.

Dr. Thomas Gordon, a psychologist and management consultant, offers the following observations for group leaders:[1]

1. Once a leader becomes like "another member" of the group, any tendency for him or her to participate too frequently can be dealt with by the group much more easily than when he or she is perceived as *the* leader. People feel free to exert some control over the participation of members, but fear trying to curb the participation of the leader.

2. The more dependent the group is on its leader, the more his or her contribution will inhibit the participation of other members.

3. A leader's awareness of the potentially inhibiting effect of his or her participation on that of the members helps control his or her participation. This awareness probably makes the leader more sensitive to seeing subtle signs that indicate that group members are inhibited.

GROUND RULES FOR MEETINGS

■ If the problem-solving session is to accomplish meaningful results, certain rules and procedures must be established and agreed upon in advance by all concerned. Imagine playing a sport in which each participant had his or her own set of rules. Chaos would be a certainty. In like fashion, most sports need an umpire or referee whose job is to enforce the rules and prevent infractions. This role is yours to play as the supervisor.

Several essential rules are listed below. Using this listing as a guide while planning and conducting your meetings should prevent most hazards from occurring or at least prevent any serious conflicts.

Before the Meeting

Defining the Problem. Make certain in advance that you know what the problem is. Then communicate this knowledge to the group members in advance of the meeting.

Defining the Limits. Be certain that the limits such as time, company policy, and the amount of authority the group will have is clear to the group. Are they empowered only to recommend solutions or to

---

1. Thomas Gordon, *Leader Effectiveness Training L.E.T.* (New York: Wyden Books, 1977), pp. 141–142.

actually choose them? In the latter case, you must delegate some of your formal authority to the group. If you alone have the power to decide, tell them so.

Providing the Research. Give your members all the relevant data you have accumulated to assist them in adopting a realistic point of view. Share your ideas and those of others in management that bear on the problem. Make them aware of any precedents.

Preparing the Agenda. Let them know where, when, what, how, and in what order the group will consider the issues.

Reserving the Facilities. Reserve the space or room you will need to meet, gather the aids necessary for the conduct of the meeting (chalk, flip charts, pencils, paper), get there a little early to make certain things are in order. Set a specific starting and ending time.

Preparing Your Subordinates. Before each meeting all who have been chosen to attend should be made aware of their responsibilities to prepare for the meeting. Specifically each member should:

1. Read the agenda and prepare a list of questions that he or she should answer before facing the group;

2. Gather the information, materials, visuals, etc., that he or she will be responsible for presenting or disseminating to the group;

3. Arrange his or her schedule to avoid being late for the meeting or having to leave early;

4. Relay the input expected from the group member to the chairperson, if a member should be unable to attend the meeting for any legitimate reason.

During the Meeting

Chairing the Meeting. Start promptly, direct the discussion, stick to the agenda and time limits, draw out each member, list the alternatives and summarize frequently. Maintain order and keep the meeting on the subject.

Determining a Solution. From the alternatives listed and analyzed, bring the group to one mind as to the best alternative or combination of alternatives that they can endorse. If the solution is to work, the majority must be behind it. Be ready to compromise in order to break any impass. Fix responsibility for the implementation of the solution.

Fixing the Responsibilities. During each meeting the group members have specific responsibilities that should be communicated to them in advance and briefly repeated to them at the start of each session. If the meeting is to be beneficial to all concerned, each member should be prepared to:

1. Be an active participant by listening attentively, taking notes, following the discussions, seeking clarification when confused, and adding input if the group member has the expertise or experience to do so;

2. Promote discussion and input from all members by respecting their rights to their opinions and attitudes, and by avoiding discourteous or disruptive behavior;

3. Practice the group-serving roles described below.

After the Meeting

Implementing the Solution. Assign tasks to those affected if need be, and put the solution into operation as quickly as possible.

Following Up. Check on the results and on the group reactions.

Assigning the Responsibilities. At the close of each meeting the participants should be made aware of any specific duties or assignments they will have as a result of the meeting. The chairperson should not allow the members to leave until each of them is clear about his or her new tasks. In addition to the specific duties each person may receive, all participants have the following general obligations:

1. To keep the results and contents of the meeting confidential by not sharing them with anyone or any group that does not have a "need to know";

2. To relay decisions and changes to those for whom the group member may be responsible and who will be affected by them;

3. To carry out promises made and assignments received as quickly as possible.

BEETLE BAILEY

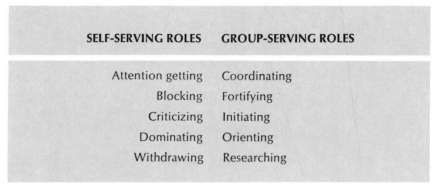

SELF-SERVING ROLES	GROUP-SERVING ROLES
Attention getting	Coordinating
Blocking	Fortifying
Criticizing	Initiating
Dominating	Orienting
Withdrawing	Researching

Figure 10-3. Group member roles.

GROUP MEMBER ROLES

■ At a meeting members of the group may play several different roles, some of which will be helpful to the attainment of the goals of the meetings while others may hinder the group's attempts to achieve the objectives for which the meeting was called. There are two categories of roles available to all members of a group, and the chances are that many of these different roles will be exhibited at each meeting. Figure 10–3 summarizes these roles.

Self-Serving Roles

Each of these roles can be either positive or negative in its effects on the meeting and on group members. Suppose as a group leader, for example, that you block another participant by not recognizing his or her raised hand. If you do so in order to get another to speak who until then has been withdrawing, you have a positive motive and effect on the group.

You may decide that as chairperson it is best to withdraw, that is, become an observer, when one of the members begins to criticize another's suggestions. In this way a participant may be forced to justify his or her proposal, new information may emerge, and others may be persuaded as to the validity of an idea more readily. Why not let a participant tell his or her peers what you want said? Attention getting is the role whereby a member focuses attention on himself or herself. He or she may be attempting to get the floor in order to add information or to redirect the discussion back to the central point. Dominating involves pushing a special interest and may involve blocking when a person continues to talk, not allowing another to get into the conversation. Whether these roles go unchecked and exhibit a positive or negative influence is up to the chairperson to determine. Just use your good sense and listen intently. Try to get at the motive behind the role a member is playing. If in your judgment the motive is positive, let him or her continue. If not, take action.

Group-Serving Roles   Group-serving roles are almost always positive in their effects. No matter who practices them, they attempt to draw members together and shed light where there was darkness. They all promote unity and harmony, and each is essential in order to reach a consensus. They tend to keep a meeting on the track, while systematically separating the unimportant from the relevant.

Fortifying is the process by which a member adds encouragement and insights to already aired ideas. It helps elaborate and interpret what has been said. Initiating introduces ideas and major points in order to get the reactions and contributions of group members. Orienting tells the membership where they have been and where they are at present. It may serve to add emphasis or to clarify ideas. Also it keeps people from traveling again over the same ground or going around in circles. Researching involves fact finding and digging up background material pertinent to the discussion so as to remove smoke from people's eyes and substitute facts for fiction.

Observe and label these activities in your group encounters from now on. You will see various positive and negative applications of all these roles in your classes at school as well as meetings at work. Study your instructor and the various roles he or she plays. You will pick up some valuable examples of each of these roles, most of which you will be able to use at work when you find yourself a group leader or participant.

In order to illustrate the influence of group decision making on employee behavior and the attitudes of group members, we shall look now at a well-known experiment in group decision making.

The Harwood Manufacturing Company sponsored one of the first experiments in group participation in management decision making in the 1940s.[2] The company was planning several changes in company methods and in their piece-rate compensation plan. Workers were divided into four groups—a control group and three experimental ones. The control-group members were assembled, and the proposed changes explained in detail to them by management. The members had the opportunity to ask questions and were given honest answers.

One of the experimental groups was told about the changes and asked to elect representatives to work with management on them.

---

2. Lester Coch and John R. P. French, Jr., "Overcoming Resistance to Change," *Human Relations*, 1, no. 4 (1948), pp. 512–532.

These elected operators cooperated with management and reached decisions which they then had to relay and help sell to their group. The other two groups participated as equals in the decision-making process with managers in several problem-solving sessions.

After forty days the results were tabulated. The control group's production under the new changes had fallen well below the standards in force before the experiment began. Some of its members had quit the company, and the remainder exhibited strong hostilities toward management.

In the group that had elected its own representatives, output had increased to meet the new standards, not one worker had quit, and a spirit of cooperation prevailed. Similar results were obtained with the other two groups. These two groups exhibited production that exceeded the old standards by an average of 14 percent.

Numerous studies carried out since the Harwood experiment have yielded similar results. Perhaps your own company has used a similar approach with you. Time and time again, participation by workers in the decisions that affect them has caused them to accept more willingly and implement more positively those decisions. Participants have exhibited a higher level of motivation and a greater measure of job satisfaction. Although not a cure-all, problem-solving sessions can do much to stimulate cooperation and receptiveness to change in the minds of participants.

PITFALLS

■ Problem-solving sessions may result in problems if there is poor leadership resulting in a violation of ground rules listed above. In addition, several other major pitfalls or traps exist that can cause a meeting to be a sheer waste of time.

The Hidden Agenda. A member's hidden agenda is his or her personal feelings toward the subject discussed, the group itself, and the individuals who comprise the group. We all have such an agenda whenever we attend a group session, whether with our formal or informal group. If a proposal or an action is put forth that conflicts with our pet beliefs, we can only try to pick it apart or live with it. Often critical remarks toward group members or their ideas are motivated by a dislike or distrust of the person or of his or her intentions. You must recognize that as a chairperson you have the duty to see behind the words and get to the motives. Often you can nullify the hidden agenda's effect by simply explaining that another person or department does not necessarily have to gain at someone else's expense. What's good for the gander can be, and often is, good for the goose.

An Improper Setting. How many meetings have you been to that were complete disasters simply because of poor ventilation, lighting, or too much background noise? Maybe the facilities were okay when they were reserved, but the timing was wrong for their use. Possibly the room was selected without regard for the number of people who would attend, so many had to stand or could not even enter the room. I am reminded of a meeting I attended in an industrial firm where the central feature was to have been a film. After the projector was started, we all soon realized that the lamp had burned out. So much for that meeting and its organizer.

A Competitive Spirit. Many sessions start out and continue to be a stage for the display of one member's accomplishments over the others' or of one group's achievements over another's. Competition is fine on the athletic field, but it has no real purpose among members of the team. Watch for the remark that attempts to build one person's reputation at the expense of another's. Nothing can ruffle fur so quickly or create defensive reactions more effectively. A quick review of the second Hawthorne study will refresh your memory with regard to intergroup competition and its dangers.

Talkative Members. Have you ever tried to carry on a conversation with anyone who only stopped talking to think about what to say next? It is quite a frustrating experience. Your voice only fills the gaps between his or her remarks. Listening is not one of that person's virtues. Also members in meetings can quickly fall in love with their own voices and viewpoints. It is the chairperson's job to prevent this. Make sure that everyone has a say and that it is duly noted. Blocking, however, can serve a useful purpose with a talkative member.

Sabotage. Group members who carry on their own conversations while another is speaking; the person who attempts to sidetrack the issues; the hidden decisions that are made without group consultation; these and similar factors represent an effort to render a meeting useless. The subversive's motivation may be that no decision will enhance the status quo. Disruptive behavior will sour the group and tear down its will to reach a decision or continue the meeting. Interest wanes and attention slips away.

INTERVIEWS

■ An **interview** can be defined as a conversation between two parties that is under the control of one of the parties and that tries to accomplish a special objective. A conversation is a two-way verbal and oral interchange of ideas and information. Thus an interview is a verbal interchange between two or more persons. It must be carefully planned and skillfully executed if its special objective is to be achieved.

As a supervisor you will be using interviews to help instruct your people, to evaluate them and to share their evaluations with them, to screen and hire new employees, to solve problems, to gather information, and to sell your subordinates on the need for changes. Interviews demand a quiet environment, a clear understanding by the parties of the special purpose of the interview, and an extensive use of open and closed questions.

The major purpose of an interview is to get the interviewee talking freely and frankly about all matters that are relevant to the accomplishment of the interview's purpose. The interviewer listens attentively, never interrupts, and usually refrains from expressing opinions or making snap judgments. The interviewee should do most of the talking.

Basically there are two types of interviews: directive and nondirective. Both may be used to give or receive information and to solve problems.

Directive Interviews

The **directive interview** is planned and totally controlled by the interviewer. It is most often used to obtain specific information, to communicate information, and to interview applicants for nonmanagement positions. Directive interviews follow a basic outline from beginning to end. They are designed to make extensive use of specific questions, mostly closed ones, in order to achieve the interviewer's special objective as quickly and efficiently as possible. The interviewer follows a script that is written out in advance.

Nondirective Interviews

The **nondirective interview** is controlled by the interviewee but planned by the interviewer. The interviewer starts the conversations with open questions—ones designed to allow the interviewee flexibility in his or her answers, and a chance to talk at length according to an outline and a pace of his or her own making. Typical open questions used in a selection or employment interview might go like this: "Why did you leave your job at Ace Supply?" or "How did you react when you were passed over for that promotion?"

Nondirective interviews avoid questions that can be answered with a simple yes or no. They allow a person to show his or her true feelings and attitudes. The interviewee speaks his or her mind while the interviewer records the responses. This type of interviewing makes great demands on both interviewer and interviewee. It takes more time to accomplish its special purpose than the directive interview. If it is not carefully conducted, it can easily degenerate into a "bull session" and a waste of time. The interviewer must keep the conversation going until all the information sought has been obtained. The nondirective interview is best used to resolve conflicts, solve problems, counsel employees, and screen applicants for management positions.

INSTANT REPLAY	This chapter has described different types of meetings and their mechanics. Both the informational and the problem-solving sessions can be quite useful, but they require planning and skillful execution if they are to be successful.

The problem-solving meeting requires your boss's approval as it necessitates your sharing formal authority with your subordinates. The limits of the group must be clearly spelled out so that its members know what they are expected to achieve. The discussion format should be used to involve each member as fully as possible. Distinct duties are yours as the group leader before, during, and after such meetings.

The roles group members play may be either negative or positive, depending upon their motivations. Each can and does serve useful purposes either to build up the group or an individual member of it. All are necessary at one time or another, and the group leader's job is to see that the roles are played in a nondisruptive manner.

Involving your people in decision making in areas that affect them most directly can release powerful motivational spirit. It is not done without risks, however, and these risks must be weighed carefully and be fully understood before you attempt to unleash these forces.

KEY WORDS	**directive interview**	**nondirective interview**
	informational meeting	**problem-solving meeting**
	interview	

1. How does an informational meeting differ from a problem-solving meeting?
2. What is the necessary prerequisite for the supervisor to obtain before he or she shares formal management authority with subordinates in problem solving?
3. State three types of problems that lend themselves to group discussion and solution by workers and manager.
4. What determines whether a self-serving role will have a positive or negative impact on a group?
5. Explain how a person's hidden agenda can prevent meaningful action at a problem-solving meeting.
6. What does the Harwood Manufacturing Company experiment add to your knowledge of group dynamics?
7. For what purpose can a supervisor use a directive interview? A nondirective interview?
8. Why is a nondirective interview more difficult to conduct than a directive interview?
9. You are chairperson for a meeting on waste reduction. What, in general, should you do before, during, and after your meeting with your subordinates?

CASE PROBLEM

The Office Party

Peter Baine closed the door to conference room A and called the meeting to order.

"It's four-thirty and, although Bill and Darrel are not here we should get started. Now our job is to plan the office party for the upcoming holidays. You're all volunteers and there is a lot to be done. Of course, I know that you all have other jobs and outside commitments, but. . . ."

Essy Jones shifted to her right and whispered to Phil Gray.

"If Peter runs true to his usual form, we'll have to send out for supper. He usually takes a day to get to the point."

"Yeh," whispered Phil.

"By the way, who appointed Peter chairperson, anyway?"

"I guess it was Hartley, the office manager. The criticism he got for last year's party must have fallen on deaf ears. Peter ran that fiasco too."

"Now, are there any questions?" Peter said in a louder-than-usual voice.

Essy raised her hand.

"Yes, Essy?"

"Pete, what are the jobs that must be performed? Let's just get volunteers for each of them, and let each person decide what he or she needs to do. Then they can meet with you to coordinate things. Time is short. We only have two weeks."

"Fine suggestion, Essy. Any others?"

There was a long pause. Bill entered the room and took a chair in the back.

"OK, here's what I propose."

Peter began to read from a list, naming tasks. With each assignment, Peter gave a detailed listing of the duties and a suggested completion date. Then he read out the names of the people assigned to each of the tasks. Phil leaned over to Essy.

"You got stuck with the refreshments. Lots of luck."

"That's OK but I don't think I'm going to like working with Bill. He's worse than no help at all."

The noise in the corridor outside the conference room grew so loud as the departing workforce left that Peter had to stop the meeting.

"Let's wait until the noise stops before going on."

Phil got up to leave, gathering his papers and stuffing them into his briefcase.

"Are you leaving, Phil?" asked Peter.

"Yes, I've got to catch the five-forty. If I miss it, I'll be waiting an hour for the next one."

"Well, if you see Darrel, give him his assignment, will you?"

"OK, what is it?"

Questions

1. Comment on Peter's handling of the group meeting.

2. What pitfalls have been illustrated in this case?

3. Why are the group members reluctant to voice their criticisms to Peter but eager to do so to the others?

4. Was this a problem-solving or informational meeting? What should it have been? Why?

5. What indications do you have that the office party will be something less than a success?

Part Three
You and Leadership

11 Leadership and Management Styles

INTRODUCTION

■ We have two objectives in this chapter: to understand the concept of leadership, and to explore the nature, potentials, and applications of each of the four styles of supervision.

In Chapter 1 we defined authority as the power to do things. Power, you will recall, is the ability to mobilize resources, both human and material. Formal power rests in the position you occupy, and is increased by delegation from a superior. Informal power comes to an individual because of his or her personality, knowledge, skills, and abilities. To be a leader, you must have informal power—the ability to get others to submit their wills to yours. To be a leader and a manager, you need both kinds of power. It is possible, therefore, to be a manager but not a leader.

LEADERSHIP

■ **Leadership** is the ability to get work done with and through others while simultaneously winning their respect, confidence, loyalty, and willing cooperation. The first part of our definition is true about **management** as well. It is the second half that distinguishes a leader from a nonleader. It is likely that while you may be a leader to some of your subordinates, you may not be to others. The goal of a leader is to be one to all of his or her subordinates. Leadership is an art that can be acquired and developed by anyone with the motivation to do so.

All leaders have three limiting factors to contend with. First, they are limited by themselves—by their knowledge, skills, attitudes, and abilities as well as by their weaknesses and inadequacies in the exercise of their roles. Second, they are limited by the groups over which they have authority—by the level of experience, skills, proficiencies, and attitudes of their subordinates as individuals and as a group. For the way in which subordinates perceive and interact with their bosses, their jobs, and each other are factors affecting both the quality and the quantity of their output. Finally, leaders are limited by their environment—by the resources and conditions available to them in their efforts to accomplish the assigned tasks and reach the established goals. All these factors undergo almost constant change, which requires the leaders to continually reassess these factors in determining the difficulties to be confronted.

Leadership Styles and Decision Making

The style of leadership you use with your subordinates, in effect, determines just how much of your formal authority you want to share with them. The autocratic leader or supervisor delegates little if any formal power. The spectator leader delegates a great deal. You will learn more about these and other kinds of leaders later in this chapter, but for now we will see how each style relates to the others.

Figure 11–1 shows how a manager's choice of a leadership style affects his or her use of authority in making decisions. At the left of the continuum model is the autocratic leader. In the middle is the democratic leader. At the right is the spectator leader. The bureaucratic manager is not shown on the continuum because he or she is not considered to be a leader.

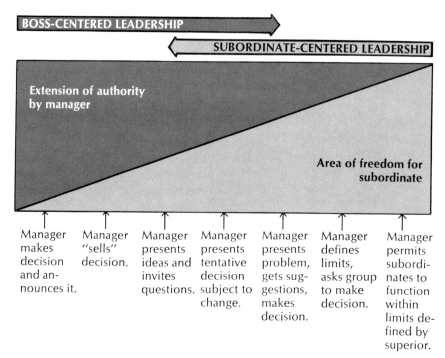

Figure 11-1. Continuum of leadership behavior.

The Managerial Grid   Many studies show that a leader's concern for or focus on his or her subordinates should be balanced against a concern for production or results. In the short run, managers who bow to organizational pressures to get results often achieve the greatest success by focusing on production and ignoring the needs of their subordinates. This kind of "crisis management" works best to put out fires and when time is short. It almost always utilizes the autocratic style of leadership, which will be described in this chapter.

In the long run, however, research tells us that the best leadership style is one that attempts to maintain a balance between the needs of your subordinates and your organization's need for results. Figure 11–2 shows the managerial grid concept developed by Robert Blake et al. According to this study, only the 9.9 position on the grid yields a satisfactory integration of the needs of people and the needs of the business organization. It leads to both an effective organization—one in which the company achieves its goals—and an efficient organization—one in which the majority of employees find it possible to achieve their goals.

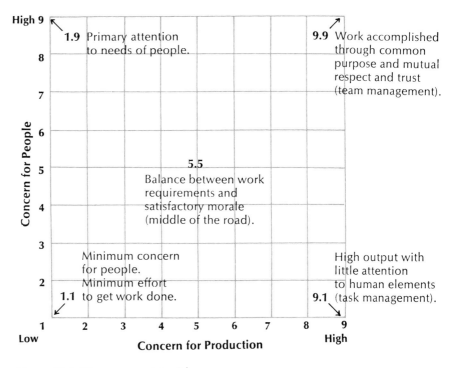

Figure 11-2. The managerial grid.

Leadership Traits

After World War II, the United States Army conducted a survey on the careers of successful military commanders. In this survey military personnel from privates to generals were asked to list the traits of commanders they regarded as successful leaders. The result was the compilation of the list of fourteen leadership traits shown here.

bearing	integrity
courage	judgment
decisiveness	justice
dependability	knowledge
endurance	loyalty
enthusiasm	tact
initiative	unselfishness

Possession of some of these traits is not a guarantee that you will be a successful leader. The absence of some or all of these traits, however, will certainly keep you from becoming a successful leader and, in fact, could interfere with your being a success in your chosen field.

1	Be technically proficient.
2	Know yourself and seek self-improvement.
3	Know your people and look out for their welfare.
4	Keep your people informed.
5	Set the example.
6	Insure that each task is understood, supervised, and accomplished.
7	Train your people to work as a team.
8	Make sound and timely decisions.
9	Develop a sense of responsibility in your subordinates.
10	Employ your resources in accordance with their capabilities.
11	Seek responsibility and take responsibility for your actions.

Figure 11-3. Principles of leadership.

Leadership Principles

What follows are proven principles or guidelines that should govern the exercise of your informal and formal authority. These principles, along with a concerted effort on your part to acquire and/or develop leadership traits, practically guarantee your attainment of leadership status in the eyes of your peers and subordinates. These traits and principles are mutually self-supporting; the exercise of the principles helps develop the traits while the person possessing the traits of a leader is inclined to follow the principles. Figure 11–3 lists eleven principles of leadership.

Each of these principles holds sound advice for you in any leadership position. They serve as concise reminders and as a checklist to which you should make frequent reference. They comprise a handy guide to help you assess your practice of management and the exercise of your authority over others. If you understand their meaning and make an honest effort to act in accordance with their wisdom, you can avoid numerous errors and problems.

ASSESSING YOUR LEADERSHIP ABILITY

■ There are four major indicators you can rely on as you attempt to determine the effectiveness of your leadership with your people. They are: (1) Morale; (2) Group spirit; (3) Proficiency; and (4) Self-discipline.

Each of these in turn can be evaluated to help measure the impact you and your methods are having on your formal-group members, individually and collectively.

Morale

People's attitudes toward all the individuals, things, and events that affect them at work constitute their morale. **Morale** can be defined as people's state of mind with regard to their job, supervisor, peers, and company. It reflects their level of involvement in their work and appreciation of the people and conditions that they must relate to every day. Through the actions and statements of people you can effectively measure their morale. If your subordinates are positive individuals who take pride in their work, they reflect favorably on you and your group. If they are absent frequently, lack attention to their duties, or dwell on negative factors, you can assume that you seem less than a leader to them.

Group Spirit

What are the major attitudes reflected by the members of your formal group and any informal groups associated with it? Are they positive and supportive, fostering teamwork and harmony? Or are they negative and destructive? Both individual and group attitudes are shaped in large measure by your human relations efforts. If your group is without team spirit, have you recently voiced your appreciation for its achievements? Are you trying to work with its members and utilize their talents? Do you know their needs and values? Do you know your group members as individuals?

Proficiency

How good are you at your job? How good are your subordinates? Is there an effort on your part to improve both your own level of competence and theirs? Are you aware of any efforts on their part to seek a higher level of competence? Are you fostering their growth and development? This indicator is tied directly to morale and group spirit. If these are low or negative, their demonstrated proficiency levels will be too.

Self-Discipline

Can your shop or office function in your absence? Do your people respond promptly and in a positive way to your instructions? Do they accept honest criticism well? Have you had to reprimand more often than praise? Do your people know the why behind what they are expected to do? Can they be trusted? If not, what are you doing about these problems?

You can rate yourself by using these indicators at any time. Chances are that your boss is doing so regularly. If you are placing the kind of emphasis that you should on your human relations, you should experience little difficulty in these general areas.

STYLES OF MANAGEMENT

There are four main styles of management available to you: the **autocratic style,** the **bureaucratic style,** the **democratic style,** and the **spectator style.** Each style has its advantages and disadvantages. Each works best for the leader and his or her subordinates in fairly precise sets of circumstances.

All four styles can have either positive or negative effects on your subordinates, depending on who the people are that are subjected to them and on the circumstances of their use. Like a firearm, they can be an instrument for winning prizes or a means of inflicting injury.

The Autocratic Style

Autocratic or dictatorial leaders keep power to themselves and do not delegate to their subordinates. The making of a final decision is reserved to the leaders alone. They keep their subordinates dependent upon them for instructions, and they allow their subordinates to act only under their direct supervision.

PREREQUISITES

The necessary prerequisites for using the autocratic style are:

1. You must be an expert in the practice of management as well as in handling your subordinates' jobs;

2. Your subordinates must be in need of this approach;

3. You must wish to communicate primarily by means of orders and detailed instructions.

LIMITATIONS ON THE AUTOCRATIC STYLE

In general, you should restrict your use of this style to the following situations:

1. When you are dealing with new employees who are unfamiliar with the tasks and methods they are expected to perform;

2. When time is short or when there is an emergency situation that does not allow you to explain the reasons for your orders;

3. When you are directing a stubborn or difficult subordinate who does not respond favorably to requests or to your use of the other three styles of supervision;

4. When your authority is directly challenged. (By putting your wishes in the form of orders, you thereby place your subordinate in the position of having to follow orders or be guilty of insubordination.)

You should restrict the use of this style of supervision to the situations outlined above. If you lack the necessary prerequisites, you cannot use it effectively. As soon as the situation changes, you will need to shift to another leadership style. Keep in mind the fact that the autocratic style can be a management style as well as a leadership style.

EMPLOYEE REACTIONS

Persons subjected to the autocratic style will generally be high-quantity producers but only for the short run. They will tend to be tense and somewhat fearful of you. If the style is used on a person too long, that is, after the need for it has ceased, he or she will become resentful and withhold his or her normal contributions to the job. It is not a style that builds team players or encourages strong ties among the workers.

The Bureaucratic Style

This style is typified by the manager's reliance upon rules, regulations, policy and procedures. They represent to him or her authority and certainty. It is management "by the book." Through the exercise of this style, the manager adopts the posture of a police officer enforcing rules religiously and depending upon superiors to resolve problems not covered in the manual.

Unlike the other three styles of supervision, those who follow the bureaucratic style cannot really be "leaders." That is because such managers are not really directing their people in a personal way. Instead, they are directing them through regulations, procedures, and policies.

PREREQUISITES

There are three major prerequisites for the use of the bureaucratic style:

1. All the other styles should be regarded as inappropriate for use;
2. Subordinates subjected to this style must be in need of it;
3. No latitude in decision making or deviations from procedures are permissible.

LIMITATIONS ON THE BUREAUCRATIC STYLE

This style is appropriate for governmental bodies, military services, and nonprofit enterprises such as public hospitals, charities, and the like. It has a very small place in businesses, and its use there should be limited to these situations:

1. During the installation of new equipment and operations when the people in charge of an operation are specialists;
2. In doing research or conducting analytical studies;
3. In training record-keeping, filing, and other clerical personnel where a faithful following of set procedures is essential for the success of the job;
4. In enforcing safety or carrying out strictly routine, highly repetitive operations.

If utilized properly, the bureaucratic approach can be an effective style that has positive effects on people. If used improperly, it can be devastating to those subjected to it who have ambition and creativity.

EMPLOYEE REACTIONS

This style does little to build motivation in subordinates. It promotes the formation of strong work habits which, after a time, become very difficult to change in even the smallest way without strong employee resistance. Employees tend to adopt an indifferent attitude toward their peers and their work. The supervisor becomes rather unimportant to the subordinates and is perceived by them as a watchdog rather than a manager. Workers will generally do what is expected but little more. There are a number of people, however, both in and out of management, for whom this style represents security, and they respond well to this style for that reason. For most people, however, it is only of value in the special situations listed above.

The Democratic Style

Democratic managers adopt a "we" approach to their work and to their subordinates. They play the role of coaches, drilling their teams in the fundamentals and sharing decision-making authority with them. They make frequent use of problem-solving meetings as outlined in Chapter 10. They delegate freely to those who have earned their confidence as well as to members of the group in general. They attempt to build a strong team spirit and to foster mutual respect and interdependence between themselves as coaches and the members of the team as well as among the team members and their peers.

This style of supervision often goes by other names, such as the consultative, general, or participative style. It is a leadership style very much in use today.

PREREQUISITES

The following conditions are needed in advance of implementing the democratic style:

1. You should have your superior's permission to use it;

2. You should be willing to accept a certain amount of mistakes and delays in the early stages of its implementation;

3. You should have a personal commitment to this style and a strong belief in its ability to motivate people—once you extend this style to your subordinates, you would find it difficult to shift to a different style;

4. You should have carefully prepared your subordinates by initial delegations of some of your authority, and you should be willing to

continue to consult with your subordinates on small matters during the early stages of the new style's use;

5. You should have a high degree of patience and the time required for group meetings on decision making and other topics.

Some supervisors may feel threatened by this style. If so, they should not attempt to use it or be asked to use it until they have been prepared through training to do so. A worker who has never in the past been asked for the time of day, let alone an opinion on new procedures, might become quite suspicious at sudden attempts to obtain his or her participation in matters affecting the department.

LIMITATIONS ON THE DEMOCRATIC STYLE

This style is best used in the following situations:

1. When your workers are highly skilled and/or highly experienced at their jobs;

2. Where time is sufficient to permit participation by your subordinates as individuals or as a group;

3. When preparing groups or individuals for changes;

4. When attempting to solve problems common to the group, such as an improvement in methods, safety, and environmental conditions;

5. When attempting to air gripes or otherwise relieve workers' tensions.

EMPLOYEE REACTIONS

The great majority of today's workers are educated enough for the democratic style of leadership. Through it they can achieve and sustain a high quality and quantity of output for extended periods. The supervisor who uses this approach is "employee-centered" rather than "work-centered," and his or her people know it. They appreciate the trust and freedom that the supervisor expresses in them through the use of the democratic style. Cooperation and group spirit are strongly promoted along with a corresponding boost to morale. Under the democratic style, workers tend to understand the contributions of their peers to a greater degree, and they get to know each other better than under any of the other styles.

The Spectator Style

This style is characterized by treating everyone as individuals. The team concept is either played down or nonexistent. Subordinates perceive of themselves and are treated as professionals, that is, experts in their fields.

The manager makes himself or herself available for consultations in accord with a strong "open door" policy, but he or she is generally physically removed from direct and frequent contact with subordinates. If the workers need help, they know where to go to find it. If they don't need assistance, the boss will tell them so. For this style is not a "cop-out" on the part of the supervisor who adopts it. Even though the boss is remote from his or her subordinates, he or she remains in touch with them and their work through conferences, reports, and records of output.

PREREQUISITES

The prerequisites of the spectator style of leadership are as follows:

1. Since the workers are treated as experts under this style, they should really be highly skilled at their crafts;

2. Controls other than direct and frequent observations must be established to monitor the workers' performance;

3. The workers must possess pride in their work as well as endurance and initiative.

LIMITATIONS ON THE SPECTATOR STYLE

The use of the spectator style should be restricted, as a rule, to the following groups or situations:

1. You have in your department highly skilled, experienced, and educated personnel;

2. You are using outside experts, such as staff specialists, consultants, or temporary skilled help;

3. You as the boss are new at your job or lack previous personal experience in the work being performed by your subordinates.

EMPLOYEE REACTIONS

Workers who work under the spectator style perceive themselves as being in business for themselves, that is, they adopt a somewhat independent air and see their boss as a kind of staff assistant who stands ready to help them if they need him or her. This style generally promotes high levels of individual output for indefinite periods of time. It fosters pride and morale better than the other styles do. But if the boss becomes too remote or inaccessible, insecurity may set in along with resulting fears and frustrations. All the workers are pretty much on their own and feel strongly the need to prove themselves to their boss and their peers. Consequently, people working under this style need constant reassurance that they are performing up to standard and that they are appreciated.

As a supervisor at any level, you must be familiar with all four of the management styles. You will have subordinates and situations at one time or another that will call upon you to use each of these styles.

During the training of a new employee, you should probably rely on either the autocratic style or the bureaucratic style or a blend of the two of them. Once the newcomer has been placed in his or her job and is performing up to standard, you should switch to one of the other styles of leadership. If you don't, your worker may rebel, and you will have gone a long way toward helping to bring about his or her termination.

If you try to use a style that is wrong for a specific subordinate, he or she will probably let you know it. Changes in a subordinate's attitudes and behavior are the first sign that you may be using an improper style of leadership. The selection of the proper style for individual workers will be easy once you have acquired some experience as a supervisor. But it may involve a bit of trial and error on your part. Don't hesitate to try a switch if the style you are presently using fails to get the desired results. Don't forget that you have a lot of help available to you through the advice and counsel of both your peers and superiors.

You may not be entirely free to select your own styles of leadership. Your boss may frown upon the use of one or another of them. You may feel inadequate in your understanding of how to implement one or more of these styles. Your tendency might be to use the one you feel most at home with on all your people. This is almost always a mistake. A subordinate who has worked well under a spectator style may, because of changes in his or her job, require an autocratic or democratic one to get him or her through a period of transition to a new assignment. You should stand ready to offer the style each subordinate needs. It is only by practice and study that you can feel confident enough to use all four styles successfully.

INSTANT REPLAY   Leadership is a precious commodity; few managers possess it. If you have your authority over others from all three sources—traditional, rational, and charismatic—you have all that is needed to be both a professional manager and a successful leader.

We have seen the various management traits so often exhibited by those in authority whom others call leaders. Without them, there is little chance for a person to become a true leader. With them and the guidance of the eleven leadership principles described in this chapter, a manager can and will win the confidence, respect, obedience, loyalty, and willing cooperation of his or her subordinates.

You can measure your success with your people through the four major leadership indicators. Your subordinates' morale, group spirit, proficiency, and self-discipline all tell you how receptive they are, individually and collectively, to your style of supervision.

The four basic styles of management offer you a variety of methods as you attempt to tailor your approach to each individual. Each style has its merits and weaknesses. Only one is right for each person you direct at any given time. If you chose the correct style, you increase your effectiveness and that of your subordinates. If you pick the wrong style, your problems will multiply.

KEY WORDS

autocratic style	**group spirit**	**proficiency**
bureaucratic style	**leadership**	**self-discipline**
democratic style	**morale**	**spectator style**

QUESTIONS FOR DISCUSSION

1. What is the essential difference between a manager who is a leader and one who is not?

2. What style of leadership or management does your boss use with you? Is is a correct one for you? Why or why not?

3. Tell the class about a person you have worked for who was a leader to you.

4. When would you use the bureaucratic style of management in a business?

5. What style of supervision would you use on each of the following and why?
   A new employee with two years' experience in a similar job.
   An old-timer who appears to be an informal leader with one of the cliques in your department.
   A neurotic employee with a good deal of experience but whose neurosis is interfering with his or her job performance.
   An employee with many more years' experience than you have and who resents you personally and your authority.

6. What do you think of the list of leadership traits prepared by the United States Army? Which are appropriate for a present-day business organization? Which are not? What other traits do you regard as important?

7. Comment on the statement "Leaders are born, not made."

8. How is it possible to be a leader to one of your subordinates while not being considered one by all your other subordinates?

A Stitch in Time

Charlie Thomas liked his work. He had an almost perfect work record and wanted to keep it that way. That's why he was becoming frustrated. Since his new boss, Greg Orchard, had arrived on the scene, Charlie was beginning to feel frustration. Not only had Greg given Charlie all the usual dull and routine tasks to do but he refused to let any of Charlie's regular work leave the area without first going over it in detail. When a few minor mistakes were found, Greg called Charlie into his office and chewed him out but good.

Charlie was so visibly shaken after one such session with Greg that Ruth, his coworker, noticed it.

"What's the problem, Charlie? You look really scared."

"Ruth, I can't seem to do anything right. Nothing I do pleases that creep. I'm used to working on my own, but now. . . ."

Ruth looked concerned. As they began walking toward the cafeteria, she asked Charlie if he wanted to talk about it.

"Before Orchard came here, I was doing fine. I got great reviews and a lot of compliments. What I did then I'm doing now, but Orchard wants it his way. Ruth, my way has worked well for three years. When I try to point this out, he just yells at me. What really burns me up is his constant nit-picking. He wants to see everything I turn out—everything. I'm ready to go see Stevens, and try to get this guy off my back."

"Listen, Charlie, going over Orchard's head will only make things worse. You are only getting the same treatment all of us are getting. Believe me, you are not alone. I think he is just worried about any mistakes leaving his area with his signature attached."

"But Ruth, everything he has found wrong so far has been minor. It's been easy to correct and really not serious. He's making me make more mistakes by treating me this way. I'm getting paranoid. I'm afraid to put the work on his desk even after checking it over several times. Now I don't mind so much doing it his way, but I can only find out what his way is after he checks my work. Then I end up revising it to meet his guidelines. It's been six weeks of hell, Ruth, and I don't know how much longer I can take it."

Questions

1. What style of supervision do you think that Charlie worked under in the past?
2. What style of supervision is Greg now using with Charlie? Why is he using that style?
3. How is the problem of role ambiguity illustrated here?
4. Should Charlie go over Greg's head and talk to Stevens? Why?
5. If you were Stevens and knew about all this what would you do?

12   The Appraisal Process

LEARNING OBJECTIVES

■ After reading and discussing this chapter, you should be able to:

1 Define the appraisal process.

2 List six major purposes in appraising your subordinates.

3 Briefly explain why clear and quantifiable standards are needed in order to prepare proper appraisals.

4 List and give examples of three types of appraisal methods.

5 List and give examples of five pitfalls in the appraisal process.

6 Describe the kind of interview best suited for an appraisal of a subordinate.

7 Recognize that, while informal appraisals of subordinates occur daily, a formal appraisal of your subordinates is required once or twice each year.

INTRODUCTION

■ One of your primary duties as a supervisor is to periodically appraise or evaluate the on-the-job performance of each of your subordinates. During the **evaluation process** you must make judgments about the person—his or her character, attitudes, and potential—as well as performance. This process is often referred to by several different terms such as merit rating, employee performance evaluation or review, and performance appraisal. Regardless of the name it goes by, the process is intended to help you fortify your relationships with your people and to give you a better understanding of each of them.

The formal **appraisal process** may take place once or twice a year. The informal appraisal process, however, takes place daily. Both of these help the individual employee of any formal organization determine where he or she stands with you and the company. They help satisfy the need to know, and they help remove fear and misunderstanding. It is through your daily appraisals that you build your case for the formal one. In the performance of your daily routine and through your daily observations, you are best able to critique a subordinate's performance and offer him or her constructive criticism and suggestions for improvement.

**GOALS
OF APPRAISALS**

■ The major goals of employee appraisals are:
1. To measure employee performance;
2. To measure employee potential;
3. To assess employee attitudes;
4. To further the supervisor's understanding of each subordinate;
5. To fortify supervisor-subordinate relationships;
6. To analyze employee strengths and weaknesses—providing recognition for the former and ways to eliminate the latter;
7. To set goals for the improvement of performance;
8. To substantiate decisions in regard to pay increases and eligibility for promotion, transfer, or training programs;
9. To verify the accuracy of the hiring process;
10. To eliminate the hopelessly inadequate performers.

If appraisals you make on each subordinate are to accomplish the above goals, they must be as objective and accurate as you can make them. They must reflect a true and definite image of the man or woman, in line with company policy and standards. This requires you to be fair in your evaluation efforts.

STANDARDS

■ Your company should furnish you with standards that help your appraisal efforts and aid you in your measurement of each subordinate's character, expected output (quality and quantity), and potential. A list of the usual standards includes standards for conduct, job descriptions, job specifications, established production rates, inspection standards, a specified uniform format for recording appraisals, and expected rates of advancement. It is only through the use of standards that have been established fairly and impartially and the comparisons you make to them that you can make accurate judgments.

Your duty to rate each subordinate cannot be delegated. It is much too important a task to be entrusted to another. The results must be kept confidential and are not to be shared with your worker's peers. Only you, your subordinate, your boss, and a select handful of staff managers should have access to the results of these formal appraisals. Since you have the primary interest and knowledge needed to properly evaluate your people, only you should be responsible for preparing their appraisals.

APPRAISAL METHODS

■ Your company is probably making use of one or more of the currently popular methods of appraising workers. Each of these methods has its advantages and disadvantages. Which one you may have to use or will be used on you by your boss is decided by company policy.

Ranking or Forced-Distribution Method

You may be required to rank your people from the most productive to the least productive or from the most valuable to the least valuable. Often such rankings are based on a normal distribution curve, requiring that no more than a certain percentage of your people fall into one or another of the categories listed. Figure 12–1 illustrates a typical ranking approach.

You may be required to make a simple list of your subordinates, ranking one over another as to their abilities and contributions. This will force you to say that one man or woman is better as an employee than another.

The major disadvantage of the **ranking method** or **forced-distribution method** is that it requires you to compare your people to one another. That might be tolerable if all of your workers perform identical tasks.

Figure 12-1. Percentage ranking method of worker appraisal.

INSTRUCTIONS TO RATER: List your subordinates by their overall rating in one or another of the categories below. Use their complete initials and do not exceed the percentages listed.

Percentage	Category	Subordinate(s)
5%	Superior	GBH
12.5%	Above average	SAB, RFL
65%	Average	PTC, BCT, LH, NPB, SDO, LMR, GSW
12.5%	Below average	
5%	Unacceptable	PBC, TFM

FACTOR	SUPERIOR	VERY GOOD	AVERAGE	FAIR	POOR
Quantity of output	Extraordinary volume and speed of output ✓	Above average output ☐	Expected output— normal output ☐	Below average output ☐	Unsatis- factory level of output ☐

Figure 12-2. Forced-choice appraisal method.

If they don't, the system requires you to compare apples and oranges. Also, it may prevent a supervisor with a large percentage of above-average performers from listing them as such because of the rather arbitrary percentage limits established for each category.

The forced-distribution method can be helpful if used in conjunction with one or another of the other methods. It does force you to make a choice and to picture your people as you may never have done before.

Checklist or Forced-Choice Method

One of the most prevalent methods in industry today is the **checklist method** or **forced-choice method** of appraisal. In it you are asked to pick the one block and statement that best describes your subordinate's standing with regard to the factor listed. These types of forms work well when summarizing the degrees to which a person has or lacks certain characteristics or traits desired of him. Figure 12–2 shows a sample.

Picking the one best choice may be difficult, especially when your workers perform many different tasks which have differing standards of output and which demand different types of skills and experiences. Also, fitting this type of form to young, inexperienced workers puts them at a disadvantage, as they appear in a bad light when contrasted to the others. Some way of compensating for these shortcomings should be designed into the system.

Critical-Incident or Narrative Method

The most flexible method, but clearly the most demanding way of appraising workers, is the **critical-incident method** or **narrative method.** In this method the supervisor must make reference to rather specific situations which highlight or illustrate a worker's abilities, traits, or potentials. Using the essay approach, the rater writes personal observations and comments in order to dramatize the particular point under examination. Figure 12–3 gives such a description.

This method offers the maximum degree of expression possible for precise and informative evaluations. It is difficult, however, because it demands an in-depth knowledge of subordinates' behavior and attitudes, which can only come from frequent and regular observations and a recording of the results. It demands that a supervisor be with subordinates daily. Although this is highly desirable, it is not always possible. Many subordinates work physically separated by great distances from their supervisors. Salesmen, construction workers, research people, and staff specialists are a few examples. In their cases, comments from the people they serve may prove quite helpful. This method applies best to managers who are rated by other managers.

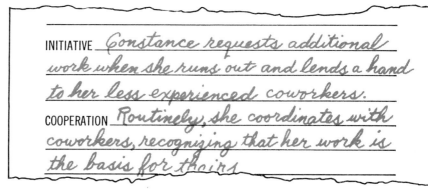

Figure 12-3. Critical-incident or narrative appraisal.

Field-Review Method The **field-review method** requires that interviews be conducted between a supervisor and personnel staff assistants (either singly or in groups). Questions are asked—usually requiring a yes or no answer—by the specialists with regard to each of the supervisor's subordinates. The staff aides record the answers and write the formal appraisals. After reading them, the supervisor must either approve them with a signature or disapprove them with comments.

This system was designed to relieve supervisors from the burdens of paper work acompanying the appraisal process. It does require, however, that each manager be prepared for the interview in as complete a manner as if he or she had to fill out the ratings himself or herself. If he or she is not well prepared, extensive revision and re-thinking may have to take place before accurate appraisals can be communicated to each worker.

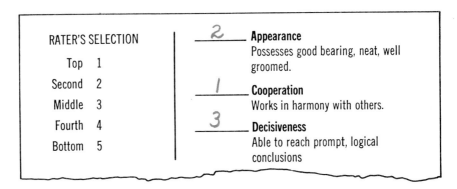

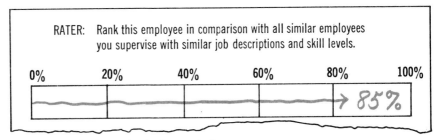

Figure 12-4. Scale method of appraisal.

Scale Method

The **scale method** combines the ranking and forced-choice methods. The rater must decide where each person stands in relation to his or her peers on the basis of a scale, with or without a specific description to go by. Two types of scales are illustrated in Figure 12–4. Some scales may attach a point value to the supervisor's choice, and total points may be used to sum up a worker's standing in his or her group.

Once again, supervisors are forced to "pick one" that may not be exactly what they would or could say if allowed freedom of expression.

All of these systems are subjective—they allow the rater to let personal interests, preferences, and prejudices flavor the rating given to each person. Even the critical-incident or narrative method puts down the situation from the supervisor's point of view and in his or her own words. No system has yet been devised that will completely eliminate this. It is up to you, the rater, to be as objective as you can by making every effort to leave personal bias and personality clashes out of each rating. Your emphasis should be first and foremost on the worker's performance on the job, in accordance with the standards established for that job. Only secondarily are you concerned with a subordinate's character and potential. State as clearly as you can what each person did, how well it was done, and what you believe the person is capable of doing.

PITFALLS

■ There are several common types of errors that can be made by raters. If you know about them, you can consciously try to prevent them from occurring in your appraisals of your subordinates. Committing any one of them will render your rating inaccurate.

The Halo Effect

One of the most frequent errors committed by raters is known as the **halo effect.** The rater allows one outstanding positive or negative trait or incident about a person to color the overall rating and image of that subordinate. Because one of your people dresses well and has good manners and bearing, you may tend to let this overshadow his or her other traits or the whole work performance. Conversely, if the most recent incident you can recall about a person is his or her commission of a major mistake, you might allow this to obscure his or her many fine qualities. Your formal ratings are supposed to reflect the whole person. You must guard against letting isolated events or appearances dominate your total impression and objectivity toward a worker.

Rating the Person— Not the Performance

There is a strong tendency for a rater to rate a person high if the rater and the individual get along, and low if they do not. Human nature is such that we perceive in a favorable way people we like most and tend to dismiss those we dislike as worthless persons. A rater's personality and attitudes may clash with those of a subordinate, and even though that worker's performance and potentials are above average, he or she may receive an overall unsatisfactory rating. If you do this, you are not being honest or fair. Your job in appraisals is to rate each person in relation to performance in a particular job. Unless an individual's personality traits are interfering with his or her work or are a great asset to him or her, there is no reason for you to bring them into the formal appraisal. You may not like an individual, but you may have to rank him or her as superior. Leave your personal biases and prejudices out of the picture you paint of the person. Avoid personal attacks.

Rating Everyone as Average

This error, which is often referred to as the central tendency, occurs when you rate everyone as average. You may be tempted to do so because you lack sufficient data to do otherwise or because you see this as the safest, least controversial method of handling your appraisals. You won't have to justify a high or a below-average rating.

Quite often, the raters fear that if they rate a subordinate as above-average, the subordinate will get a "big head" and become more difficult to direct or control. Or supervisors may fear that if they rate a person below average, they will face a confrontation at the appraisal interview or criticism from their boss for allowing a poor performance. In other words, supervisors may fear that when they are appraising their people, they themselves are being appraised—that the major purpose of appraisals is to find out how good a boss the supervisors have been and not primarily to evaluate the workers. If you have cause to believe this to be the case where you work, you have a very unfortunate appraisal system. How well your people perform does influence your future. But making out phony appraisals that show them all average or above cannot be justified by the facts, and your boss will know it. Simply saying someone is good does not make it so. If you falsify their ratings, your people will know it too. And if you think it might be hard to supervise an employee who earns a good rating and is told about it, how much more difficult to supervise would the employee be who feels you have been dishonest with him or her?

The only safe road to travel is that of integrity. Arm yourself with the facts by careful and frequent observations. Be with your people as often as you can and make on-the-spot corrections and comments about their work and their attitudes. Let them know where they stand with you regularly. Be open and available. If you do, there will be no shocks or surprises at the appraisal interview. Your informal appraisals will have prepared them for what you will say. They will expect what they receive, and you will have the facts and events to support their ratings.

The Rush Job

Related to most other appraisal errors is the last minute, hurry-up job of rating that occurs at midnight, the day before the interviews, or at lunch or breaks on the day you must relay the results. If you have two or twenty subordinates, you have to give yourself enough lead time for thinking things through and searching your memory and your files for tangible data upon which to prepare your case. How would you like it if your boss summed up your past six months at work with a fifteen-minute effort on your appraisal form?

A great deal rides on your formal appraisals. Your people know that it represents in writing your opinion of them and their performances. They know that what you say will directly affect their futures and their earnings. They know also that you go on record with your superiors in these appraisals. Your relationships and credibility are at stake. Don't muff this great opportunity to cement your relations; pass out deserved praise, and build programs for their improvement. This should be a task that you tackle with great concern and eagerness. You are laying foundations that will have to support future plans and programs. Make those foundations firm and strong.

Comparisons

If you try to rate a man or woman by comparing one with another, you are making a big mistake. We know that people are unique and dynamic. No two people look alike, think alike, act alike. Even if your people have the same job, they cannot be compared because their experiences, training, education, attitudes and skill levels are different. To say that Paul is better than Peter has no meaning unless you know exactly how good Paul is and should be. The questions then arise, "How long has Peter had a chance to be as good as Paul?" and, "Has he the potential to be so?"

The only comparisons that you should make are to the standards that have been established for each job and for worker conduct. You can say that Suzy meets the standards of her job while Helen does not. Or that Joe exhibits the cooperative spirit necessary for success in his job while Jeff does not. These are not comparisons of one person to another; instead, they are comparisons to the standards and expectations you have for each subordinate in relation to his or her duties.

Not Sharing the Results

We have been under the assumption that whatever your formal appraisal of a worker is, it will be discussed with that worker. To do otherwise really defeats the whole purpose behind appraising people— to better their performance individually and collectively. Yet some companies promote systems for the evaluation of employees that actually prohibit or discourage the communication of the results to the rated individuals. They do so because they assume that the daily appraisals have said all that has to be said. Or they see the formal appraisal as primarily a communications device between supervisor and middle manager or between line and staff. This unfortunate perception of the process denies the supervisor and every other manager the opportunity to accomplish all the goals we have mentioned previously. If this situation exists in your company, you must realize how it affects your workers. A sense of fear and distrust is created by this secrecy, and frustration will result from not knowing what the formal reports about a person's abilities have to say. Work for a change in policy if you live under such a system.

Lack of Proper Training

All too often companies sow the seeds for management failures by failing to provide each supervisor with the proper training he or she needs to appraise people properly. A supervisor who has not been taught how to appraise, how to prepare for an appraisal interview, and how to conduct such an interview will make mistakes that could have been prevented. If you are uncertain about how to do your appraising, seek counsel from your peers and superiors. If the company fails to give you the proper training in this vital area, it will be up to you to fill the gap by yourself. Self-study, conferences with your boss, courses in personnel management at a college, and management seminars are all good ways to pick up or improve your skills in this area.

Lack of Standards of Performance

Unless supervisors have clearly defined and properly communicated standards of performance to refer to as they gather information and make observations of their subordinates, they will not be capable of making and sharing an adequate appraisal. Your people must know what is expected of them. You must know how they perceive their jobs. Unless both the supervisor and the rated employee know these standards ahead of time, the appraisal process and its accompanying interview will yield something less than the goals listed at the beginning of this chapter.

Lack of Proper Documentation

When you attempt to criticize an employee's performance, you must be prepared to give specific information. You must have concrete evidence to back up your observations and criticisms. In noting an employee's tardiness, be specific by giving the dates and the amount of time missed. We should expect that each criticism will not be a surprise to the rated employee. Rather each should have been discussed when it happened. The formal appraisal interview should only be a review of past events that exhibits a concern for the prevention of past infractions as well as a focus on improvement in the future.

THE APPRAISAL INTERVIEW

■ All your daily contacts should provide you with the facts you need to prepare and support your formal evaluations. The big event for both you and your worker is the appraisal interview where you both can discuss the judgments you have made. This meeting should occur in private and without interruption.

There are three stages related to sharing the results of your appraisal efforts. They are the preparation for the interview, the conduct of the interview, and the follow-up to check on its results.

Preparation

The interview should not just "happen." It must be planned with the same thoroughness you would apply to the planning of any important event. Then you can foresee and prevent most of the problems and misunderstandings that could permanently damage your relationship.

Be certain that you review each rating in detail before you attempt to meet and discuss it with your worker. Even though you wrote it, you probably wrote several others at the same time, and it is amazing how easily you can confuse them in your own mind. Anticipate the areas or individual remarks that might give rise to controversy. Be clear in your own mind why you rated a person below average on a given point, what led you to that conclusion, and what supports it now. If you have recorded a failure that the person has overcome and is not likely to repeat, be sure that you have so stated on the rating. You don't want to put much emphasis on such a situation. After all, most of our learning takes place through trial and error, and we learn best from the analysis of our mistakes.

Imagine students who are first introduced to the mathematical process called addition. They receive an explanation of the process and are guided through several examples. Then they are asked to add the numbers 3 and 6. The students try and get the wrong answer. The instructor reviews the process and the students' individual application of it to find out where and how they made their errors. When the errors in application are pinpointed, the students try again. This time they get the correct answer. After adding for several days they master the process and never repeat their original errors. Would you now hold their initial error against them? You wouldn't and shouldn't. More recent performance indicates quite strongly their mastery of the concepts, and they have proven that they won't fall victim to those errors again.

Having analyzed your subordinate's weaknesses as probable points for discussion and questions, construct a list of the person's strong points. Label what the person does extremely well. Identify favorable personality traits. These represent excellent introductory material to get the interview going. Some managers use what is referred to as the "sandwich approach." This technique gives the worker a strength, then a weakness, then a strength, and so on. It tends to soften the blows to a person's ego and promote confidence in the person being rated. Use whatever approach you feel is best for both you and your worker. Watch his or her reaction and be ready to adjust your approach as necessary.

Finally, set down a list of goals or objectives you would like to see the person set for himself or herself. These should relate most specifically to the improvement of his or her performance and character. Then determine the possible ways in which he or she might go about achieving each one. For example, suppose your subordinate has recurring difficulty in making logical and practical decisions. Be ready to get his or her views as to how he or she might improve. Have a suggested plan on hand, and recommend that he or she follow it if he or she does not have a plan. For every weakness you should stand ready with a suggestion for improvement—let us hope that your subordinate will concur.

Conducting the Interview

Make arrangements for adequate time and facilities, and be certain that you will be free of unnecessary interruptions. This is time for just you two and should not be interfered with.

Begin the interview by emphasizing that its purpose is to promote improvement in both the individual and the department. Then move into the specifics. Keep it short and to the point.

One good approach is to begin with some rather general questions such as, "Well, Tom, how would you rate yourself on your progress since our last interview?" or, "If you had to appraise yourself for the past six months, what would you say about your performance?" This method gets your subordinate talking and gives you additional insights into his or her way of perceiving things. Also, it makes the point that this interview is supposed to be a dialogue and an interchange of points of view. Avoid the lecture format, and get his or her feelings and observations into the open. You should work for mutual agreement and accord.

At some point during the interview give the worker a copy of the appraisal. Allow him or her time to read it and understand its contents. Ask him or her for reactions, and take each as a lead into the why behind the rating. With each weakness noted, give a validation of it. Then discuss how it can be overcome. If your subordinate sees no immediate way to attack it, introduce your thoughts on the matter.

Finally, set some specific short-range goals with your subordinate to remedy the list of shortcomings. These should tackle the questions of what should be done, by what time it should be completed, and how to reach each goal. You will be instilling hope for each person you interview, and, more concretely, you will be showing a way out of the present difficulties. Here again is a chance to convince your subordinate of your honest concern for his or her welfare and progress.

The Follow-Up

After the interview and through the exercise of your normal performance of your duties, check on each person's progress toward the goals set in the interview. If Ann said she would brush up on her basic skills, visit with her to see if she has. If Wally said he was going to try a new method, find out how well he is doing. Your people will soon realize, as you do, that appraisals are daily routines that are only summarized periodically through the formal appraisal report and interview. This realization should cause them to give of their best regularly and not just

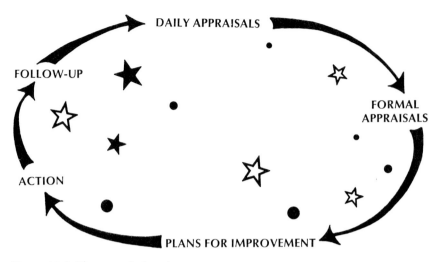

DAILY APPRAISALS

FOLLOW-UP

FORMAL APPRAISALS

ACTION

PLANS FOR IMPROVEMENT

Figure 12-5. The appraisal cycle.

at appraisal time. Figure 12–5 shows this concept as a cycle that is never ending and always repeating itself.

Rewards

Just how much you can do to provide tangible rewards for your people who excel is related to many factors. The extent of your authority, your control over the purse strings through budget requests, your boss's willingness to delegate to you—all these are a few of them. Often all you can do from a dollar-and-cents point of view is to recommend a fixed amount as a raise. A worker who is near or at the top of the wage rate may only be eligible for a token amount. Until a worker gets a promotion to a higher pay grade, he or she will have "peaked out." That may be the incentive for that person to work at an above-average pace to hasten the promotion. Or, if he or she is trapped by being the least senior person, it could mean frustration.

You have many intangible awards you can give each person, however: the pat on the back for a job well done, the frequent appreciation you show each person both in public and in private. Your demonstration of your dependence on each team player goes a long way toward satisfying his or her need for esteem and status. A letter of commendation sent upstairs for the exceptional contributions your people give when they don't have to, passing over the outstanding performer when some occasional dirty jobs come along, and the granting of time off if you have the authority to do so—these things can go a long way toward proving to your people that you are aware of each of them and of the value of their individual efforts. Besides the other things we have discussed, the appraisal process should make you keenly aware of which of your subordinates are carrying the load in your department and just how dependent you really are on them.

The following checklist should help you review the major principles that govern the appraisal process. Refer to it now and when you rate each person.

1. Am I with my people regularly? If not, have I some way of measuring their performance, attitudes, and potential?

2. Do I let them know how they stand with me often? Am I honest when I do so?

3. Do I really know each of my people as individuals? If not, what am I doing about it?

4. Can I detail in writing each of their specific duties? Would my list agree with theirs?

5. Do my appraisals emphasize an individual's performance on the job? Am I using established and approved standards for comparison?

6. Can I back up my opinions with facts? With specific incidents?

7. Have I commented on my subordinates' potentials?

8. Have I planned well to share the results with each person?

9. Have I thought about ways that each can improve his or her rating?

10. Is this rating something I will be proud to put my signature to?

INSTANT REPLAY   Every manager has the responsibility to evaluate subordinates and their contributions on a regular basis. Informally you appraise your subordinates through the normal conduct of your duties. Formally you appraise them in accord with company policy; you must rate each person through an interview either on an annual or semiannual basis. Regardless of the frequency, your evaluations must include judgments on the worker's character, potential, and performance.

If the evaluation process is to be effective, standards for comparison must be established and referred to. If these standards are well known to both the rater and person being rated, little difficulty will be encountered in making and justifying your judgments.

Your duty to rate each employee in your charge cannot be delegated. You are the best qualified individual to make the decisions and observations that constitute each appraisal. The results must be kept confidential.

There are many approaches and methods available to a rater but they all share one common shortcoming: they are subjective and allow the rater to interject or be influenced by personal biases and preferences.

This means that you must be aware of the many pitfalls and errors that you could fall victim to in preparing appraisals so that you can do your best to prevent their occurrence.

The real value in the appraisals lies in sharing them with each person you rate. Plan for the event by setting aside enough time and proper facilities. Review what you have written about each worker, and be ready to defend your opinions. Involve the rated individual in a dialogue to get at his or her observations and objections. Your object should be to reach a mutual understanding and agreement on the contents of the rating. Work with each person to help establish definite goals that will provide improvement in the future. Then follow up to be sure that your subordinates are achieving some measure of success.

Your efforts will be rewarded by strengthening your relationship with each person and watching it improve and develop. You can take pride in your subordinates and their progress, and you will benefit through their greater contributions to the department and their pride in themselves. As old mistakes vanish, new ones may creep in. That is why the appraisal process is a cyclical one—the end of each appraisal interview triggers the resumption of the informal appraisal process.

KEY WORDS

appraisal process	evaluation process	narrative method
checklist method	field-review method	ranking method
critical-incident method	forced-check method	scale method
	halo effect	

QUESTIONS FOR DISCUSSION

1. What is the difference between the formal appraisal process and the informal appraisal process? How are they related?

2. How often are you appraised by your superior? How does he or she share the results with you?

3. What should be the primary purpose of the appraisal of subordinates?

4. How can the appraisal process help a company determine if its hiring practices are adequate?

5. Of what use are previous appraisals of his or her workers to a supervisor? Should they become "permanent" documents?

6. Why is it necessary to rate personal traits of individuals in an appraisal?

7. How can the appraisal of subordinates promote cooperation among them?

8. Why is it important for a supervisor to make the appraisal interview a participative process?

9. Which method of appraising subordinates do you prefer? Why?

CASE PROBLEM

The Facilities Committee

The Facilities Committee had been established four months ago to help plan the move from the Stevens Company's rented offices to its new corporate headquarters building, which was to open in thirty days. The five committee members had been appointed by J. R. Stevens, and they represented all the major departments that would occupy space in the new building. All five were either supervisors or middle-management personnel. Mary McCarthy, the credit department supervisor, had been elected chairperson by the other four members at the committee's first meeting.

The Committee's report and plans for the move were almost ready for a final typing. All that remained for Mary to do was to complete the formal appraisals on each of the members. Mary decided to list the specific contributions made by each member and to rank the members on the basis of how actively each had participated in discussions at the twelve meetings Mary had chaired. The evaluations were not required to be a part of the formal report, but Mr. Stevens had asked Mary for "some feedback on how things went at the meetings."

Mary decided to rate each person through a brief narrative description, noting both their good and bad points through the use of quotes from the minutes of each meeting. Mary had taken the minutes at each meeting and had recorded her personal observations about the members after each meeting. Thus she felt she had more than enough data to do accurate appraisals.

After Mary wrote the appraisals, she attached them to the formal report, labeling them Appendixes A-D. She gave the entire report to the typing pool on Monday for a final typing and instructed the pool supervisor to

deliver copies of the report only to the individuals named on its title page. Mary was the only member of the committee listed to receive a copy.

Mary had no sooner arrived at work on Thursday than she was confronted by an angry committee member, George Aikens, the head of the data control department.

"Where do you get off sending that report to Stevens without committee approval?"

"George, if you had attended our last meeting you would know that the committee approved the report as I submitted it."

"Mary, do you mean to say that all the members approved the total report or the report *minus* the appendixes?"

Mary blushed and sat down at her desk. She began to go through her mail.

"I'm waiting for an answer, Mary. I should warn you that I've already talked to the others, and they were not aware of the fact that we were being evaluated in any way by you or by anyone else. Hell, we nearly all outrank you here. And it seems the whole building knows that I missed a few meetings and was ranked last in participation. For a report that was supposed to be confidential, I would say it is pretty public knowledge. What did you do, post it in the employee lounge?"

Questions

1. How did the confidential report get to be public knowledge?
2. Comment on Mary's method of appraising the committee members.
3. What pitfalls did she fall victim to?
4. If you were one of the committee members, how would you react?

13   Discipline

LEARNING OBJECTIVES

■ After reading and discussing this chapter, you should be able to:

1 Define discipline.
2 Differentiate between positive discipline and negative discipline.
3 Explain the role of punishment in the exercise of discipline.
4 List and briefly explain four principles of discipline.
5 List and briefly explain four common pitfalls that can affect a supervisor's efforts at discipline.
6 Explain what it means to be fair when you discipline your subordinates.
7 Describe why supervisors should know themselves and their subordinates well before they attempt to discipline their subordinates.

INTRODUCTION

■ Nearly everything we have discussed since Chapter 2 relates directly or indirectly to the contents of this chapter. What we shall discuss here must be considered in the light of what has gone before. Discipline is a necessary management duty that is fundamental to building and maintaining your human relationships with your people.

By **discipline** we mean two distinct and related concepts: education and training to foster obedience to reasonable rules and standards; and the dispensing of appropriate punishment for wrongdoing. Both sides are essential, for one without the other would not accomplish the purpose of discipline: to promote reasonable and safe conduct among and between your people so as to protect lives and property and promote individual and group success.

For the purposes of our discussion we shall divide the whole subject of discipline into two approaches: **positive discipline** and **negative discipline.**

POSITIVE DISCIPLINE

■ Successful discipline promotes understanding and self-control. The primary aim of discipline by any manager at any level in the hierarchy should be to inform. You must communicate what is expected of each individual in regard to his or her behavior on the job. This process begins with the arrival and induction of each new employee and continues throughout his or her employment.

The subject of your communications should be the limits placed upon each individual by company policies and regulations, departmental rules and procedures, the person's job description, and the union contract if one exists. By communicating in advance of an infraction the expectations you have of each worker and the limitations under which he or she has to work, you have forewarned your subordinate about the type of conduct you want him or her to exhibit while on the job.

Each person is evaluated at work by certain standards and norms. Most situations involving the need for discipline center around a failure to communicate these standards adequately. The need for punishment arises because of an individual's failure to meet one or more of the standards set up to govern his or her performance and conduct.

Figure 13–1 points out the visible boundaries on a worker's conduct. If employees stay within these borders they risk nothing, but if they

Figure 13-1. Boundaries placed on human conduct at work.

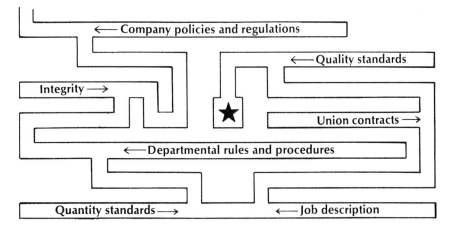

step outside them, they can expect punishment. Once established, these borders must be maintained through adequate enforcement and a judicious application of fair punishments.

When employees know their jobs and the standards they must meet, they gain security. They are aware of the degree of freedom allowed and have definitive limits over which they know they must not step. If they cross one or another of these limits, they must be certain that a punishment will follow the violation.

Positive discipline can be illustrated by a police officer traveling in the flow of traffic in a well-marked, easily identifiable police car. He or she is visible to other motorists, serves as a reminder to obey traffic regulations, and represents a warning that violators will be apprehended and given a penalty. There is nothing sneaky or subterranean about his or her behavior, and the officer's main purpose is to prevent violations from occurring. Now contrast this comparison with that of an unmarked squad car parked out of sight of passing motorists. In this case there is a deemphasis on prevention and an emphasis on detection and punishment.

Don't leave your people guessing about the limits imposed on them or about their chances of getting caught in wrongdoing and being punished. Be visible and obvious, and let them have no doubts about your intentions and your punitive powers. You are not trying to trap anyone. Rather you are serving to inform them by your actions and words that you wish to promote reasonable behavior and prevent any unacceptable conduct.

People resent rules when they consider them unnecessary or unfair. It is often not enough to give them prohibitions. We all need to know why we cannot do certain things. For example, if we cannot smoke in Department A, explain why we can't. If your subordinates are not to use company tools at home on a loan basis, tell them why not. Resentment follows a lack of understanding or misunderstanding of the need for rules or regulations. Be sure your people have adequate explanations so that their obedience will be based on logic. This procedure should provide an incentive to cooperate.

NEGATIVE DISCIPLINE

■ Negative discipline places an emphasis on the detection of wrongdoing and punishment. It usually becomes bureaucratic and impersonal, and relies heavily on records, rules, and procedures. It is characterized by a lack of trust in subordinates, demands for blind obedience and willful disobedience of rules and regulations on the part of the employees. Many employees play a game with their supervisors when they work in such an environment. They become covert and

1 Reprimanding should be done in private whenever possible.

2 Disciplinary action should be looked upon as *corrective* in initial stages and *punitive* when training and counseling have little or no effect.

3 Good discipline is more effectively maintained if the manager has a written set of guidelines to follow.

4 Make certain you have all the facts before taking disciplinary action. Reversal of a penalty is detrimental to morale and lowers respect of employees for management.

5 Sarcasm should be avoided when dealing with employees.

6 Don't threaten, argue, or show anger.

7 Suit reprimands to the individual and situation.

8 Discipline promptly.

9 Criticize the behavior, not the employee.

10 Suit the severity of the discipline to the seriousness of the offense.

11 Disciplinary action requires follow-up.

12 It is important for the manager to reestablish friendly contact with an employee soon after disciplinary action is taken.

13 An employee should be told when he is doing poorly on the job.

14 The immediate supervisor should be involved with any disciplinary action involving a subordinate.

15 An employee who is a chronic disciplinary problem is not likely to improve simply through a transfer.

16 Managers must take disciplinary action on continued infractions of rules even though the infractions are minor. Laxity breeds laxity.

17 Remember that the primary function of disciplinary action is to prevent recurrence.

Figure 13-2. Guidelines for improving the disciplinary process.

Reproduced by permission from *Personnel Management* by Elmer H. Burack and Robert D. Smith. Copyright © 1977, West Publishing Company. All rights reserved.

sneaky in their behavior. They deliberately plot to break rules to see if they can "beat the system" and get away with it or to keep the management off balance and irritated. They do so because they resent the approach to discipline taken by their employer and supervisors, and take delight in frustrating their efforts. They have not developed the attitudes that support a willing compliance with and obedience to their organization's rules.

A climate in which negative discipline thrives should be examined and restructured to promote willful obedience and positive discipline. Individual counseling is absolutely essential in order to turn the situation around. Human relationships need development, nourishment, and maintenance. Supervisors must initiate and play properly their roles in human relations. Rewards and merit awards should be established for the good performers. The disciplinary system must become more professional and worthy of the respect and confidence of your employees. Figure 13–2 lists seventeen solid guidelines for improving the disciplinary process. Take a few moments to study its suggestions, and see if any of them are needed where you work.

THE SUPERVISOR AND DISCIPLINE

■ You are forced by the nature of your position to make judgments about your people and their conduct. When you become aware of an infraction or improper behavior, you are expected to act. You are the chief enforcement officer where workers are concerned and cannot escape that duty. You must get the facts—all the facts that relate to the offense. Then you are asked to be both judge and jury—determining the degree of guilt and deciding upon an appropriate penalty to fit the wrongdoing.

Knowing yourself and your people well will prevent a great deal of trouble for you in your role of disciplinarian. Practicing sound human relations and demonstrating proven leadership principles and traits to your subordinates should minimize your need for punitive actions. Only a small fraction of your people will cause you any difficulty— usually those we have discussed who have character disorders or lack maturity. And even with these few, many of the infractions they commit are not a reflection on you or your leadership. Often an individual is affected by outside influences or people like family members and friends that distract him or her from the duties of the job and lead him or her into trouble. An employee's mind may be on his or her child or on a financial problem that may cause him or her to act without proper precautions or in an emotional way—the way we all sometimes do. This is why knowledge about each person you supervise is so essential. You can assess a subordinate's intention from past records and thus determine whether or not the misconduct is deliberate or accidental. As was the case with the assessment of attitudes, you must often look beneath an action to discover its real cause.

Most individuals who repeat offenses do so because of immaturity or personality defects. These people may need a firm hand and successively more severe penalties if they do not respond to your counseling efforts. But you should be certain that you are not adding to their difficulties by being a problem supervisor.

If your workers like their jobs and respect you as their supervisor, they have the best reasons for avoiding the need for punitive action on your part. Such workers are not bent on disruption but on construction. Workers who appreciate that your concern is for their welfare will not let you down intentionally.

PUNISHMENT

■ An important aspect of discipline has to do with the punishment of wrongdoers. Sometimes, as with controls, prevention devices and actions may fail, and then the need for prompt and fair action takes over. Your power to take action in dealing with infractions is probably limited. Typically, most supervisors can:

1. Give an oral warning;
2. Issue a written reprimand;
3. Suspend a person from the job without pay.

Whether you have the powers mentioned above or not is largely a matter determined by your job description, your company's policies, and the union contract's stand on this issue, if your company has a union. Often the union contract will have much to say about your powers to discipline and management's powers in this area. Be certain that you know the limits placed upon your disciplinary powers and that you stay within those limits.

The decision to fire a person usually rests with the person or persons who have the authority to hire. In most disciplinary cases this is the course of last resort and should only be followed when *all* else has failed. There are some situations, however, that usually demand that the guilty party receive an immediate dismissal. These are:

1. Gross insubordination such as refusal to obey a direct, lawful order;
2. Drunkenness on the job;
3. Willful destruction of company property;
4. Dishonesty or theft.

Certainly there will be exceptions to these situations, and whatever circumstances surround each of these exceptional cases must be considered. It is nevertheless true that a large majority of companies require that the penalty for these infractions be automatic dismissal.

PRINCIPLES OF DISCIPLINE

■ Just what action you take when your subordinates violate rules and regulations should be governed by the following principles:

1. Know each subordinate, his or her record, and the nature and causes of the offense;

2. Know your powers as laid down in your job description; when in doubt, check with your boss and your peers;

3. Check on the precedents, if any, that governed similar situations in the past;

4. Be consistent—if you have given an oral warning on the first minor offense, as a general rule do so in every like case;

5. Consider the circumstances surrounding the misconduct. Was it willful or accidental? Was the person aware of the limits placed upon his conduct? Is this his or her first offense?

6. If a subordinate has made the same mistake more than once, make the punishment progressively more severe. Generally you progress from an oral warning to a written reprimand and eventually to a suspension. But try to find out the causes of the violation;

7. Be certain that you have the facts to prove your action is warranted. Have you gotten the offender's point of view? Do you have witnesses?

8. Be reasonable and fair.

Whatever action you decide upon as appropriate, be sure that you inform the guilty party and the union if such an action is required by the union's contract. You don't need permission from the union or your steward to discipline, but it is wise to let them know your decision. Don't ask the steward for advice. If the union is dissatisfied with your decision, its leaders will file a grievance.

Keep in mind that you are not the final voice in matters of discipline. Your company and the union may have provisions providing for review of your decision, as matters of discipline are considered too important to entrust to any one manager's decision. Chapter 14 will have much more to say on this matter. If you are wrong, you will be overruled. If not, you should be able to count on your boss for backing. Your subordinates will hear about your disciplinary decisions too. Don't jeopardize your relations with them by hasty or irrational actions. You could damage your relationships with each worker and his or her group if you are unfair. Just be sure that you have the facts and that you have put them together properly.

Consider the case of a supervisor named John who has given an oral order to a subordinate, Harry. Harry has failed to respond. Orders are intended to provoke an immediate positive response, and usually do if they are not overutilized, so John immediately assumes that Harry is being insubordinate. Without any further investigation John suspends Harry for one week while he and the company decide whether to fire Harry or not. But wait a moment. Aren't there several legitimate reasons why Harry could not have followed the supervisor's order? Here are but a few:

1. Harry didn't hear the order;
2. Harry has been told to do something illegal;
3. Harry has been told to perform a task outside of his job description or beyond his capabilities or training;
4. John was unclear in his order, and Harry didn't understand it.

All of these and more could get Harry off the hook. If John goes solely upon his observations without any further investigation, he is likely to make an improper decision and be reversed. Harry could be back at work with pay for his time off. John will have damaged his reputation and alienated Harry, among others. It pays to get the other employee's point of view.

An associate during my high-school teaching days told me about his method for handling cheating in his classroom. He began each new term by defining his policy on cheating as follows. Anyone caught cheating on an exam, project, or quiz would receive a failing grade for it, and his or her parents would be notified to this effect. If a student was caught cheating twice in the same course, he or she would receive a failing grade for the course, and his or her parents would again be notified. For most students, such a warning in such clear terms would be sufficient. However, it seems that there are always a few who either don't believe you or who feel cheating is worth the risk.

When my friend caught a student cheating, he would simply take up the student's paper and ask him or her to see him after class. Before he picked up a paper, however, the teacher was certain in his own mind that cheating had occurred. When they met after class, the teacher told the student what he had witnessed and asked the student to verify his observations. If the student would not admit the offense, the teacher was prepared to let him or her complete the exam. In point of fact, however, my friend was never confronted with this situation. In every case during the five years the teacher used this system, the student readily admitted his or her wrongdoing. In no case did that student, once caught, do it again.

This method is simple and direct. The teacher practiced it without exception. At no time during five years did this teacher have two students who were caught cheating in the same class. The word got around that this teacher meant what he said, and the students respected him for it. The honest students felt secure that their hard work and study would pay off and not be jeopardized by the cheating of their dishonest fellow students. The grades in this teacher's class reflected each student's ability and not someone else's. Not once did parents complain about this system. In fact, some of them expressed their complete agreement with it and indicated that they were more involved with their children as a result. Eventually, this teacher's methods were adopted by the school as policy.

One lesson from this story is that you must start out firmly with your people. You cannot afford to be too lenient or permissive. Don't look the other way when you witness an improper situation, but don't go looking for trouble either. You certainly don't want to be accused of spying or setting traps for your people. That is totally improper. Get your subordinate to admit his or her mistake and to accept the punishment. If you get yourself into a swearing match (where it is his or her word against yours), you have a poor case indeed. Get a witness or at the very least an admission of guilt upon which to build your case. And remember, criticize the action—not your subordinate as a person.

When you punish, you must look at the person and the circumstances. This does not mean that you do so in order to exercise prejudice or "get even." If you are vindictive or carry a grudge, you are bound to attack people personally. They will know it, even if you won't admit it. You will be basing your actions on a personal dislike for people and not on their actions. As in making appraisals, you have to be as objective as you can in order to prevent criticism of your motives or intent. Don't open yourself up to base complaints. Your job and your reputation are too valuable to risk on immature behavior.

Don't be the cause of your subordinates' mistakes either. Set the example and let them know you mean what you say. Give them the security that comes with knowing what they must do and why.

A man who audited stores for a large retail chain for over thirty years once told me that where he uncovered dishonest employees, there was usually a dishonest manager who seemed to encourage them. This type of manager, he said, on the way out of the store each day would help himself or herself to a handful of peanuts or candy. At other times such a manager might be too lenient in the enforcement of rules or regulations or deal weakly with dishonest employees. Honest employees began to resent the "extras" enjoyed by their peers and decided to get into the action too. It may start with a pen or pencil, but it may not end until the "take" reaches some pretty high figures.

Being fair means many things, but the most important part of it involves basing your decisions on the circumstances. What would be an appropriate punishment for one party to an infraction of the rules may not be so for another. For example, assume you find two of your people in a shoving match; before you can break it up, one of them hits the other. Both people are guilty of fighting, but can you think of reasons why justice might dictate coming down harder on one than on the other? I'm certain you can, if you remember to consider the circumstances and the motives beneath the action you observed. Someone started the fight. Shouldn't that person be dealt with more severely than the person who was provoked? What if one of the people had done this before while the other had a clean record? Wouldn't these facts influence your decision?

Being fair doesn't mean treating everyone the same. You are not a machine that operates automatically or in the same manner, no matter who drops in the coin. When we talk about precedents, we mean treating like offenses in a like manner. But the key word is *like*. Be careful that what you are dealing with and the people you are dealing with are sufficiently similar to warrant concern for precedents. An old-timer who should and does know better should not be treated in the same fashion as you would treat a new employee. One has learned while the other is learning. One has more responsibility to set a good example than the other.

PITFALLS

■ We shall now discuss the major problems you may encounter when you attempt to carry out your duties in the area of discipline. As was the case with the pitfalls we discussed in the last chapter, they can be eliminated or at least minimized if you are aware of each of them and consciously try to prevent them from interfering with your efforts.

Starting Off Soft

Supervisors, especially those who are new at the job, are apt to relate being lenient with being liked. They sometimes feel that if they look the other way on occasion or mete out less than a deserved penalty for an infraction, they will endear themselves to their subordinates. Nothing could be further from the truth. In actuality, their leniency will be the cause of more trouble. If Mary arrives late and you say nothing, she will be encouraged to do it again. So will the others who witness the event and your failure to take constructive action.

We have stated before in this book that when you take office, your people will adopt a "wait and see" attitude toward you. They can be expected to test you on numerous occasions and in numerous ways. Each of them wants to know if you mean what you say. They need to know the limits and where the hard-and-fast boundaries lie. They want to know specifically what to expect if they commit a violation. If you talk one kind of game and play another, or if you promise punishment and don't deliver, you will affect your relationships adversely for months to come.

It is always easier to start out tough with an emphasis on the letter of the law. As you gain self-confidence and additional knowledge about your duties and your people, you can shift the emphasis to the spirit of the law as well, tempering your judgment within the framework of your understanding of your people, their personalities, and the group pressures at work on them. This is what is meant by justice. Each person and most events are unique and should be dealt with as such.

If you are soft, those that "toe the line" will resent you for it. They will see no tangible reward for proper behavior while they witness some for improper conduct. Your softness will be interpreted as weakness, and you can expect many more "fishing expeditions" on their part to find the limits.

Incomplete Research and Analysis

Let us assume that you see a man stretched out on a packing crate thirty feet away and, because he has his eyes shut, you jump to the conclusion that he is sleeping on the job or, at the very least, goofing off. You should know by now from your past experience and from this book that appearances are not always what they seem. It takes more than one observation to make a sound case where discipline is involved. Unless you go to the man, preferably with a witness you can count on, and ask him some questions, you can't really be sure that your observations are, in fact, correct.

If you intend to punish someone, be certain that you have a firm case that will stand up to a review by higher authority. Have the details clearly in mind and make some notes on your observations for later reference. The mind loses certainty and eliminates details with the passage of time between a disciplinary action and the appeal of that action. Answer such questions as who was there and what was said by each. If all you have is a swearing match, you'll lose the case, especially where a union is involved.

Acting in Anger

How many times have you wished you could take back remarks made to another in anger? If you are like most people, the answer is "too often." With emotions influencing your observations and judgment, you will seldom make a sound decision. Too often you will have to back down and apologize for a demonstration of your lack of self-control.

Count to ten or to one hundred if necessary, but cool down before you decide anything. It helps to move away physically from the situation and the environment of a wrongdoing in order to regain your composure. Tell the individual you have caught in a violation to report to you in your office in a few minutes. This will give you both time to recapture your sense of balance.

Disciplining in Public

The only thing you should do with your people in public is to praise them. If you have some critical remarks for an individual, pass them along in person and in private. Each person has a reputation to uphold both with you and with his or her peers. He or she has pride and self-esteem which need protection. He or she does not wish to be subjected to ridicule or embarrassment. It's not punishment your people may fear; it's your way of dispensing it. Your methods may make the difference between a constructive and a destructive kind of discipline.

Exceeding Your Authority

Keep in mind that, like your people, you too have limits on your power and conduct. To paraphrase an oil company slogan, you have "power to be used, not abused." Check with your boss and your peers when you are in doubt about what course of action to take. There is really no legitimate excuse for falling into this trap. There are too many ways open to you that can prevent it.

Being Vindictive

The best defense one of your subordinates can have in a disciplinary case is that you are picking on him or her or making a personal attack. Be sure that the reasons behind your action and words are not based on personality clashes or personal prejudice. Put your biases aside, or they will shine through with a neon brilliance for all to see. If you single one person out for disciplinary action, and your methods rest in your personal biases, you will certainly lose your case and face the wrath of those who must review your actions.

Like your subordinates, you have likes and dislikes. It would not be reasonable to expect you to like all your people. But you are being paid to serve all of them regardless of their personal feelings toward you or yours toward them. Unless a subordinate's personality is defective and interferes with his or her performance, you cannot in conscience hold it against that individual. You are not out to win your subordinates over as friends or to socialize with them. Sure, it is tough to be fair to those whom we dislike. But if we are to be of service to our company and ourselves, we must make every effort to do so.

Leaving It to Others

Like appraising your people, disciplining them is your exclusive right and duty. You cannot be asked to part with it if you are expected to control and properly direct your workers. Some companies allow the personnel department or some other outside authority to mete out discipline. This reduces the supervisor's role to that of an arresting officer. Your subordinates will soon realize that you cannot punish, only report violations. Your status will be greatly reduced. This represents a tremendous handicap to a supervisor. While some managers prefer this arrangement because it releases them from a difficult responsibility, they fail to see that the giving up of this power makes them impotent and subjects them to additional and needless harrassment from above and below.

What would be even worse than losing disciplinary powers to a higher authority is the giving away of them to a top worker or straw boss. Knowing how difficult it is to discipline properly, how much more likely do you think it is that such people might make a mess of it? Remember, these people are extensions of yourself and, as such, represent you to your other subordinates. Don't give them the power to cause you and themselves trouble. You and only you are responsible for your people and their actions. If your top worker or straw boss made the wrong decisions, you would have to correct them, thus hurting their already difficult position, possibly beyond repair. Most straw bosses don't want such authority, but if they try to assume it, make it clear that they cannot have it.

Failure to Keep Adequate Records

In order to gain and keep a perspective on each of your people, you should keep records on each of them as to their performance appraisals, reprimands, peculiarities, and needs. These files will prove quite helpful when you face tough personnel decisions. Also, they come in very handy when you want to justify your opinions or take specific disciplinary actions.

INSTANT REPLAY

We have examined in some detail the necessary and demanding job of discipline. Keep in mind that there are two sides to discipline: the need to train and educate for obedience, and the need to punish wrongdoers. Both are essential, and neither can stand alone.

The number one goal of all managers is to communicate to their people the precise limits or boundaries that surround their behavior and performance. Beginning with the induction of a new employee, the boss must define the newcomer's responsibilities and outline the expectations placed upon him or her. The emphasis should be on prevention of trouble and the nurturing of mutual respect, integrity, and self-control.

The need for punishment is apparent to all, as we know what the world would be like without it. People don't resent punishment, but they often resent the methods used to mete it out. If a punishment is deserved and the worker was forewarned, he or she knows he or she has no complaint.

The majority of your subordinates need little or no disciplinary action. They will probably like you and their work well enough to concentrate on getting ahead. There are always a few, however, who won't take you at your word and will probe to see if you really mean what you say. Don't let them down. These people often are the problem workers we discussed in Chapter 6. If you have any subordinates of the types we discussed there, you are certain to have a need for punitive measures at times.

In the final analysis, discipline is either easy or hard, depending upon how well you have built your relationships with your people and how sincere you are in fulfilling your responsibilities toward them. If they doubt your sincerity, you will have trouble. By being fair and treating each situation on its merits, you can and will find that the need for punishment diminishes while the degree of cooperation increases.

By practicing the principles of constructive discipline and being aware of the problems discussed in this chapter, you can head off the major difficulties others encounter and lessen the need to take punitive action.

QUESTIONS FOR DISCUSSION

1. What are the two distinct and related concepts related to discipline?
2. Why are both parts of the definition of discipline essential to a supervisor?
3. What does it mean to say that discipline should be fair?
4. What are some outside pressures that may have gotten you into trouble at work or in school? How did they cause you to get into trouble?
5. Explain briefly how this chapter is related to the chapter on attitudes (Chapter 6). How is it related to the chapter on motivation (Chapter 7)?
6. Describe your boss's methods for dealing with wrongdoers.
7. Why are the circumstances surrounding an act of misconduct important to a supervisor?
8. How do you feel about getting a subordinate to admit wrongdoing before taking punitive action against him or her?
9. Is it a good idea to request a shop steward or some union official to recommend the proper punishment before you discipline one of your subordinates? Why?
10. Why is disciplining subordinates considered a task that should not be delegated?

CASE PROBLEM

Lucid Lennie

Lennie Dawson swung around in his swivel chair to greet Shirley Masters and Ruby Blake.

"Sit down, Shirley and Ruby. Now what has gotten into you two lately? Shirley, you have been with us two months, and I don't have any record of trouble with you before this morning. How come all of a sudden you get yourself in trouble?"

"I haven't been myself lately, Mr. Dawson. My husband and I are having difficulties. My mind can't seem to concentrate on anything else."

"And what's your excuse, Ruby?" asked Lennie.

"Shirley has been getting on my nerves lately. She's become unbearable. We work side by side, and all day long she mutters and mumbles to herself under her breath. I ask her a simple question and she won't answer.

I can't take it anymore. You have to separate us."

"Look here, you two, I've got a department to run and have no time for petty squabbles. Ruby, you can't get along with anyone so far as I can see. Two months ago it was Hazel Dumbrowski, and before that you picked a fight with Liz Turner."

"Mr. Dawson, you know I tried to get on with them. I really did. It's not my fault that they were jealous of my bonus checks and higher salary. They just resented the fact that I earned more than they did."

Lennie was getting upset and beginning to show it.

"That's ancient history. What I want to know, Ruby, is did you or did you not throw Shirley's purse at her?"

"Yes, but...."

"That's all I need to know. Take three days off without pay, starting

Discipline / 221

now. The next time you goof off, I'm going to make it a week. I. . . ."

"Mr. Dawson," Shirley interrupted, "it was really my fault. I started it by telling Ruby to shut her face, and when she didn't, I pushed her work off her desk. That's when she threw my purse."

"Shirley, it is noble of you to try to get Ruby off the hook. But she has had too many of these incidents before. Her file has several warnings for similar occurrences. She needs time off to cool off. Now, since this is your first offense, Shirley, I am going to give you a written reprimand which will go into your personnel file downstairs. If you get involved with Ruby like this again, you will join her with a week at home."

Ruby then turned to Lennie and asked, "Are you going to separate us?"

"No. You two have got to learn to get along."

The two women left the office together.

"Ruby, why didn't you tell him I started the whole thing?"

"Listen, Shirley, you're new here. Once that guy gets something on you, he never forgets it. He had already made up his mind that I was at fault. There's no use arguing. I'll see the shop steward and file a grievance. Don't worry! I'll get three days off with pay."

Questions

1. Evaluate Lennie's efforts at getting the facts.
2. Was Lennie correct in mentioning Ruby's previous difficulties in getting along with her coworkers? Why?
3. Why do you suppose Lennie did not believe that Shirley had started the incident?
4. What facts did Lennie uncover but fail to develop?
5. Do you think Ruby will win her grievance? Why?

14 Gripes, Grievances, and Unions

LEARNING OBJECTIVES

■ After reading and discussing this chapter, you should be able to:

1 Define what a union is.

2 Define what a grievance is.

3 Differentiate between a gripe and a grievance.

4 List three prohibitions of the Wagner Act.

5 List three prohibitions of the Taft-Hartley Act.

6 Explain what is meant by the phrase *collective bargaining.*

7 List and briefly describe the basic steps in handling grievances.

8 List two basic reasons why workers join unions.

9 Compare the roles of supervisors and stewards in labor relations.

10 Differentiate between arbitration and mediation.

INTRODUCTION

■ This chapter discusses the proper ways of dealing with the complaints of employees. First, we take up how to handle complaints you might encounter in a company where there is no union. Next, we discuss briefly what unions are, and why workers join them. Finally, we learn how complaints are handled in a company where there is a union contract.

GRIPES

■ For our purposes a **gripe** is defined as any complaint about working conditions or on-the-job relationships that comes to a manager's attention.

Complaints involve (1) objects that can be seen and touched (the switch is broken, or the machine needs adjustment); (2) sensory experiences other than touch and sight (the ventilation is poor in here, or the office is too noisy); or (3) nonsensory situations (my pay is too low, or they don't reward experience around here). The first of these complaints is easily dealt with by personal observations and inspection. It is either true or not true and offers little difficulty in resolution. The other two types of gripes are different, however, as they are quite difficult to pin down and verify.

Complaints are often symptoms of a much different problem than the one they seem to state. The worker may be complaining about his or her level of pay or job classification, but the real issue may be dissatisfaction with the job. In the worker's mind he or she may feel that more pay or a higher job classification will make the job more bearable. Therefore, even after a careful explanation about why a certain level of pay goes with the labor grade, the worker will remain dissatisfied because the real problem has not yet been dealt with.

Often complaints are imaginary. Take the case of an old, high-ceilinged plant structure that had been recently air-conditioned. Both before and after this renovation the workers complained about feeling too hot and working in a stuffy atmosphere. The air-conditioning ducts had been mounted nearly twenty feet above the plant floor so that the individuals in the area could not feel any cool air circulating. In fact, many of them accused management of not turning the system on. They were convinced that it was not functioning.

Management's answer was to install thermometers on the plant pillars and to tie colored streamers to the air outlets. The workers could now see for themselves that the temperature was proper and the air was in fact circulating. Their complaints stopped immediately. Seeing was believing.

HANDLING GRIPES ■ Since we are talking at this point about how to resolve the complaints of workers in a nonunion setting where, as a rule, no clear-cut procedures for dealing with such problems exist, we shall examine a recommended procedure.

To begin with, your attitude toward the gripes of your workers should be to treat them seriously. Your subordinates think that their complaints have merit or they wouldn't bring them to your attention. Often you may overhear a complaint of your workers. Their actions as well as their words will provide you with clues about their true feelings. Watch for any sudden changes in established patterns of behavior. If complaints are not dealt with as soon as they are discovered, they can soon spread to other workers and begin to interfere with your department's cooperation, production, and morale.

An open-door policy is the best way to prevent trouble from getting out of hand. If your people feel that you care about them, and if they have confidence in your judgment, you will find them willing to air their irritations and observations. This can only come about, however, after you have established sound human relations with them as individuals and a group. So don't be discouraged if you only hear about gripes through the grapevine. It takes time to develop proper attitudes and relationships. If you find that your people don't come to you, it simply means that you have some more work ahead of you. Find out why, and then go to work on the problems.

The six-step procedure that follows is a proven one, and in the absence of a prescribed company procedure, you should find it quite helpful:

1. *Listening.* When your subordinates bring you a gripe, give them your undivided attention. If it is an awkward time for you, set up an appointment with them in the near future when you will be free of distractions. If a group of your subordinates seems to share a common complaint, use the problem-solving meeting we discussed in Chapter 10. Remember that quite often all people want is to talk with someone about their problems. By talking, they are expressing confidence in you and showing respect for your opinion. Often the workers know that the solution to their difficulty is beyond both their control and yours. In discussing such a situation, we often find a clarity and perspective that it is almost impossible to discover alone. The workers may come to realize that the problem is really not so serious as they originally thought, or they may actually discover a solution as they attempt to explain their views.

By listening attentively and drawing people out, you may find that what began as the major complaint gradually slips away as the real and underlying issue comes to the surface. When that happens, you will have hit pay dirt. It may be the first time that the workers were able to express what was really on their minds. Gradually all the facts will emerge in your subordinates' words, and the problem will come into focus. Then and only then can it be intelligently resolved.

2. *Remaining calm.* Even if the workers are agitated and emotional, you cannot afford to be. If you are, the meeting may degenerate into a shouting match, and the workers will leave more upset than before. The complaint may slip underground where it will fester. The workers will stop talking about it to you but not to their peers. What started out as a small problem of an individual may soon become a big problem for your subordinates as a group.

3. *Getting the complainers' solutions.* Once your subordinates have talked themselves out, and you feel that you know the real issues, ask

them for their solutions. What would they do if they were in your shoes? What do they think would be a fair disposition of their complaint? What you want to know is what they think will make them happy. If it is within your power to grant such a solution, and if you believe it to be a wise one, then do so. If you need more information or wish to check out their side of the story, defer your answer and give them a specific time for receiving it.

4. *Explaining your decision.* Whether you can give your subordinates a decision that they think is just or not, you should give them the why behind it. If company policy is involved, let them know which one, and how it was interpreted. The same goes for rules and regulations. They may not receive the answer they were hoping for, but they will know that you went to bat for them and did your homework. You "did something" about their problems, and they can't help but respect you for it.

5. *Explaining how to appeal.* If your workers are dissatisfied with your decision and want to pursue the matter further, tell them how to do so. Let them know whom they should see and how they can make an appointment. If your workers decide to appeal your decision, you should not hold that action against them, and you should let them know that you don't.

6. *Following up.* Regardless of the outcome, it is sound management practice to get back to the people who have made a complaint within a reasonable time after its resolution. Assess their present attitudes, and make it clear that you want your people to come to you with their gripes. Be sure that you keep a record of the proceedings for future reference.

By being sincere, listening attentively, asking exploratory questions, and acting on each complaint promptly, you will minimize conflicts and reduce barriers to productivity and cooperation.

LABOR UNIONS

■ So far in this chapter we have discussed gripes and grievances in companies where there is no union. Let us now shift to companies that are unionized. Before we consider what happens in a company with a union contract, however, we need to take a brief look at unions in the United States.

A **labor union** consists of a group of workers employed by a company or an industry or practicing the same skilled craft who have banded together to bargain collectively with employers for improvements in their wages, hours, fringe benefits, and working conditions. Craft or trade unions are made up of workers in the same skilled occupation. For example, the International Brotherhood of Electrical Workers

Unions	1964	1974	1976
	Membership (in thousands)		
Teamsters*	1,507	1,973	1,889
Automobile workers*	1,168	1,545	1,358
Steelworkers	1,250	1,300	1,300
Electrical (IBEW)	806	943	924
Machinists	808	943	917
Carpenters	760	820	820
Retail clerks (RCIA)	428	651	699
Laborers (IUNA)	432	650	627
State, county (AFSCME)	235	648	650
Service employees (SEIU)	320	550	558

*Indicates independent unions. Others are affiliated with the AFL-CIO.

Table 14-1. America's ten largest unions and their membership.
Source: *Statistical Abstract of the U.S., 1977,* and U.S. Department of Labor.

(IBEW) and the International Brotherhood of Teamsters, Chauffeurs, Warehousemen and Helpers of America (usually called the Teamsters) are unions organized to represent skilled craftsmen and tradesmen. Industrial unions include all workers in a company or an industry, regardless of their specific occupations. The United Auto Workers (UAW) and the American Postal Workers Union are examples of industrial unions. Table 14–1 shows the ten largest craft and industrial unions based on their 1976 membership; also shown are membership figures for 1964 and 1974.

Union Membership: The Figures

According to the Bureau of Labor Statistics, 19.4 million Americans held membership cards in 177 national and international unions at the beginning of 1977. A union is considered international if it has members outside the fifty states. In 1976, American international unions had 1.5 million members working outside the United States, most of them in Canada and Puerto Rico. Of the 19.4 million union members, about 79 percent belong to 111 international and national unions directly affiliated with the AFL-CIO (American Federation of Labor and Congress of Industrial Organizations).

Union Trends

Union membership is declining in the United States both in actual numbers and as a percentage of the work force. More than 760,000 people left the ranks of organized labor between 1974 and 1976. The percentage of unionized employees in nonagricultural areas dropped from 34 percent in 1955 to about 24 percent in 1977.

In 1977 women were nearly 41 percent of the total civilian labor force in the United States, but were only 21 percent of the total union members. In that year there were 4.1 million women in labor unions out of a total of about 37.4 million working women.

LABOR LEGISLATION

■ From colonial days until the 1930s, unions and employee associations were prosecuted and banned by the courts as illegal conspiracies in restraint of trade. Courts uniformly held, in case after case, that these groups of employees wrongfully interfered with the right of employers to run their businesses as they saw fit. Nearly every employee was hired during this period on the condition that he or she would not join a union or engage in union activities. A worker who did was considered to have breached the contract of employment and was subject to immediate dismissal.

In the 1890s an additional burden was placed on unions by their inclusion under the provisions of the Sherman Antitrust Act (1890) and related antimonopoly legislation. Courts took the position that unions might be considered monopolistic, and their efforts at collective bargaining were viewed as attempts to interfere with a free market mechanism. This was the first instance in U.S. history that any federal law dealt with the rights of workers to bargain collectively with their employers. Actually the Sherman Act did not specifically state that unions were monopolistic, but its wording was so general that unions could be—and were—considered to fall under its provisions. However, in 1914, the Clayton Act removed unions from the jurisdiction of the antitrust laws.

Norris-LaGuardia Act (1932)

Further relief came in 1932 with the enactment of the Norris-LaGuardia Act, which severely restricted the use of court orders (**injunctions**) against organized labor engaged in labor disputes with employees. It also outlawed the use of **"yellow dog" contracts** by which employees were forced to agree not to join a union. There were no laws, however, that required an employer to recognize an employees' union or that prevented an employer from starting a company union. Employers began to require that new employees join the company union, which was controlled by the management and operated for its benefit. The union leaders achieved for their members only those benefits that management wanted them to.

The Norris-LaGuardia Act did not attack the practice of blacklisting nor did it forbid the discharge of employees for union activities. Companies were still in control; and by locking their employees out of their shops **(lockout),** they could outlast, in most cases, the workers' enthusiasm for unionization. Since many workers lived on only subsistence wages, they could not survive for very long.

National Labor Relations Act (1935)

As the Great Depression dragged on, Congress began to analyze the causes for it and soon realized that the mass impoverishment of so many workers had been a significant factor. To achieve a balance of power between labor and management, the National Labor Relations Act (often called the Wagner Act) was passed as one of the measures of the New Deal. It has often been referred to as organized labor's *Magna Carta,* because it guaranteed the rights of unions to exist free from prosecution. It gave the individual worker the right to join without fear of persecution by his or her employer. In the words of Section 7 of the Act:

> employees shall have the right to self-organization, to form, join or assist labor organizations, to bargain collectively through representatives of their own choosing, and to engage in concerted activities for the purpose of collective bargaining or other mutual aid or protection.

The Wagner Act also listed five unfair labor practices and prohibited these management activities. Employers could not:

1. Restrain employees from joining a union;
2. Contribute financially to or interfere in any way with union operations;
3. Discriminate in any way against a worker because of his or her union affiliation;
4. Punish union members who reported management violations of the Act;
5. Refuse to bargain in good faith with a duly elected union of their employees.

Prohibition numbers 2 and 3 are most significant to supervisors. These provisions have been interpreted as forbidding management from making threats or promises of financial gain to employees who are considering union affiliation or are about to engage in an election to determine a bargaining agent.

The Wagner Act also established the National Labor Relations Board (NLRB), consisting of five members appointed by the President of the

United States and empowered to investigate any alleged violations of the Act and to oversee elections to determine a bargaining unit. Its decisions have the power of law and bind both unions and employers. The Wagner Act was challenged in the courts, but it was declared constitutional by the Supreme Court. It was so prolabor, however, that it eventually had to be amended to curb some of the labor excesses it helped to create.

Labor-Management Relations Act (1947)

During the years between the passage of the Wagner Act and the end of World War II, the country witnessed a phenomenal growth in union membership and also in abuses of union power. Organized labor grew from about 4 million members in 1935 to over 15 million by 1947. Unions were becoming a powerful force and exercising sizable financial and economic power which was almost totally unchecked. Postwar strikes threatened the economy. While management's hands had been tied, organized labor's hands were not.

Congress again felt compelled to balance the two forces. Despite the protests of labor and a veto of the bill by President Truman, it passed the Labor-Management Relations Act, usually called the Taft-Hartley Act. The Act was intended to take away much of the power that organized labor had gained in the 1930s. It amended the Wagner Act to include a list of provisions against specific unfair practices on the part of the unions:

1. Workers could not be coerced to join or not join a union;
2. The closed shop was prohibited;
3. Unions were required to bargain in good faith;
4. Complex restrictions were placed on certain kinds of illegal strikes and boycotts. The **secondary boycott,** by which the union forces an employer to stop dealing with or purchasing from another company not directly involved in a labor dispute, was prohibited. (A **primary boycott** is the union's refusal to deal with a company with which it does have a labor dispute.) So were jurisdictional strikes, designed to force an employer to give work to one union rather than another.
5. Unions could not charge their members excessively high initiation fees.
6. Employers were not required to pay for services not performed (**featherbedding**).

The Taft-Hartley Act also gave management the right to sue a union for violating the collective bargaining agreements. Other provisions required unions to make annual disclosures of financial records and prohibited them from making political contributions. (Certain Taft-Hartley provisions were later amended through legislation.)

An emergency provision in the Taft-Hartley Act allows the President of the United States, through the Attorney General's office, to seek a court injunction that will stop a strike or lockout that threatens the nation's general health or welfare. The injunction can last for up to eighty days. During this "cooling-off" period, the federal government attempts to mediate the disputes that are separating the parties. The National Labor Relations Board can hold a secret ballot vote among the striking or locked-out union members after the injunction is sixty days old to see if the company's last offer will be acceptable.

THE BENEFITS OF UNION MEMBERSHIP

■ Workers join unions because of the benefits they hope to receive. These benefits fall under two main headings. They are: (1) a better bargaining position and (2) a fair and uniform treatment.

Better Bargaining Position

Individuals have little bargaining power compared with their employers. A company can simply make an offer on a "take it or leave it" basis—or make no offer at all. The employee is free to say yes or no. The individual's bargaining power rests on his or her ability to refuse to accept an employment offer or to quit when dissatisfied. But if all the employees at a company in a trade or department bargain as one with the employer, the company will have to shut down or operate under severe handicaps if the whole group of workers goes on strike.

Fair and Uniform Treatment

Pay raises, disciplinary actions, promotions, and eligibility requirements for company training programs could and might be decided on an arbitrary basis without union checks on management's powers. Favoritism and discrimination could influence these decisions, resulting in inequities and injustices with little hope for appeal. Unions have increasingly pushed for a greater reliance on uniform, published procedures when management makes such decisions. This explains the unions' heavy reliance upon seniority provisions in the event that a company wishes to fire, promote, or take similar actions. The best man or woman may not always get the benefit, but objectivity will bear on the decision. Workers are constantly trying to protect themselves and their financial futures from insecurity.

One of our most basic needs relates to safety and security. Safer working conditions have been brought about through union demands and through state and federal legislation. Fringe benefits such as insurance and pension plans are major examples of the unions' quest for greater security for their members.

Union Security Provisions

Unions have fought for years to win recognition from employers and are constantly striving to increase their strength by requiring all employees to belong to the union, once it is recognized as their legitimate bargaining agent. In an election for recognition, a union may only win by a slim majority. Those workers who voted no may not wish to join the union unless they are forced to do so. To counter this resistance, various types of shop agreements have been formulated and won through favorable legislation and collective bargaining.

The Closed Shop. A union security provision that requires employers to hire only union labor is known as the **closed shop.** This type of union shop agreement was supposedly outlawed by the 1947 Labor Management Relations Act, but it still exists because of hiring practices in some industries. For instance, in the construction industry, contractors normally hire only union workers in order to get qualified, skilled labor and to avoid trouble with other already employed unionized workers.

The Union Shop. Under a **union shop** agreement, all current employees must join the union as soon as it is certified as their legitimate bargaining agent. Newcomers have to join after a specified probationary period—normally 30 days.

The Agency Shop. Employees do not have to belong to the union under the **agency shop** agreement, but must pay a fee to the union. The reason for this is that union negotiations benefit all employees, members and nonmembers alike. Since all employees benefit, each should pay his or her share of the costs of winning those benefits.

The Open Shop. Under the **open shop** agreement, membership in the elected union is voluntary for all existing and new employees. However, members and nonmembers alike share in the benefits won by the union.

LABOR RELATIONS

■ The area of **labor relations** includes all the activities within a company that involve dealings with a union and its members, both individually and collectively. Specifically, there are two main areas that are the most important and time-consuming: **collective bargaining**—arriving at a contract that covers workers' wages, hours, and working conditions; and **grievance processing**—dealing with complaints that allege a violation to the collective bargaining agreement.

Collective Bargaining

Bargaining collectively—the union representatives on one side of a table, management's representatives on the other—is the traditional way in which labor disputes are settled. Some time in advance of the expiration date of a labor contract, the two groups begin a series of meetings that will ultimately lead to the signing of a new agreement. Bargaining may take place on the local level, where only one local union and employer are involved, or on an industry-wide basis, where the agreement sets the standard for the industry, as in the automotive and trucking industries.

The usual process involves a specialist in labor relations from the company's labor relations department (usually at vice-presidential level) and the union's negotiating committee. Both sides employ the services of labor lawyers who are well versed in the most recent developments in labor law and who help them in hammering out specific contract provisions and wording.

Both sides bring to the bargaining a list of demands and assign to each in their own minds a priority that will become apparent as negotiations develop. Some demands are made merely to be used as trading material. Negotiating involves give-and-take, so each side must be prepared to bargain away some of its demands in order to obtain others.

Each side attempts to resolve the many minor issues as quickly as it can, reserving the major issues for the final meetings immediately preceding or following a strike. It is then that the pressure for a settlement is greatest. Ultimately, through compromises and trading, a new contract emerges. No one is anxious to be labeled a winner or a loser. Rather, both sides seek to improve their positions and eliminate problem areas that stand in the way of harmony and efficient output. The agreement is then offered to the union membership, who vote to accept or reject it. A simple majority vote is usually required.

The union contract with management spells out in rather precise terms the rights of workers with regards to rates, hours, and conditions of employment. It is a formal written document that both managers and stewards must thoroughly understand. It can and does limit management's authority. Both parties must operate within the restrictions it lays down if they are to avoid costly and time-consuming work stoppages and disagreements. As always, there are experts available who stand ready to help supervisors and stewards with interpretations of the contract.

Enforcing the Labor Contract

Enforcement of the terms of the agreement worked out through collective bargaining depends upon communication of the contract provisions and the demands they make on labor and management. Managers, especially those who direct workers, must be made aware of their rights and duties. Copies of the agreement are made available to each manager along with an explanation in terms that are easy to understand. Any questions that may arise in a manager's mind can be quickly answered by consultation with the personnel department and labor-relations officials.

The union also must make its members aware of their rights and duties. Copies of the contract are distributed to each member, and meetings are held locally to explain the contract's terms. At the plant and department levels, workers may turn to their steward for guidance in understanding the contract and dealing with any alleged violations of it.

The Supervisor and the Steward

The **steward** is first of all an employee and a worker. He or she has the additional responsibilities of a union office because the union members have elected him or her. Stewards receive released time from work to carry out their duties. Figure 14–1 lists the differences and similarities that exist between the roles of supervisor and steward. Note that there are more points that draw them together than keep them apart.

Just as a supervisor is management's spokesperson, the steward is labor's. He or she has the duty to represent workers in the early stages of the grievance process. The steward must be able to interpret the contract to both the supervisor and to fellow workers if he or she is to carry out the role intelligently. A complaint usually cannot become a grievance without the steward's consent. He or she must decide if the gripe has sufficient merit to promote it to the first step of the grievance procedure.

Stewards, like managers, have a difficult and demanding position. They are workers and must conform to company standards or risk disciplinary action. On the other hand, stewards have the status of elected union officers who, if they wish to retain their posts, must be effective representatives of and counsels to their constituents. They may, therefore, feel a good deal of pressure to push gripes to grievance status, even though their best judgment says they should not. Or, in cases where there are few complaints or grievances, stewards may feel the need to dig for some issues or manufacture some discontent in order to justify their position and prove that they are serving a useful purpose.

Just how stewards behave is largely an individual matter affected in part by their supervisors and the kind of relationship they have. Where there is room for interpretation, stewards are bound to take the union's view, just as supervisors are bound to accept management's. Therein lies the stuff of which grievances are made.

SUPERVISORS	STEWARDS
Know the contract	Know the contract
Enforce the contract	Enforce the contract
Look out for the welfare of subordinates	Look out for the welfare of constituents
Are spokespersons for both management and subordinates	Are spokespersons for the union and constituents
Settle grievances fairly (in line with management's interpretation of the contract)	Settle grievances fairly (in line with union interpretations of the contract)
Keep abreast of grievance solutions and changes in contract interpretation	Keep abreast of grievance solutions and changes in contract interpretation
Maintain good working relationships with stewards	Maintain good working relationship with supervisors
Keep stewards informed about management's decisions and sources of trouble	Keep supervisors informed about union positions and sources of trouble
Protect management rights	Protect labor rights

Figure 14-1. The responsibilities of supervisors and stewards.

Handling Grievances   When a worker is dissatisfied with a supervisor's disposition of a work-related complaint, he or she may appeal that decision by filing a formal charge called a **grievance.** All grievances allege that a violation has occurred to one or another of the provisions of the labor agreement. A gripe that is improperly handled can and usually does become a grievance. Managers consider every gripe about wages, hours, and working conditions a potential grievance.

A grievance is not a personal attack or insult to a supervisor—it is a problem to be solved. The first thing you must do is to keep calm and listen. Don't start an argument. Grievance discussions can become heated debates, and words may be said that will be regretted later. Grievances that are not properly settled in their early stages can grow into very costly and damaging disputes.

If the details of the grievance are not clear to you after you hear the complaining employee's case, ask questions. Find out the what, when, where, why, and how. Find out exactly what the person believes will make him or her happy and what provisions of the labor contract are involved.

Conduct your own investigation to determine whether or not the facts presented to you are complete and true. If they are not or if you are uncertain about any of them, list your questions and gather the evidence needed to clarify the situation. If you are unsure about the proper interpretation or application of the specific language of the labor contract, seek counsel from the labor-relations specialists.

If you determine that the grievance is without merit, give the worker and the steward your facts, your (management's) interpretation and application of the labor-contract provisions, and your specific reasons for denying the grievance.

Your oral answer to the complaining employee may not be acceptable to him or her or to the steward. If it is not, your involvement may be far from ended. You will probably be given a written copy of the complaint and asked to spell out in specific language the answer you have given orally. You will probably be questioned by various labor-relations people and union officials during later phases of the grievance procedure.

If your oral answer has been accepted by the complaining employee and the union steward, prepare a written record of the complaint and your disposition of it. Just be certain that the remedy you grant is within your power to give and has your boss' approval.

When writing up a grievance, use the following checklist to make certain that you have included all the necessary information. It might become necessary to refer to your records later when similar situations arise or when the same employees are involved in another grievance.

1. *Who is affected?* List the names, numbers, and departments of all workers and management representatives involved.

2. *What is it about?* Lost time? Pay shortage? Seniority violation?

3. *Is it a contract violation?* If so, state the clause and how company or union action violates it.

4. *When did it happen?* Report the exact time or period the grievance was suffered. If it concerns lost time or retroactive pay, report the exact dates for which time or pay is due.

5. *Where did it happen?* This is especially important in cases involving a health or safety hazard.

6. *Why did it happen?* Was the incident simply a clerical error? Was a worker unjustly penalized?

7. *What is the demand?* What specific action did the worker and the steward request? What remedy was granted?

8. *Did you obtain signatures and dates?* If any written petition was handed in, did you obtain the signatures and dates of the writer and steward?

9. *Did you distribute copies to the proper persons?* If you prepared a report on the grievance incident, have you made certain that all the interested parties have a copy of it?

The Grievance Procedure

If a company has a labor contract with a union, there is bound to be a formal procedure for the processing of grievances. How it operates is spelled out in the contract. This is a typical procedure:

Step 1. The Supervisor Meets with the Steward and the Employee Filing the Grievance. After the steward has agreed with a worker that the handling of his or her complaint was inadequate and that there is the possibility of an infringement on the contract terms, the steward brings the formal grievance back to a supervisor and attempts to work out a solution.

Every effort is made in this initial step to resolve the conflict. Both the union and management want to eliminate the time and expense of further discussion and debate.

If, after hearing them out, the supervisor believes nothing new has been added to change the situation, he or she will stick to the original decision. However, it is understood that the manager has researched the issue carefully and consulted with the various specialists available before reaching the decision that led to the grievance.

Step 2. The Supervisor's Immediate Superior and/or a Representative from the Labor-Relations Department Meet with the Union Grievance Committee. The union grievance committee is usually composed of several stewards from different areas of the business and may or may not include a staff member of the local union involved, such as a business agent. A middle manager, usually with the counsel of a labor-relations expert, sits down with these persons and examines the issues. The first thing they try to agree on is the matter of precedent, that is, similar cases that have already passed through the grievance process at one time or another. Cool heads must prevail, and again every effort is made by the parties to resolve the dispute at this level.

If a solution cannot be agreed upon, both the union and management feel that major issues are at stake and neither side is yet willing to yield to the other.

Step 3. The Labor-Relations Director and/or the Plant or Division Manager Meet with the Union Grievance Committee. Again, if the procedure so states, a representative from the local union administration may be present to augment the grievance committee. Costs and time now are beginning to mount, and both sides will want to solve the issue as quickly and adequately as they can.

Step 4. A Member or Members of Top Management Discuss the Issues with a Representative or Group from the National or International Union that Chartered the Local Union Whose Member Initiated the Grievance. If a local independent union is involved, which has no affiliation with a national or international union, the local's attorney and business agent will meet with management's representatives.

Step 5. *Mediation or Arbitration.* A neutral third party intervenes, meeting with the personnel involved in the dispute at steps 1–4.

Mediation

Mediation brings in the expertise of a neutral outsider who is allied with neither labor nor management. He or she is invited to try to bring the two sides together and, after hearing both points of view, to recommend a solution. The decision is not binding on either party. Often the mediator is a distinguished public official, such as a mayor or a judge, who has a fine reputation and whose insights, wisdom, and power are respected by both sides. He or she usually serves without pay of any kind in the public interest.

Arbitration

In arbitration also, a neutral third party is called in. He or she is a professional arbitrator recommended by the American Arbitration Association, the Federal Mediation and Conciliation Service, or one of the various state agencies set up for this purpose. Arbitrators usually serve with pay. In 1975, the AAA and the FMCS processed 23,529 grievances through arbitration—almost double the 12,000 handled in 1974. About as many other grievances were arbitrated through other agencies.

The arbitrator conducts hearings into the dispute, calling witnesses, recording testimony, and, in general, conducting the proceedings in much the same manner as a court of law conducts a hearing. It may be quite informal, however, depending on the arbitrator's style. When he or she announces a decision, it is binding on both union and management.

Normally, grievances are not put into writing until they progress from the first step to the second. This is especially true in large corporations, where the number of grievances is quite large and where the majority are usually solved at the steward-supervisor level. From this step on, the number of people involved increases, as does the need for precise language. Since the complainant and the steward are not present in the later steps, their thoughts and those of the supervisor must be put in writing.

We have examined the similarities and the differences between the handling of gripes in both a nonunion and a union setting. It should be clear to you that gripes are all potential destroyers of morale and team play if they are not handled properly and promptly. They are not to be treated lightly. Sometimes your people will come to you directly with their complaints, and sometimes you will hear about their dissatisfaction indirectly. Investigate the circumstances and involve your subordinate in a discussion so that the facts may be uncovered and assembled. Then render your decision.

If a worker decides to appeal your decision, and he or she has no union to back up the appeal, explain the company's appeals procedure and help him or her to get started. Don't consider this as an attack on you personally. Don't hold it against the worker. If your company has a union, then the worker will begin his or her appeal by getting the shop steward involved. After meeting with the two workers, you must again decide the issue. If you stick to your original decision, they will probably proceed with the grievance procedure.

Make yourself familiar with both federal and state labor laws that affect your company and your workers. Read the company publications in the area of labor relations and keep abreast of grievance settlements both inside and outside your company. Be sure you know your company's interpretation of the various sections of the labor agreement and consult regularly with the staff specialists. Keep your steward informed of your disciplinary decisions and develop a spirit of cooperation with him or her. The union is telling him or her to do the same. If you do these things, you will be preventing the likelihood of your being overruled in a complaint or a grievance, and you will be an accurate and effective spokesperson for the management team.

KEY WORDS

agency shop	**grievance processing**	**open shop**
arbitration	**gripe**	**primary boycott**
boycott	**injunctions**	**secondary boycott**
closed shop	**labor union**	**steward**
collective bargaining	**labor relations**	**union shop**
featherbedding	**lockout**	**yellow dog contracts**
grievance	**mediation**	

1. What is the difference between a gripe and a grievance?
2. How many unions are there in the U.S.? What percentage of union members is female?
3. What did the Wagner Act do for labor's attempt to organize?
4. What is the difference between collective bargaining and grievance processing?
5. How does arbitration differ from mediation? In what way are they similar?
6. What can a union do for its members in regard to helping them satisfy their social needs?
7. Why do you think more white-collar employees are turning toward unions today than ever before?
8. How will you be able to tell if an employee's gripe is real or an expression of something much deeper?
9. What would be your reaction if you overheard a subordinate's conversation in which he or she stated a specific complaint?
10. Why must a supervisor always treat a worker's gripe as a serious matter?

CASE PROBLEM

From Gripe to Grievance

When Harold Volkert, the supervisor of the central accounting office, walked into his office, one of his office workers, Dorothy Klaus, and the shop steward, Francis Seng, had been waiting about ten minutes for him.

"I think I know what you are here for," said Harold. "You think Dorothy should have been promoted to the new job."

"That's right," replied Francis, "and we are here to give management a chance to correct its error."

"I gave the job to Regina McNally because she has the edge on Dorothy. Her experience before she joined our company was in line with the duties of the new job. Also she has completed two college accounting courses since that time."

"Wait a minute, Harold. Dorothy is the most senior bidder and, according to the contract, she should have first choice. The wording is pretty clear to me," said Frank as he opened his copy of the agreement. "Here it is. Section 8, paragraph 2c, which states, and I quote:

where workers have comparable abilities, the most senior bidder shall receive preference in promotions."

"Look, Frank, I won't argue the fact that Dorothy has two years more service than Regina. But the key words are 'comparable abilities.' Both bidders took our accounting tests, and Regina scored higher than Dorothy."

"Harold, did Dorothy pass that test or didn't she?"

"Yes, but her score was twelve points lower than Regina's."

"All right, then. She passed the test, has three years bookkeeping experience, and the most seniority. Besides, she has a high-school diploma, and that is all the new job calls for."

"Hang on, Frank. The job description and specifications were posted with the job notice. I have a copy of them here. The new position requires a high-school diploma *and* college level accounting or its equivalent."

"I have three years accounting experience right now, Mr. Volkert," said Dorothy.

"Dorothy, all you have been doing is taking information provided to you and moving it to different places. You have been posting, compiling, and transferring information from one account to another or from accounts to routine financial statements. The new job requires accounting ability and the ability to reconcile conflicting data, analyze and prepare financial statements and records, and determine profit contributions from each of our various chemical divisions. What you have been doing is not accounting, only recordkeeping."

Frank spoke up. "As I see it, you just don't want to train Dorothy. She has received excellent ratings for the past three years and has proved her ability to learn new tasks. She has the prerequisites and could do the job if she were shown how."

"I admit, Frank, that the question of training time and expense did influence my judgment. But Regina has excellent ratings too and is better able to handle the duties of the new job because her past performance con-firms this capability. Therefore, she and Dorothy do not have comparable abilities. Regina has much more ability to cope with the new duties than Dorothy, so the question of seniority doesn't really matter."

Questions

1. Whose interpretation of the labor contract do you feel is correct in this case? Why?

2. Is there any evidence that Harold consulted higher authority before he made his decision? Should he have done so?

3. Do you think both Dorothy and Regina have "comparable abilities?"

4. If Harold sticks to his promotion decision, what do you think Dorothy and the steward will do?

5. What stage of the grievance procedure are these people in?

6. Who should get the job and why?

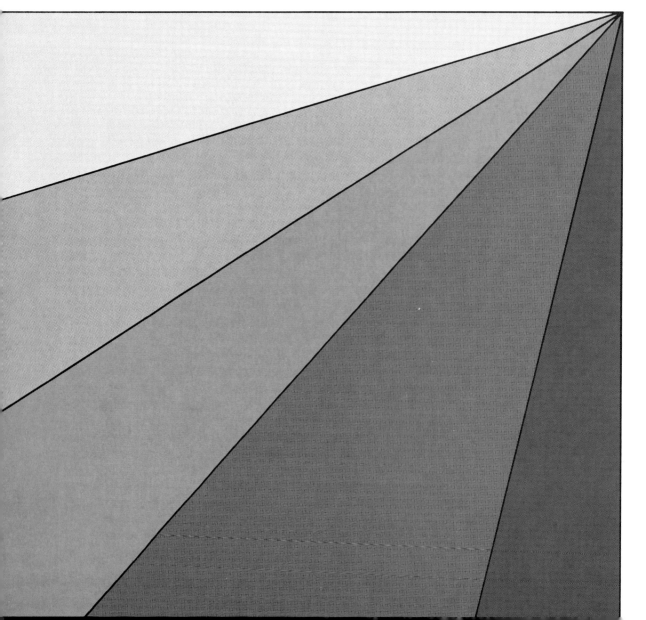

Part Four
The New Worker

15 The Selection Process

■ After reading and discussing this chapter, you should be able to:

1 Define selection.
2 Explain the role of a supervisor in the selection process.
3 Describe the role of the personnel department in the selection process.
4 Define recruiting.
5 List and briefly explain four selection devices.
6 Describe a situation that requires a direct selection interview and one that requires an indirect selection interview.
7 Describe what each supervisor should do to prepare for a selection interview.
8 List and briefly explain four pitfalls that can plague the selection process.
9 Describe what the federal laws and the Equal Employment Opportunity Commission (EEOC) guidelines allow in the area of discrimination, and what they forbid.

INTRODUCTION

■ **Selection** is the personnel management function that determines who is hired by a business firm and who is not. It is the process by which applicants are evaluated so as to determine their suitability for employment. Selection begins with the recruiting of potential candidates for each job the company wishes to fill and ends with the decision to hire one of them. In the case of workers, this decision is usually made by the supervisor.

This chapter looks at this extremely important function from a supervisor's viewpoint. In some companies the supervisors have nothing much to say about hiring new workers. They are told that new people have been assigned to their departments, and they then must accept that decision. This is not as it should be. Therefore, we shall turn our attention to the kind of selection in which the supervisors have a significant role to play.

ADVANTAGES OF SUPERVISOR INVOLVEMENT

■ If adequate selection is to take place in a business, the decision to hire a new worker should be made by the person who will become his or her boss. This is because the manager has firsthand knowledge about his or her department, workforce, and the job that must be filled. He or she is best equipped to assess each applicant's suitability and potential for both performance of the duties he or she will inherit and for getting along with the existing workforce. It makes a great deal of sense, therefore, to involve supervisors in the selection process and, in particular, to give them the power to make the final decision to hire a new employee.

If a new person is dropped into your lap or shoved down your throat, your receptiveness and interest in his or her ultimate success on the job is somewhat less than it would be if you had had a say in the hiring.

When you know that your decision is the final and binding one, you are putting your reputation on the line. Before you pick a person for your department, you will probably look over all the applicants carefully in order to select the best from among the many individuals you interview. Since the person is one you have chosen, you will feel a personal commitment to him or her that otherwise would be missing. You will want him or her to "make it" because, if this is not the case, it will affect you as well as the new employee. Part of your success and that of your department will be riding on your choice. If you are the department head in fact, then you should have a voice in adding new people to it.

If the new employees stumble a bit or have troubles of one kind or another, you as supervisor will be more concerned with helping them through their difficulties if you yourself hired them. When you are responsible for selecting new employees, their chances for success are much greater.

THE PERSONNEL DEPARTMENT'S ROLE

■ The selection process is extremely important. In fact, it is so important that it cannot be entrusted to a single individual. Depending on the size of your company and its philosophy of management, the selection of new employees can be a more or less intricate and complex operation.

"Can you type?"

Supervisors trigger the selection process by notifying the personnel department of their needs for employees. You must keep the personnel people informed as to your needs and, most importantly, keep them up to date on the descriptions they have on file for each job that you supervise. When a change is made in a job, such as enlarging it, eliminating one or more of its duties, or merging it with another job, let the personnel people know about it immediately. Otherwise they will be looking for a person to fill a job that no longer exists. As a job's description changes, so too may its specifications. The people in the personnel department must know about any changes if they are to recruit, test, and interview intelligently.

As a rule, the personnel department will not send you an unqualified applicant for final selection. Every candidate you interview should have the potential for success on the job available and should have the personnel department's approval. All you must do is to pick the best person from the qualified applicants you receive. The personnel department will have done all the legwork and analytic work through its team of specialists.

THE FINAL INTERVIEW

■ There are two objectives that you should keep in mind as you conduct the final selection interview: (1) you must gather enough information about the applicant to enable you to make a decision to hire or not to hire; and (2) you must provide the applicant with enough knowledge so that he or she can make an intelligent decision to accept or reject the offer of employment if you give it. You should strive to leave the applicant with a positive and accurate picture of your company and its people while interviewing. If an applicant is turned down by you, he or she will at least walk away with no ill will toward you or the company.

During the interview, all you can hope to do is to assess what the person has done and what you believe him or her to be capable of doing. You can't assess what an applicant will do, only his or her potential based upon past performances. You should concern yourself most with the person's ability to handle the duties of the job in question. This is the most important consideration. Second, consider the composition of your present workforce and the applicant's likelihood of getting along with its members. Keep in mind that the applicant's proper induction and introduction to the workers is your responsibility. You will have a great deal to do with teaming him or her up with the positive members of the group. Chapter 16 will have more to say about this important area.

Recruiting

The personnel department is usually charged with the recruitment function. It must find people who would make good applicants or candidates and attract them to the company. The people in your personnel department must be told what kind of people to look for, so they rely upon an up-to-date job description and its specifications. Then they have to decide where and how to find likely applicants. Like a salesperson, they are looking for suitable candidates who will be receptive to their recruitment efforts.

Some of the best sources of new workers are your present workers. Many of them have friends and acquaintances who might make good new employees of the company. They know people who are looking for new positions and are well enough acquainted with the company to recommend it to friends. This source of new talent is so highly regarded by some companies that they pay their employees a "finder's fee" for each person they recommend who is later hired. Most employees are careful with their recommendations because, like yourself, they are putting their stamp of approval on the new recruits. If the new employees do not work out well or are grossly unqualified, the judgment of the persons who recommended them would not be well regarded by the company.

After receiving a request for a new employee from a supervisor, the personnel department does its research and searches its files for a suitable applicant who has applied for a position in the past. Usually they also post the job vacancy throughout the company. This gives present employees who might be interested in the vacancy a chance to apply for a transfer or promotion into it. Where unions are involved, this is a common practice that is usually called for in the labor contract. If the job cannot be filled internally, the personnel recruiters will have to go outside to find applicants.

Selection Devices

The first selection device used with an applicant is the application form. Each interested recruit must fill one out, listing personal and work-related data which will be examined to determine the candidate's qualifications for the position. From the application the personnel people can decide whether or not the applicant meets the minimum criteria for the job. If he or she does not, the application is usually kept on file because a job may open up in the future for which that person is qualified.

The second selection device is a preliminary selection interview with each applicant who has the prerequisites for the job. During this interview the personnel interviewer asks various questions designed to fill in the gray areas and to assess the interests and attitudes of the candidate.

The third selection device involves the administration of pertinent tests and a physical exam. There may be several different kinds of tests that are designed to give information about the candidate's aptitudes, interests, personality, and achievements. If the applicant performs well on the tests and physical health is no barrier, the candidate will proceed to the fourth selection device, the final selection interview. Figure 15–1 illustrates the selection process and shows the selection devices as steps 4, 5, 6, and 8.

Figure 15-1. The selection process.

Supervisor

1 Request for a new worker

Personnel Department

2 Posting the job

3 Recruiting of applicants

4 Filing of applications

5 Preliminary interview

6 Testing and physical exam

7 Evaluation of results and sending records and applicant to final interview

8 Final interview
Reject ☐
Accept ☐

9 Processing of paper work

TYPES OF INTERVIEWS

■ There are basically two types of employment interviews available to you: the **direct interview** and the **indirect interview.** They get their names primarily from the types of questions each utilizes and partly from the way in which each is conducted. Take a few moments to review what Chapter 10 had to say about interviews.

The Direct Interview

The direct or patterned interview is a thoroughly planned, highly structured interview based on a format of specific questions set down in advance and followed exactly. These questions make up the outline for and the direction to be followed during the interview. The questions ask for specific and detailed information that the interviewer considers crucial and essential in assessing the candidate. The answers will supplement and help verify the information already gathered by the personnel people on the applicant.

Here are some examples of the kind of questions you should ask: "What did you do between your job with the ABC Company and your employment at XYZ, Incorporated?" or, "Why did you leave the ABC Company?" These questions ask for facts and leave little room for opinions on the part of the candidate. The only opinions you should look for are those that directly affect how the person views the job and type of working conditions that he or she will experience if hired.

Generally, the interviewer will ask the set of questions (questions he or she has written down in advance) in the order in which they are listed. Feel free to record the applicant's responses as they are given. Certain questions may be more important than others as they will reveal more valuable information. These questions should be marked in some way to highlight them to make certain that you do not forget to ask them. You will probably do as much talking as the applicant does, as you must both ask questions and supply information. Be sure that the applicant knows the nature of the job for which he or she is being interviewed and that he or she has an opportunity to ask questions too.

This type of interview works best when you are dealing with applicants for routine production or clerical positions. It allows you to obtain the maximum information while spending a minimum amount of time.

The Indirect Interview

The indirect interview is also planned in advance but is generally more unstructured and flexible. Questions are written down, but they are designed to be open or loose in order to allow the applicants more freedom in their responses and, in so doing, to reveal the attitudes behind their words.

Typical questions that might be asked include: "Why did you apply for this job?" or, "Which job have you held that you liked best (least) and why?" The object of these open questions is to let the applicants talk so that their aspirations, goals, and preferences can come out.

The interviewer is not bound to a rigid format with the indirect approach. One question can lead to others with the applicants' responses determining the direction and flow of the interview. Quite often you will find out a great deal more by an applicants' detailed explanations and will uncover much more than you otherwise would in the direct interview. People left to talk on their own will say more than they normally would, because they are not sure how much you want to know. They will seize the opportunity to speak their minds if they are relaxed and encouraged to do so.

Either type of interview may include an on-the-job performance test if you think it necessary. Such a test is designed to let the applicants demonstrate their capabilities at running a machine, meeting close tolerances, filing correspondence, typing correct copy, and the like. If this type of test has not been done already by the personnel department, then you have an excellent opportunity to do it during the final interview.

There is no hard-and-fast prescription for the final interview. You may mix these two types if you wish or stick to just one. The point is that you know what you are looking for, so you should pick the best methods you can to help you find the right new employees. The only real restrictions you have are yourself and the time you have available for the interview.

PREPARATION FOR THE INTERVIEW

■ As with all types of interviews, whether for counseling, sharing your evaluations, or interrogation and fact finding for disciplinary actions, the final interview should be held in private and in an environment as free from interruptions as you can make it. Since you usually know well in advance when an applicant is due to report, set aside enough time to do the kind of interview you desire and do your homework in advance of the meeting. Read the candidate's application form thoroughly and the comments, if any, from the personnel interviewer. Look over the candidate's test scores and make a list of any deficiencies that you feel will interfere with his or her successful performance. Prepare a brief checklist of the essentials you wish to cover so that you don't waste time and overlook an important area. Figure 15–2 is such a list.

From your list, make a set of questions that are designed to fill in the gaps and to give you the additional information you need to reach your decision about the applicant.

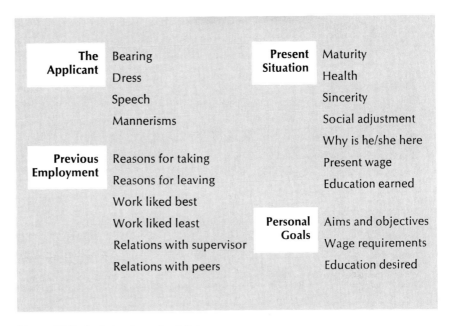

Figure 15-2. An interview checklist.

The Applicant
- Bearing
- Dress
- Speech
- Mannerisms

Previous Employment
- Reasons for taking
- Reasons for leaving
- Work liked best
- Work liked least
- Relations with supervisor
- Relations with peers

Present Situation
- Maturity
- Health
- Sincerity
- Social adjustment
- Why is he/she here
- Present wage
- Education earned

Personal Goals
- Aims and objectives
- Wage requirements
- Education desired

CONDUCTING THE INTERVIEW

■ No matter what type of interview you choose, you should follow the basic procedure outlined below.

1. *Put the applicant at ease.* Keep in mind that the applicant will probably be a bit nervous, so do what you can to eliminate this barrier to successful communications by planning to make him or her comfortable as soon as you meet. A comfortable chair, a quiet room, good ventilation, a cup of coffee, an ash tray close by, and a smile along with your handshake will go a long way toward relieving his or her tension.

2. *Stick with your schedule.* If you have planned your questions and prepared an outline to follow, stay with them. Watch the time so that you cover what you must before your time runs out. There may be a temptation on both your parts to wander from essential areas and talk randomly about whatever arises. You have several points to cover, and you won't usually have the luxury of unlimited time. If you don't get what you are there to get, you will have to make a decision on less than complete knowledge about the applicant.

3. *Listen.* By now you are probably sick of reading about listening. But it is of the greatest importance to the communications process, especially when you are engaged in a discussion. If you do all the talking, you will learn nothing. If you use the time between your questions in planning for what you will cover next, you will miss the applicant's

answers. If you are not attentive to the applicant, you will shut him or her off.

4. *Remain neutral.* Retain your impressions and opinions until the end of the interview. Mask your reactions, whether favorable or unfavorable. If the applicant senses your feelings one way or the other he or she will begin to tailor responses to your reactions. You will receive what you have indicated you want to hear, not what the applicant wants to say. When you disagree with a response, ask the applicant for his reasons. Try to uncover his or her way of looking at things. You will gain a perspective on the individual and his or her attitudes that otherwise would be denied to you. As with appraisals, you should not concern yourself with an applicant's opinions that are not related to the nature of the job or the working environment. If an applicant's attitudes or feelings are contrary to yours, simply ask yourself if it really matters. Will those opinions keep the applicant from a successful job performance? If not, forget them.

Avoid leading questions. Questions that lead a person to the answer you want to hear will do just that. An example is, "You got along with

HERMAN

MANAGER

"I've got two other applicants to see before I make my final choice."

© 1976. Universal Press Syndicate.

your boss, didn't you?" If a person answers no, he or she is pretty stupid. These questions simply waste time. They tell an applicant where your values are but you won't learn the applicant's values.

5. *Give the applicant your decision.* If you have decided that a person is not right for the job, let him or her know it. It is not fair to keep people hanging or to put them off when you have definitely ruled them out. They have other plans to make and need to know where they stand as soon as possible. If you like a candidate but wish to interview one or two others before you decide, let the applicant know that as well. He or she may be interviewing several employers and may not be ready to give you a decision either. But give a specific time by which he or she will have your final decision. Then stick to that time limit as best you can. If you delay your decision too long, you may lose your prospect. If you know this person to be the best you have seen thus far and totally qualified for the position you have vacant, offer him or her the job. You have what you need. Further searching may be expensive and may yield nothing better. You may be surprised to hear the applicant tell you that he or she is not sure and wishes to examine other opportunities. If you really want the person, set a time by which he or she should give you a definite answer.

PITFALLS

■ As with most of your duties, there are a number of pitfalls that may snare you if you are not aware of them. Since there is a strong similarity between appraisals of subordinates and appraisals of applicants, some of the same pitfalls we discussed in Chapter 12 apply here as well. Those we have discussed before are:

1. *The halo effect.* If you make this mistake, you will be letting your personal biases or prejudices influence your appraisal of an applicant.

2. *The rush job.* If you are inadequately prepared for an interview, how can you find out all you need to know about an applicant?

3. *Comparisons.* It is not fair to compare, for example, an applicant to someone who has had years of experience on the job. You should ask yourself if the applicant can meet the standards set by the job description. (For example, you have no reason to expect that the new person can replace right away all the skills of a retiring worker like Willy who has had thirty years' experience on the job.)

In addition, you should consider the following other pitfalls:

4. *Failing to follow the principles of sound interviewing.* After you have completed this chapter, you should have a good grasp of what these principles are.

5. *Overselling your company or the job.* By overstatements, puffed-up generalizations, and inaccurate or untruthful information you might

be sowing the seeds that eventually would cause the new person frustration and lead him or her to quit. The person may be taking the job with false hopes and on the basis of your inaccurate promises. He or she will soon discover that his or her mental images don't coincide with the hard realities encountered on the job. Selection is an expensive process. If the person you select only stays a short time, you will have to repeat the whole process all over again. You will have been unfair to both your company and the employee. You will probably be worse off than you were before because of the further disruption to your work force and production schedules. Your subordinates may begin to suspect that your judgment is not what it should be.

6. *Omitting pertinent information.* If you leave out some vital facts with regard to the applicant's duties or working conditions, he or she will be forced to make a decision on the basis of incomplete information. If the applicant had known all the facts he or she might not have accepted the position. Therefore, once they become known, the applicant may decide that you have misled him or her and quit. You may experience a tendency to leave out the unpleasant aspects of the job or to skip over them lightly. This can only lead a person to think badly of you and may give rise later to gripes and frustration. Give the facts as clearly as you can, leave out the sugar coating and be complete in your description of the job.

7. *Neglecting sound public relations.* By either overselling or omissions you may be paving the way for a later termination. Also, if your decision at the close of your interview is a negative one, and you haven't left the person with a good impression about your company and its people, you will be promoting unfavorable public opinion about your organization which could cause a decline in job applicants and even in sales. Treat the applicant as you would a guest in your home. You want to make an honest but favorable impression so that no matter what happens, when the visit is over both parties will leave with positive impressions.

8. *Asking questions of a discriminatory nature.* Companies can get into major difficulties with the federal and state governments if they seek information of a discriminatory nature on application forms and during interviews. Antidiscrimination laws and the Equal Employment Opportunity Commission (EEOC) guidelines forbid employers to ask for information about a person's race, religion, marital status, and country of origin.

Figure 15–3 illustrates the types of inquiries an employer may legally make with a job applicant. It is intended only as a guide since governmental regulations and laws keep changing the definitions of what is and what is not discriminatory.

	ACCEPTABLE INQUIRY	DISCRIMINATORY INQUIRY
Name	Additional information relative to change of name, use of an assumed name or nickname necessary to enable a check on applicant's work records.	The fact of a change of name or the original name of an applicant whose name has been legally changed.
Birthplace and residence	Applicant's place of residence. Length of applicant's residence in Illinois and/or city where the employee is located.	Birthplace of applicant. Birthplace of applicant's parents. Requirement that applicant submit birth certificate, naturalization, or baptismal record.
Creed and religion	None.	Applicant's religious affiliation. Church, parish, or religious holidays observed by applicant.
Race or color	General distinguishing physical characteristics such as scars, etc.	Applicant's race. Color of applicant's skin, eyes, hair, etc.
Photographs	None.	Photographs with application. Photographs after interview, but before hiring.
Age	If hired, can you furnish proof of age?	Date of birth or age of an applicant except when such information is needed for or to: 1. Maintain apprenticeship requirements based upon a reasonable minimum age. 2. Satisfy the provisions of either state or federal minimum age statutes. 3. Avoid interference with the operation of the terms and conditions and administration of any bona fide retirement, pension, employe benefit program. 4. Verify that applicant is above the minimum legal age (21), but without asking for a birth certificate. Age specifications or limitations in newspaper advertisements which may bar workers under or over a certain age.
Education	Academic, vocational, or professional education, and the public and private schools attended.	
Citizenship	Are you in the country on a visa which would not permit you to work here?	Any and all inquiries into whether applicant is now or intends to become a citizen of the U.S., or any other inquiry related to the aspect of citizenship.

Figure 15-3. What employers may and may not ask for on application forms and in employment interviews.
Reprinted courtesy of *The Chicago Tribune*. All rights reserved.

	ACCEPTABLE INQUIRY	DISCRIMINATORY INQUIRY
National origin and ancestry	None.	Applicant's lineage, ancestry, national origin, or nationality. Nationality of applicant's parents or spouse.
Language	Language applicant speaks and/or writes fluently.	Applicant's mother tongue. Language commonly used by applicant at applicant's home. How the applicant acquired ability to read, write, or speak a foreign language.
Relatives	Names of relatives already employed by the company. Name and address of person to be notified in case of accident or emergency. Name and/or address of any relative of applicant.	
Military experience	Military experience of applicant in the Armed Forces of the United States. Whether applicant has received any notice to report for duty in the Armed Forces.	Applicant's military experience in other than U.S. Armed Forces. National Guard or Reserve Units of applicant. Draft classification or other eligibility for military service. Dates and conditions of discharge.
Organizations	Applicant's membership in any union or professional or trade organization. Names of any service organizations of which applicant is a member.	All clubs, social fraternities, societies, lodges, or organizations to which the applicant belongs other than professional, trade, or service organizations.
References	Names of persons willing to provide professional and/or character references for applicant. Names of persons who suggested applicant apply for a position with the employer.	The name of applicant's pastor or religious leader.
Sex and marital status	Maiden name of applicant.	Sex of applicant. Marital status of applicant. Dependents of applicant.
Arrest record	Number and kinds of convictions for felonies.	The number and kinds of arrests of an applicant.
Height	None.	Any inquiry into height of applicant, except where it is a bona fide occupational requirement.

Figure 15-3 continued from preceding page

■ According to the EEOC, people are members of a minority group and therefore protected by federal law from discrimination in employment if they meet one of the following definitions:

Hispanics: Spanish-surnamed Americans
Asians or people from the Pacific islands: Oriental Americans
Blacks not of Hispanic origin: Negroes
American Indians: Natives of North America
Alaskan natives: Eskimos

Women are also protected by law from discrimination in employment but are *not* considered to be a minority.

In 1977 women made up about 41 percent of the labor force of the United States, numbering about 40 million women aged sixteen and above. In 1977 blacks were our largest minority, representing about 11.5 percent of the total population. In that year, Hispanics who were citizens or legal residents numbered about 17 million, or about 8 percent of the total population. If we also include the estimated 7 to 8 million Hispanics who are in America illegally, however, the size of this minority group is significantly greater. Minority groups represent less than 50 percent of the United States' labor force.

Federal antidiscrimination laws prevent employers from denying employment to applicants on the basis of their race, color, sex, age, religion, or national origin. Prior to 1968 business and industry were little troubled by the federal laws because they were poorly enforced and lacking in adequate judicial interpretation. Since that time the federal government has proved its commitment to the elimination of discrimination in employment by vigorous court actions and additional laws. Figure 15–4 lists the major laws in this area.

Recent court decisions have clarified these laws and reinforced the guidelines established by the Equal Employment Opportunity Commission (EEOC) and their state affiliates, the Fair Employment Practices

Figure 15-4. Federal anti-discrimination laws.

YEAR	LEGISLATION
1963	Equal Pay Act (Amendment to the Fair Labor Standards Act of 1938)
1964	Civil Rights Act
1967	Age Discrimination in Employment Act
1972	Equal Employment Opportunity Act (Amendment to Title VII of the Civil Rights Act)

Commissions. In general, it is unlawful for employers to discriminate against employees with respect to pay, working conditions, and privileges of employment because of race, color, religion, age, sex, or nation of origin. Discrimination is permitted if such factors as sex, religion, or national origin are necessary occupational qualifications. While anti-discrimination laws apply most directly to actions by management, unions may not interfere with their implementation. In fact, most unions today may be counted on to support and cooperate with management's efforts to eliminate discrimination in employment.

The guidelines handed down by EEOC in 1970 affect all employee selection devices and procedures. A "test" under these guidelines means "any paper-and-pencil or performance measure used as a basis for any employment decision." Whether the selection involves the hiring of new employees or the eligibility of existing employees for promotion, transfer, or training, employers involved in interstate commerce are required to adhere to these guidelines. For example, any scored selection interviews and personal or work histories are included in the above definition of a "test."

There are two major guidelines to be considered before a particular selection device or procedure is used: (1) **validity;** and (2) **disparate effect.**

Selection devices or procedures are "valid" according to EEOC if they are directly related to and predictive of a person's job performance. For instance, if a high percentage of people score average or above on a particular test and demonstrate successful performance on a job, while a high percentage of the people who score below-average on the test do not perform successfully on the job, the test may be considered valid. If a high percentage of both groups demonstrate successful job performance, the test would be considered not valid.

A selection device or procedure is considered to have a "disparate effect," that is, an adverse effect, if the number of minority group members excluded by it is significantly greater than the number of whites excluded. In other words, if 50 percent of the blacks fail a test while only 30 percent of the whites do, the test is considered to have a disparate effect on this minority group. In order to meet the EEOC guidelines, selection devices must be valid *and* exhibit no disparate effect.

THE SUPERVISOR'S ROLE IN MINORITY HIRING

■ After extensive interviewing of managers and employees in forty-three companies representing retailing, service, and industrial areas, Professor Lawrence A. Johnson of the University of Massachusetts found that the supervisor is a major key to the minority worker's success or failure.[1] In companies committed to employment of minority groups, coaching the minority newcomer's supervisor is as important as training the worker. If the program is to be a success the supervisors must:

1. Learn to listen to and understand the minority worker's point of view;

2. Communicate effectively;

3. Expect considerable testing and probing from the minority worker as to the company's standards and the supervisor's attitudes and sincerity;

4. Be made aware beforehand of their own possible reactions to probable situations in their relationships with minority workers.

With the increased emphasis on recruiting and hiring minority members today, you are more likely now than ever before to encounter these persons in every department of your company.

They, like all of us, expect an even chance for success. They may need extra training to fill the gaps left in their formal education and previous employment experiences. They want and need to be respected and appreciated for their good points and potentials. They want to carry their own weight.

You must realize that a minority worker may arrive expecting the worst: resentment, rejection, hostility, and isolation. He or she may tend to read into your actions and words or those of peers more than is in them. He or she may be considered to be hypersensitive. In a way, he or she may be looking for signs of discrimination as well. What a white worker might brush aside, a minority member may consider an insult or personal attack. Until all of your subordinates feel that they are being treated as individuals, you can expect a measure of discontent.

All the roles you must play in order to achieve the sound human relations described in Chapter 8 are even more necessary when you deal with minorities, and they may demand additional effort and diligence on your part in order to relate successfully to each of them. This is particularly true when such a person first joins your department.

There are always a few workers, however, regardless of ethnic background, who will try to take advantage of you or the situation. Some workers will be looking for special privileges. They may want to use the fact that they are women or members of minorities as a lever in attempts to gain favored treatment. This inequity, though clearly understandable, must be prevented. Your success and that of your workers

1. Lawrence A. Johnson, "Employing the Hard-Core Unemployed," *Research Study No. 98*, American Management Association (1969).

will be hampered if you don't. You will suffer most of all through alienation of your other subordinates and their accusation that you are playing favorites.

Enforce the standards of performance and conduct impartially. Let all your workers know their rights and the avenues open to them when they feel that they have been treated unjustly.

PLANNING THE NEWCOMER'S FIRST DAY

■ Assuming that you have offered the job and the applicant has accepted, you must now begin your planning to welcome the new arrival. During the interview and after it, you should have a fairly good idea as to the need for training that exists. If you know some training will be needed, begin to map your plans out and get the program organized in such a way that you are ready to begin as soon as possible. Prepare your people for the new person by communicating all that you know that is positive and not confidential. Get the work area ready, the passes if any, and all the necessary items he or she will need to get right to work. In short, plan to make that first day a truly positive experience, one that will tell the applicant that his or her decision to work for you was correct. Chapter 16 will explore the special duties you and your company must perform to properly welcome your new subordinate.

INSTANT REPLAY

Although not every supervisor is directly involved in the hiring of new employees, he or she should be. The advantages of doing so include a greater commitment to the new person's success, a better understanding of the new person's attitudes and personality at the start, and a better understanding on the new employee's part of what it is he or she has agreed to and what his or her chances are for success.

The supervisor has a choice as to the nature and scope of the interview he or she wishes to use to help make a final decision. He or she knows that every applicant has been screened initially by personnel. The supervisor has the assurance that all the applicants meet the minimum standards for the job. What must be done through the final interview is to assess their willingness to achieve and to determine their capabilities for doing so.

The selection process is both an information-gathering and information-giving situation. You must give the applicant as much truthful information as he or she needs to make a sound decision. If you oversell or omit critical data, the applicant will be laboring under misinformation or incomplete knowledge. Therefore, he or she may tend to feel cheated and will either put forth legitimate gripes or quit.

KEY WORDS

KEY WORDS	direct interview	Equal Employment Opportunity	minority
	discrimination	Commission (EEOC)	recruiting
	disparate effect	indirect interview	selection
			validity

QUESTIONS FOR
DISCUSSION

QUESTIONS FOR DISCUSSION

1. Why is it good policy to involve a supervisor in the hiring process?
2. Do you have a voice in the selection of your subordinates at work? If you do not, would you like to? Why?
3. For what type of applicants do you believe the indirect interview works best? Why?
4. Is there such a thing as underselling your company or a job to an applicant? Explain.
5. If you knew that tomorrow morning at 8 a.m. you would be interviewing an applicant for a job in your department, what would you do before meeting with him or her?
6. How can the halo effect interfere with a successful final interview?
7. Why is it important for the interviewer to mask his or her reactions to the applicant's answers and statements?

CASE PROBLEM

Belle's First Job

Ever since the First Trust and Savings Company hired Belle Walker for the summer, she has been a thorn in Kay Farrel's side. As head cashier, Kay is responsible for supervising the bank's eight tellers. When Wilma Banks left three weeks ago, Belle was hired as Wilma's replacement without any consultation with Kay. Kay was openly critical of the way in which Belle had been hired because it was a significant departure from past practices and company policy.

Kay had inquired about why exceptions were made in Belle's case but was only given terse and evasive answers. After some checking on her own, Kay discovered what she believed to be the real reason. James B. Walker, Belle's father, is one of the most important merchants in town. He keeps large personal and business accounts at the bank and is a member of its board of directors.

Kay does not have any serious doubts about Belle's ability to become a good teller. Belle is a high-school graduate and has been an above-average student for most of her school years. She is a bright and personable young lady and very good with customers. She has learned her job well enough and why shouldn't she have? Her instructor has been Wilma Banks, who was the best teller at First Trust and Savings Company.

During the first two weeks of training Belle, Wilma had mentioned on several occasions that Belle's heart didn't seem to be in her work. She would often say she understood, but then make some simple mistake when left on her own. She enjoys talking to the customers more than she does handling their banking transactions, and more than a few times they had let Belle know this. Belle is also fond of saying that she really didn't need this job or the money it pays but wants to work for the experience and to meet new people. She is headed for college in the fall and wants to fill some time.

This week Belle has been unable to balance out at the end of her shift on Tuesday and Thursday. She had a significant excess of cash she could not explain on Tuesday and a shortage of cash on Thursday. Kay is also concerned about Belle's tardiness—another departure from her behavior pattern of the first two weeks on the job. Twice this week she has been late in opening her window. This creates problems for the other tellers, who do not hesitate to let Kay know how they feel about it. When Kay spoke to Belle about her tardiness on Monday, she had been assured it would not happen again. But Belle was late again today.

Kay knows that Belle will only be around for another eight weeks and wonders if it is worthwhile to raise the problem over her performance. She has doubts about her boss' willingness to stand behind her in any attempted disciplinary action. He has let her down before, even when a big depositor's daughter wasn't involved. Kay is afraid, however, that letting things go unchecked might lead to more serious problems in her department.

Questions

1. What special treatment has Belle already received? What are the consequences?
2. Suggest a selection system that might have avoided this problem.
3. What special consideration should Belle receive from Kay before Kay takes any action?
4. What should Kay do now?

16 Induction and Orientation

LEARNING OBJECTIVES

■ After reading and discussing this chapter, you should be able to:

1 Define induction.

2 Define orientation.

3 List four basic goals of an orientation program.

4 List five questions answered for new employees through an orientation program.

5 Describe a follow-up procedure for an orientation program.

INTRODUCTION

■ After a new employee has been recruited, interviewed, tested, and hired, you must begin to prepare for the newcomer's arrival and initiation. Some groundwork for this procedure has already been laid throughout the selection process. The applicant was informed as to the nature of the job, the company's operations in general, and the wage and fringe benefits that go with the job. What remains to be done is the careful planning for and the execution of the new employee's formal introduction to the company, the job, the supervisor, and the working environment in depth.

ORIENTATION

■ **Orientation** includes the planning of a program to introduce the new worker to his or her company, job, working environment, and peers as well as the execution of that program. Planning must begin as soon as the applicant accepts the offer of employment, and it continues until he or she reports for the first day of work. Goals must be established and a program for their accomplishment must be drawn up. You must do all this carefully in order to insure your new subordinate's successful first impressions of the new job.

The importance of adequate planning of the orientation program cannot be overemphasized. Things don't just "happen." They must be arranged in advance. If the new employee is in need of training, the details of the training must be thought through and outlined. A training schedule needs to be drawn up, and the goals that the newcomer is to achieve must be established. All the necessary aids and materials have to be obtained in advance, and the persons to be involved in the training must be given advance notice about the parts they will play so that they can prepare for the training sessions by brushing up on the skills they will need to demonstrate.

The personnel department must be contacted, and the necessary forms, passes, booklets, and so forth procured so that they are available on the first day. As the newcomer's supervisor, you will want to brush up on the forms and content of the booklets so that you can guide the employee through the maze of paperwork effectively and smooth out the wrinkles that might overwise interfere with a constructive first impression.

The person's work area must be prepared so that the basic inventory of tools, equipment, supplies, and materials is on hand. It must be put into a clean and polished state of readiness so that the new employee starts off with the desirable standards of housekeeping and maintenance firmly in view and in mind. Everything must be in its place and in working order so that there are no surprises waiting for the new person or yourself.

Arrangements must be made for the new person to be a part of one or another of the groups of workers in your department. It is a good idea to get someone to act as the new employee's *mentor*—a guide and tutor who will be available to answer questions and help once you have finished your orientation. A mentor should be a volunteer who knows the ropes and whose judgment and abilities you respect. This person can provide immediate acceptance and social companionship on and off the job during breaks and lunch.

The formal group must be informed as to the qualifications possessed by the new person in advance of his or her arrival. Share all the positive features you know about the new person that are not confidential in nature. Pave the way for his or her acceptance by the positive group or groups to help in shaping his or her attitudes. There is much to do, so don't waste time and put things off too long. What happens the first day may determine the difference between a successful career employee and one who will quit in the near future. It is in your hands, and

Orientation step	Personnel department	Department head	Coworker
Welcome	87%	51%	8%
Explaining daily routine	17%	89%	26%
Procedures and regulations	70%	67%	9%
Job introduction	15%	92%	27%

Table 16-1. Companies and orientation steps.
Source: Dartnell Institute of Business Research.

you will usually have the responsibility for a proper introduction and orientation.

In 1977 the Dartnell Institute of Business Research[1] in Chicago made a survey of 350 companies throughout the United States and Canada to find out how new employees are welcomed. Table 16–1 shows the results of this survey; 85 percent of the companies in the survey offered some kind of orientation program.

Of the companies surveyed, 61 percent have described their orientation policies in writing, thus making the orientation of their new employees a formal and routine process. Thirty-nine percent have not formalized their initiation programs. More than 87 percent of these firms issue an orientation manual or handbook to newcomers.

According to a recent survey conducted by the American Society for Personnel Administration and the Bureau of National Affairs, Inc., 86 percent of the 196 companies in the survey provide some type of informal orientation program.

GOALS

■ The goals or objectives of an orientation program for new employees are four in number:

1. To instill favorable first impressions and attitudes with regard to the company, its purposes, and its people;

2. To satisfy the new employees' need for security and social acceptance;

3. To design and provide initial experiences that foster motivation and promote early success;

4. To prevent problems initially and in the future.

---

1. "How Employers Say a Formal 'Hello,'" *Chicago Tribune,* October 12, 1977, sec. 12, p. 35.

In order to accomplish these goals, base your planning on them. Your planning should be concerned with the construction of an orientation program whose procedures and practices will enable you to achieve each of the above-mentioned goals. In the light of these goals, determine what specific steps you wish to accomplish and in what sequence you wish each step to occur. Then determine what resources and facilities you will require. In short, you must decide what to do, how to do it, and who will assist you. You may wish to delegate some of the tasks to your most reliable assistants.

The following checklist may prove useful to you as you plan your orientation program.

Have I planned for his or her:
1. Introduction to the job and peers?
2. Tools, equipment, uniforms, passes, and forms?
3. Inclusion on the payroll and related schedules?
4. First day's work?
5. Training program and its personnel?
6. Familiarization with regulations and rules that govern performance and conduct on the job?
7. Mentor?
8. Understanding of the standards of quantity and quality?
9. Follow-up interview?

INDUCTION

■ **Induction** is the process of initiating or welcoming the new employee to the organization and his or her place of work. It is the part of the orientation program that is usually carried out directly by the new person's supervisor.

As soon as the new employee arrives, the induction or initiation procedure begins. The typical induction answers the following five basic questions for the new worker:
1. Where am I now?
2. What are my duties?
3. What are my rights?
4. What are my limits?
5. Where can I go?

Where Am I Now?

After greeting the new arrival warmly, you should explain in words and graphic form just where he or she fits into the entire company's operations. By starting with a copy of the company's organization chart you can move from his or her slot in your department all the way up the chain of command to the chief executive. Explain the jobs performed in your department and the departments adjacent to it. Name the personalities involved in each, with particular emphasis on those the new employee is most likely to encounter. Give the newcomer a good idea as to how his or her job and department relate to the ultimate success and profitability of the company.

Answering this question in full will help accomplish all the goals of a successful orientation program.

This initial explanation can be followed by a tour of the department and a look at the work area. Introduce the person to his or her co-workers and mentor and give them a chance to chat. Next, familiarize the new person with the facilities within the department that he or she will need to use from time to time such as the storage areas, supply room, tool room, washroom, water fountain, and the like. This is also a good time to point out the bulletin board, time clock, and various signs that are posted about the area. Give the newcomer a chance to ask any questions that relate to what he or she sees. Anticipate the likely problem areas and, if he or she doesn't get to each of them, be certain that you do.

From the tour of the immediate work area and your department, take a walk through the adjacent areas and explain the functions that go on in each. Introduce the newcomer to the people you meet along the way in such a manner as to demonstrate your enthusiasm and pride in having him or her join your operation. Something like this should do the trick: "Bill, I'd like you to meet Howard Kramer. Howard, this is Bill Watkins. Howard has just joined our team, and we are lucky to have him." This gives your new worker a chance to know your true feelings about his or her decision to come aboard. The newcomer will quickly begin to sense that he or she is respected and well thought of, as well as needed. Bill will not remember the names of all those to whom he has been introduced, but he will remember your enthusiastic welcome. When he meets these people later, chances are that they will remember him and exchange a greeting.

During your walk through the company you have an excellent opportunity to review the company's history. By sharing knowledge of the company you will let the new person feel like an important part of a big operation. There is tremendous value in this, as we all like to feel we belong to groups that are bigger and more powerful than ourselves. Review the company's line of products or services and point out when major events took place that have built the company and contributed to its present position. Pass on all the positive information you have that is not confidential so that a positive image is created of the company, its people, and its future.

When you tour the cafeteria or lounge area, treat the new arrival to a cup of coffee. Some companies pick up the tab for the first day's snacks and lunch and some do not. If your company does not, why not pay for the coffee yourself? It's hard to think of a better way to say "Welcome." Lunch time is a good time to visit in a relaxed and personal way and to assess the impact of the morning's events upon your new person. It gives him or her a chance to clear up any questions.

A student once told me that he has a simple philosophy about induction and orientation. In his words, "I just treat them like I would an old friend I haven't seen for some time. There's so much to talk about and share that conversation is never a problem."

What Are My Duties?   After you return from your tour, take the new person back to the work area. All the supplies, materials, tools, and equipment needed will be there because you made sure that they would be. The area will be clean and orderly, thus demonstrating the standards of housekeeping and maintenance you expect to be continued.

Give a copy of the job description to the new person and go over each duty. Explain the details implied by this general listing and check his or her understanding of each. Wherever you can, demonstrate each duty either by performing it or by specific examples.

Issue any passes or identification cards needed for parking, entrance to the cafeteria, obtaining tools, and the like. Help the newcomer fill out all the necessary forms, which are sometimes a bit confusing and difficult to follow. By answering questions for your new worker you will be helping to accomplish goals 1, 3, and 4 of your orientation program.

What Are My Rights?   By rights we mean receiving what is owed or due each employee. All workers are entitled to receive their wages according to a prearranged schedule. Explain the pay periods and how pay is calculated. Explain fringe benefits such as group life- and health-insurance plans, the company's profit-sharing plan, paid holidays, incentive awards, the suggestions plan, and the like. In particular, communicate the eligibility requirements, where they exist, for each of the benefits.

If there is a union, be certain to introduce the steward and explain the rights a person has in regard to union membership. Where this is voluntary, say so. Don't give your views about unions. Simply advise the newcomer of what he or she needs to know.

Review the overtime procedures you follow and the way in which workers become eligible for it. Go over the appraisal process and what will be rated in it. If there is a union, explain the grievance process and how to file a grievance complaint.

Cover all the areas that you know from past experience have been sources of misunderstanding in the area of workers' rights. For instance, workers often confuse sick days with personal-leave days. Be sure that your employee knows the difference and what the company policy is with regard to these matters.

Answering this question in detail will help accomplish goals 2, 3, and 4 of the orientation program.

What Are My Limits?   You may recall from our discussion on discipline in Chapter 13 that your first and most important duty in this matter is to inform each employee about the limits or boundaries placed on their conduct and performance. Discipline starts with the induction and orientation of each person. The do's and don'ts that you intend to enforce should be explained along with the penalties attached to each. Each employee should have copies of the company regulations and department rules.

Pay particular attention to the areas affecting safety. Each worker should not only know the rules but company policy as well. If safety equipment is needed, be sure that it is issued or purchased, whichever is required. Then be certain to include an emphasis on safety throughout the newcomer's training. Instill safe working habits and conduct right from the start. Enforcement then becomes easier.

Orientation goals 1, 2, and 3 will be furthered by answering this question in full.

Where Can I Go?   This question involves the opportunities for advancement that exist for each new person. Explain his or her eligibility for training and advanced programs that increase both work skills and the opportunities for promotions. State the criteria you use for making promotion and transfer decisions. People need to know what is required of them in order to advance. Finally, explain the standards he or she must meet in order to qualify for a raise.

Orientation goals 3 and 4 are furthered by answering this question for your new workers.

FOLLOWING UP   ■ Plan a follow-up interview to talk with the newcomer about the first day's experiences and answer any questions that may have accumulated. See if you can get a handle on how he or she really feels.

At the end of the first week, schedule another informal meeting with the new person and determine if he or she is making an adequate adjustment to the new job. Your personal daily observations should tell you if he or she and the group are getting along and if any personal problems are beginning to surface. Watch for the warning signals such as fatigue, chronic complaints, lack of interest, or sudden changes from previous behavior patterns. If you spot any of these signals, be prepared to move swiftly to uncover the causes.

You must be prepared for the possibility that the new person may not work out. He or she may not, in spite of your efforts and those of the personnel department, be cut out for the type of work that has been assigned. If your observations and his or her responses seem to indicate this, get together with your boss and discuss the matter. You may be able to work something out such as a transfer to a different job within or outside your section. It may also be possible to re-define duties to compensate for the difficulties. You want to try your best to salvage the new arrival and to avoid costly termination and replacement proceedings.

REASONS FOR QUITTING

■ Employers are eager to prevent employee turnover because it is a source of great expense and it is also upsetting to the flow of work within the organization. By finding out why its employees quit, a company may be able to eliminate some causes of future resignations. The **exit interview** with all employees who quit their jobs is a device that can help uncover causes of employee dissatisfaction and frustration.

Crawford Williams[2] has listed the various reasons for quitting that employees gave in numerous surveys and exit interviews. The following reasons are of particular interest to supervisors:

1. Poor selection;
2. Poor placement;
3. Inadequate training and supervision;
4. Unsatisfactory working conditions;
5. Safety hazards;
6. Lack of opportunity;
7. Failure to receive credit for good work;
8. Favoritism shown relatives of bosses and/or senior employees;
9. Unwillingness of supervisors to hear complaints or suggestions;
10. Time lost because of breakdowns or bad scheduling.

These complaints were connected with 45 to 60 percent of all voluntary job changes. You can see that supervisors are directly related to each of them and are usually in a position to do something about them. Knowing how difficult and time-consuming, not to mention expensive,

---

2. Crawford Williams, "Why workers say 'I quit.'" From a reprint of *Supervisory Management Magazine,* July 1968.

the hiring process is, don't you think that you should do your best to eliminate these causes of resignations whenever you can?

Supervisors should make the decision to hire, and they are in the best position to see to it that new employees achieve success. Your most important resource is the individual worker. Your aim should be to conserve all your resources, especially your human resources.

All you have to do is to treat the new person like a guest in your home whom you wish to impress favorably. If you have his or her welfare uppermost in your mind, you won't go wrong. Be honest. Keep the channels of communications open. Through adequate planning, a warm welcome, and a constructive orientation program, you will be doing all that you can do or are expected to do.

INSTANT REPLAY	After you have decided to hire an applicant and he or she has accepted the offer of employment, the induction process or phase begins. In this phase you should plan for the newcomer's arrival by constructing a program of orientation that will welcome him or her into your organization.

Once the new employee arrives, the orientation or introduction begins by explaining to him or her the various policies, regulations, and rules as well as the rights and opportunities that are his or hers to enjoy.

The first day is the most crucial one because it is the first real taste of your leadership and the working environment. It can be a frightening and unpleasant experience, especially if there's neither a formal orientation program nor a coworker or supervisor to soothe those first-day jitters. The opinions and attitudes that the newcomer will carry for most of his tenure with you and your department have their roots in this first experience. Every effort should be made to convince the new person that he or she is a necessary, vital part in a dynamic whole.

In view of the fact that security and social acceptance are two of the most basic human needs, you should design your orientation program to include some measure of satisfaction for them. The assignment of a mentor and your own open attitude toward your subordinates will go far to help provide these needs for your new subordinate. The future of your new employee is in your hands to a considerable extent. If you expect the newcomer to serve yourself, your group, and your company, you must be willing to serve his or her needs too.

KEY WORDS	**exit interview**	**induction**	**mentor**	**orientation**

1. Design an orientation program to welcome a new student to your college.
2. Tell your group about the way in which you were inducted into and oriented to your present job. What was not done that should have been?
3. How is the induction process influenced by the selection process?
4. What should be included in the first day's orientation program?
5. How can the personnel department assist a supervisor in the orientation planning? In the orientation process?
6. Using the list of reasons employees give for quitting, mention one way in which the supervisor can deal with each reason.
7. During your orientation program, were you misinformed in any way? If so, describe its effect on you.
8. Of what value is a mentor to a new employee?
9. Why do you think that 39 percent of the companies surveyed by the Dartnell Institute of Business Research have not formalized their orientation programs?
10. Why do some companies fail to offer any formal orientation program to new employees?

CASE PROBLEM

Fitting In

Burly Mike Gunderson is foreman of the central warehouse operations of York Products Company. He has seven men who work for him in loading, order picking, stocking, inspecting, and general clerical work. Company policy requires that new employees be requisitioned and hired by the central personnel office, which is located in the company headquarters about fifteen miles from the warehouse. In the past, Mike has been quite satisfied with the new employees he has received from the home office and, for the most part, all of them have fit in well with the group in the warehouse. That is to say, all have fit in until recently, when Walter Perry appeared.

Nearly a month ago, Mike requested a replacement for Jim Yost who was leaving to start his own business. Jim worked alongside Mike in the small office where all the records and orders of the warehouse were processed. He had agreed to stay on an extra week to help train his replacement, Walter Perry.

Mike had met Walter briefly before introducing him to the other men, and he suspected that he might have trouble with Walter who was shy but willing to learn. Walter was quite thin and tall, only twenty years old, and looked like a scarecrow. He seemed sensitive and withdrawn. Mike had introduced Walter to the group at lunch on Walter's first day of work. That was three days ago and, ever since, things have gone from bad to worse.

The warehouse group is a rough bunch of guys who like to horse around and kid each other. They work hard and play hard. They have a softball team and a bowling team, and like to frequent a neighborhood tap after work for a little spirited eating and drinking. Most of the men are in their thirties and have known each other for several years. They have an unwritten code that seems to dominate their every action: "Act like a man!"

Jim Yost is finding it increasingly difficult to work with Walter and doesn't mind telling Mike why.

"Mike, that kid really irritates me. Every time he speaks I want to throw up. I've been getting the raspberries from the other guys about working with Perry. He won't join any of the teams. He brings books to work and prefers to read and eat alone on his breaks. Some of the guys think he's a chicken or sissy or something. I can't take much more. Look, he knows most of my job now because he learns fast. Can't you teach him the rest? I just want out. I want to get on with my new business venture."

"I knew the guys were kidding a lot about Perry. I even expected it, but I didn't expect that you would be so uptight about it."

"Look, all the guys are uptight. In fact, they're downright mad about that kid being part of their group. They're afraid the guys on the other teams are going to find out about Walter and that they will start kidding them about him. Mike, you ought to get rid of him. You two are going to have to work together here when I leave, and then they'll start to kid you! Are you ready for that?"

"I don't know the kid very well yet. He's spent all his time with you and I wasn't aware of all this until now. Jim, just stick it out for two more days. Then I'll take over."

Mike begins to reflect on the happenings of the last three days. When Jim left, who would Walter have breaks and lunch with? He would have no friends if all the guys feel so strongly about him. He doesn't seem to fit in with any of the other workers, and Mike definitely doesn't want the kid's image to rub off on him.

Questions

1. How have the warehousemen formed their image of Perry?
2. What can Mike do as the formal leader of the work group to integrate Perry into the group?
3. Do you think it important that all employees "fit in" to the existing group or groups at work? Why?
4. If you were Mike, what would you do now?

17   Training

LEARNING OBJECTIVES

■ After reading and discussing this chapter, you should be able to:

1 List three things that are taught through training.

2 List three advantages that you as a supervisor derive from training your subordinates.

3 List three advantages of training for your subordinates.

4 Describe three qualities that a person should have before attempting to train other people.

5 List and briefly describe seven principles that govern training.

6 Describe various stages in the training cycle.

7 List and briefly describe four pitfalls connected with training.

INTRODUCTION

■ Immediately following induction and orientation comes another important duty—the training of your subordinates. The process of training involves helping the trainees acquire the necessary skills, knowledge, and attitudes which will enable them to carry out their present duties as well as to prepare themselves for increased responsibilities.

Training becomes necessary by the very fact that you have subordinates. Whether they are all old-timers, newcomers, or a mix of the two, you will always have to concern yourself with their development. Old-timers have the need to periodically update their skills and to form new attitudes. Newcomers need to be shown what is expected of them now and what may be expected of them in the future.

This chapter is concerned with how to train your people. Whether you do it yourself or rely on others to help you with the training, you must see to it that your people are properly trained.

THE TRAINING PROCESS

SKILLS

Many jobs require the mastery of certain motor **skills,** that is, activities that require muscular coordination blended with technical abilities such as typing, equipment operation, and the use of precision machines. What you are imparting when you seek to develop such skills is a proficiency or technical ability related to a trade or craft.

The best way to teach a skill is to involve the learners as quickly as possible in doing or performing the skill. Practice and more practice are keys to the successful acquisition of motor skills. Moving from an in-depth understanding of the tools, equipment, or machinery to an actual working knowledge of the trade or craft, the trainees experience a controlled exposure to both the technical and manipulative sides of their jobs.

Early successes are essential, and extremely close supervision must be exercised so that improper working habits are not acquired and so that confidence is instilled as soon as possible. Often you may have to ask the trainees to unlearn certain procedures or habits acquired by earlier experiences before you can substitute the proper methods. This is a difficult and time-consuming task which requires a great deal of patience of both teachers and students.

KNOWLEDGE

Knowledge is the body of facts, ideas, concepts, and procedures that enable people to see or visualize what it is that must be done and why. If trainees can understand the whole job and its relationship to the work of others, they have a better chance to master their own jobs. They must understand the theory (fundamental principles and abstract knowledge) that govern their work before they can adequately perform their own tasks. Then they must (with your help) translate the theory into practice through the training process. Knowing what to do is one thing, but applying the knowledge is the most important thing.

ATTITUDES

Much has already been said about attitudes, and all of it is related to the training process. You must remember that when you train you are attempting to instill positive attitudes, either as replacements for improper ones or to fill a void in the minds of your trainees. Attitudes are taught primarily by your example and secondarily through your words. Workers learn an attitude by what you do. If you talk safety but act in an unsafe manner or skip over safety lightly during the training period, your workers will adopt the same casual attitudes. The most important attitudes that you must help form in learners are those that involve their job and their safety.

ADVANTAGES OF TRAINING FOR THE SUPERVISOR

■ Just what do you yourself get out of training a subordinate? What is in it for you? The following are but a few of the many benefits you receive when you train your people properly:

1. *You get to know your subordinates.* When you are dealing with new employees, you hasten the process of learning about their needs, wants, and potentials. With your other subordinates you get a chance to update your knowledge of each person, thereby making your personnel decisions and recommendations easier with regard to promotions, raises, transfers, and the like.

2. *You further your own career.* As your people grow in abilities, proficiency, and reputation, so too will you. As each individual increases his or her efficiency and effectiveness, the whole group benefits. As your subordinates look better, feel better, and perform better, they strongly affect your reputation as a supervisor and leader. As we have stated before, your reputation is a product of their making.

3. *You gain more time.* As a result of training your people become more self-sufficient and confident. You will find that as their performances improve, you have more time for the essentials. You will spend less time on corrections and deficiencies and more on planning, organizing, controlling, and coordinating. You may be able to shift from an autocratic style of supervision, so necessary during the training, to a less time-consuming one.

4. *You promote good human relations.* One of your primary roles in developing good human relations with your people is that of educator. You give them logical reasons to support sound working relationships with you and their peers. They gain self-confidence, pride, and security through their training, which promotes cooperation and respect for you. Many will see you as the cause of their improvement and will rely on you more for advice and direction in the future.

5. *You reduce safety hazards.* By emphasizing safety rules, procedures, and attitudes through your proper conduct and words, you will be reducing the likelihood of violations and the resulting accidents and injuries. How tragic it would be to have to live with the knowledge that a subordinate's injury might have been prevented had you done all that you should have in the area of safety.

ADVANTAGES OF TRAINING FOR SUBORDINATES

■ Training gives your workers as many advantages as you receive (if not more). Here are a few:

1. *They increase their chances for success.* Through training, workers gain new knowledge and experiences which help to reduce the risks of personal obsolescence and increase their value to themselves and the company. By exposure and practice workers gain new techniques that

HERMAN

"This is my nephew. I want you to spend the morning grooming him for your job."

© 1976. Universal Press Syndicate.

enhance their abilities and their enjoyment of work. By successfully completing training, workers confront change, meet challenges, and decrease fears.

2. *They increase their motivation to work.* By successful training experiences and proper guidance, individuals experience a greater measure of achievement. They find ways to reduce fatigue, increase contributions and expend less effort to accomplish their tasks. These accomplishments tend to fortify a desire to work harder. We all need the security that comes with really knowing our jobs well so that we are free to learn new skills and to advance in our careers.

3. *They promote their own advancement.* As workers become more proficient, they earn the right to receive additional duties either through delegation or a job change. By proving themselves through the learning process they justify the investment of additional company time and money in their development. They become more mobile members of the organization.

4. *Their morale improves.* Mastery of new responsibilities inevitably leads to new prestige and importance. This newfound pride can be

translated into higher earnings, a greater commitment to the company, and a renewed self-image. As the spirits of group members rise, they can and often do infect the group. Workers see themselves as necessary and now more valuable parts of the whole and as greater contributors to the group's success.

5. *Their productivity increases.* Their output will be less problem-ridden, exhibit less wasted effort and materials, and result in a higher quality and return to themselves and the company.

Some or all of these benefits will accrue to everyone who takes part in training. The degree to which an individual receives such benefits is a variable that cannot be predicted. But training does tell your people of both your company's and your personal interest in their welfare and development. That says a great deal.

REQUIREMENTS FOR TRAINERS

■ Ideally, you as the supervisor should plan and execute the essential function of training. This is true primarily because of the many personal benefits available to you when you do. After all, the workers on your team are your responsibility.

There are times, however, when you cannot train subordinates. Either you may lack the time or the firsthand knowledge of the job to be taught, or both. In such cases you may have to delegate the training duties to a subordinate or rely on the various staff specialists your company may provide. In either case, you are accountable for their actions and the results. Therefore, it would be wise for you to assist, when you are able, in the planning of the training and to check up periodically on its execution. Better one ounce of prevention than pounds of cure.

If you delegate the training function to a subordinate, he or she should meet the following basic requirements.

1. Be willing to train;
2. Know the body of knowledge, attitudes, and skills to be taught;
3. Know how to train—possess a working knowledge of the principles and procedures that govern the training process.

Unless your subordinate possesses these prerequisites, you must either do the training yourself or train another to train.

We shall be assuming throughout the remainder of this chapter that you, the supervisor, will be conducting the training.

THE PRINCIPLES OF TRAINING

■ There are several established and proven principles that you should keep in mind while planning and conducting a training program. These principles should be used as a checklist to make certain that you have not overlooked anything important. They are summarized by the catch-word *Mirrors* to facilitate your remembering them:

M otivation
I ndividualism
R ealism
R esponse
O bjective
R einforcement
S ubjects

These principles are interdependent and interrelated.

Motivation

Both you and the learner must be motivated, or the training process will achieve something less than is desired. Your motivation should be no problem as there is much that you will gain by training. If you delegate to a subordinate, you again should have no problem because he or she willingly accepted the responsibility. It is the learner or trainee that poses the greatest concern. New employees are usually anxious to get through training so as to gain some level of independence and security. Your training of new people should start as soon after their arrival as possible.

When training experienced workers to gain new skills or update old ones, you may have a problem. Chapters 8 and 11 deal at some length with this situation so you may want to review them. Just remember to point out to all your trainees what personal advantages they will be receiving. Give them all the incentives you can to encourage them to be willing learners.

Individualism

The principle of individualism states that the training you prepare and present must be tailored to meet the needs and situations of individuals. In order to do this, you must know what skills, knowledge, and attitudes the people possess already so that you can start from there in designing your program. By building on what they already know, you can use their past experiences as a frame of reference. What is to be added can be linked to their present abilities.

By individualizing your approach, you can adjust the sequence of what is to be taught to best fit present conditions. For instance, if people already know how to operate a particular piece of machinery that is similar but not the same as the one they must now operate, begin by pointing out the similarities and then show the differences or exceptions.

BEETLE BAILEY

© King Features Syndicate, Inc., 1973.

Finally, this principle states that you must vary your presentation of material to fit people's ability to assimilate it. Let the learners advance at a comfortable rate and don't give too much at once. You will only frustrate and confuse people if you do.

Realism

Make the learning process as close to the real thing as you can. For most training situations you should teach people on the job, using the actual equipment, tools, or machinery that must be mastered. In the case of office or clerical employees, use the actual forms, manuals, procedures, and practices. This is not always possible because of various limitations. Noise levels may interfere with proper communications; space may not be adequate for proper demonstrations or explanations; equipment or machines may not be available for training use because they are being fully utilized in current production. When you can't train on the job, or deem it wiser not to do so, set up conditions that are as close to the actual working situation as you can. Use examples and situations that accurately reflect actual problems the worker is likely to encounter. Then move from the simulated conditions to the actual environment as soon as possible.

Response

The principle of response reminds you to check on the learners' receptiveness and retention regularly. Involve the trainees in a two-way conversation. Ask questions and encourage them to do the same. It is only by checking frequently that you can be sure that lasting progress is taking place.

Response also includes the concept of evaluation. Besides oral questions and answers, you can evaluate or measure the trainees' progress by means of performance tests or written quizzes. Use whatever you believe will yield the information you seek. Involve the learners in feedback throughout the training process.

Objective

The principle of the objective states that trainees and trainers should always know where they are headed at any given point in the training process. As a trainer you have to set goals for the training program and for each of the individual training sessions you conduct. These must be communicated to the trainees so that they know where they are headed and can tell when they get there.

The trainees' goals are targets to shoot for during each session as well as throughout the entire program. They should be realistic, specific, and within the learners' ability to achieve. They tell employees that their training is planned and professional.

Ask yourself this question: "What do I want the trainee to be able to accomplish?" Reaching this conclusion will guide you in choosing the most appropriate training methods.

Reinforcement

According to the principle of reinforcement, if learning is to be retained, it must involve all the senses or as many as possible. When you first explain an idea, you may involve both sight and hearing with a demonstration coupled with an explanation. Then you can let the trainees try out their understanding by repeating the demonstration and explanation in their own words. They will then be using sight, touch, and hearing and will be reviewing the concepts as well. By using frequent summaries and reviewing points you know to be crucial, you will be practicing reinforcement. By repetition and practice you lend emphasis and greatly increase retention.

Also, put the knowledge and skills that must be learned to work in a real situation as soon as possible. Studies reveal that we retain about 50 percent of what we hear immediately after we hear it and about 75 percent of what we experience immediately after the event. As time passes without further reference to our knowledge or application of our skills, our retention of them diminishes still further.

Subjects

The principle of subjects is two-sided: you must know as much about the trainees as possible, and you must have a mastery of the subject to be taught. By research and rehearsal before the main event, you will be aware of the likely trouble spots both in the presentation and the learning of the material.

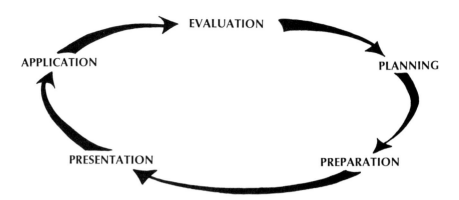

EVALUATION

APPLICATION

PLANNING

PRESENTATION

PREPARATION

Figure 17-1. The training cycle.

THE TRAINING CYCLE

■ Figure 17–1 illustrates the training cycle. It is a cycle because training never really ends. As the jobs change or new equipment and procedures are introduced, even the most experienced veterans will have to be exposed to the changes.

Planning

As we stated earlier, during this first step you must construct a training program for individuals on the basis of your knowledge of these people and their needs. You will have to determine the objectives you wish to reach, the methods (lecture, demonstration, discussion) you wish to use, and the equipment and environment necessary for successful re-sults. A timetable must be worked out for the entire program as well as for the individual sessions or lessons.

Breaking Down the Job for Training Purposes

Study the job to be taught. List its duties and responsibilities. Reduce its content to identifiable steps, and arrange them in a sequence that is logical and by which they can best be taught. Then identify key steps—steps that are crucial or critical to the mastery of the process being taught as well as steps which historically have been the source of trouble or difficulties to the persons holding the job. Safety is always critical to any operation as well as to each step associated with safety.

After you have a list of the key steps and their corresponding critical concepts, break the job into learnable units—units small enough to be effectively taught and absorbed in one session. If the units are too big, the learner will be unable to digest them. It is far better to have less material—leaving ample time for review and practice—than to have too much. A good rule of thumb is to attempt to teach no more than three key points in every sixty-minute session.

Preparation

When you are finished with your planning, the execution begins with the preparation of the training area. Have everything on hand and in working order so that the session can flow smoothly and without interruption. Have the area properly arranged and in the same condition you expect your workers to keep it.

Prepare the workers by:
1. Putting them at ease;
2. Stating the objectives to be achieved during the session;
3. Pointing out the advantages to be received from the training;
4. Explaining the sequence of the events that are about to follow.

You should stress the fact that when you and the company take the time and make the effort necessary to train workers, it is positive proof of concern for the workers and an expression of confidence in their abilities. Training is costly and the trainees should know the costs and why management is willing to incur them. If eligibility for training was competitive, let each trainee know of your pride in his or her selection. Let your trainees know that there is no harm in making mistakes. In fact, we learn more by the analysis of our mistakes than we do by listening to a teacher who says all the right things. It is through the examination of our failures or incorrect examples that we discover their causes and can prevent their reoccurrence.

Presentation

During your presentation you attempt to communicate to the workers what you wish them to learn. It is best to use examples and illustrations wherever and whenever you can. Demonstrate the process, one step at a time, and allow time for questions. Stress the important points in each step. By doing things "by the numbers" or in slow motion, the learners have a chance to examine each step in detail and to check their understanding. If they have no questions, ask some of your own. Watch your pacing. It is as probable that you are going too slow as that you are going too fast.

Stick with your timetable and lesson plan as closely as you can. It's best to take a break after each fifty or sixty minutes so that you and the learners return refreshed. Most adults don't have an attention span greater than this period of time. If you run out of time before you run out of materials, stop anyway. You should be flexible enough to allow for such happenings. You can't predict all the problems you may encounter, so leave your lesson a little loose to accommodate the unexpected.

Be patient. Try not to show your emotions or frustration to the trainees. Any criticism you make should be constructive and aimed at the person's actions rather than the person.

Application

This phase of the training cycle lets trainees get their feet wet. They must perform the process or activity as it was demonstrated and explained. Get trainees active in the application of what they learn as soon as you can. Even though we are treating the presentation and application separately here, they may be and should be intermixed. This happens when you let the trainees repeat a demonstration you have given or when you let them try their wings on one or more of the key steps as you take them through the motions. By mixing the two you are practicing the principle of reinforcement and providing the early and measured successes that are so essential to mastery of the material and motivation in the learner.

Provide trainees with frequent and immediate feedback. Let them know when they are correct and ask them to spot their own mistakes. Let them examine the product of their efforts and try to spot any defects. Once they discover an error, explain, or get them to do so, just how it can be prevented from happening again. Point out how one error, the one just made, for example, can lead to others. Use each mistake as a point for review, and then conduct a critique to summarize the entire lesson.

There is a technique of great merit in use in different types of apprenticeship programs. The master mechanic or teacher will "bug" a machine by deliberately planting a problem within it. The student must troubleshoot the item to uncover its problem and then correct the deficiency. This technique may fit your needs, so give it some thought. Just be sure that the bug you plant does not permanently damage the equipment!

Evaluation

In this phase you attempt to check on the trainees' grasp of the who, what, when, where, why, and how. You can and should include evaluation in any of the phases of training as well as at the end. Performance tests, oral quizzes, and silent observations are part of every phase of the training cycle. As with the summaries, evaluation should be frequent and the results shared with the trainees.

Through evaluation you can quickly ascertain the need for reteaching a point. Also, you will soon realize just how fast you can place people on their own, free from your strict supervision and control. Put people on their own, but gradually. Don't let them feel that when the training ends, it's sink or swim. Be available to them and let them know that you are. Simply make your visits and observations less frequent as each person demonstrates an ability to perform to standards. Your follow-up should tell you whether lasting effects have been achieved or whether an individual needs additional training.

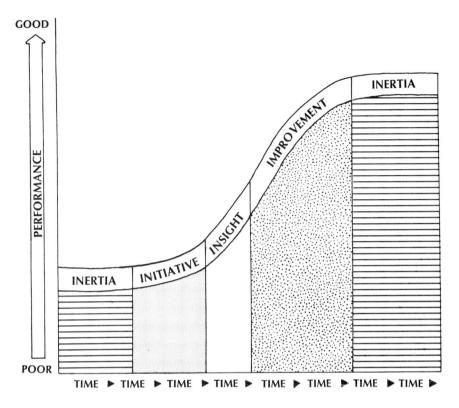

Figure 17-2. The improvement cycle or learning curve.
From *The Nine Master Keys of Management* by Lester R. Bittel. Copyright © 1972
McGraw-Hill Book Company. Used with permission of McGraw-Hill Book Company.

THE IMPROVEMENT CYCLE

■ Figure 17–2 summarizes the training process. Trainees move from a state of inertia through the training cycle to a new but higher state of inertia and so on.

The Inertia Stage

Lester Bittel states that the learner "begins from a standing start."[1] Inertia is the tendency a body at rest has to remain at rest. With each worker there may be a tendency to resist training. As in the case of a person's resistance to change, personal or social reasons may be behind this resistance. The **inertia stage** must be overcome if the training is to be effective.

---

1. From *The Nine Master Keys of Management* by Lester R. Bittel. Copyright © 1972 McGraw-Hill Book Company. Used with permission of McGraw-Hill Book Company.

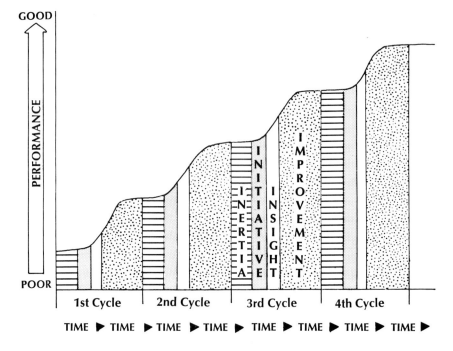

Figure 17-3. Long-range improvement curve.
From *The Nine Master Keys of Management* by Lester R. Bittel. Copyright © 1972
McGraw-Hill Book Company. Used with permission of McGraw-Hill Book Company.

The Initiative Phase

The **initiative phase** represents the learner's movement from a state of inertia to active participation in the learning process. He or she may be pushed but it is far better to have him or her want to learn by incentives and explanations that will instill the will to learn.

The Insight Phase

Insights are sensory, intellectual, and procedural. Sensory insights involve the concepts of tight, smooth, and the like. Intellectual insights include an understanding of an entire operation and its parts, the relationship of the newly acquired knowledge to what was previously known, and the why behind events. Procedural insights "establish the necessary sequence for successful accomplishment of objectives; safety precautions; stress on accuracy rather than speed."[2]

Bittel explains that what happens in each session or program with a trainee is repeated with each new program or session as shown in Figure 17–2 so that a cycle is set in motion as illustrated in Figure 17–3.

---

2. Ibid., p. 249.

THE TRAINING ENVIRONMENT

■ Training can be carried out with and by individuals or groups either on the job or in a controlled environment such as a classroom or laboratory. Instruction or training given on the job is generally conducted on a one-on-one basis with a teacher/trainer working with a pupil/trainee. Examples are the master worker or artist who teaches an apprentice or the boss who teaches an understudy or assistant.

The training environment in a classroom or laboratory tries to simulate real working conditions but eliminates the noise and confusion that often surround an actual working area with its customary production disturbances and routine activities. Individual instructors or instruction teams may conduct lectures and discussions or put on demonstrations. Machines and training aids can help make the training seem more realistic and thus are used more readily in such a training environment. This type of environment works well for the training of individuals and groups.

TRAINING METHODS

■ There are three basic training methods that can be used to train workers: the buddy system, machine-based systems, group sessions. All have advantages and disadvantages. Some are appropriate for certain training tasks but not for others. We shall define and give examples of each method.

The Buddy System

The buddy system is a person-to-person or one-on-one method of training. It may be known also as the teacher-pupil method or the master-apprentice method, but regardless of what it is called, this method utilizes one trainer and one trainee; a person who knows the job teaches someone who needs to know it. When the person doing the training is properly prepared, the buddy system has the following major advantages:

1. It is flexible—learning can take place in a classroom, a laboratory, or on the job. Changes can be introduced quickly. The system can be tailored as to pace and content to meet the individual needs of trainees.

2. It provides for immediate feedback—the teacher/trainer works directly with the trainee and can personally and quickly evaluate the learner's progress or lack of progress, offering corrections and reviews to improve retention and mastery.

3. It is personal—it "humanizes" the training process and allows for questions and answers, reviews, and additional drills or practices at any time. Personalized corrections may be made and personalized instructions given throughout the duration of training. Also, it frequently helps the learners to satisfy some of their social needs.

The disadvantage of the buddy system are:

1. It is costly—the salary or wages of the trainer go to pay for the training of just one trainee during any training session. Expensive equipment and machines are tied up and utilized by only one trainee at any given moment. The time and talents of the trainer are utilized for only one trainee per session.

2. It is difficult—to prepare for and conduct adequately. If the real advantages of the buddy system are to be realized, the instructor must assess adequately the needs of the learner, tailor his or her instruction to meet those needs, and avoid passing along attitudes, prejudices, and shortcuts that differ from what the worker needs and what management wants taught.

Machine-Based Systems

Automated or programmed instruction methods are referred to as *machine-based systems of instruction and training* because they rely heavily upon a machine to relay information and evaluate learner responses. Computers and machines that use filmstrips, videotapes, audiotapes, records, and the like can enhance the learning environment and enrich the kind of training that takes place. But all machine-based instruction requires people to: (1) prepare the learner and materials; (2) monitor the training process by keeping track of time and handling questions or making adjustments to the equipment; and (3) evaluate the progress or lack of progress made by each trainee. This method is more often used to supplement other types of training rather than as a substitute for them. It works well when used to complement the other methods.

The advantages of machine-based training are:

1. It is uniform—it insures that the same material is presented in exactly the same way to each trainee.

2. It is flexible—it can be adjusted, or can adjust itself, to fit the needs and pace of the trainees. It involves the learners in the learning process. It frees trainers for other duties and allows them to handle more than one trainee per session. By periodically checking on each person's progress and by remaining available to each trainee, the trainer will often be able to accomplish other tasks while the machines do part of the instructing.

3. It is inexpensive—while the materials and machines may be expensive to prepare, install, and keep in repair, these costs can be spread over dozens or hundreds of trainees and over a long period of time, and they can be slowly absorbed as an operating expense through allowances for their depreciation.

The disadvantages of machine-based training are:

1. It is impersonal—machines cannot fully replace the need for human interaction. They cannot provide the warmth of a smile and compliment from an instructor for a job well mastered in training. They cannot sense an employee's fear or frustration or the lack of comprehension of a video or verbal message.

2. It requires expertise—learning materials require a great deal of money, know-how, and time to prepare. To be economical they must use materials that will not require frequent changing and that will not become obsolete over a short period of time.

3. It can be boring—for trainees with short attention spans, for those who learn quickly, and for those who already know a significant portion of the material to be mastered, the teaching machine method of training can become frustrating and boring.

Group Sessions

Lectures, conferences, and role-playing sessions can be quite effective methods of training more than one person at each session. Lectures present basic principles and individual points of view, and they can be used to introduce, summarize, or evaluate training sessions or performances. Conferences and discussions can inform, solve problems, clarify situations, and help participants critically evaluate their opinions, attitudes, and methods. Role playing helps people act out a situation to what they see as its logical conclusion. Participants see one another in different lights and have a chance to evaluate critically the solutions of others while trying out their own solutions on the group. All group sessions deal with two or more trainees and require expert planning and leadership if they are to be successful.

The major advantages of the group-sessions method are:

1. It is uniform—two or more persons are exposed to the same material in the same way and at the same time.

2. It is inexpensive—compared to other training methods, the group sessions offer savings in hours and salaries for training purposes.

The major disadvantages of the group-sessions method are:

1. It is impersonal—it does not allow for individual differences, individual participation, or close involvement in the training.

2. It magnifies errors—the impact of each involuntary mistake or bit of misinformation is magnified by the number of trainees.

In designing your training program, try to utilize more than one method of training. For most training a single method will not do. A blend or mix will probably suit your purposes better. When you know what has to be taught, and the human and material resources you have available, think about which method should work best for you and your trainees.

PITFALLS

■ There are four basic pitfalls that may cause you to stumble or that may interfere with your training efforts. Besides violations of any of the above-mentioned principles of training, the pitfalls are:

1. Letting George do it;
2. Assuming something;
3. Fearing a worker's progress;
4. Getting too fancy.

"Letting George do it" means that by delegating or using the assistance of staff specialists, you hope that proper training will take place. Since you are not directly involved, you may tend to wash your hands of the process and rely on their efforts. Remember that you have accountability and must participate in both the planning and execution to the extent necessary to know what is being done and what goals are being achieved. You will be stuck with the results, so make them as beneficial as possible.

"Assuming something" simply means that you assume that the training has been effective or that, since you taught the material according to plan, all of it has been assimilated. There is an old axiom a boss would be wise to cite to a subordinate: when you assume anything, you make an *ass* out of *u* and *me*. Rely on facts and observations that can provide you with a proper evaluation of the program and its effectiveness, not on hunches or your intuition.

The third pitfall reminds you that some people fear the successes and increasing abilities of others, as they view them as threats to their own security. Have you known a manager who refused to train a subordinate because he or she was afraid that if someone could do the job he or she might lose it? Managers may refuse to delegate in order to keep their people dependent upon them and may deliberately deny a subordinate the chance to advance, fearing that the subordinate may challenge their position. Keep in mind that unless you have a trained successor, you are locking yourself into your present position. Training is the job of every manager who has subordinates. By not doing it, you are neglecting a very important duty. This neglect will be reflected in your ratings.

"Getting too fancy" means that trainers may get too caught up in methods and training aids and lose sight of what it is they must teach. Too much flash and too little substance. Have you ever listened to a speaker or lecturer who talked for hours and said nothing? If you have ever seen a fireworks display, you know what is meant by this error.

Training imparts skills, knowledge, and attitudes. Through training you provide many advantages to yourself and your trainees. Your performance rating is determined in large measure by the efforts of your subordinates. The better you can make them, the more you will benefit. The better they become, the more they themselves will profit.

You may have to delegate your training responsibilities or may prefer to do so. When you do, you must oversee the process and check on the results. Delegation implies accountability.

The principles of training will help you direct your efforts and serve as a reminder about what to consider in both the planning and execution of your training program. Each has to do with a major aspect of training, and to ignore them will hamper your efforts severely.

Training is cyclical in nature; no sooner do you end one program than the need arises for another. From evaluation of your workers' strengths and weaknesses comes a recognition of their needs for training.

The improvement cycle illustrates the movement of individuals from a state of rest to an eagerness to learn, thence to the reception of insights, and finally to a personal growth and period of improvement. When the training ends, the trainees return to the inertia stage.

KEY WORDS

individualism	**knowledge**	**response**
inertia stage	**objective**	**skills**
initiative phase	**realism**	**subjects**
insight phase	**reinforcement**	

1. What is meant by the word *skills?* What is the best way to teach skills?

2. Why are early successes important to a trainee in the learning process?

3. How would you teach someone an attitude?

4. Pick two of the principles of training and explain how they are interrelated and interdependent.

5. Why do we refer to training as cyclical in nature?

6. You are planning a program to teach a subordinate how to teach. What identifiable steps would you include? What are the key steps in your estimation? What would be two of your objectives?

7. Explain how the various stages in the execution phase of the training cycle can be intermixed.

8. What is meant by the term *insight?* What kinds of insights are there?

9. Why is it that some managers refuse to train their subordinates? If you were such a manager's boss, what would you do about it?

CASE PROBLEM

Wally Chambers

"Just between us fellas, what I told you in class is pure theory. Tomorrow when you guys get out on the shop floor and start working on your own machines, you'll know that the classroom ain't the real world."

Wally Chambers is a highly experienced and skilled craftsman. Few people know their fields as well as Wally knows his and his students know it. That's why the new group of trainees listen attentively when he speaks— inside or outside the classroom. He knows his stuff alright. That's why he was picked to train four new workers at the Colonial Furniture Company's Louisiana plant.

"Why did we have to learn it all if it isn't the real world, Wally?"

"Listen, kid, you'll learn about the real world fast enough when you realize that the more pieces you guys can turn out, the bigger your paycheck's gonna be. That's when you learn all the short-cuts and how to save time. Stuff like that ain't Kosher to teach you yet. You've got to discover it for yourselves. But I'll give you guys a clue— watch old Elmo Jackson. You can learn a lot of tricks from him."

"Wally, I'll bet watchin' you could teach us a thing or two."

"A few things, kid, but don't let no boss know where you learned 'em. I got my own methods, see. Some of which ain't Kosher if you know what I mean. Well, it's been fun teachin' you guys. You been good students. Good luck!"

Wally shook hands all around and left the four new employees to finish their coffee break.

"Gee, he sure was a swell teacher, wasn't he?"

"Yeah, and a great guy, too."

"I hope I get to work next to Elmo or Wally. Any tricks those guys know, I want to know too!"

"What do you think he's talking about when he says his methods aren't Kosher?"

"Well, I'm not sure, but I think he gave us some clues in his lectures. You guys, remember when he was talking about safety? He said then that the safest method isn't always the best or fastest method, but that's what the company wanted taught, so he was going to teach it."

"Yeah, and I think we got another clue when he took us on the plant tour and showed us how Ernie had rigged his machine to get a higher cutting speed."

"You know, I'm beginning to think our training really begins tomorrow."

Questions

1. Why was Wally picked to train the new employees?

2. Judging from Wally's words, what knowledge and attitudes were taught outside of class?

3. What do you think Wally means by the word *Kosher?*

4. What do you think the trainee means by the last sentence in the case problem?

Part Five

You and Your Environment

18

Security, Safety, and Health

LEARNING OBJECTIVES

■ After reading and discussing this chapter, you should be able to:

1 Define security, safety and health.

2 Outline what supervisors can do to prevent theft by employees.

3 Describe what supervisors can do to avoid hiring dishonest persons.

4 Outline security measures for safeguarding an office and shop.

5 Describe a supervisor's duties in fire prevention.

6 Describe what a supervisor should do in the event of a fire.

7 Outline procedures for preventing losses due to vandalism.

8 Explain a worker's rights under worker's compensation.

9 Describe the purposes of the Occupational Safety and Health Act (OSHA) of 1970.

10 Describe the enforcement procedures and devices used by OSHA inspectors.

INTRODUCTION

■ As the title of this chapter implies, we are concerned here with the supervisor s duties with regard to: (1) **security**—protecting physical facilities and nonhuman resources from loss or damage; (2) **safety**—protecting human resources from accidents and injuries; and (3) **health**—preventing illness and treating injuries when they occur.

Our focus will be on prevention, that is, the ways in which supervisors can head off trouble and minimize damage to their company's human and material resources. We shall explore what supervisors are expected and required to do to help protect these resources. Your duties with regard to security and safety begin with the screening of new applicants and continue on a daily basis as you carry out your managerial functions.

In directing the employees, you can help them avoid accidents and prevent theft through training and discipline. In organizing your department, you can build a structure for the prevention of accidents and the enforcement of safety rules. In planning, you can design programs, procedures, and practices that will help carry out management policies and coincide with state and federal safety standards. You can construct effective preventive, diagnostic, and therapeutic controls to deal with safety and security problems. Through effective communications, committee action, and peer-group cooperation, you can insure the coordination of safety and security efforts throughout the company.

PHYSICAL SECURITY

■ During 1976 about $25 billion was lost by the 1.7 million business corporations of the United States because of crimes committed against them and the necessity to spend money on crime-prevention measures. (See Table 18-1.) If we add to this figure the crime losses experienced by our nation's 9.8 million sole proprietorships in that same year, we discover that there are each year business losses in excess of $50 billion because of criminal activity.

Thefts by customers raise the cost of doing business, and ultimately they lead to higher prices. The average retail business loses an amount equal to 2 percent of its total sales each year to shoplifters. According to the Commerce Department, this represents price boosts on products of $89 for every person in the United States. In 1974, retailers spent

Table 18-1. The cost of crimes against business. Crimes include bad checks, inventory shortage, robbery, vandalism, and counterfeiting.
Reprinted courtesy of The Chicago Tribune. All rights reserved.
Data: U.S. Department of Commerce.

Business sectors	Billions of dollars				
	1971	1973	1974	1975	1976
Retailing	4.8	5.2	5.8	6.5	8.1
Manufacturing	1.8	2.6	2.8	3.2	4.3
Wholesaling	1.4	1.8	2.1	2.4	3.4
Services	2.7	3.2	3.5	4.3	6.7
Transportation	1.5	1.7	1.9	2.3	2.5
Totals	12.2	14.5	16.1	18.7	25.0

nearly $2 billion to protect themselves from thefts committed by customers. A security firm in New York City was hired to follow five hundred shoppers around a large department store. The firm reported that one out of every twelve customers stole something!

Employees and owners who steal from their own companies raise the cost of doing business and reduce the firm's profits; as a result, their own returns from their companies are decreased. Internal crimes committed by employees cost American businesses about $15 billion annually. Retailers alone lose about $6 billion in "inventory shrinkage." Employees steal everything from paper clips to electric typewriters. Nearly all internal crimes are theft-related, but there are cases of arson and sabotage as well. By 1984 it is estimated that businesses will spend $1.3 billion each year for security systems and devices to protect themselves against such internal crimes.[1]

There is not a lot that supervisors can do to prevent theft by customers, but there are a number of precautions that they can and must take to reduce **pilferage,** that is, theft by employees.

CRIME PREVENTION

■ Preventing crimes committed by employees begins with the selection of each new employee. In most companies supervisors are involved in the selection of new employees, as they certainly should be. During the screening process both the supervisors and members of the personnel department should be alert for the telltale signs of a potentially dishonest employee. (See Figure 18–1.) In addition to this list of clues, you should check the applicant's life-style for any hints that the person is living above his or her level of income.

Ask for and verify a recommendation from the applicant's most recent employer. This precaution won't always uncover a person with a history of theft or willful destruction of company property, however, because many employers simply ask an employee caught stealing to resign. They often do not fire such an employee or prosecute him or her in the courts because they don't want to air their dirty linen in public. Few employers pass on to a potential new employer negative information about a former employee because they fear being accused of violating that person's civil rights and having a lawsuit filed against them. In addition, the courts have been notoriously lenient toward white-collar criminals, who have often received only small fines or jail terms of less than a year in convictions for thefts amounting to thousands of dollars in cash or goods.

---

1. *Chicago Tribune,* 23 September 1975, sec. 4, p. 9.

Here are some clues on what to look for
in an applicant's background. None of these is infallible,
but they are good tools for measuring up a job hunter.

Frequent job changes	There may be good reasons why a person is a "job jumper." Pursue the question and find out why.
Periods of unemployment	If the reasons are economic, okay. But let the applicant explain, and pay attention to possible inconsistencies.
Frequent changes of residence	How come you moved so often? You have a right to ask and to examine the reasons given.
Financial overinvolvement	Is the person deep in debt?
Overqualified	Why is a college graduate or and experienced person applying for a job that does not call for such a background? There can be important clues to revealing past hanky-panky.
Falsification of application	Pick up inconsistencies and ask about them. While most companies will fire an employee who lied on the application, the harm may have been done by then!

Figure 18-1. Some warning signs of a potentially dishonest applicant.
Reprinted from "Safety & Security for Supervisors," a monthly publication
of Business Research Publications, Inc., 799 Broadway, New York, N.Y. 10003.

Efforts at crime prevention have to begin with a hard stand in company policy, and they depend upon all the supervisors at every level for strong enforcement. Consider this policy statement in a large life insurance company's employee manual:

Any employee found stealing, or attempting to steal, company money or property—whether by wrongfully taking it or by fraud or embezzlement—will be subject to immediate appropriate disciplinary action, including termination of employment.

The company will be the sole judge of the sufficiency of the evidence in these cases. Where the evidence so warrants, the company will also bring the matter to the attention of appropriate law enforcement agencies.

Many law-enforcement officials and security firms recommend this kind of hard line to prevent dishonest employees from practicing their thievery at more than one company. Get to know your company's security policies and procedures. Then enforce them without exception!

OFFICE SECURITY

■ Most companies have on their premises tangible assets such as office machines and equipment to protect as well as valuable, highly sensitive information. To protect these assets some basic, commonsense approaches work well alongside sophisticated and sometimes quite expensive equipment.

The number one problem in protecting office equipment, machines, and sensitive information is to prevent access by unauthorized personnel. People must be kept separated into two groups in the minds of office supervisors: those who belong, and those who do not.

It should not be possible for someone to enter an office without being screened at the entrance. To make this screening process easier, many offices have only one entrance; it is usually the only nonfire exit as well. Someone like a receptionist should be on hand at all times to greet each visitor from the moment the office is opened until it is closed for the day. Persons who have no legitimate reason to go farther should not be allowed to do so. People admitted beyond the reception area should have a specific destination. In the case of messengers and delivery people, the receptionist should accept the parcel or message, or should request the addressee to come forward to receive it if a specific signature is required. Parcels should be checked into a central cloak room or, if this is not practical, they should be periodically spot-checked by security personnel. Briefcases, packages, lunch pails, and similar objects can easily be used to carry company property or sensitive information out of an office.

The protection of the employees' personal property can be best achieved by alerting people to the ever present dangers of loss and theft. Office personnel should be asked to keep their valuables with them or safely locked away. A purse or a pocket calculator left on a desk is just too big a temptation for some people, whether strangers or regular employees. Advise your people to take their valuables home after work, especially when the office is to be unoccupied over a weekend or long holiday period when a burglary or fire is most likely to occur. Unfortunately, warnings are often not enough for some people, and losses are almost certain to happen.

When a theft occurs, an investigation is called for on your part. It should involve security people if they are available. Use any past experience as a reminder that losses have occurred. There is nothing quite

```
┌─────────────────────────────────────────────────────────────────┐
│                    DAILY SECURITY CHECKLIST                       │
│                                                                   │
│     1. File cabinets locked.                            [_____]   │
│                                                                   │
│     2. Safe locked.                                     [_____]   │
│                                                                   │
│     3. Personal valuables secured.                      [_____]   │
│                                                                   │
│     4. Windows locked.                                  [_____]   │
│                                                                   │
│     5. Machines off.                                    [_____]   │
│                                                                   │
│     6. Night lights on.                                 [_____]   │
│                                                                   │
│     7. Non-essential lights off.                        [_____]   │
│                                                                   │
│     8. People out.                                      [_____]   │
│                                                                   │
│     9. Doors secured.                                   [_____]   │
│                                                                   │
│    10. Alarm on.                                        [_____]   │
│                                                                   │
│    Remarks: _____   │
│                                                                   │
│    _____   │
│                                                                   │
│    Date: _____  Time: _____    │
│                                                                   │
│    Checklist completed by: _____   │
└─────────────────────────────────────────────────────────────────┘
```

Figure 18-2. Daily security checklist for closing an office.

so effective as an actual loss to drive home the need to safeguard one's own property. Figure 18–2 gives a short security checklist to follow at the end of each day. Whoever is in charge of securing the office should refer to such a list before leaving.

SECURING THE SHOP

■ Shop or plant security has some definite parallels to office security. Again the prevention of access by unauthorized personnel is the number one problem to insure safety and security. Controls can be exercised over people who enter the area in similar ways. Personal belongings can be secured in employee lockers or checked with the company's security personnel upon entering the plant or shop.

But there are some special security problems that go along with plant security. Besides protecting property and information from theft, you must be concerned with the prevention of fires and vandalism.

Security, Safety, and Health / **301**

FIRE PREVENTION

■ About every fifteen seconds a fire results in property damage somewhere in the United States. Such fires often result in the loss of life and jobs as well. While you are not expected to be a professional firefighter, you are expected to minimize the risks of a fire starting in any area over which you have some control. The job is not yours alone. You must have the support of management as well as of your peers and subordinates. Without their cooperation your efforts will be of little use.

Most fires are a result of carelessness and might have been prevented. Piles of rubbish, oily rags, the improper use of smoking materials and flammable liquids represent common causes that people with good common sense should recognize as likely hazards. Proper training of personnel, which includes fire prevention and how to extinguish various kinds of fires, can go a long way toward reducing and eliminating fire hazards. A concern for fire prevention begins with the initial training of each new employee and continues to be reinforced by fire-prevention programs throughout the year.

Periodic inspections should be conducted by every department on a regular schedule. All your people represent potential causes of fires, just as they also represent detection and prevention devices. All employees should be made to feel that fire prevention and detection depend upon them personally. Such attitudes are instilled through actions and words and by responding in a positive way each time a subordinate tells you about a potential fire hazard or takes time to remove one.

Be certain that all pieces of fire-fighting equipment such as extinguishers and hoses are in proper working order, visible, and accessible, and that you and your people know where they are and how to use them. Different kinds of fires require different kinds of fire-fighting equipment. The wrong type of extinguishing agent—such as water used on a grease fire—can spread the fire and increase the likelihood of injuries and property damage.

If and when a fire occurs, you will have three jobs to do in a hurry:
1. Get your people out of danger;
2. Call the fire department;
3. Fight the fire if you know how to, and have the proper means and training to do so without putting yourself in jeopardy.

PREVENTING VANDALISM

■ **Vandalism** is generally considered to be wanton or willful destruction or damage to another's property. Sometimes it is done by disgruntled employees and sometimes by outsiders. Regardless of who does the damage, some simple precautions can help prevent or minimize losses.

To begin with, all equipment, machines, tools, and other expensive pieces of company property should be the responsibility of specified people for control and security purposes. Portable pieces of equipment should be issued only upon request and returned by the persons to whom they were issued. The responsibility for levels of maintenance should be associated with the operator and the maintenance department so that each item will be properly cared for and checked periodically in order to record its condition. Any damage or changes should be reported immediately.

Physical facilities must be kept clean and under observation at regular and irregular intervals. Storage areas require extra security measures if they contain sensitive or highly valuable materials. Illumination of inside and outside areas will help avoid trouble and unwelcome visitors. Closed-circuit television, guards, proximity devices, and alarm systems are popular yet expensive prevention and detection measures. But locks are still the primary means of security used by any business firm. They cannot prevent trouble or efforts to bring about vandalism if they are not used or left open. Locks and guard routes should be changed periodically.

PROTECTING PEOPLE

■ Protecting people from illness, accidents, and injuries is not only smart business, but it is required by law as well. By law a business is responsible for injuries suffered by its employees if the injuries occur during or arise as a result of the employees' employment.

An **accident** is defined as any unforeseen or unplanned incident or event. Damage to people or property need not occur to have an accident. Workers who slip on a wet floor but who do not suffer any injury are victims of an accident. People who pound a nail into a wall and miss the nail without damage to themselves or the wall are also victims of an accident.

While accidents are usually unforeseen, many are not unforeseeable. Planning and safety programs can and do yield significant decreases in accidents. Through the three Es of accident prevention established by the National Safety Council—engineering, education, and enforcement—the probability of accidents can be reduced and their severity can be minimized.

WORKER'S COMPENSATION

■ Prior to 1910 workers were injured frequently on the job. Their lost wages and medical bills were usually their own problems unless they could prove in a court of law that their employers were the sole force or cause of their injuries. If a worker contributed in any way to the injury suffered or if a worker knew his or her work to be dangerous, the employer could usually avoid legal responsibilities for damages.

Today worker's compensation laws exist on both the federal and state levels. If a worker suffers an illness or injury on the job, he or she can file a claim with the state's compensation board. An employer will be directly responsible and liable for accidents and illnesses that arise out of and in the course of a worker's employment. Benefits are paid to individuals according to schedules of benefits containing fixed maximums that may be awarded by compensation boards. Nearly all business firms carry some kind of worker's compensation insurance of the type sold by nearly every casualty insurance company.

The various states have either compulsory or elective worker's compensation laws. Under elective laws, a company may provide the protection the law requires on its own. But if the company rejects the law, it loses its common-law defenses against claims of negligence. Employees (or their families) would therefore be free to sue the employer for damages for injuries, illness, or death.

Under compulsory worker's compensation laws, every employer within the state's jurisdiction must accept the application of the law and provide the benefits required. They may self-insure to provide the benefits of worker's compensation insurance policies. When the company provides on its own the protection required by law through worker's compensation insurance, the employee who suffers an injury or illness may not sue.

Benefits from worker's compensation insurance compensate employees for medical and disability expenses as well as for income loss because of illness or injury. The cost of this insurance varies with a company's history of worker claims. The more claims against a company, and the more benefits paid by an insurance company, the greater the premium charged for worker's compensation protection. Every business, therefore, tries to insure workers' safety through the latest in equipment devices and work safety rules not only to protect its workers from injury but also to protect its profits from the drain of insurance premiums and self-insurance funds. Figure 18–3 shows a sample checklist for an on-going safety program.

OSHA'S ACTIVITIES

■ In 1970 Congress passed the Occupational Safety and Health Act that created the Occupational Safety and Health Administration **(OSHA)** "to assure so far as possible every working man and woman in the Nation safe and healthful working conditions to preserve our human resources." The law, which became effective in April 1971, applies to all employers engaged in any business affecting commerce and em-

Indicate discrepancy by ☒

General Area		Tools	
Floors condition		Power tool wiring	
Special purpose flooring		Condition of hand tools	
Aisle, clearance/markings		Safe storage	
Floor openings, require safeguards		Other	
Railings, stairs temp./perm.		**First Aid**	
Dock board (bridges plates)		First aid kits	
Piping (water-steam-air)		Stretchers, fire blankets, oxygen	
Wall damage		**Fire Protection**	
Ventilation		Fire hoses hung properly	
Other		Extinguisher charged/proper location	
Illumination—Wiring		Access to fire equipment	
Unnecessary/improper use		Exit lights/doors/signs	
Lights on during shutdown		Other	
Frayed/defective wiring		**Security**	
Overloading circuits		Doors/windows, etc. secured when required	
Machinery not grounded		Alarm operation	
Hazardous location		Dept. shut down security	
Wall outlets		Equip. secured	
Other		Unauthorized personnel	
Housekeeping		Other	
Floors		**Machinery**	
Machines		Unattended machines operating	
Break area/latrines		Emergency stops not operational	
Waste disposal		Platforms/ladders/catwalks	
Vending machines/food protection		Instructions to operate/stop posted	
Rodent, insect, vermin control		Maint. being performed on machines in operation	
Other		Guards in place	
Vehicles		Pinch points	
Unauthorized use		**Material Storage**	
Operating defective vehicle		Hazardous and flammable material not stored properly	
Reckless/speeding operation		Improper stacking/loading/securing	
Failure to obey traffic rules		Improper lighting, warning signs, ventilation	
Other		Other	

Keep on file as evidence of on-going safety program.

Figure 18-3. Monthly safety checklist for an on-going safety program.
Reprinted from "Safety & Security for Supervisors," a monthly publication of Business Research Publications, Inc., 799 Broadway, New York, N.Y. 10003.

ploying people. Its terms apply to all the states, territories, and possessions of the United States but do *not* apply to government employees or to working conditions protected under other federal occupational safety and health laws such as the Federal Coal Mine Health and Safety Act, the Atomic Energy Act, and the Migrant Health Act.

According to OSHA, each employer has the duty to furnish employees a working environment free from recognized hazards that cause or that are likely to cause death or serious physical harm. Each employee has a duty to comply with safety and health rules and standards established by the employers or OSHA. Administration and enforcement of OSHA are vested in the Secretary of Labor and the Occupational Safety and Health Review Commission, a quasijudicial board of three members appointed by the President. Research and related functions are vested in the Secretary of Health, Education, and Welfare (HEW) whose functions will for the most part be carried out by the National Institute for Occupational Safety and Health. The Institute exists to develop and establish recommended occupational safety and health standards; to conduct research and experimental programs for developing criteria for new and improved job safety and health standards; and to make recommendations to the Secretaries of Labor and HEW concerning new and improved standards.

Occupational Safety and Health Standards

In general, job safety and health standards consist of rules aimed at preventing hazards that have been proven by research and experience to be harmful to personal safety and health. Some standards apply to all employees. An example of these would be fire protection standards. A great many standards, however, apply only to workers engaged in specific types of work, such as handling flammable materials.

It is the obligation of all employers and supervisors to familiarize themselves and their subordinates with the standards that apply to them at all times. Any person or business adversely affected by a government standard may challenge its validity by petitioning the U.S. Court of Appeals within sixty days after the new standard is imposed. Variances from standards may be granted to employers if extra time is needed to comply or if an employer is using safety measures as safe as those required by federal standards.

Compliance Complaints

Any employees who believe that a violation of a safety or health standard exists which threatens them with physical harm may request an inspection by sending a signed written notice to the Department of Labor. A copy should be provided to the employer. The names of the complainants will not be revealed to the employer. If the Department finds no reasonable grounds for the complaint and a citation is not issued, the complainants will be notified in writing. Employee complaints may also be made to any local OSHA office.

OSHA Inspections

When OSHA compliance officers (inspectors) call, they may be on a routine inspection or they may be responding to an employee's complaint. In the latter case the inspectors may not limit their visits to the complaint. Other areas may be investigated as well. Any violations spotted will be discussed and written up on a citation, which must be posted at or near the location of the violation for three working days or until the violation has been corrected. Extra penalties or fines have been assessed for failures to correct violations or because the citation was removed before the violation had been corrected.

An OSHA inspector may ask the supervisor or any person in charge of an area to accompany him or her on an inspection, or the inspector may conduct the inspection alone. Employers do not have an absolute right to accompany inspectors. It is good practice for any supervisor to tag along on any inspection that involves his or her work area. You may spot violations that the inspector does not, and you will be present to give explanations and to make on-the-spot corrections of minor problems.

Don't rely on the manufacturer's words that new machinery meets OSHA standards. You should inspect it and supervise its installation. The primary responsibility rests with your company, not with the manufacturer. Many cases of violations and fines accompanying them have been reported for companies that thought they could rely on a manufacturer's safety guarantees. Your machine operators may be of some assistance in pointing out potential as well as actual safety problems.

Don't expect the OSHA inspectors to tell you how unsatisfactory machinery should be made safe. They will only alert you to unsafe conditions. The OSHA Review Commission puts it this way: "An employer's own abilities and that of an industry may be relied upon to devise suitable ways to conform to the requirements of a standard."

Enforcement

Since the Federal Occupational Safety and Health Act took effect in April 1971, fines of from a few dollars to $227,700 (against Texaco in 1977) have been levied against employers. In the first two years, OSHA inspectors conducted over fifty-three thousand inspections and found over one hundred and seventy thousand violations. Employee complaints filed with OSHA average several thousand per year.

It's not enough to warn and instruct employees about safety hazards. Supervisors must also *enforce* instructions and *remove* or *eliminate* hazards. Supervisors who ignore company or OSHA safety rules and standards can cause a doubling of the penalties if accidents are the result of such behavior. (See Figure 18–4 for two novel ideas on safety enforcement.)

Figure 18-4. Two novel ideas on safety enforcement.
Reprinted from "Safety & Security for Supervisors," a monthly publication of Business Research Publications, Inc., 799 Broadway, New York, N.Y. 10003.

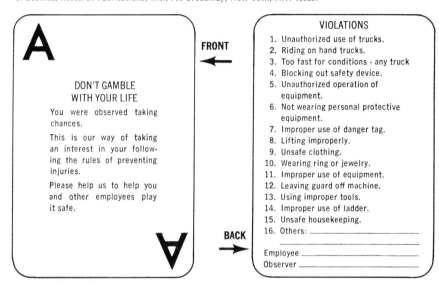

A

DON'T GAMBLE
WITH YOUR LIFE

You were observed taking chances.

This is our way of taking an interest in your following the rules of preventing injuries.

Please help us to help you and other employees play it safe.

FRONT

BACK

VIOLATIONS
1. Unauthorized use of trucks.
2. Riding on hand trucks.
3. Too fast for conditions - any truck
4. Blocking out safety device.
5. Unauthorized operation of equipment.
6. Not wearing personal protective equipment.
7. Improper use of danger tag.
8. Lifting improperly.
9. Unsafe clothing.
10. Wearing ring or jewelry.
11. Improper use of equipment.
12. Leaving guard off machine.
13. Using improper tools.
14. Improper use of ladder.
15. Unsafe housekeeping.
16. Others: _____
   _____

Employee _____
Observer _____

Harry J. Hahn, safety supervisor, Hammermill Papers Group, Erie, Pa., supplies supervisors a set of cards with a safety message on each side.

You were just doing something that could have caused an injury or accident. Perhaps you didn't realize it, but think over what you've been doing in the last few minutes and you may recall the unsafe act.

I am giving you this card as part of our safety program, to make all of us **Think, Plan, and Work Safely.**

Keep it until you see someone else on the job doing something in an unsafe way —and then pass it along to him or her. I hope I don't get the card back!

Safety Division

We believe in safety!

For Thomas Mahoney, post safety director, Fort Benjamin Harrison, Ind., "everyone is a safety director" with these pass-around calling cards.

The safety-minded supervisor:

1 Takes the initiative in telling management about ideas for a safer layout of equipment, tools, and processes.

2 Knows the value of machine guards and makes sure the proper guards are provided and used.

3 Takes charge of operations that are not routine to make certain that safety precautions are determined.

4 Is an expert on waste disposal for housekeeping and fire protection.

5 Arranges for adequate storage and enforces good housekeeping.

6 Works with every employee without favoritism.

7 Keeps eyes open for the new employee or the experienced employee doing a new job.

8 Establishes good relations with union stewards and the safety committee.

9 Sets good examples in safety practices.

10 Never lets a simple safety violation occur without talking to the employee immediately.

11 Not only explains how to do a job, but shows how and observes to insure continuing safety.

12 Takes pride in knowing how to use all equipment safely.

13 Knows what materials are hazardous and how to store them safely.

14 Continues to "talk safety" and impress safety on all employees.

Figure 18-5. Profile of the supervisor with low accident rates.
Source: U.S. Department of Labor.

As a supervisor you may be able to fire an employee who willfully fails to comply with federal safety standards or requirements and/or other reasonable company safety standards or rules. Employees do not have the right to walk off a job or refuse to perform work they consider potentially unsafe *unless* the existing conditions present "a real danger of death or serious injury." Employees who feel that their working environment is unsafe may file a complaint with their employer, union, or OSHA. Obviously, workers are free to leave a job anytime that they want to, but they must be prepared to take the consequences of such action. We hope that your people trust you enough to feel that you will do something about their complaints. If you do not, you will find the union or government officials demanding that you correct unsafe working conditions and that you follow federal standards. Figure 18–5 provides a profile of the safety-minded supervisor.

Damages

Workers injured on the job may collect damages awarded by worker's compensation or OSHA. They may not sue employers in a civil action for injuries suffered because of violation of the OSHA safety standards. If a penalty is assessed, the Labor Department notifies the employer who then has fifteen working days to contest the citation. The Occupational Safety and Health Review Commission can then grant a hearing and render a ruling to affirm, modify, or reject the citation and its recommended penalty. Appeal of the Commission's rulings can be made through the U.S. Court of Appeals.

Willful or repeated violations of the Act's requirements by employers may incur monetary penalties of up to $10,000 for each violation. Citations issued for serious violations incur mandatory monetary penalties of up to $1,000 for each violation, while penalties in the same amount may be incurred for lesser violations. A serious violation exists when there is a substantial probability that death or serious physical harm could result. Any employer who fails to correct a violation for which a citation has been issued within the prescribed period may be penalized up to $1,000 for each day that violation continues.

A willful violation by an employer which results in the death of any employee is punishable by a fine of up to $10,000 or imprisonment for up to six months. A second conviction doubles these criminal penalties. Criminal penalties also exist for making false official statements, and for giving unauthorized advance notice of any inspections to be conducted.

Requirements to Keep Records

Employers are required to keep and make available to the Labor Secretary (and also to the HEW Secretary) records and periodic reports of work-related deaths, injuries, and illnesses. A record must be made if an injury or illness involves medical treatment, loss of consciousness, restriction of work or motion, or transfer to another job.

Employers may also be required to maintain accurate records of employee exposures to potentially toxic materials or harmful physical agents which are required to be monitored or measured. Employees must be told of any excessive exposure and of the corrective action being taken. The Secretary of Labor, in cooperation with the Secretary of HEW, can issue regulations to provide employees an opportunity to observe the monitoring or measuring, and to have access to records that indicate their own exposure to toxic materials or harmful physical agents.

You cannot consider plant and office security problems in a vacuum. Security measures, if they are to be effective, depend upon the commitment of every member of management's team. Through these people, all the company's policies, programs, procedures, and practices are developed, communicated, executed, and enforced. Security for property and information basically depends upon the enforcement efforts of every supervisor. Security procedures in a manual are of little use unless they become a reality in the office or shop.

Safety is everyone's responsibility. The production of safer machines and equipment is only a beginning of safety efforts. The safest machine can still cause injuries if its operator is careless, poorly trained, or poorly supervised. Education about and the enforcement of safety standards, rules, and procedures are the keys to a safer working environment and to the reduction of accidents and injuries.

Since 1971 the Occupational Safety and Health Administration (OSHA) has represented the federal government's efforts to protect Americans from work-related accidents, illnesses, and injuries. It establishes safety standards that must be followed by employers and employees. OSHA inspections, citations, and fines help enforce these standards.

Supervisors who really care about safety and security are attentive to their subordinates and their working environment. They listen to workers' complaints about unsafe methods and machines, and act promptly when they discover breaches of security. Supervisors should consider every worker as an additional pair of eyes and ears that can help reduce losses and damage to the company's physical and human resources.

KEY WORDS

accidents	pilferage	vandalism
OSHA	safety	worker's compensation
	security	

1. How are efforts at plant and office security similar? Are they unique or different in any way? If so, how?

2. What can supervisors do to prevent theft in an office?

3. What should you look for when you screen applicants for employment in order to avoid hiring a thief?

4. What should supervisors do in the event of a fire?

5. In what ways will good housekeeping help reduce accidents and damage to property?

6. How do the states' workers' compensation laws aid injured workers?

7. Why is it a good idea for supervisors to escort an OSHA inspector on his or her inspection through an area?

8. An OSHA inspector has just issued you a citation for violation of a federal safety standard. What should you do?

9. Your people use toxic chemicals. What does OSHA require you to do?

CASE PROBLEM

Safety First

"OSHA regulations clearly state that employees may not walk off the job or refuse to perform a job just because they think it is unsafe," said Art Price, the personnel manager of Hadley Products Company.

"That's right," said Andy Prachak. "As the foreman out in that yard, I know what those men go through every day. I don't blame Ed for wanting safer conditions. But I draw the line at open protests and insubordination to get them."

Rick Sczebo, head of the union's grievance committee, interrupted. "You guys are talking about firing Ed for leaving a damn hazardous job. You ought to be grateful Ed hasn't complained to OSHA about conditions out in that yard. There have been two serious injuries already, due mainly to the company refusing to fix known hazards. Does someone have to be killed or permanently injured before people do something about safety?"

"Don't cloud the issue, Rick," said Art. "We are talking about a serious breach of discipline. If we let Ed get away with a clear case of insubordination, Andy will have to suffer for it for a long time to come. Ed was given a direct order to finish stacking those skids with his worklift. He refused and left the yard before quitting time and without a pass. What's worse, he refused in front of three other workmen who heard Andy's order."

"Look, Art, this is not a case of insubordination. Andy will be the first to tell you that Ed is a good worker. Right, Andy?"

"Right, one of the best. That's why I'm shocked at his leaving like he did. It just wasn't like him."

"Well," said Rick, "that ought to tell you how bad things must have been in Ed's mind. You were asking him to risk his life and limb. As the grievance says, and I quote Ed's words, 'Those skids were broken and piled in a dangerous way. They were stacked badly and were already too high. When the foreman told me to add another layer, I knew they would be too unsteady to stay up for long. I wasn't going to put my buddies and myself in any more danger by adding another layer.' "

"You see," Rick continued, "Ed saw a clear danger and acted the way any normal person should. He refused to carry out a stupid order that never should have been given in the first place."

"Now see here," said Andy, "I resent that. If Ed thought the job was that dangerous, why didn't he tell me what he thought? He didn't explain anything until he wrote that grievance in response to his firing. All I know is that I don't want him back in the yard. He's fired now, and if he's rehired, I'll quit."

"Wait a minute, Andy. Let's not lose our heads here," said Art. "Let's have a cup of coffee and relax a minute. I'll get some. Be back in a minute."

Art left the room. Andy and Rick glared at each other through a long silence. Then Rick spoke up.

"The union tells me that any worker can leave his job if he believes there is a *real* danger of death and serious injury."

"Well, what your union doesn't say is what OSHA cases have said: that a worker can leave *only* when the company knows about the hazards *and* refuses to do anything about them. Ed never told me what he thought. I'm not a mind reader."

Art returned with three, steaming cups of coffee for two, steaming employees. Art spoke as he set the cups down. "What's it going to take to settle this case, Rick?"

"Art, what the union wants is to correct the bad conditions out in the yard as soon as possible, and to reinstate Ed with back pay and seniority. If we don't get some action soon, we're going to call in the OSHA inspectors."

"If you do," replied Art, "you could shut this place down with violations. Your members would be out of a job for Lord knows how long. You know how government red tape can foul things up. Let me propose a compromise here. If it's OK with Andy, we will get started on a safety program and fix the problems your boys think are the most serious ones. Give us a list, and we will do as much as we can as fast as our budget will allow. Second, we will bring Ed back with no back pay for the two weeks he's been fired and give him his seniority minus those two weeks. What do you say, Andy?"

"OK, if that's the best we can do."

"What do you say, Rick?"

Questions

1. Comment on the union's and the company's views of OSHA.

2. What are the central issues in this case?

3. If you were the union's spokesperson, how would you answer Art's suggested compromise?

4. Comment on the supervisor's view of the importance of safety versus the importance of maintaining discipline.

19

Getting Along with Management's Team

LEARNING OBJECTIVES

■ After reading and discussing this chapter, you should be able to:

1 Define who a supervisor's peers are.

2 List five purposes of maintaining good human relations with your peers.

3 List and briefly describe the application of the four human relations roles to the relationship between a supervisor and his or her peers.

4 Describe how a middle manager's job is different from a supervisor's job.

5 Describe what a supervisor's boss owes to the supervisor.

6 Describe what a supervisor owes to his or her boss.

7 Describe how a supervisor can maintain good human relations with his or her peers.

8 Describe how a supervisor can maintain good human relations with his or her boss.

INTRODUCTION

■ This chapter is concerned with the personal relationships you should develop with your peers and superiors. We shall consider what these people have the right to expect from you, and what you have the right to expect from them.

Much of what we are about to discuss is directly related to the concepts we first explored in Chapter 8. Note the many similarities and some differences that may occur to you as you study Chapter 19. Before you start on it, it would be a good idea to review the concepts of Chapter 8.

YOU AND YOUR PEERS

■ Your **peers** are all the other managers who are on the same level of the management hierarchy as you are. You work more closely with some than with others, but situations can change rather rapidly in business. What we say here should aid you in developing a mutually beneficial relationship between yourself and your fellow supervisors.

The most important reasons for establishing good human relations with your peers are:

1. To know and understand all of them as individuals;
2. To approach and cooperate with all of them as individuals;
3. To provide what help you can to enable all of them to achieve the measure of satisfaction they desire from their job;
4. To foster a spirit of cooperation and teamwork among your peers.
5. To tap their funds of knowledge, skills, and experience.

DEVELOPING SOUND HUMAN RELATIONSHIPS

■ Your success as a manager is linked to your peers and what they think of you as a person and as a supervisor. Your personal and professional reputation with them is important for a number of reasons. If they think highly of you, they will be drawn to you and be willing to associate with you. They will freely give of their time and energy on your behalf and help you with advice. How you measure up with them, and their reactions when your name is mentioned are factors that may carry influence with your boss as well. When your boss looks at his or her subordinates—you and your peers—for someone to delegate to or train for a higher position, the boss can't help but compare you to them. If you can't get along with, or are avoided by, your peers, your boss will know it.

Your peers represent an enormous pool of talent and experience that is yours to tap and contribute to if they view you in a favorable way. For this reason if none other, it is to your advantage to cultivate their friendship both on and off the job.

Your peers should constitute your friends at work and share in your social activities as well. In many ways you need each other, and all of you stand to benefit from a partnership or alliance based on mutual respect and the need to resolve common problems.

If you are off in your own little world and unwilling to share your knowledge and know-how, you deny yourself the advice and experience they stand ready to give. You may be branded as uncooperative or antisocial and destined, at best, for a career as a supervisor. Higher positions have no need for isolates. You will find, if you have not already done so, that the more you give of what you have, the more you will receive from others.

Your Human Relations Roles

The four fundamental roles we spoke about in Chapter 8 apply to your peers as well as to your subordinates. They take on a somewhat different meaning and application, as this chapter will illustrate. Here, as in our earlier discussion, the roles are interdependent and interrelated. They now become two-way in nature as there is both a give and a take involved in each. As you give to others, you should expect to receive from them in return.

Your Role as Educator

The two-way nature of this role includes assisting your fellow supervisors in their growth and development as well as enlisting their help on your own behalf.

You have a great deal to give your peers. You have talents and skills that may be developed to a greater degree in you than in some of them. You have knowledge about human nature, your job, and management in general which can be beneficial to others. You have attitudes and a personality which can be the basis for friendship and which can sustain a fellow manager when he or she needs it most.

Most people have experienced the joy that comes with sharing what they have with others. A father and mother know the pleasure they receive when they give of themselves to their children. They have seen the delight when they show their children how to do things and when they assist the children to develop their skills and increase their knowledge. Do you remember what fun it was to take a friend for a ride in your new car? Can you recall the enjoyment you received when you helped younger, less experienced persons solve a problem that was so difficult for them yet so easy for you?

Besides the momentary joy you receive when you share your knowledge and your "tricks of the trade," you also get something much more lasting—a good reputation. Psychologically, all your peers who profit through your efforts on their behalf are in your debt. They may not always show overt appreciation (and you should not always expect it), but they will find it hard not to reciprocate, to share what they have with you. When you need a favor, a bit of advice, or a helping hand, your colleagues will respond when and if they are able to do so.

Your peers' advice and know-how can't be found in books. You will receive in a relatively short span of time, if you are wise enough to ask, what it might take you years to discover on your own. Which is easier and more fun: reading about how to do something difficult, or having someone who knows how to do it show you how it is done? Your peers probably feel the same way about this as you do.

If you know yourself well, you know your strengths and weaknesses. Where you are weak, a peer may be strong and vice versa. The more peers you know well, the greater the quantity of help available to you. Give what you have and take advantage of what they have to give. Don't bury your talents and don't let them bury theirs.

Your Role as Counselor

Counsel is a *mutual* exchange of ideas and opinions. Counselors are people to whom you go for advice and to try out your ideas. They provide you with guidance and a plan in the absence of one of your own. The key to counseling your peers is empathy—the intellectual and imaginative understanding of another's feelings and state of mind. From this develops a mutual respect and appreciation.

As with subordinates, just being available and favorably predisposed toward your peers may give them what they need at precisely the moment they need it—a sympathetic ear. By listening to others who have difficulties, you provide emotional first aid. By responding when asked and when qualified to do so, you may give people the support they need to find a way out of their trouble.

When a friend asks you for advice and you have empathy for that person, speak your mind freely. Without empathy (which usually means without friendship) you should confine your guidance to work-related matters. Steer clear of personal advice unless you know the person well.

A few words of caution. It is one thing to be asked for your opinion and quite another to give it without being asked. You don't want a reputation as a "butt-in-ski," so avoid any counsel unless it is solicited.

We all have known the value of being on the receiving end of good counsel. An interested, sympathetic adviser and friend cannot only temper our views, but he or she may resolve our difficulties as well. When we consult a friend, we are either looking for answers we think he or she possesses or a shoulder to lean on. The value in either cannot be measured but is tremendously helpful, nevertheless. Our counselor brings a certain neutrality and objectivity to bear on the issue which we are powerless to muster on our own.

In order for the give and take of counseling between friends and associates to work, we must have communication channels open to the left and to the right. Do your best to avoid arguments and displays of temper with your associates. Don't burn any bridges so that you can't return to a pleasant relationship once a momentary storm passes. If for a time you alienate a peer, stand ready to apologize when you have been in the wrong. Be quick to forgive a colleague who injured you. You don't have to call all of your peers your friends, but you should not call any of them enemies. By sharing the successes of others, you enrich the returns to them. By sharing the sorrows of others, you capture their friendship. So it is also when the other people reciprocate.

**Your Role
as Judge**

Closely allied with the counseling role in human relations is the role of judge. As is the case with your subordinates, you have four specific duties to attend to: enforcement, settling disputes, evaluating, and dispensing justice. The latter will be discussed under your role as spokesperson.

ENFORCEMENT

The duty you have to enforce company policies and regulations affects your peers as well. There is an urgent need for all supervisors to be uniform both in the interpretation and the application of these policies and regulations. You have experienced the unhappy situation that results when one supervisor is lenient and another severe. Imagine a situation in which you are trying to get your workers to arrive and leave on schedule, while the supervisor in the adjacent department allows his or her people to come and go as they please. How much more difficult has this supervisor made your job? Where two managers interpret or enforce the same regulation or policy in different and conflicting ways, a wedge is driven between them. This wedge acts as a barrier to both communications and cooperation. Managers at every level must agree with and work parallel to each other if they are to act in a unified and effective way.

SETTLING DISPUTES

Where you find yourself at odds with a peer over an interpretation of policy or the way to enforce a rule, get together with that individual and work it out between you. Quite often your duties overlap those of another supervisor. A meeting and polite discussion are all that are usually required to resolve the difficulty. If you two cannot work the matter out, get together with your boss and his or hers. Don't let the conflict continue any longer than necessary. Take action as soon as you are aware that a problem exists.

Periodically you may be called upon by circumstances to serve as a peacemaker. For example, two of your associates are engaged in an argument and their emotions have taken over. As a witness to the dispute, you may be able to intervene with a calmness and logic the others lack. Do so when you find yourself in such a situation. It does managers no good to squabble, especially in public. Workers read all kinds of things into such events. You may save a friend or associate the embarrassment that comes from making a fool out of himself or herself.

EVALUATION

Study your peers for an understanding of their management techniques. All of them have their unique characteristics and methods. Hold your standards up to theirs and see how they compare. Where you discover significant differences, make every effort to determine which is the better set to follow. In the final analysis both your and their techniques may prove to be inferior to yet another set of standards.

Your peers make excellent working "models" to be observed and evaluated. Try out your theories and applications on your associates and get their reactions to them. Watch how they handle themselves in difficult as well as routine matters. Test your attitudes against theirs, and see if you can't refine your viewpoints and pick up some of their methods.

CRITICISM

When you observe a peer engaged in improper or forbidden conduct, you owe him or her a bit of friendly correction. You and your fellow supervisors are a team of managers who must not work at cross-purposes if you wish to succeed. When one of your number engages in unauthorized and harmful activities, he hurts all other supervisors. Others, especially workers, who observe a supervisor's improprieties draw conclusions that inevitably are harmful to his or her reputation and to yours. You are all "in this together" so to speak.

When a peer's actions and objectives are contrary to yours, you must confront him or her with your observations. Let him or her know, in a tactful and sincere manner, what you know. Of course you want to do so in private. After all, if you know what he or she is up to, it is quite likely that others—including the boss—do too. You may find more often than not that a peer is unaware that he or she is doing anything wrong and will appreciate your drawing his or her attention to the matter.

You, in turn, must stand ready as well for constructive criticism. We all need it occasionally and, in fact, stop growing without it. Contentment and smugness creep in, and a false sense of security takes over. We begin to believe that we are consistently right and gradually close our minds to the new and different.

The strongest kind of friendly correction you can exert is your own good example. By promoting the things in which you believe and by opposing the things you believe to be wrong, you take a stand and exhibit principles for others to see.

Don't go looking for problems or the failings of others. But when you discover them, you have a duty to alert the other person. A friendly warning or a few words of counsel to let the manager know that he or she may be on thin ice are all that is called for.

There is a tendency we all have when we see a friend or peer in trouble to "cover" for him or her. If you do, you may gain a few temporary benefits. But in the long run, you stand to lose far more than you could ever gain. You will identify yourself as an ally of improper conduct and demonstrate wholly unacceptable attitudes for any manager to hold. You are not in a position of power and trust to shield your friends from earned discipline. That would constitute an inexcusable abuse of your position. Nor should you punish. That is a superior's duty. You need not inform on a peer as, in time, things have a way of surfacing and getting to those who should know. But don't compromise your own position of trust and personal integrity to help anyone. You will only be hurting yourself. You have too much to lose for too long.

Your Role as Spokesperson

You owe loyalty to your peers, but only when they are in the right. Allegiance to someone is a precious gift not to be given lightly. It must be earned as well as respected. Loyalty implies mutual trust and confidence. Where it is not mutual, it cannot persist.

You should never spread a rumor about anyone. But when you hear one, it is your job as a spokesperson to refute it if you can. If you cannot, ask the other person to substantiate his or her statement. Inquire as to the source. The person will know what you are thinking—that he or she is spreading gossip. When this bit of gossip relates to a peer, let that individual know its content and its source.

When an untrue rumor pertains to you and when you view its content as serious (all attacks on your character are), defend yourself. Trace it to its originator and confront that individual with your knowledge. Control your temper but make your point as forcefully as you feel is necessary. Then bury the incident and try to avoid carrying a grudge. If a rumor is minor and not related to your character, let it go. You haven't the time to track down all rumors, nor should you try to do so.

Respect legitimate demands for your silence as is the case when conversing about personal matters with a friend. Information revealed to you by a peer that pertains to him or her alone should not be a topic of conversation with others. If you reveal a secret or break any confidence, your peer is sure to find out about it. What will happen to your reputation then?

The role of spokesperson also pertains to spreading the "good news" or praising the ideas, contributions, and accomplishments of your peers. Giving credit where it is due and expressing your appreciation for benefits received, especially in public, is a pleasant duty one manager or friend has toward another.

When you receive information from a peer, such as orders or instructions, be sure that you verify its content for yourself. If you act upon it without doing so, you may be in for a shock. He or she may be passing along secondhand data and much accuracy can be lost in handling and translation. Be certain also when you relay information from the boss to a peer that you preserve its original form and intent. If what you received was written, pass it along in the same format.

Finally, remember that you are also a spokesperson for your subordinates. When another supervisor interferes with them or their work, make it clear to the other person that you resent the interference. Such an action challenges your authority. You must shield your subordinates and yourself from outside interference and conflicting orders or instructions.

YOU AND YOUR INFORMAL GROUP

■ As we have stated before, you are probably a member of several formal groups and of one or more informal ones. Chapter 9 also told you how informal groups can affect your behavior and attitudes. The informal group you choose or that chooses you will have a dramatic and lasting impact on your reputation and your future. Choose any informal group with the same caution you would exercise when choosing a friend. Pick out the ones who will have the greatest positive effect on your growth and those that have the most to offer. In that way, some of their luster and brilliance will rub off on you. You are judged in part by the company you keep. Why open yourself to criticism or end up having to defend your companions or yourself? You don't have to alienate those bent on self-destruction. Simply avoid any permanent bonds or relationships with them. Remain civil but apart.

One of the hazards inherent in membership in an informal group is the restrictions it places on your contacts with others. Once you have reached either the transformation or confirmation stage of induction, you probably have begun to confine your socializing at work to a specific few. In time, you may become rather narrow and cut off from differing opinions. You may be denying yourself the valuable companionship and variety that others have to offer. Don't take yourself out of circulation. Break your routine on occasion and mix and maintain contacts with others of similar rank. It's foolish to restrict your explorations to the same mountain. After awhile there is nothing left to explore.

COMPETITION WITH YOUR PEERS

■ Keep in mind that although you should maintain good relations with others and develop cooperation with them as suggested in Chapter 6, you are still in competition with your peers. In much the same manner as a professional athlete, you have to maintain a balance between individual displays of talent and ability, and the need for team play. All great athletes achieve their greatness in this way. You must be willing to take a back seat now and then and let another manager's talents come through. If you "hog the ball," you do so at the expense of team play. Eventually you'll find out that the ball will stop coming your way.

Just remember what we have said all along: your reputation and performance evaluation are primarily in your subordinates' hands. Only secondarily will your peers play a part. And if you are wise, that part is yours to write, produce, and direct. You have the ability to influence it through your human relations efforts and interactions with your peers.

A HUMAN RELATIONS CHECKLIST

■ Use the following checklist as a guide to evaluate your human relations efforts in dealing with your peers. Any "no" responses indicate a need to make an adjustment:
1. Do I carry my own weight?
2. Do I lend a hand where needed?
3. Do I look out for the other person?
4. Am I loyal to my peers?
5. Do I respect their confidences?
6. Do I share my know-how?
7. Am I willing to give of myself?
8. Have I earned the respect of my peers?
9. Do I show them respect?
10. Do I cooperate?
11. Do I share information?
12. Do I avoid passing the buck?
13. Am I a team player?
14. Do I defend my peers in their absence?
15. Do I offer constructive and friendly criticism?
16. Am I quick to forgive?
17. Have I avoided making enemies?

The best way to maintain good human relations is to develop yourself into the best person and manager you have the potential to become. You will gain both rational and charismatic power in so doing, which will draw people to you. In giving what you have and drawing upon what others have to give, you will build bonds of friendship and strengthen your reputation with your peers.

GETTING ALONG WITH YOUR BOSS

■ Before we get into specifics about your relations with your boss, a few words are in order about your boss—how your boss' job is similar to yours, and how it is different from yours.

As a supervisor your boss is a middle manager. He or she is accountable for your actions. Your boss is similar to you in that he or she is both a follower and a staff or line manager. He or she executes all the functions of management and is evaluated on the basis of his or her subordinates' performances. Your boss, like yourself, must develop sound working relationships with subordinates, peers, and superiors. Also, he or she probably served an apprenticeship as a supervisor, so you can count on an understanding of your situation on his or her part.

When compared to a supervisor, however, a middle manager has more differences than similarities. The differences are that your boss:

1. Directs the work of other managers;
2. Exhibits strongly promanagement attitudes;
3. Spends more time on planning than on any other function;
4. Spends less time with subordinates;
5. Spends more time with peers and superiors;
6. Is more of an adviser than a director;
7. Has more freedom of action and flexibility;
8. Has more information and a broader perspective;
9. Is less concerned with procedures and practices (tactics) and more concerned with planning and programs (strategy);
10. Is more concerned with tomorrow than with today;
11. Is more concerned with the causes of management actions than with their effects.

In the case of the last item on the above list, a supervisor and his or her subordinates often evaluate a management decision on the basis of its effect or impact upon them. This is quite natural and to be expected. What affects your people adversely or is the cause of gripes or worse is always of great concern to you. The way you react to management decisions reflects upon you and your potential to take on the duties of a higher position.

To illustrate this point, suppose that higher management has recently reduced the plant budget for overtime. This decision is translated at your level to mean less overtime for the department and less income for the workers. Your people see this decision as it affects them—a reduction in their potential earnings. If you and they have grown dependent on overtime or see it as necessary to the current operations, your section may be in for some trouble. Your boss was in on the initial decision. He or she knows the reasons for it and the management objectives it was designed to achieve. For instance, a decision to reduce overtime expenses may conserve income, allow your company to price its line more competitively, and reduce overall expenses. Your boss is concerned with these matters because they affect him or her more directly than your problems do. The boss sees all of these objectives as logical and sound and supports them. Once the whys behind a decision are known to you, you should support the decision as strongly as your boss does. Give what facts you can to your subordinates to soften the blow. Emphasize that the conservation of income may mean the prevention of layoffs and the saving of jobs. You must be flexible enough to meet rapidly changing situations such as this. Add to this flexibility a readiness to adjust to situations as they are, not as you would like them to be.

YOUR BOSS' EXPECTATIONS

■ Primarily, most middle managers expect their subordinate managers to be loyal followers. Your boss, like yourself, needs the respect and support of subordinates. He or she must be able to count on your willingness and ability to enforce company policies and standards. He or she is relying on you to carry out decisions with the proper attitudes. You must not let him or her down. In the eyes of your subordinates, the boss' reputation is as important to them as your own. They have a right to believe that they have good leadership, that their boss and his or her boss consistently exercise good judgment. Don't let any action or innuendo on your part jeopardize your boss' reputation.

Take this short quiz to assess your attitudes toward management. If you can honestly answer yes to each question, your attitudes are strongly promanagement:

1. In a labor dispute, do I take management's side?
2. Do I believe in my company, its policies, programs, and products?
3. When I disagree with a decision from higher management, do I implement it, hide my feelings from my subordinates, and relay my displeasure to those who can change things?
4. Do I defend management and managers when they are unjustly attacked?
5. Do I accept accountability for the actions of my subordinates?
6. Do I avoid attempts to cover up or shield my subordinates or peers from discipline they have earned?
7. Do I consider myself a contributing member of management's team?
8. Do I routinely exhibit respect and loyalty to my superiors?
9. Do I demand and encourage the best from my people?
10. Do I evaluate my subordinates fairly and objectively?

Your boss expects you to get along well with your peers and the company's various staff specialists as well as with your subordinates. If you are able to resolve your disputes on your own, without arguments and displays of temper, you are demonstrating resourcefulness. By developing and maintaining a cooperative spirit, you open the channels through which aid and advice will flow.

Initiative is an extremely important characteristic for any manager to possess. Are you the kind of manager who waits for orders or instructions before acting? Do you need "something in writing" before you implement a change? If you do, you lack this essential quality. We are not talking here about assuming anything. That is always a dangerous practice. But when you have the authority to act in a situation and you know what must be done, you must not be afraid to respond. Unless you are completely at a loss as to what you should do, you should act. You won't always be right or pick the best method. But you won't appear paralyzed either. If you wish to make progress, you must be able to perceive what is needed and, when you have the power, see that the need is satisfied. Don't forget that besides your boss, your peers and the company's staff specialists stand ready to help.

Finally, your boss expects you to keep him or her informed. What you know about essential operations your boss should know also. Nothing can injure you quite as effectively as for the boss to be surprised—to find out about something secondhand. The boss hates surprises where you and your people are concerned. You can make your boss look awfully stupid if you fail in your duty to keep him or her abreast of developments. Share what information you have with the boss without betraying any confidences.

WINNING YOUR BOSS' CONFIDENCE

■ If you meet your superior's expectations, you are well on your way toward gaining his or her confidence. In addition, learn from your mistakes. Each error you make has a lesson or two for you. Study your errors to avoid their repetition. Whatever else you do that demonstrates an effort at self-development should be brought to your boss' attention. The courses you take in school and recent articles or books you have read that have been helpful in your work are all worthy topics of conversation with your boss.

Consider the following five courses of action. See if you agree with the thousands before you who have tried them and found them to be of great benefit.

Finding a Better Way

Long ago, as an undergraduate student in management, I learned four magic words on methods improvement that have served my students and myself well. They are:

> Combine
> Eliminate
> Rearrange
> Simplify

When you look at a plan, program, procedure, or practice with these words in mind you have an essential tool for evaluating them. Nothing is as valuable on your personnel record as the initiation and discovery of a better way to do something. The time, effort, and money that can be saved are important, but the effect on your reputation and career are even more important. Just be certain that the idea is yours before you take credit for it. Where help was received, credit should be given to that individual.

As a manager you should give methods improvement a high priority. No matter how smoothly an operation is running, there is usually room for improvement. Turn your attention to the most costly operations first. That is where you stand the chance of effecting the greatest savings. Then work your way systematically through the rest of your operations. Don't keep your successes to yourself. Share them with your peers and superiors. Others can profit from your innovations.

Keeping Your Promises

A "can do" attitude is great if you really can do what you promise. Before making such a promise, be as certain as you can of the resources at your disposal and the limits on your operations. If, in your best judgment, you have what it will take to get the job done, then commit yourself and your people to the endeavor. It is better to be a little bold than to be too cautious. If circumstances change dramatically for reasons beyond your ability to foresee, let your boss know. He or she will understand, and adjustments can be made. If you should have known about or suspected the changes, your reputation will suffer. Just try to avoid "going out on a limb" that is too weak to support your position.

Speaking Positively or Not at All

Whatever the topic of conversation and wherever it takes place, be sure that what you say is positive. There is a temptation to engage in gripe sessions and to put the other guy down. Such displays are clearly negative and completely without redeeming qualities. If your gripe is justified, reveal it to those who can act upon it. If the person you wish to criticize is a subordinate, approach him or her in private and keep it constructive. The point here is that no one, especially your boss, finds a benefit in associating with a person who is always negative. Few activities are as futile as gripe sessions. Names are dropped and things are said that all too often you wish you could retract or forget. If you have nothing of a positive nature to say, you are better off to say nothing.

Constructive criticism, whether of an individual or an idea, is not negative, and you are perfectly right to engage in it as long as the environment is correct. When an argument is put forth that favors a course of action and you see a disadvantage to it, you must air that point if the advocate of the proposal fails to do so. When the boss or anyone else puts forth a proposal in your presence, he or she wants your honest reactions. Loyalty demands that you do your best to prevent a person from making a mistake or suffering some humiliation when and where you can. Don't refuse a subordinate, peer, or superior such aid when you have it to give.

Taking a Position

You are a thinking human being and a member of management's team. But you must be a contributing member—one who carries his or her own weight and stands ready to help teammates. If you want the respect of others, you must have convictions. These convictions or beliefs tell others what you are and where you stand. Your character and principles are demonstrated when you take a stand on an issue. Before you do, however, be sure that you think it through and anticipate the possible drawbacks as well as your supportive arguments. Then prepare your defense.

When you take your stand and find it untenable, don't be reluctant to yield to superior forces. Bullheadedness is not a quality that endears you to anyone. Be reasonable. You want to be thought of as a person of principle, as a man or woman who thinks things through and fights for what he or she believes in. The corollary to this is equally important: you want to oppose those things you believe to be improper or wrong.

Involving Your Boss in Major Decisions

Just as you stand ready to help a subordinate or peer with a problem, your boss stands ready to help you. The boss' time is too valuable for trivial matters, so reserve your requests for assistance to the critical items.

Most middle managers have regular meetings for both individual and group discussion. Others maintain an "open-door" policy, relying upon their subordinates to bring in their problems. You should know and adjust to your boss' approach.

When you have a problem with which you have wrestled but to which you have no certain solution, set up a meeting with your boss, explaining in advance what it is you wish to discuss. Assemble your research and facts. Construct a list of alternatives you have considered. Then be sure to report to the meeting on time.

During the meeting follow the advice of the catchword *KISS (Keep It Short and Simple)*. You want the maximum benefits from the shortest possible time. What the boss wants most is to see that you have considered the matter and given it your best effort. He or she will not make your decisions for you, except when you have reached an impasse. Even then most bosses only offer suggestions and direct your attention to additional items you may have overlooked. That method may be a little frustrating, but the learning experience is invaluable to you.

Each contact you have with your boss should be as professional as you can make it. Be yourself but be prepared.

OBTAINING SOME OF YOUR BOSS' POWER

■ It is your job to know yourself well and to seek self-improvement. It is your task through human relations to know and approach your subordinates, peers, and superiors as individuals. Fundamental to your relationship with your boss is getting to know him or her well—his or her needs and ambitions, strengths and weaknesses. You can learn from a strong boss. You may be able to help a weak one.

The boss, like yourself, is probably looking for subordinates who can assume time-consuming details and routine. By delegating them, the boss creates time for more important tasks—the ones he or she alone must tackle. Also, your boss is gaining time to devote to taking on a larger portion of his or her boss' duties, thus training for advancement. So it goes from supervisor to chief executive. Through delegation each trains another. While providing for a subordinate's growth and progress the boss helps to insure his or her own advancement. A manager who has not trained a subordinate to move up may himself or herself be unable to move up. The manager who won't grow or help others to do so is not generally a manager for long. His or her lack of mobility acts as a ceiling on those with ambition and ability below. A manager's failure to grow may mean the loss to the company of promising young talent.

When you have proved to your boss that you are worthy of his or her respect and confidence, the delegation of duties to you will begin. You will get details and routine at first. If you handle them well, you can look forward to increased responsibilities with the challenges they represent.

If your boss is reluctant to delegate, you should urge him or her to do so. First you must free yourself from your details and routines in order to make time available. Then go to your boss with "time on your hands" and a plea for additional duties. If you have your eye on specifics, let the boss know what they are and why you feel qualified to take them. As we have stated earlier, take a stand, then sell it and defend it. You may not be successful at first; old habits die slowly. But you have planted a seed and a good manager will not let it die. Your boss will be disturbed by your idleness and impressed by your initia-. tive. If you persist, the boss will respond.

A few words of caution. Don't assume any of your boss' duties or anyone else's without consultation. There is a tendency for a bright and eager young supervisor to spot something that needs doing and do it. This is fine as long as you have jurisdiction over the matter. But when the duty you usurp belongs to another, you are guilty of grabbing power from another. This will be interpreted to your disadvantage. After all, how would you react if a peer or subordinate took on your responsibilities without first consulting with you?

Don't get yourself into a position where your boss becomes too dependent upon you. If the boss views you as indispensable, he or she may consciously or unconsciously restrict your chances for advancement. He or she will fear your loss through promotion or transfer and the corresponding upset this may represent. Your best defense is to train a successor. When the opportunity arises and the time is right, you can then point to a subordinate with pride and confidence as your logical and well-trained successor.

YOUR EXPECTATIONS OF YOUR BOSS

■ Besides respect and loyalty—which are essential prerequisites for a working relationship—your boss should provide you with the following:
1. Constructive criticism;
2. Fair evaluations;
3. Essential guidance;
4. A constant flow of necessary information;
5. Recognition for jobs well done;
6. An appropriate management style;
7. Training for growth and development;
8. A good example.

Where one or more of these items is lacking, look first at yourself for the cause. Something in you or your performance may be missing. If you don't give respect or loyalty, you have none coming. If you don't respond well to criticism, you may not receive it. If you don't think your boss' evaluations of your performance are fair, why did you accept them without protest? You may not be receiving guidance because you have not asked for any. Is the guidance you seek really essential? If you don't get information, maybe it is because you can't keep a secret or have no need to know. If no recognition is due you, you won't receive any. Don't expect recognition for simply doing your job. If your boss' management style with you is not to your liking, have you discussed it with him? If your boss won't delegate, have you enough time to take on the additional duties? Have you asked your boss for more things to do?

You may find, as many management students do, that the more you learn about management principles and practices the more critical of persons in authority you become. If this is happening to you, don't be alarmed. You are experiencing what all children growing up experience: the realization that the adult who occupies a position of trust and authority is really just a human being. As children realize this, they must search for a new understanding and relationship with their parents. No longer are the children content with blind obedience. No longer can they accept instructions or orders without knowing the why behind them. They are becoming critical and questioning and are now armed with standards upon which to base their questions and criticism.

The beauty of all this is that you will now know when something goes wrong and why. How you react to your new knowledge and act upon it determines whether you remain always a freshman or become a senior and graduate. Knowledge is power, and power needs controls on its use. As you are maturing, you will discover flaws where you saw none before. An inadequate manager often provides a better learning situation than a real professional does. When things run smoothly, you often don't know why they do. But when things go sour, you have a chance to ask and determine why. That goes for your mistakes as well as those of the boss. It is through your analysis of your boss' shortcomings that you can prevent their plaguing your own efforts. All the cases in this book and in every management text portray managers with flaws and inadequacies for just this reason.

THE PROBLEM SUPERVISOR

■ A supervisor may be the main cause of a poor working relationship with the boss. Through their actions or failure to act supervisors can and do influence their boss' behavior. Your boss makes his or her reputation as a result of your effective execution of the tasks and responsibilities assigned to you. Your boss is very much aware of your conduct and accomplishments. If your relationship with your boss is not what it should be or what you would like it to be, consider the following check list. If one or more of these questions stings a bit, set a new course of conduct now:

1. Am I predictable to the boss in my behavior and attitudes?
2. Am I a mature person?
3. Do I keep my promises?
4. Do I keep confidences?

5. Do I issue conflicting information and reports?
6. Do I hold a grudge?
7. Do I set standards realistically?
8. Am I loyal?
9. Do I criticize the boss in public?
10. Do I carry out my duties well and on time?

INSTANT REPLAY

As a group, your peers can offer you skills, knowledge, and experiences that will complement and enlarge upon your own. By sharing what you have with them, you open the way for them to do the same. You can learn through them faster than through any other method. Draw on what they have to give whenever you can. Learn by observation, conversation, and association.

All the roles in human relations apply to your peers as well as to your subordinates. It is up to you to practice sound human relations with them and maintain the good relationships you have established.

You win the boss' respect and confidence by meeting his or her expectations of you. For this reason you must try to get to know your boss as thoroughly as you can through observation, conversation, and association. Become familiar with his or her ways of doing things and with his or her standards. If you are ever in doubt as to what the boss means or expects, don't hesitate to ask for clarification.

Just as you train subordinates by delegation, so does your boss. But you must be receptive to his or her delegation in both ability and attitude. Unless you have the time and predisposition, don't expect additional duties. Where your boss is reluctant to train you, you must take the initiative. Prove by your actions and words that you consider yourself capable of handling parts of the boss' job.

Your boss owes you certain things. If they are not forthcoming, look at your attitudes, performance, and reputation before you condemn your boss. Chances are that you are not ready to receive the missing items in your boss' eyes. Try to see yourself as he or she sees you. When changes are called for, implement them as quickly as possible. Where the boss is weak, help him or her become strong—learn from his or her successes as well as failings. Give the best you have to give. Then you bargain from a position of strength when you request what is rightfully yours.

KEY WORD **peers**

1. Explain why your human relations role as educator is two-way.
2. Cite a major difference between your human relations efforts with subordinates and with peers.
3. Give an example of a conflict with a peer that required your boss' intervention to resolve.
4. Give an example from your own experience that illustrates how a manager's reputation was harmed by peer-group actions.
5. What do you stand to lose if you engage in a cover-up of a peer's wrongdoing?
6. What advice would you give a fellow supervisor who makes the following statement: "My boss doesn't appreciate me"?
7. Why is it important·for your subordinates to think highly of your boss?
8. In what way has your boss helped you the most?
9. Why do you think your boss is more concerned with tomorrow than with today?
10. How should supervisors act when their boss is criticized in their presence?

CASE PROBLEM

Who's Kidding Whom?

As Sara Herman was picking her coat off the rack in the employee's coatroom, she heard loud laughter and spirited conversation from down the hall. Will and Rosalyn were having one of the lighthearted interchanges for which they had become famous recently. Sara was about to join them when she heard her name mentioned, so she decided to stay hidden and listen.

"Listen, Roz, just between you and me, Sara is a gossip. You really have to watch what you say to her 'cause it's going to come back to you. I criticized the hotel manager at lunch with her one day and sure enough, he let me know about it just one day later."

"You know what really gets me about her is that phony smile she gives everyone. She's always so syrupy sweet. If she were my subordinate, I'd give her a real talking to. Why don't you?"

"Come on, Roz, I thought you two were buddies, being in the same jobs and all. I'm her boss but one thing I've always found difficult to do is to correct a subordinate. She does her job alright, it's just her personal traits I find offensive. I can't really criticize her personality if it doesn't interfere with her work. Why don't you talk to her if you are bothered by her?"

"Get smart, Will, she criticizes you all the time. I can't talk to her, because she's a friend. How do you criticize a friend? Say, now that I think about it, she'll probably hear about all her faults like she usually does—by listening in on other people's conversations. Come on, we're running late. Let's get our coats."

At that moment Sara stepped out of the coatroom, walked past Will and Roz, and left the building without saying a word.

Questions

1. What seem to be Sara's faults? How should they be brought to her attention?
2. What are Will's faults? How should they be brought to his attention?
3. What are Rosalyn's faults? How should they be brought to her attention?
4. If you were Will's boss and knew about this incident, what would you do?
5. If you were Will, what would you do?

20 You and Your Future

LEARNING OBJECTIVES

■ After reading and discussing this chapter, you should be able to:

1 Describe the value of a college education to an individual's economic status.

2 List and describe five aptitudes that can be assessed through testing.

3 List and describe five interests that can be assessed through tests.

4 Explain the concept of obsolescence as it relates to employees and machines.

5 List six steps in planning a career.

6 Explain how an individual can take a personal inventory.

7 Explain the importance of a commitment to success in career planning.

INTRODUCTION

■ Your yesterdays are history. Your todays will be history tomorrow. Your tomorrows represent your future. What happens to you as they unfold is up to you. What you are willing to invest in your future today will determine your returns tomorrow.

Where you have been influences where and who you are now. Where you would like to be will dictate what and who you must become. Have the seeds you planted years and months ago sprouted or have they withered and died? Any gardener knows that the ground must be prepared to receive the seed before it is planted. Following the planting of the seed comes the difficult task of nurturing its growth. Weeds must be pulled, the ground must be cultivated, water and nutrients must be furnished in just the right mix before the seed will develop into a healthy plant and yield fruit. So it is with your career.

If you are not happy with your past or your past efforts to determine your future, you have the necessary prerequisite for change. If you really want some specific objective or state in life and you have the capacity to achieve it, all you need is a plan in order to obtain it. This chapter is concerned with your future—with your need to avoid personal obsolescence through planning.

OBSOLESCENCE

■ **Obsolescence** exists when a person or machine is no longer capable of performing to standards or to management's expectations. What choices does management have when confronted with an obsolete person or machine? Figure 20–1 highlights a company's alternatives.

You can see from this analogy that the best you can hope for from your company are training and some incentives for self-development. In theory, every employee is eligible for training, but in practice not everyone is qualified for it. Since it is your future we are discussing, you are the one who should be most concerned with it. Don't wait for your company to make the first move. You must take the initiative and maintain it. Your boss is waiting for you to do so. Let your company know you are ready and worthy of additional investments of its efforts and resources.

Figure 20-1. Alternative ways of dealing with obsolescence in a person or machine.

PERSON	MACHINE
Invest in the person through training and development, and offer incentives for efforts at self-improvement.	Keep the machine and modify it, when economically feasible to do so, to improve its efficiency and longevity.
Tolerate the person and his or her limitations and inefficiencies.	Keep the machine and live with its limitations and inefficiencies.
Tolerate the person, but reduce his or her role in the organization by deletion of duties or demotion.	Keep the machine but reduce its role in production, relegating it to back-up or temporary use.
Discharge the person and replace him or her with a better-qualified individual.	Scrap the machine and replace it with a more up-to-date model.

A person can become obsolete in attitudes, knowledge, skills, and abilities. Obsolescence in any one of these areas marks a person as a potential candidate for the scrap heap. He or she may become too costly to keep or maintain.

Personal obsolescence can happen quite suddenly. Overnight changes can take place that will render an individual's performance inadequate. Computers have had this impact on workers as well as managers. When one company buys or merges with another, changes take place in a rapid and unpredictable manner. New skills and knowledge are necessary for the changes in personnel and job descriptions that will take place. Those who possess the potential and have prepared themselves for bigger things will be playing more important roles when the dust settles. Those who have not will be looking for new positions outside the company.

Ask yourself the following questions to determine your degree of personal obsolescence:

ATTITUDES

1. Is my mind free from anxiety over personal matters while I work?
2. Do I believe in myself—my knowledge, skills, and abilities—and in my associates?
3. Am I open and receptive to advice and suggestions regardless of their sources?
4. Do I look for the pluses before looking for the minuses?
5. Am I more concerned with the cause of management's action than with its effect?

KNOWLEDGE

1. Am I curious—do I still seek the "why" behind actions and events?
2. Do I read something and learn something new every day?
3. Do I question the old and the routine?
4. Do I converse regularly with my subordinates, peers, and superiors?
5. Have I a definite program for increasing my knowledge?

SKILLS

1. Is what I am able to do still needed?
2. In light of recent trends and developments in my company and industry, will my skills be required one year from now?
3. Do I practice my skills regularly?
4. Do I regularly observe how others perform their skills?
5. Have I a concrete program for the acquisition of new skills?

ABILITIES

1. Do my subordinates, peers, and superiors consider me competent?
2. Do I consistently look for a better way of doing things?
3. Am I willing to take calculated risks?
4. Do I keep morally and physically fit?
5. Have I a specific program for improving my performance?

All development is self-development. Your efforts at personal growth, once begun, should never cease. Education by formal and informal means is a lifetime process. The day you stop learning is the day you begin your regression. Continuing your education is the best insurance you can have against the risk of becoming obsolete. Through it you keep your mind alert and nimble. You will be making the necessary modifications and refinements that are so important to flexibility and progression.

THE VALUE OF FORMAL EDUCATION

■ College enrollment figures indicated an all-time high in the numbers of students attending colleges and universities in 1975. While the numbers have increased, so has the percentage of high-school seniors who plan to enter college. Few college graduates, whether from a two-year college or a four-year school, will dispute the value—both economic and personal—of their years of formal education. According to official Census Bureau figures:

1. Adults who have completed college earn from two to three times as much, on the average, as do those with only a grade-school education;

2. Over their lifetimes, adults with five or more years of college (some postgraduate work) will earn on the average about $500,000 more than those with only a grade-school education;

3. If you begin your career at age twenty-two after graduating from a four-year college, the present value of your total future earnings will be nearly $760,000. If you start your career at age eighteen with only a high-school diploma, you can expect total future earnings of about $480,000.

One proof of the economic security provided by a college degree can be seen in the unemployment rates. In 1969, less than 1 percent of members of the labor force with college degrees were unemployed. In 1975, the year of the worst recession since World War II, only 2.9 percent of people with a college degree were unemployed. Contrast this with 9.1 percent—the percentage of the total labor force that was unemployed during the same year.

The value of a college degree lies not only in the wages and salaries a person earns, but also in the increased earnings potential it gives him or her. Degree-holders are eligible for many more jobs, fringe benefits, greater challenges, less physical work, and greater opportunities for advancement.

If you continue with your studies in business, you will join a group that includes about 12 percent of your fellow students across the country. Each year, about this number of college-bound high-school graduates choose to major in business and commerce.

PERSONAL GROWTH ■ Besides meeting the need we all have to avoid personal obsolescence, a program for growth and development is necessary just to stay even with the changes taking place around us. Your job security and promotability rest upon your efforts at self-development. But most important, your quality of life is determined by what you do now and how you do it. The road to a richer, happier, more rewarding life is yours to travel. But you must take the time to chart your course carefully.

Commitment to an ongoing program is fundamental to achieving personal growth. Sacrifices are and will be necessary as well. Some of your time, energy, and money will have to be reserved for the execution of that program.

In this life we have two choices: to go to the next life a bright, shiny, uncirculated coin, or to wear ourselves out in the service of others, which means to acquire the coveted patina that comes through constant use and circulation. A coin is both a medium of exchange and a measure of value. You can either become impotent and inert, gathering dust in a vault or become an instrument to enrich yourself and others. Successful men and women have spent themselves willingly in the service of their families, friends, subordinates, peers, superiors, and their God.

PLANNING YOUR FUTURE ■ Like any solid object, your plan for personal growth should be three-dimensional. The first dimension—length—involves a concern for timing and establishing priorities. Once you have determined your needs, they must be translated into goals. Then you must consider their relative importance and establish priorities. Finally, you need to consider the amount of time you will need to reach each goal.

The second dimension—height—involves looking down as well as up. Just as a tree cannot grow taller except with a bigger base, you need to know what is necessary to have in your personal inventory in order to qualify for the position you seek. Then you must plan the route to get you there.

The third dimension is depth. Under this heading should be included a concern to probe more deeply into problems and concepts. Also some effort should be made to broaden your interests and perspectives—to branch out into new and related fields of knowledge. Along with pursuing your specialty through reading and study, you should increase your fund of knowledge about business in general. The higher you wish to go, the greater are the demands for depth and breadth.

You must reach out—up, down, and to the sides—if your growth is not to be stunted. Whatever you do, do it to the best of your ability. When that ability is something less than desired, it must be improved. Thus better performance will follow. Widen your interests and make new acquaintances. Expose yourself to the new and different. When you open yourself to others, you open your mind in the process.

Your career needs a plan if you wish to control it. You start by knowing where you have been and where you are now. Then decide where it is that you want to go. The six steps in planning your career are:

1. Take a personal inventory;
2. Analyze your present situation;
3. Set your improvement objectives;
4. Develop a program;
5. Set your program in motion;
6. Evaluate your progress periodically.

Taking a Personal Inventory

Take a good, honest look at yourself. Try to see yourself as others see you. Your boss' appraisals will help. So too will the honest assessments of friends and family members. As we have stated before in this book, you must know your strengths and weaknesses. Label your successes and failures, what you do well and what you can't do. Make a list of your personal commitments to insiders and outsiders that affect your role at work. From this effort will emerge a list of what's in stock and what must be procured.

Have you progressed in your supervisor's eyes as well as your own since your last appraisal? Have you acted on his or her suggestions for increasing your efficiency and effectiveness? Have you convinced your boss that you desire regular and honest appraisals? Have you asked for and made time for some of his or her duties? These questions boil down to a willingness on your part to improve. If you sincerely wish to do so, transmit your commitment to your boss in words and deeds.

Refer to the checklist that follows: Ask yourself the questions and record your responses carefully. Be specific. If you cannot, you have some work to do before you can make intelligent decisions about your future:

1. How well am I executing my present duties?
2. How well have I prepared for my boss' job?
3. What higher positions hold the greatest appeal to me? Am I prepared for them?
4. What types of additional training or education would be most beneficial to me?
5. What kind of work gives me the most satisfaction? The least?
6. What type of work gives me the most difficulty? Why am I having these difficulties?
7. What distractions in my life interfere with my job? What can I do about them?
8. What new developments have occurred in my field in the last year?
9. Does my current job offer a challenge, and an opportunity for growth and advancement?
10. What do I want from a job?
11. What are my personal goals for the next twelve months?
12. Where will I be one year from now? Five years from now?
13. What are my weaknesses in human relations with subordinates, peers, superiors? What am I doing about them?
14. What are my weaknesses in terms of executing management functions such as planning, organizing, directing, controlling, coordinating? What am I doing about them?
15. What do my superiors, peers, and subordinates really think about me as a person and about my performance on the job?

Assessing Your Aptitudes

Unless you possess extraordinary ability and talent in some area, you may be concerned about whether or not you are in or will choose the right career. **Aptitude tests** have been developed to assess your ability, talent, or capacity to perform certain kinds of mental processes. The ones most frequently measured by these aptitude tests are shown in Figure 20–2.

By taking a battery of aptitude tests through your college's counseling office, you will gain a knowledge of which aptitudes you have and what kinds of jobs you would be most capable of handling. Nearly every job demands one or more of these aptitudes from the job holder. Through proper interpretation of the test results, you will know also the kinds of jobs you are best suited for. Failure to assess your aptitudes may well prevent you from discovering any false perceptions you have of your own capabilities.

Abstract reasoning	The ability to think logically without using numbers or words. Skilled craftsmen, technicians, engineers, scientists, and computer programmers must have this capacity.
Verbal reasoning	The ability to think, comprehend, and communicate effectively through the use of words. Authors, teachers, administrators, salespeople, and secretaries require this ability.
Mechanical reasoning	The ability to recognize the mechanical principles that govern the use of machines and tools. Draftsmen, repairmen, engineers, mechanics, and skilled craftsmen require this ability.
Numeric ability	The capability to solve mathematical problems and think in numbers. Bank tellers, economists, accountants, designers, and technicians must feel comfortable with numeric reasoning.
Spatial relationships	The ability to make things three-dimensional and to imagine the shapes and sizes of things. Depth perception and the ability to estimate distances are also part of this aptitude. Drivers, assemblers, draftsmen, scientists, and technicians share this aptitude.
Manual dexterity	The ability to move the hands skillfully and easily. Nearly every assembly operator, craftsman, and technician needs this aptitude. So do artists and musicians.

Figure 20-2. Mental processes tested in aptitude tests.

Assessing Your Interests

Aptitudes are not the whole story, however, in picking a job. Your personal interests matter a great deal. Even though you have the aptitudes for a given profession or job, you may not want to do it for a living or for the rest of your working career.

Another kind of test of your preferences or interests can help you pinpoint the kinds of activities you like the most. The Kuder General Interest Inventory, which is a widely used test in this area, breaks human interests down into ten general areas: Artistic, clerical, computational, literary, mechanical, musical, outdoor, persuasive, scientific, social service.

Remember that aptitudes and interests tell you only what you are *now*, not what you are likely to become. Other factors will influence your choice of a career—your financial needs, responsibilities, and expectations; your personality and individual motivations; your desire for status and security; and many other factors. Tests can tell you only what you might enjoy doing or the occupational areas you should consider. You are the only one who can decide upon your career.

You should know your likes and dislikes, your strengths and weaknesses. Ask yourself what you want from your job and career. Which needs are most important to you? What kinds of rewards do you want to receive from working? The following list of twenty questions should get you started in taking an inventory of your personal traits and preferences.

1. Am I aware of my major strengths?
2. Am I aware of my major defects? Do I have a specific program to improve?
3. Am I in good physical and mental health?
4. Do I have an ongoing program of physical activity and follow a proper diet regularly?
5. Am I willing to work at a fixed location, confined to a specific work area?
6. Am I willing to work nights and weekends regularly? As the need arises?
7. Am I willing to work outdoors, exposed to extremes of weather and temperature?
8. Do I seek responsibility? Am I a responsible, dependable person?
9. Can I follow orders and directives?
10. Am I a team player?
11. Do I want close supervision?
12. Am I able to work alone, without close supervision?
13. Do I like working with details?
14. Do I like repetitious work, and am I comfortable with routines?
15. Am I looked upon by others as a leader?
16. Do I want to see the results of my labors—to follow tasks from beginning to end?
17. Do I enjoy solving problems and meeting new situations?
18. Do I prefer to work with ideas rather than with tangible things?
19. Do I get along well with other people?
20. Do I work well under the pressure of deadlines?

Analyzing Your Present Situation

What has transpired to get you where you are? Can you honestly say that where you are now was a product of your own efforts? What are the specific skills and abilities that account for success in your present job? Will they be needed where you want to go? By weighing what you have now against what you will need to have, you can determine which of these qualities are already in stock and which will have to be developed.

Setting Your Objectives For Self-Improvement	As clearly and precisely as you can, put the qualities you wish to obtain and the skills and abilities you wish to develop in writing. Be specific. Determine which of these you need most urgently and make them objectives for the short run. Set a time limit by which each is to be procured. Then stick to it as well as you are able. Set the remainder of your needs as long-term goals—goals to be achieved within a year or two. Finally, consider the means you wish to use to reach each goal. Be realistic and a little conservative. Don't take on too much at once. You'll only be in for a letdown and frustration. Start with the goals you need most urgently, and select the one that appears easiest to achieve. As with a diet, early success is important to both commitment and continuation.
Developing Your Program	The program you formulate should contain the answers to who, what, when, where, why, how, and how much. Break it down into phases, each with specific goals and time limits. Keep it in writing and in front of you so that you constantly remind yourself of the targets you wish to hit. Share its contents with your loved ones. They can boost your willpower.
Setting Your Program in Motion	Begin your execution of the program as soon as it is formulated. If you meet heavy resistance in one or another of its phases, leave that phase and divert your attention and efforts to another. Then come back to that phase and try again.
Evaluating Your Progress Periodically	If certain goals you have stated appear to be impossible, you may have to abandon them. With each goal you abandon or achieve, establish another in its place. Remember that the program is a continuing effort at improvement and personal growth. Check your progress against the time limits you established. Were you realistic? Are you on course? Share your successes and setbacks with your husband or wife. Seek counsel from the sources you feel are best qualified to help. But keep working at your program!
	Most companies offer their managers many opportunities for growth and development. Programs range from reading materials to college degrees underwritten by the company's funds. Find out what is available to you and what the requirements are for taking advantage of each of them. Pick the ones that you and your boss feel will be most beneficial to you. Be selective and don't overcommit yourself. It is better to do one or two things splendidly than to do several only adequately.

If your company has few opportunities for you, turn to your local colleges and junior colleges. All of them have excellent, adult, evening- and day-programs with professional counselors available. You can take courses for credit or for personal enjoyment. Don't worry about gaining admission. Where there is a will, there is a way. Today you don't have to be a high-school graduate to attend a junior or senior college. You'll find a few peers in your classes. Take one with you who feels as concerned as you do about the future and the need to prepare for it.

CAREER KILLERS

■ Based on interviews and discussions with nearly twenty business executives, both active and retired, a list of reasons for the failures of managers was formulated. Each of these individuals was asked to recall a subordinate who had met with failure and to state the reasons they believed to be behind this event. The reasons are listed below in the order of the frequency with which they were mentioned. One or more of them were cited by each person interviewed:

1. Too many wrong decisions;
2. Lack of motivation to achieve;
3. Lack of enthusiasm for the job;
4. Lack of standards to govern personal conduct and performance;
5. Lack of goals;
6. Lack of self-control;
7. Lack of integrity;
8. Lack of loyalty;
9. Failure to stay current in one's field;
10. Lack of a system of values;
11. Inability to maintain a balance between home and career;
12. Burdensome and distracting financial and family problems;
13. Lack of potential or ability to succeed.

Keep this list in mind as you plan for your future. All of these reasons are linked to personal obsolescence in some way or another. If any of these career killers is present in your life, what are you going to do about it?

CHANGING JOBS

■ There may come a time in your career when you feel the need to change jobs. If you cannot serve your boss or your subordinates by giving them the best you have, you know that that time has arrived. If you don't look forward each morning to going to work, it is a very good sign that you need a change. When a promotion is not near and you foresee no promising future in your present position in spite of your best efforts, it may be best to move.

When you are considering a move, consider this: look for a job with no ceiling and work you know you will like. Look first at your present company. Is there another position for which you are qualified and in which you would rather work? What is the company policy on transfers? Will your boss let you move? Will he or she endorse the move? If you know the answers to these basic questions and you still want to move, evaluate your competition. If you feel you have better than an even chance, go ahead and apply.

The advantages of seeking a transfer or lateral move within your company are many. You are a known quantity to management. Your records of production and accomplishments mean more to you with your present employer than they will any place else. You know the company and its personnel as well. Just be certain that what you are moving to is better than what you are leaving.

If you decide to leave your present employment, *don't quit before you find a new position*. This will enable you to bargain from a position of strength, without the pressures of unemployment and the immediate need to gain income. Once you have obtained the new job, be certain that you give your old employer proper notice before leaving. This will avoid complications later when your new employer seeks references from your former company.

Whatever the job you hold now or the job you wish to obtain, stay with it at least one year. This gives you time to learn about the company and to take advantage of its several benefits. It gives your company a chance to get its money's worth from you also. If you change jobs too frequently, you may find yourself locked into a level of responsibility and pay that you can't get above. Each change you make should represent growth, not merely a dollar increase. A job that teaches you more and offers you a better potential is far more valuable to your career than just more money. Consider each move carefully. Know as much about the new job and company as you can before you accept the position.

INSTANT REPLAY   Your future is in your own hands. If you take the time necessary to plan for it, what happens to you in the future will be predictable and beneficial. You must take the initiative and provide both the goals and the means that you need in particular to grow and develop. In so doing, you provide the best protection against the threat of personal obsolescence.

Any plan for your career development must start with a firm commitment. This commitment is to both excellence in all your undertakings and persistence in your efforts. Once you have the commitment to proceed, you must formulate plans and incorporate them into a program for action. Such a program should be three-dimensional, containing length, height, and depth.

As soon as your plans are consolidated, they should be executed in phases, your most urgent needs taking priority over the others. Periodically assess your progress and stick with your time limits. Start off slowly and work at the easy goals first. As each goal is achieved, substitute a new one. Share your desires and progress with those to whom your progress is most important. Seek counsel and advice where and when you can.

Don't restrict your efforts to opportunities within your company. Outside sources are available that will greatly increase your knowledge and the rate at which you can acquire it.

KEY WORDS	**aptitude tests**	**obsolescence**

QUESTIONS FOR DISCUSSION

1. What do managers have to do if they are to avoid personal obsolescence?
2. Why is a plan for your future necessary?
3. In constructing a plan for your future development as a manager, to whom should you turn for counsel?
4. Do you think it is a sound idea to share your plans for your future with your loved ones? Why or why not?
5. What do you think are your greatest strengths?

6. Pick any two of the career killers listed above, and indicate what managers can do about each of them if they fall victims to it.
7. How is a plan for your future similar to a diet plan?
8. Is it a good idea to separate your objectives into short- and long-range objectives? Why or why not?
9. What advice would you give a peer who is considering a job switch to another company?

The Exit Interview

Ms. Campbell, the assistant personnel manager of the Harlequin Stores, had just conducted an exit interview with Sherman Wu and had recorded his candid comments. (See Exhibit A.) She was sorry to see Sherman leave after only four months on the job. When she recruited Sherman, she had been impressed by his personality and eagerness to succeed. He also was helping the company's affirmative action program, which called for more minorities in management positions. Ms. Campbell still did not understand well why Sherman had decided to leave.

As she reviewed her notes in preparation for her formal report to her boss, Ms. Campbell went back in her mind to the week when she had first welcomed Sherman and other management trainees to the company. They had all been anxious and nervous. They were a good mix, she recalled thinking at the time, all of them young and fresh out of college. They represented a fine blend of ethnic and academic backgrounds. Three had been business majors while three others were from the liberal arts. All showed above-average results on the tests they had taken and on their college transcripts.

Ms. Campbell remembered how the recruits had been officially greeted by the President of the Harlequin Stores,

Exhibit A

```
                EXHIBIT INTERVIEW

        NAME:   Sherman Wu

        AGE:    23

        INITIAL ASSIGNMENT:   Management Trainee

        DURATION OF TRAINING:   2 months

        PLACEMENT FOLLOWING TRAINING:   Retail sales -- Men and Boys
                Wear, 2nd Floor, Main Street Store

        REASONS FOR LEAVING:

                1.  Training program was too high-level for job
                    assignment.  Trainee claims he was groomed for
                    top management position and given a clerk's job.
                2.  Failure to get along with coworkers.  None of
                    his peers were his equals educationally.  Found
                    them somewhat hostile.
                3.  During first two months on job, trainee had no
                    formal contact with fellow trainees and few
                    encounters with management.
                4.  Trainee was groomed for a job requiring innovative
                    and creative thinking and sound decision making
                    in line with his liberal arts training in college,
                    but was given a job requiring none of these
                    characteristics.
                5.  Found no one in management willing to listen to
                    complaints.  Department supervisor generally
                    unavailable and somewhat hostile.  Trainee felt
                    he could not serve his remaining four months
                    under Mr. Wiley's supervision.

        REMARKS:

                1.  Pay and benefits received were adequate from
                    trainee's point of view (placed on salary that
                    was higher than the average clerk's salary plus
                    commission).
                2.  Has no immediate job to go to and has no definite
                    career goals.  Wants to travel for while before
                    returning to work.  Says he knows what he doesn't
                    want but uncertain what he does want.
                3.  Mr. Wiley rates Mr. Wu as a below-average per-
                    former and a loner.
```

and they had all received a royal treatment during their first two months on the job. For a moment she thought Sherman must be ungrateful and impetuous. She reconsidered that judgment, however, because Sherman had shown none of those traits while a trainee or a sales clerk.

Perhaps the real reason for Sherman's departure had not yet appeared in Ms. Campbell's notes. Sherman had known that he would be a sales clerk in at least three departments for six months after his initial training. After that "ground-floor" experience, however, he would be an assistant supervisor and have his own department within two years from the date he finished his training—earlier perhaps if those new stores on the drawing boards opened up on schedule. Sherman knew all this and had known it when he accepted the trainee's position. If Sherman could have stuck it out a few more months, he surely would have earned a responsible job in the future, especially in view of his minority status.

Ms. Campbell began to feel somewhat annoyed again. That kid had cost the company a lot of money to train, she concluded, and we didn't get half of it back. He took a valuable seat in an expensive training program that could have been offered to another individual who might have stayed on and been more grateful. She picked up her pen and added these final words to her notes:

Like most minority members this interviewer has dealt with, Mr. Wu has a chip on his shoulder and wants instant success without having to earn it. Would not rehire.

Questions
1. Why did Sherman decide to leave?
2. What, if anything, would you do to change the training program?
3. What accounts for Ms. Campbell's change in her attitudes toward Sherman? Do you agree with her diagnosis of him? Why or why not?
4. What lessons are there in this case for a college graduate about to start a career in business?

Appendices

APPENDIX A: HOW TO TAKE CLASS NOTES

A.   Never write while the instructor is covering material verbally.

1.   Listen carefully.
2.   Wait for a natural interruption, pause, or delay—then write.

**B.   While listening, ask yourself mentally, "What is the instructor saying?"
and "What is the key idea?"**

1.   If you find it hard to restate the key idea, ask the teacher to restate his
or her concepts.
2.   Put the key ideas (main points) in your own words, not the teacher's.
Your notes should be you talking to yourself
3.   Think in "shorthand"—use key words and phrases.

C.   Write your notes when you find a logical pause.

1.   When a student asks or answers a question.
2.   When the teacher answers a question.
3.   When the teacher moves to the board or uses it.

D.   Review your notes as soon as possible following class.

1.   Make sure you still understand the concepts you recorded.
2.   Expand upon them at your leisure and write a more detailed account
if necessary.
3.   Read your notes over before reviewing reading assignments. This will
give you a feeling for what the teacher felt was important in the readings and
tell you what was covered in class that is not in the text. You will then know
your teacher's emphasis.

APPENDIX B: HOW TO PRESENT A CASE PROBLEM IN CLASS

A. Getting the facts.

1. Read the entire case problem through.
2. Before reading the questions that follow it, ask yourself where the problems lie. If you have no clear insights, reread the case. Recall that the case appears in conjunction with a chapter in the text. The major purpose of a case is to dramatize an incident within which you can apply the knowledge you have gained from that chapter and the ones preceding it.
3. Read all the questions following the case problem. Consider each in a sequence that you feel makes the most sense. If you read about a person taking action, ask yourself, "What will be the effect of that action on the people in the case problem?"
4. If a question calls for your opinion, back it up with specific examples from your own experiences when possible.
5. When you feel that you cannot answer a question without additional information, try to read into the case problem and between its lines. Look for clues that will allow you to deduce or create what is probably true from what you are given. Most cases give you symptoms rather than a disease. Try to get under the surface of the wording. This will become easier for you with each new case.
6. Make notes on your answer to each question. Quote from the case and cite specific references from the chapter(s) that is (are) related to the case.

B. Presenting the case problem in class.

1. Start with a capsule summary of the facts as you see them. Identify the key persons in the case problem and put their names and titles on the blackboard so that you can refer to them as you speak.
2. When answering each question, be as specific and factual as you can. State your decision and give the audience the benefit of your research and analysis. Cite your references and quote from the case to prove a point. Let the class know where you are when you do so, so that they can follow your argument.
3. Keep in mind that there is no one right answer to the case problem's questions. There are many wrong ones, however. You are far better off to base your conclusions on facts than to guess. You can expect the greatest resistance and objections from the class when you state decisions that require deductions or assumptions. If you can show the group your logic, they will probably accept your reasoning. Be prepared for different sets of assumptions—possibly as valid as yours—with correspondingly different conclusions. Allow time for questions. If you are stuck, defer the answer to a classmate.

APPENDIX C: HOW TO TAKE EXAMS

1.   Come prepared. The night before, review your notes and get a good night's sleep. Just before the test, eat a light snack and visit the washroom. Bring the required references, your eyeglasses, pencil, eraser, pen, and paper.

2.   Read the exam's instructions carefully. Before you begin, know how many questions should be on the exam and how your answers to each should be presented.

3.   Answer the questions that you are sure of first. Save the more difficult ones for later.

4.   Trust your first impression. Studies prove that your first impulse in response to an objective-type question is correct more often than not.

5.   Calculate numerical answers on scratch paper. Put your answer(s) in the space provided and be sure to label each answer. Reread the question and see if your answer "looks right."

6.   Check the time periodically. Use any extra time to review the exam and to rethink the questions you are not sure of. Be certain that you give what was wanted in the desired form and in the space provided.

7.   Ask your instructor for any clarification you may need to understand a question.

8.   Ignore those around you. Those who talk and look around are headed for trouble. Those who leave early are either stupid or foolish.

9.   Don't leave any questions blank. You are a *sure* loser if you do. Try your best guess at objective questions and write *something* for the essays.

10.   Reread your answers. Touch up your punctuation, spelling, and grammar. Fill in any missing answers and be sure your name and any other required data appear where they should.

APPENDIX D: AN INTRODUCTION TO STATISTICS

In this brief look at the world of "ordered numbers," you will learn the basic terms and concepts used so frequently to influence your opinions. *Statistics* is the science of collecting, arranging, and presenting numerical data to provide information about a subject. Textbooks, newspapers, and magazines present tables and charts that show specific facts, trends, and changes affecting a subject under discussion. Phrases like "the average consumer" or "the median income of the American worker" or "of the 400 consumers surveyed . . ." lead readers into persuasive presentations that attempt to influence their understanding and reactions to the numbers that follow.

Collecting numerical data.

Ben Franklin, the personnel manager of the National Widget Company, has been asked by the company's president to calculate the average salary paid to its seven managers. The payroll department sent him the data in Table A.

Notice that the data Franklin received are listed in alphabetical order. In reviewing the data Franklin realized that these salary figures would be more useful to him and more clearly represented if they were listed numerically from the highest paid executive to the lowest. So he rearranged the data as shown in Table B.

Manager	Annual salary
Adams, J.	$26,500
Franklin, B.	31,000
Hamilton, A.	28,500
Jefferson, T.	28,500
Jones, J.	19,000
Revere, P.	24,500
Washington, G.	45,000
	$203,000

Table A

Annual salary	Manager
$45,000	Washington, G.
31,000	Franklin, B.
28,500	Hamilton, A.
28,500	Jefferson, T.
26,500	Adams, J.
24,500	Revere, J.
19,000	Jones, J.
$203,000	

Table B

At a glance Franklin knows that:

Washington is the highest paid manager.

Both Hamilton and Jefferson receive the same salary.

Jones is the lowest paid manager.

Finding the arithmetic mean.

Most of us like to group facts in our minds. It helps us to understand and relate to things better. Franklin is no exception. He knows that the figures he has could be more useful if he could deal with them in the aggregate or in a total in some way and thus relate each salary to that total. So he decides to calculate the average pay for managers by adding the salaries they receive and dividing that sum by the number of managers. This average is known as the *mean* or *arithmetic average*. By dividing the total salaries ($203,000) by the number of managers (T), Franklin arrives at $29,000 as the average or mean salary received by managers at National Widget:

$$\$203,000 \div 7 = \$29,000$$

Note that while the average pay is $29,000, no manager actually receives that amount. Also there are only two managers who receive more than this amount while there are five who receive less. Because of these considerations, Franklin decides not to use the $29,000 average-pay figure because it would be misleading. Although it is the actual average, it is not representative of the salaries paid. Franklin decides to use a figure that falls more toward the middle of the salaries listed.

Finding the median.

The *median* is the number in an array of figures that falls exactly halfway between the highest and the lowest figures listed. The median divides an array exactly in half. Returning to his second list and counting from the top or bottom of the figures listed, Franklin finds the middle number of the seven amounts listed: $28,500, the salary received by Jefferson. Half the salaries listed are below this figure. The median salary of $28,500 is more representative of the salaries paid to the company managers than the mean salary of $29,000, so Franklin decides to use this figure.

Finding the mode.

The *mode* in an array is defined as the number that appears most frequently. In Table B the salary of $28,500 appears twice, while all other salaries appear only once. Thus $28,500 is the mode figure or *modal* salary. Modes are used to determine what sizes are best for hats, shoes, clothing, and other items. The measurements that people have in common establish the sizes for manufactured models.

Finding the frequency distribution.

If you have a perfect distribution in an array of figures, the mean, median, and mode for that array will be equal. To illustrate this concept, look at the numbers listed below. They represent the grades received by 18 students who took the same test:

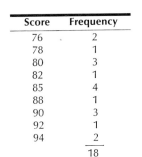

Score	Frequency
76	2
78	1
80	3
82	1
85	4
88	1
90	3
92	1
94	2
	18

Table C

76, 76, 78, 80, 80, 80, 82, 85, 85, 85, 85, 88, 90, 90, 90, 92, 94, 94,

Writing these test scores in another way gives what is called a *frequency distribution,* shown in Table C.

The frequency column allows us to list our data in a shortened way. By multiplying the frequency (the number of times a figure appears in the array) times the score, we can find the totals as shown in Table D.

The mean for these scores is found by dividing the total scores by the total number of scores in the array (the total of the frequency column):

$$1530 \div 18 = 85.$$

The mean or average grade in this array is 85.

The median is the score that falls halfway between the highest and the lowest scores. We find the median in Table D by counting into the array halfway. As there are 18 scores, halfway would be between the 9th and 10th scores listed. The 9th and 10th scores are both 85. Since there is no difference between these two scores, the median is 85. (If the 9th score were 85 and the 10th score were 86, the median would be 85.5—still halfway between the 9th and 10th scores.)

The mode is the score in the array that appears most frequently. The score 85 is listed four times. No other score appears as frequently, so 85 is the modal score.

In this array we find that the mean, median, and mode are the same. All are the number 85.

Score	Frequency		Total scores
76	x 2	=	152
78	x 1	=	78
80	x 3	=	240
82	x 1	=	82
85	x 4	=	340
88	x 1	=	88
90	x 3	=	270
92	x 1	=	92
94	x 2	=	188
	18		1530

Table D

THE AVERAGE SOLDIER

Statistically speaking, these are the characteristics of the average soldier in the United States Army:

- Is male or female.
- Is 23 years of age.
- Has 3 years of active military service.
- Males are 5′10″ tall and weigh 167 pounds.
- Females are 5′4″ tall and weight 130 pounds.
- Has a high-school diploma.
- Comes from a community of 25,000 people.
- Comes from a family whose average annual income is about $10,000.

Do you think any soldier in the Army would fit this description exactly?

Glossary

accidents: Any unforseen or unplanned incident or event that results in damage or harm (Ch. 18).

accountability: The responsibility to answer for a subordinate's use of your formal authority (Ch. 1).

activities: In the PERT method of planning, the activities are described as an easily defined sequence of jobs (Ch. 3).

agency shop: Under an agency shop agreement, employees do not have to belong to the union, but must pay a fee to the union since all employees benefit from union negotiations (Ch. 14).

appraisal process: Periodic evaluations of each subordinate's on-the-job performance as well as his or her character, attitudes, and potential (Ch. 12).

aptitude tests: Tests developed to assess people's abilities, talents, or capacities to perform certain kinds of mental processes (Ch. 20).

arbitration: A process that involves settling a labor dispute through a neutral outsider or arbitrator. The arbitrator conducts hearings into the dispute, and his or her decision is binding on both union and management (Ch. 14).

attitude: Our willingness or predisposition to react in a predetermined way to certain stimuli, such as individuals, groups of individuals, or events (Ch. 6).

authority: The power to do or get something done; it may be formal or informal in nature (Ch. 1).

autocratic style: A management style characterized by the retention of all authority by the leaders, who keep their subordinates dependent upon them for instructions (Ch. 11).

boycott: The refusal to trade or deal with a person or company.

> *primary boycott:* A union's refusal to deal with a company with which it has a labor dispute.

> *secondary boycott:* An action by which a union forces an employer to stop dealing with or purchasing from another company not directly involved in a labor dispute (Ch. 14).

bureaucratic style: A management style characterized by the manager's reliance upon rules, regulations, policies, and procedures (Ch. 11).

checklist method: This method of appraising subordinates, which is also known as the forced-choice method, requires a supervisor to pick the one block and statement out of several that best describes a subordinate's standing with regard to a particular characteristic (Ch. 12).

clique: Informal group of two or more people who come together by choice to satisfy mutual needs or share common interests. There are three primary types of informal groups: horizontal, vertical, and random (Ch. 9).

closed shop: A union security provision that requires employers to hire only union labor. This type of union shop agreement was supposed to have been outlawed by the 1947 Labor Management Relations Act (Ch. 14).

collective bargaining: A traditional way of settling labor disputes that involves placing union representatives on one side of a table and management's representatives on the other (Ch. 14).

communications: Transmission of information and

understanding from one person to another through the use of common symbols. Such symbols are both verbal and nonverbal, and may involve the use of language, color, pictures, objects, facial expressions, gestures, or actions to carry a message (Ch. 5).

communications barriers: Conditions that interfere with or prevent effective communications. Six major barriers to successful communications are uncommon symbols, improper timing, atmospheric disturbances, improper attitudes, background differences, and sender/receiver relationships (Ch. 5).

concentration: Mental receptiveness coupled with physical alertness during the act of listening (Ch. 5).

controlling: A managerial activity that involves the ability to prevent, identify, and correct deficiencies in all phases of business operations; an integral part of all the other functions of a supervisor (Ch. 4).

cooperation: Working together to reach common goals or objectives (Ch. 6).

coordinating: A managerial function that insures that all the parts of an organization operate in harmony. It involves the integration of all details necessary for reaching a supervisor's goals (Ch. 4).

critical-incident method: This method of appraising subordinates, which is also known as the narrative method, requires a supervisor to make reference to rather specific situations that highlight or illustrate the workers' abilities, traits, or potentials. The rater makes use of the essay approach in preparing personal observations and comments (Ch. 2).

critical path: In production planning, the calculation of the total time required to produce a product is the critical path (Ch. 3).

delegation: The giving away of all or some of a person's formal authority and the corresponding responsibility to another, usually a subordinate (Ch. 1).

democratic style: A management style characterized by the sharing of authority with subordinates through delegation and problem-solving sessions, with the corresponding development of a team spirit (Ch. 11).

deviate: A person who does not aspire to join or belong to a group (Ch. 9).

direct interview: A thoroughly planned, highly structured interview based on a format of specific questions set down in advance and exactly followed. Used for assessing candidates for a position, it supplements the information on the candidates that has been gathered by the personnel department (Ch. 15).

directing: This managerial function involves recruiting, selecting, and placing new employees —three activities often lumped together under the heading *staffing*. Directing also involves training and offering incentives to subordinates as well as evaluating, disciplining, and promoting them (Ch. 4).

directive interview: An interview planned and totally controlled by the interviewer. It follows a basic outline from beginning to end according to a script written out in advance. Usually used to obtain specific information, to communicate information, or to interview applicants for non-management positions (Ch. 10).

disciplining: This managerial duty involves two distinct and related concepts: education and training to foster obedience to rules and standards; and the dispensing of appropriate punishment for wrongdoing.

> *negative discipline:* An aspect of discipline that places an emphasis on the detection of wrongdoing and punishment.

> *positive discipline:* A process that promotes understanding and self-control by informing subordinates of what is expected of them in regard to on-the-job behavior (Ch. 4).

discrimination: Unlawful denial of job opportunities or advancement on the job to individuals on the basis of their race, color, sex, age, religion, or national origin (Ch. 15).

disparate effect: Term used to characterize a selection device or procedure that excludes a significantly greater number of minority group members than whites from a job opening (Ch. 15).

drive: A force within us fueled by human needs common to all people. These needs provide the motives for our efforts to achieve goals in life (Ch. 7).

Equal Employment Opportunity Commission (EEOC): Federal governmental agency that establishes and maintains guidelines to prevent discriminatory practices in employment (Ch. 15).

evaluating: A management practice that requires supervisors to make periodic appraisals of their subordinates' on-the-job performance (Ch. 4).

evaluation process: This process, which is often referred to as merit rating, or employee performance evaluation and review, requires supervisors to make periodic appraisals of their subordinates' performances (Ch. 12).

events: In the PERT method of planning, the individual jobs or activities have definite starting and ending points called *events* (Ch. 3).

exit interview: An interview conducted with an employee who has announced his or her decision to leave the company in order to determine the reasons for the decision (Ch. 16).

explanation: One of the basic ingredients of spoken communications. An explanation identifies the key points or ideas and groups them in a logical sequence (Ch. 5).

featherbedding: An unfair labor practice whereby unions require employers to pay for work that is not performed (Ch. 14).

field-review method: According to this method of appraising employees, the supervisor is interviewed by staff assistants in the personnel department. The supervisor answers questions about each of his or her subordinates. The staff assistants write up the formal appraisals, which the supervisor either approves with a signature or disapproves with comments (Ch. 12).

flow of planning: Various steps in the planning function, including the philosophy of management; goals; policies; rules; programs; procedures; practices; and outcomes (Ch. 2).

Force Field Analysis: A method of visualizing the driving and restraining forces at work within an individual so as to assess more accurately what is needed to effect a change in his or her attitudes (Ch. 6).

forced-check method: This is the same method of employee appraisal described above under *checklist method* (Ch. 12).

formal authority: Authority that comes with the position a person occupies in a formal organization (Ch. 1).

formal group: Two or more people who come together by management decision to achieve specific goals (Ch. 9).

frustration: Mental state that arises when the goal we are seeking and the satisfaction it represents are viewed as unobtainable (Ch. 7).

functional authority: Power given to a manager of a department, usually a staff department, enabling him or her to make decisions that are binding on another department (Ch. 1).

Gantt chart: A planning tool used for planning small-scale work on the basis of time (Ch. 3).

goal: A precise, specific objective the top management of a company decides to be worthwhile. Once decided upon, a company's goals should be described formally (Ch. 3).

grapevine: Informal channels within a company that are not specifically designed for the dissemination of information but are used for this purpose by nearly every employee (Ch. 5).

grievance: A formal complaint filed by management or a labor union alleging that a provision of the collective bargaining agreement has been violated (Ch. 14).

grievance processing: A formal procedure for handling labor disputes within a company under the terms of a labor contract (Ch. 14).

gripe: Complaint about working conditions or on-the-job relationships that comes to a manager's attention (Ch. 14).

group: Two or more people who are consciously aware of one another; who consider themselves to be a functioning unit; and who share in a quest to achieve one or more goals or some common benefit (Ch. 9).

group dynamics: Forces for change that are brought to bear on individuals when two or more of them come together to gain some mutual benefit or to achieve some common goal (Ch. 9).

group spirit: Major attitudes reflected by the members of a formal group and the informal groups associated with it (Ch. 11).

halo effect: Error frequently made by people appraising others. It consists of allowing one outstanding trait—either positive or negative—to color the overall rating and image of the subordinate (Ch. 12).

hierarchy: Group of people picked to staff an organization and make all the necessary plans and decisions that allow it to function (Ch. 11).

horizontal clique: Group consisting of two or more people from the same functional area and on the same level of authority (Ch. 9).

human needs: Needs common to everyone that provide the stimuli or motives for change within ourselves. They include our physical needs, safety needs, social needs, esteem needs, and self-realization values (Ch. 7).

human relations: Development and maintenance of sound, on-the-job relationships by a manager with subordinates, peers, and superiors (Ch. 8).

incentives: Benefits a company believes will have a strong appeal to its employees and encourage them to give a better than average performance in their jobs (Chs. 4 and 7).

indirect interview: Loosely structured employment interview that utilizes open questions designed to secure not only information from applicants but also their opinions and attitudes (Ch. 15).

individualism: Training principle that requires a trainer to learn about the prior skills, knowledge, and attitudes of the people he or she is to train so that the training sessions can be properly suited to the trainees' needs (Ch. 17).

induction: Process or initiating or welcoming a new employee to his or her place of work in a new company. A part of the orientation program, it is usually carried out by the new employee's supervisor (Ch. 16).

inertia stage: Tendency of each worker to resist training, which must be overcome if the training is to be effective. During a training process, the trainees move from a stage of inertia through the training cycle to a new but higher state of inertia (Ch. 17).

informal authority: Authority a person has over others because of his or her personal traits. It is something others freely give to the other individual (Cr. 1).

informal group: Two or more people who come together by choice to satisfy mutual needs or share common interests (Ch. 9).

informational meeting: Meeting held for the purpose of disseminating pertinent information affecting a department or some department members (Ch. 10).

initiative phase: In the training process the initiative phase represents the learner's movement from a stage of inertia to active participation in the learning process (Ch. 17).

injunctions: Court orders in labor disputes that direct one or the other of the parties to do something or to refrain from doing something (Ch. 14).

insight phase: In the training process the trainees move from the inertia stage through the initiative phase to the insight phase where they receive insights that lead to an understanding of the operation in which they are being trained (Ch. 17).

interview: Conversation between two parties that is under the control of one of the parties and that tries to accomplish a special objective (Ch. 10).

introduction: In spoken communications the introduction attempts to get the listener's attention, arouse interest, and state the subject matter and purpose of the communication (Ch. 5).

isolate: Person who would like to belong to a clique but is denied membership for some reason (Ch. 9).

job description: Listing of the duties and responsibilities of a job or formal position in an organization (Ch. 3).

job enlargement: Increasing the number of tasks a worker has to perform. The extra tasks may or may not offer a degree of variety or challenge (Ch. 6).

job enrichment: Concept of providing employees with work variety, a deeper personal interest and involvement, a greater autonomy, and an increased amount of responsibility (Ch. 6).

job specification: Personal characteristics required of a person to fill a position (Ch. 3).

knowledge: In the training process, knowledge is a body of facts, ideas, concepts, and procedures that enable people to see or visualize what must be done on a job (Ch. 17).

labor relations: All the activities within a company that involve dealing with a union and its members either individually or collectively (Ch. 14).

labor union: Group of workers employed by a company or an industry or practicing the same skill who have banded together to bargain collectively with their employer for improvements in wages, hours, fringe benefits, and working conditions (Ch. 14).

leadership: Ability to get work done with and through others while simultaneously winning their respect, confidence, loyalty, and cooperation (Ch. 11).

line manager: Manager in an organizational hierarchy whose activities or department directly influences the profitability of the business (Ch. 1).

linking pin: Key individual in a business organization who is a member of two or more groups and who links or locks these groups together (Ch. 2).

listening: In the communications process, listening involves paying close attention to the speaker in order to hear his or her words (Ch. 5).

lockout: Management practice that consists of denying the workers access to their jobs in order to discourage union activities (Ch. 14).

management: Team of people in any formal organization that occupies positions of formal authority and is charged with the coordination of the organization's human and material resources through the functions of planning, organizing, directing, and controlling the work of others for the purpose of achieving stated goals (Ch. 1).

mediation: In a labor dispute mediation means bringing in a neutral third party who is allied with neither labor nor management. After hearing both parties to the dispute, the mediator recommends a solution, but his or her decision is not binding on either party (Ch. 14).

medium: Channel or means of communications. One of the basic components in any attempt to communicate thoughts or ideas to others. The other basic components are the message, the transmitter, and the receiver (Ch. 5).

mentor: Experienced employee who volunteers to act as a guide and tutor to a newcomer. The mentor should be able to explain about the company and provide a degree of immediate social acceptance (Ch. 16).

message: In the communications process, the message is one of the basic components, along with the transmitter, the medium, and the receiver (Ch. 5).

middle management: Occupying the center of the management pyramid, the middle management level is the location of all managers below the rank of vice-president and above the operating level (Ch. 1).

minority: According to EEOC, the following are members of minority groups protected from discrimination in employment: Hispanics (Spanish-surnamed Americans); Asians or people from the Pacific Islands (Oriental Americans); blacks not of Hispanic origin (Negroes); American Indians (natives of North America); and Alaskan natives (Eskimos) (Ch. 15).

motivation: Drive within a person to achieve a personal goal. It is fueled by the individual's wants and needs (Chs. 7 and 17).

motives: Internal causes or reasons for action, based upon an individual's recognition of his or her own needs and wants (Ch. 7).

morale: A person's attitudes toward all the individuals, things, and events that affect him or her at work (Ch. 11).

narrative method: See the *critical-incident method* of appraisal above (Ch. 12).

nondirective interview: Interview controlled by the interviewee but planned by the interviewer. The interviewer starts with open questions designed to allow the interviewee flexibility in his or her answers and a chance to talk at length according to an outline and pace of his or her own choice (Ch. 12).

objective: In planning a training program, the principle of the objective states that trainers and trainees should always know where they are headed during the training process (Ch. 17).

obsolescence: State that exists when an employee or a machine is no longer able to perform to standards or to management's expectations (Ch. 20).

open shop: Under an open shop agreement, membership in the union is voluntary for all long-time and new employees (Ch. 14).

operating management: Lowest level on the management pyramid; the place where supervisors and foremen are found (Ch. 1).

opinion: Judgment about a person or event that can be put into words and that probably reflects one's general attitude or outlook on life (Ch. 6).

organization development: According to the Conference Board, organization development is a planned, managed, systematic process used to change the culture, systems, and behavior of an organization in order to improve the organization's effectiveness in solving problems and achieving its objectives (Ch. 6).

organizing: Involves the following steps: (1) determining the tasks to be performed; (2) establishing a framework of authority and responsibility among the people who will accomplish the work; and (3) allocating appropriate resources to accomplish the tasks and reach the objectives (Ch. 3).

organizing principles: Include unity of command, span of control, delegation of authority, homogeneous assignment, and flexibility (Ch. 3).

orientation: The planning and execution of a program to introduce a new worker to his or her company, job, working environment, and peers. It includes giving explanations about the newcomer's rights, duties, limits, and future prospects (Ch. 16).

OSHA: Occupational Safety and Health Administration, or less frequently, Occupational Safety and Health Act of 1970 (Ch. 18).

peers: A manager's peers are all other managers at the same level of the hierarchy. A worker's peers are all other workers in the company (Ch. 2).

perception: Ability to separate a speaker's facts from his or her feelings so as to comprehend the meaning of what is being said (Ch. 5).

personality: An individual's habitual way of acting, feeling, and thinking with regard to people and events (Ch. 7).

PERT: Popular, precise method used in the critical-path scheduling of production. PERT (Program Evaluation and Review Technique) lends itself to any task that has an easily defined sequence of jobs or activities with definite starting and ending points called events (Ch. 3).

Peter Principle: Concept that in every hierarchy each employee tends to rise to his or her level of incompetence (Ch. 2).

philosophy of management: Way in which the top management of a company looks at the people and events that have an impact on the business (Ch. 3).

pilferage: Theft by employees (Ch. 18).

planning: Construction of a program for action in order to achieve stated goals through the use of people, procedures, and practices (Ch. 3).

policies: Attempt to coordinate and provide uniformity in the conduct of a business and the behavior of employees. They are basically plans

for insuring the smooth, harmonious running of a company (Ch. 3).

practices: Procedures that deal with the "nitty-gritty" of the small details that need to be decided in order to complete work. Usually established by individual managers for their own departments (Ch. 3).

problem-solving meeting: Meeting conducted in order to reach a group consensus or solution to a problem affecting the group. It uses the discussion format, which allows members to participate actively under the direction of a chairperson (Ch. 10).

procedures: General ways or methods for carrying out individual programs and handling the day-to-day routine of a business (Ch. 3).

proficiency: Level of competence that an employee or group of employees exhibits in accomplishing the work. Often tied to morale and group spirit (Ch. 11).

programs: Plans for each division, department, or section developed by managers at every level. Programs list goals to be achieved and answer general questions about the use of a company's resources (Ch. 3).

promoting: One of a manager's duties includes preparing recommendations, ratings, and formal evaluation of subordinates as a basis for promoting them. Promotions usually require the approval of two or more levels of management, and may also require the endorsement of the personnel department (Ch. 4).

random clique: Clique composed of two or more persons from two or more functional areas (Ch. 9).

ranking method: The ranking (or forced-distribution) method of appraising employees requires the manager to rank his or her employees from the most valuable to the least valuable (Ch. 12).

realism: Training principle that requires the learning process to be as close to real-life conditions as possible, for example, by using actual equipment and tools in a training situation (Ch. 17).

receiver: In the communications process, the receiver is one of the basic components along with the message, the transmitter, and the medium (Ch. 5).

recruiting: Usually an activity of the personnel department, it involves finding good applicants or candidates for employment openings in a company (Ch. 15).

reinforcement: Training principle that states the need to involve all the senses (or as many as possible) in training in order to insure retention (Ch. 17).

response: Training principle that reminds the trainer to check regularly on the learner's receptiveness and retention (Ch. 17).

responsibility: Having to answer to someone, usually one's immediate boss, for the use of one's formal authority in a company (Ch. 1).

role ambiguity: Situation that occurs whenever a manager is not certain of the role he or she is expected to play or how to play it (Ch. 2).

role conflict: Situation that occurs when conflicting or contradictory demands are made of managers (Ch. 2).

role prescription: Expectations and demands placed on managers by their superiors, subordinates, friends, and family, and that help shape the managers' perception of their jobs (Ch. 2).

rules: Specific, inflexible guidelines for the behavior of employees while at work (Ch. 3).

safety: Protecting human resources in a company from accidents and injuries (Ch. 18).

sanctions: Negative means, such as threats or punishments, used by a company to encourage workers to play their roles according to the rules prescribed by the business organization (Ch. 2).

scale method: This method of appraising employees combines the ranking and forced-choice methods. The rater decides where each subordinate stands in relation to his or her peers on the basis of a scale (Ch. 12).

security: Protecting physical or nonhuman resources from loss or damage (Ch. 19).

selection: The personnel management function that determines who is hired by a business and who is not. It is a process by which applicants are evaluated as to their suitability for employment (Ch. 15).

self-discipline: Ability to regulate and correct ourselves in order to improve our conduct and efficiency (Ch. 11).

sensitivity training: Technique that makes use of small groups of people engaged in unstructured discussions for the purpose of changing the participants' attitudes and breaking down their resistance to change (Ch. 6).

skills: Activities that require muscular coordination blended with technical abilities, such as typing or the use of precision machines (Ch. 17).

spectator style: Management style characterized by a strong reliance of the supervisor on the knowledge, skills, and initiative of his or her subordinates, with a corresponding development of a high level of independence and pride among the subordinates (Ch. 11).

staffing: Process involving the recruiting, selecting, and placing of new employees in their jobs (Ch. 4).

staff manager: Specialist who supervises an activity or a department that does not contribute directly to the major goals of a company. A staff manager's primary mission is to help other managers who need his or her specialized knowledge Ch. 1).

steward: Employee of a company elected to a union office by the union members who has the responsibility of representing the workers in labor disputes with the company (Ch. 14).

subjects: Training principle to the effect that a trainer should know as much as possible about the trainees, and should also have a mastery of the subject to be taught (Ch. 16).

summary: In spoken communications the summary is used to restate important points and to aid the memory of the hearer (Ch. 5).

supervision: Directing human resources, including the training, appraisal, and disciplining of subordinates (Ch. 1).

supervisor: Member of management's team on the operating level who directs the work of non-management people (Ch. 1).

synergy: Increased effect as a result of combining forces that goes beyond the total of all the individual forces on their own (Ch. 9).

Theory X: Theory adopted by managers with respect to human nature and motivation. According to Douglas McGregor, managers who follow Theory X believe that workers have a natural dislike for work, must be threatened or coerced to do a fair day's work, and require constant supervision (Ch. 7).

Theory Y: Theory of human nature and motivation directly opposite to Theory X. Managers who follow Theory Y believe that the average person likes work, is capable of directing himself or herself if committed to achieving a goal, desires responsibility, possesses initiative, and is underutilized intellectually in the average industrial setting (Ch. 7).

top management: Company's chief executive, his or her immediate subordinates, and the secretary and treasurer if the company is also a corporation (Ch. 1).

training: Teaching of skills, knowledge, and attitudes to both new and long-time employees (Chs. 4 and 17).

transmitter: In the communications process, one of the basic components along with the medium, the message, and the receiver (Ch. 5).

union shop: Under a union shop agreement all current employees of a company must join the union as soon as it is certified as their legitimate bargaining agent (Ch. 14).

validity: Necessary characteristic of all selection devices or procedures. According to EEOC, devices and procedures are "valid" if they are directly related to and predictive of a person's job performance (Ch. 15).

vandalism: Wanton or willful destruction or damage to an employer's property (Ch. 19).

vertical clique: Two or more people from the same functional area who are on different levels of the hierarchy (Ch. 9).

worker: Nonmanagement employee (Ch. 1).

worker's compensation: Federal and state laws designed to compensate employees for illnesses and injuries that arise out of and in the course of their employment (Ch. 18).

yellow-dog contracts: Unfair practice by which management requires employees to agree not to join a union as a condition of their employment (Ch. 14).

Bibliography

Benton, Lewis R. *Supervision and Management.* New York: McGraw-Hill Book Co., 1972.

Bittel, Lester. *What Every Supervisor Should Know.* New York: McGraw-Hill Book Co., 1974.

_____. *The Nine Master Keys of Management.* New York: Mc-Graw-Hill Book Co., 1973.

Blake, Robert R.; Mouton, Jane S.; Barnes, Louis B.; and Greiner, Larry. "Breakthrough in Organization Development." *Harvard Business Review* 42, no. 6 (November-December 1964).

Boyd, Bradford B. *Management Minded Supervision.* New York: McGraw-Hill Book Co., 1972.

Buffa, E. S., and Taubert, W. H. *Production-Inventory Systems: Planning and Control,* rev. ed. Homewood, Ill.: Richard D. Irwin, 1972.

Burby, Raymond J. *An Introduction to Basic Supervision of People.* Reading, Mass.: Addison-Wesley Publishing Co., 1966.

Coch, Lester, and French, Jr., John R. P. "Overcoming Resistance to Change." *Human Relations* 1, no. 4, (1948): 512–32.

Dalton, Melville. *Men Who Manage: Fusions of Feeling and Theory in Administration.* New York: John Wiley & Sons, 1959.

Davis, Keith. *Human Relations at Work.* New York: McGraw-Hill Book Co., 1962.

Dessler, Gary. *Management Fundamentals: A Framework,* Reston, Va. Reston Publishing Company, 1977.

Donnelly, Jr., James H.; Gibson, James L.; and Ivancevich, John M. *Fundamentals of Management.* Austin, Tex.: Business Publications, 1971.

Dowling, Jr., William F. and Sayles, Leonard R. *How Managers Motivate: The Imperatives of Supervision.* New York: McGraw-Hill Book Co., 1971.

Drucker, Peter F. *The Practice of Management.* New York: Harper & Row, Publishers, 1954.

Evans, Chester E. *Supervisory Responsibility and Authority.* Research Report No. 30. New York: The American Management Association, 1957.

Gardiner, Glenn L. *Foremen in Action*. New York: Harper & Row, Publishers, 1959.

Gellerman, Saul W. *Motivation and Productivity*. New York: The American Management Association, Inc., 1963.

Gordon, Thomas. *Leader Effectiveness Training: L.E.T.* New York: Wyden Books, 1977.

Greenwald, Douglas. *McGraw-Hill Dictionary of Modern Economics*. New York: McGraw-Hill Book Co., 1965.

Guest, Robert H. "Of Time and the Foreman," *Personnel 32* (May 1956): 482.

Hepner, Harry W. *Perceptive Management and Supervision*. Englewood Cliffs, N. J.: Prentice-Hall, 1961.

Herzberg, Frederick; Mausner, Bernard; and Block, Barbara. *The Motivation to Work*. New York: John Wiley & Sons, 1959.

Kahn, R. L.; Wolfe, D. M.; Quinn, P. R.; Snoek, J. D.; and Rosenthal, R. A. *Organizational Stress: Studies in Role Conflict and Ambiguity*. New York: John Wiley & Sons, 1964.

Kohn, Mervin. *Dynamic Managing: Principles, Process, Practice*. Menlo Park, Cal.: Cummings Publishing Company, 1977.

Koontz, Harold, and O'Donnell, Cyril. *Principles of Management*. New York: McGraw-Hill Book Co., 1964.

Labor, U. S. Department of: Division of Employment Standards, Employment Standards Administration. *Federal Labor Laws: A Layman's Guide*, Bulletin 262. Washington, D.C.: Government Printing Office, 1971.

Likert, Rensis. *The Human Organization*. New York: McGraw-Hill Book Co., 1967.

————. *New Patterns of Management*. New York: McGraw-Hill Book Company, 1961.

Maslow, Abraham H. *Motivation and Personality*. New York: Harper & Row, Publishers, 1954.

Massie, Joseph L. *Essentials of Management*. Englewood Cliffs, N. J.: Prentice-Hall, 1964.

McGregor, Douglas. *The Human Side of Enterprise*. New York: McGraw-Hill Book Co., 1960.

————. *Leadership and Motivation*. New York: McGraw-Hill Book Co., 1966.

Merrill, Harwood F., ed. *Classics in Management*. New York: The American Management Association, 1970.

Miner, John B. *Management Theory*. New York: The Macmillan Company, 1971.

————. *The Management Process*. New York: The Macmillan Company, 1973.

Peter, Laurence J., and Hull, Raymond. *The Peter Principle*. New York: William Morrow & Co., 1969.

Pfiffner, John M., and Fels, Marshall. *The Supervision of Personnel*. Englewood Cliffs, N. J.: Prentice-Hall, 1964.

Pigors, Paul, and Myers, Charles A. *Personnel Administration*. New York: McGraw-Hill Book Co., 1973.

Plunkett, W. Richard. *Introduction to Business: A Functional Approach*. Dubuque, Iowa: Wm. C. Brown Company Publishers, 1977.

Roethlisberger, F. J., and Dickson, W. J., *Management and the Worker*. Cambridge, Mass.: Harvard University Press, 1939.

Rudkin, Donald A., and Veal, Jr., Fred D. *Principles of Supervision*. Philadelphia: Auerbach Publishers, 1973.

Sartain, Aaron Q., and Baker, Alton W. *The Supervisor and His Job*. New York: McGraw-Hill Book Co., 1972.

Schein, Edgar H. *Organizational Psychology*. Englewood Cliffs, N. J.: Prentice-Hall, 1970.

Sirota, David, and Greenwood, J. Michael. "Understand Your Overseas Work Force." *Harvard Business Review* 49, no. 1 (January-February 1971): 53–60.

Sisk, Henry L. *Principles of Management*. Cincinnati, Ohio: South-western Publishing Company, 1969.

Stewart, Charles J., and Cash, William B. *Interviewing: Principles and Practices*. Dubuque, Iowa: Wm. C. Brown Company Publishers, 1974.

Sutermeister, Robert A. *People on Productivity*. New York: McGraw-Hill Book Co., 1969.

Tannenbaum, Robert, and Schmidt, Warren H. "How to Choose a Leadership Pattern." *Harvard Business Review* 36 (March-April 1958).

Walker, C. R., and Guest, Robert H. *The Foreman on the Assembly Line*. Cambridge, Mass.: Harvard University Press, 1956.

Index